HOMES

TODAY AND TOMORROW

Second Edition

HOMES

TODAY AND TOMORROW

Second Edition

by
Ruth F. Sherwood

Former Chairperson, Division of Human and Consumer Service
Garland Junior College, Boston, Massachusetts

with
George H. Sherwood, Architect

Bennett & McKnight Publishing Company

Peoria, Illinois

Previous copyrights 1972 and 1976.

Bennett & McKnight Publishing Company
809 W. Detweiller Drive
Peoria, Illinois 61615

85   KP   5

ISBN 0-02-664530-0
(Previously ISBN 0-87002-326-8)

Library of Congress Catalog No. 80-68008

Printed in the United States of America

Editor: Marlene Weigel
Production Supervisor: Gordon Guderjan
Production Assistants: Pat Schultz, Carol Owen
Contributing Artists: Steve Justice, Forward Productions
Cover Design: Forward Productions
Cover: home courtesy of Gina and Ken Kaeser; accessories courtesy of Baurer Furniture, Inc.

PREFACE

The material in this book is designed to help you understand your own housing needs and to help you in making decisions about your home. The purpose of this book is to help you to evaluate the ideas of others, to develop your own ideas, and to have confidence in your decisions.

The book is divided into six parts. Part 1 discusses how homes fulfill human needs through design. Part 2 is devoted to housing styles from colonial to modern times. Part 3, which emphasizes the value of good design, tells how a house is made and the relation of a house to natural resources and the environment. Part 4 discusses furnishings and interior design. Part 5 helps you learn about budgets and mortgages and the other financial aspects of housing. Part 6 gives information on career opportunities in the trades and professions related to housing.

Throughout the book, photographs and drawings illustrate the principles discussed in the text. Suggested activities and case problems give you an opportunity to apply the information in each chapter and relate it to your own needs now and in the future.

Each chapter includes "Terms To Know." These words appear in boldface in the text where they are defined or explained. At the end of the text is a bibliography including many books and periodicals you may find of interest.

TABLE OF CONTENTS

Table of Contents

PART 1 HOW HOMES ARE DESIGNED

1 Human Needs and Home Design

Left: In this studio apartment, the sofa opens into a bed, the chest and trunk store clothing, and the table doubles for study or dining. (Celanese House)

Right: Can you think of things that the apartment might have in common with this primitive hut?

WHAT WILL THE FIRST HOME OF YOUR OWN BE LIKE?

What appears in your imagination when you think of the first home of your own? Remember places which appealed to you. Try to recall details. Would you like a home as modern as the "spaceship" in Fig. 1-1? Do you dream of a home that is old-fashioned like this young woman's first apartment in Fig. 1-2? The images that come to your mind will tell you about much that is important to you. They will help you decide what you like.

Your favorite possessions also indicate your taste. Do you have a collection or a favorite pic-

1-1. This home has been molded from fiberglass.

Terms To Know

adobe	functional
apprentices	heirloom
archaeologists	mass production
culture	prefabricated
design honesty	self-actualization
esteem	traditions

ture to display? Do you like some of your things because they are useful or because they have sentimental value? A true "dream" home is one where you feel you belong. It reflects your ideas and the things you enjoy.

Also, you have probably formed opinions about the practical features that are important.

You may have lived in several houses or apartments. Was there enough storage space? Enough bathrooms? What did you like about each home?

Your dream may be to have a room of your own, an apartment, or, in the future, a house. Dream homes are not necessarily large and expensive. Perhaps you would like to do as the young person shown in Fig. 1-3 has done—build your own house. Maybe you would like to find an old house and restore or remodel it. The small apartment in Fig. 1-4 is modest but fun for its renter. She has one cherished piece of furniture, the secretary, and is collecting the stained glass windows. In this small apartment the renter enjoys independent living while acquiring furniture for a future home.

Sue Scott

1-2. The trunk and dresser were found in family attics.

What you want from a home depends on your needs—the needs you have in common with all other people and the needs which you have as an individual.

HOUSING HELPS FULFILL HUMAN NEEDS

The dictionary defines housing as the buildings or shelters in which people live. But housing provides for more than basic physical needs. The house that satisfies one person may be totally wrong for another. In addition, people's needs change as they go through life. In general, however, the needs which housing helps fulfill have not changed much since primitive times.

What are some of the needs one should consider in selecting a home? The late psychologist, Abraham Maslow, ranked human needs at five

1-3. Log cabins such as this are pre-cut and include instructions for building them yourself.

UPI

Georgia Pacific

1-4. Do you recognize the object used as a stool?

levels within a pyramid, Fig. 1-5. The five groups of needs are basic physical needs, safety, love and belonging to a group, esteem, and self-actualization. Because human beings are complex, a list cannot include all there is to say about them. Sometimes, too, the items on the list overlap. But Maslow's pyramid is a useful tool in helping people understand themselves. In many ways homes provide opportunities to satisfy the human needs in Maslow's pyramid.

Basic Physical Needs

At the bottom of Maslow's pyramid are the most basic physical needs—food, air, and shelter. People could not live long in freezing temperatures or under a desert sun without some kind of protection. From earliest times, homes have provided shelter from the weather. They have also served as storehouses for the food supply. Primitive homes were often clustered around water holes, sources of food, easily defended sites, or other natural attractions. Early people lived in either a tent, a cave, or a pit.

Today wandering tribes such as the Bedouin of North Africa, hunters, explorers, soldiers, and vacationers use tents in almost all parts of the

world. The first tents were made of poles covered with skins or branches. Two tepees are shown in the foreground of the early painting in Fig. 1-6. The impressive four story high council house, Fig. 1-7, was built by women of the Wichita tribe. Pine poles, split in half, were set in the ground in a circle and joined together at the top. This framework was covered with willow branches and then finally swamp grass to provide a completely weatherproof dwelling.

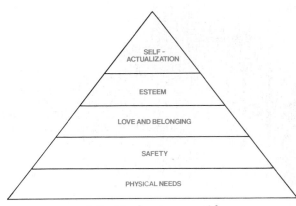

1-5. Maslow's pyramid.

Museum of Fine Arts, Boston
1-6. This painting is of the Hudson Bay Trading Post in the Montana Territory.

Because these homes could be easily taken down and moved to new locations, they were used for centuries by nomads who moved from place to place in search of food or to follow their grazing herds.

A cave is the most primitive type of shelter. **Archaeologists,** people who study history from relics and remains of old civilizations, have studied the bones, charcoal, and pottery chips found in caves. They know from their study that some caves were occupied for centuries. An example of a cavelike shelter that was used by the Pilgrims is shown in Fig. 1-8.

The temporary "foxholes" soldiers make when they are fighting in open areas are an example of the pit. Archaeologists have found remains of elaborate pits that must have been comfortable homes such as the one in Fig. 1-9. They had strong roofs and included fireplaces for cooking, places to store food, and mounds that were covered with skins to be used as beds.

Today our homes still help satisfy basic physical needs. They shelter us from the weather and provide food storage.

Safety

At the second level of Maslow's pyramid is safety. Early homes kept people safe from ani-

Indian City, U.S.A.
1-7. An early "mobile home."

1-8. This shelter was dug into a bank and roofed over with bark.

15

1-9. *How do you suppose this roof was made watertight?*

mals and other humans who might harm them or steal their belongings. Safety was one of the reasons people grouped homes together and formed the first towns and villages. They thought they could help protect one another.

Today, homes still provide a place of safety. Many people build fences around their property or install special locks and chains on their doors to give them a sense of security, or of being safe.

Of course certain people should be in a home environment for reasons of safety because they must be cared for. For example, a tiny baby or a very sick person may need constant attention and should be near others at all times.

Love and Belonging to a Group

The need for love and belonging to a group includes the need for friends and family and for being a member of a larger community. These needs are on the pyramid's third level. Homes give family members space to live and work and play together and to share the things which help build affection. Houses can be designed to en-

courage togetherness. A house built on the "open" plan, for instance, has large spaces and few dividing walls and provides for family unity.

The average American moves 12 times in a lifetime, making this one of the most mobile societies in the world. People who move a lot may achieve belonging by maintaining a sense of family history or "roots." Most families have some object or piece of furniture which they keep because some relative owned or made it. Fitting these treasured possessions from the old

1-10. *Pioneer women sewed quilts like this by hand.*

16

1-11. This home is decorated using African designs.

location into the new one helps make up for the impermanence of their homes. The quilt in Fig. 1-10 was made by a Pioneer Kansas farm wife. It was carried on horseback to Wyoming and eventually California. Now a cherished **heirloom,** or family treasure, it still provides a feeling of roots for the descendants of that pioneer woman. Other families might decorate an entire house around their family heritage, Fig. 1-11.

Some people choose homes in a certain town because they wish to belong to the group who live in that town. They enjoy being a part of what happens in the community. This is an-

other reason early towns were formed. People desired company and friendship. The well-planned apartments in Fig. 1-12 offer close neighbors. The elderly people who live here may be alone if they wish, but neighbors, a community hall, and town facilities are nearby.

Esteem

Esteem means worth or value. If you esteem someone you think well of that person. Esteem is at the fourth level of Maslow's pyramid, and it includes a person's need for the esteem of others and the need for self-esteem. People want

1-12. This apartment complex offers planned social activities to the tenants.

to feel that others respect and think well of them. They also need to feel good about themselves.

Esteem can take many forms. For instance, a family who builds a fancy, expensive house might do so because they believe others will recognize and respect them for it, Fig. 1-13. They deliberately select the style, location, and decoration which they hope will impress others. Studies have shown that almost all people, consciously or subconsciously, view every change in residence as a step up or down.

Esteem can also have to do with a person's rights. Everyone needs to feel that others respect his or her right to privacy, for instance. The home in Fig. 1-14 is owned by people who like to be off by themselves. The way a home is designed can influence how much privacy each person has. The open plan, discussed earlier, does not offer much privacy.

Self-actualization

At the top of Maslow's pyramid is **self-actualization.** It is the need each person has to fulfill him- or herself as an individual. Part of the satisfaction people feel about their housing comes when they believe it is an accurate reflection of themselves. While house hunting, people often say, "This is MY house," "This is really ME," or "I couldn't stand this place!" These reactions may not be based on considerations as cost or location, but on how the people see the homes as images of themselves. Self-actualization can take many forms. Creativity, and independence, and a sense of values are three forms of self-actualization which housing can help people achieve.

The first apartment or house marks a milestone for most young people. No matter how makeshift it may be, its shortcomings might be overlooked if it is viewed as a symbol of inde-

1-13. This house is unlike any other in its neighborhood.

1-14. Can you think of disadvantages to this much privacy?

Janell Gauwitz
1-15. This sofa, loveseat, and chair were purchased at a furniture company's liquidation sale.

pendence. Fig. 1-15 shows the first apartment of a young working woman. Although she was able to furnish it inexpensively, the investment was, for her, a large one. Yet she felt it was worth the independence she has as a result.

Everyone has a sense of values, but individuals value different things. Homes give people the opportunity to build their values into their daily lives. For instance, someone who could afford it and who valued physical fitness might want a home with a swimming pool on the property. Another person who valued the beauty of nature might choose to live in a cabin in the mountains.

Creativity is the ability to make something that is different from what someone else would make. For instance, if two people were to paint a picture of the same house, the house would

look different in each painting. Each of us is different and we often express that difference by being creative.

In early times objects for daily use were often skillfully made and decorated. The primitive spoon shown in Fig. 1-16, is an example of a creative design. Although it was intended for everyday use and was seen only by the maker or the maker's family, it was carefully decorated with a carved animal head.

1-16. The wood used for this spoon was one of the few materials used in primitive homes.

1-17. What does this pottery have in common with the wooden spoon?

The pottery in Fig. 1-17 is an excellent example of handicraft and represents a current design trend. Because it is one-of-a-kind and because of its beautiful form, color, and texture, this pottery affords its owners something unique and personal.

The way a home is decorated can also be an expression of creativity. People like to surround themselves with the things which they feel are beautiful or which express some part of their own personalities. Primitive people sought beauty as well as comfort in their homes. Centuries ago the homes of the Pueblo Indians in Taos, New Mexico, were several stories high. They contained underground chambers where the chiefs held council and where religious ceremonies were conducted. On the walls of these apartments are decorations depicting storms and the plants and animals in the world around them.

The young person who lives in this apartment in a 150-year-old house, Fig. 1-18, likes to collect antique cooking utensils. The apartment she chose and the accessories she used to decorate are an expression of herself.

OTHER INFLUENCES ON HOUSING DESIGN

Housing is designed to help human beings fulfill their needs. But the way housing evolves may be affected by other things, such as the materials available to build a home. Following are several of the more important factors which determine housing designs.

Function

A **functional** design is one suited for a specific use. A home which did not include a place to sleep, for example, would not be functional.

Sue Scott
1-18. This kitchen has the "country" look.

Part 1: How Homes Are Designed

Study the baking dishes in Fig. 1-19. They are designed to eliminate a problem in microwave cooking. When cooked in a microwave oven, foods must be stirred to prevent slow cooking at the center. The dishes' circular shape with a hole in the middle eliminates the need for stirring. These dishes are examples of good functional design.

Let's consider the two high-intensity lamps in Fig. 1-20. The lamp on the right is of simple, modern form. It is shaped to give the best pattern of light, and the lamp height may be adjusted to any convenient level. The base is designed to provide balance and to allow the lamp to be used in several positions. The designer was not limited by any traditional form for there was no tradition established for this type of lamp. The new and different shape is expressive of the function of this lamp, which is to concentrate light on a small area.

What do you think of the second lamp which appears to be an antique telephone? Does its form reflect its function?

The question, "What is it?" is usually an indication of bad design; it suggests that the object's function is not apparent. This does not

mean to imply than an object should not be decorative; it means that, in general, useful objects should not be disguised.

However, in some instances it may be desirable to disguise the function of an object. For example, you might choose to make a bed in an efficiency apartment seem less conspicuous by selecting a model which folds up into a cabinet. For secrecy, a painting might actually be the door to a wall storage space or a safe. If an object is attractive in itself, however, it is normally poor judgment to make it resemble some other object. A television set is a modern and desirable item. It is poor design to disguise it so it appears to be a dry sink or some other kind of furniture.

What do you think of the roof line of the apartment building in Fig. 1-21. One of the functions of a roof is to provide shelter from bad weather. This roof slopes down over the entrance. What will happen to anyone who approaches this entrance on a rainy day? Can you think of other examples that illustrate the lack of appropriateness in houses or furnishings?

It is a simple matter to outline the requirements for an item as uncomplicated as a dish or lamp. However, to specify just what to expect from a design as complex as a room arrangement may not be so easy. First, you must think of the functions to be performed and then experiment with different room arrangements to see which one best meets the requirements.

Study the two rooms shown in Fig. 1-22A and B. The room settings reveal a contrast in function. The smooth, easy-to-clean surfaces and decorative items in A suggest an informal

Corning Glass Works
1-19. Can you explain what is meant when people say, "Form follows function?"

1-21. Is this roof design functional?

style of living. The room is arranged for multi-purpose activities. The desk-bookcase unit offers a convenient study center. The sofa and low table provide a conversation area. The colonial parlor in B, however, suggests a more formal way of life. The furniture arrangement has one purpose—conversation. The decorative objects in this room form a background and are less a part of the activity which takes place in the room.

The function of a home may be altered somewhat by the lifestyle of the people who live there. Fig. 1-22 shows how the way we use a living room has changed in the past 150 years. Such changes are always taking place. At the present time, technology, increased mobility,

working mothers, and increased leisure time are some of the factors influencing the functional design of housing.

MOBILITY

Statistics show that about 20% of the people in this country move every year. This mobility, along with the increase in population, has resulted in a boom in apartment construction. Vast apartment complexes are common in most of the cities across the country, Fig. 1-23. With the apartment boom has come a unique furniture style designed for mobility and apartment living—it is lightweight, small in scale, and multipurpose.

Because mobility has created a demand for easy-to-move furnishings, apartments and many houses are now usually equipped with built-in storage and appliances. When families move today, they generally do not have to take stoves, wardrobe cabinets, linen chests, or kitchen cabinets.

Since few young adults today expect to live in their parents' homes, houses are no longer being built to hand down from one generation

1-20. How might the design of the "telephone" lamp impair its function?

1-22. Are both these rooms appropriate for their intended use?

24

1-23. This complex houses 92 apartments.

to another. Instead, today's house plans are designed to meet the needs and interests of the current owners, with attention given to the possible resale value of the house.

TECHNOLOGICAL CHANGES

Fast transportation and communication have almost eliminated regional styles in home design. The same furniture styles can be found in almost any city or town. Even national differences tend to disappear.

The automobile has had a noticeable impact on housing. At the time many older residential areas were developed, only a few people owned cars. Streets were generally narrow and no provision was made for parking. Later, as cars became more common, separate garages were built to house them. Today, parking the family cars poses an increasingly serious problem if no provisions are made. The house in Fig. 1-24 has no garage but a carport.

In new construction, the garage is considered

Lorenne and Edwin Weigel

1-24. Why are carports more common in the south than in the north?

25

Corning Glass Works

1-25. Would these dishes be easy to store?

POPULATION TRENDS

For the first time in American history the average household consists of fewer than three persons. Young people are waiting longer before entering into married life. The percentage of single persons in the 25–39 age bracket has increased. More adults today than in the past will never marry. Apartments and condominiums meet the needs of many singles. Twenty percent of house and condominium buyers are women.

There are more elderly people in the population than ever before in history. The number of elderly in the west and south has increased more than 20%, and the number of children under five in the north central states has decreased almost 15% and 22% in the northeast.

Housing has already responded to some of the changes that are occurring in the makeup of the population. For example, some cities are

a part of the house design. The number of cars a family has usually determines the size of the garage, which greatly influences the design of the house as well as increasing its cost. Now the energy shortage promises to affect the use of cars. If no substitute for gasoline is found, the car, as we know it, may disappear. Once more there may be no garages added to homes. New forms of transportation will be developed which may influence the shape of housing in new ways.

CHANGES IN FAMILY ROLES

Today, it is not uncommon for mother, father, and children all to have different time schedules during the week. In many cases, it is almost impossible for the entire family to be together for a meal, except perhaps on weekends. Living patterns such as this influence the design of household equipment. The dishes in Fig. 1-25 are designed for fast food. They are the size and shape of the most popular packages of convenience food, and the glass-ceramic material is designed for use in a microwave oven which can cook frozen food in minutes.

1-26. How does the design of this building add to privacy?

Charles Cole, Architect

26

1-27. How would you decorate this room to accommodate your own leisure interests?

turning unused elementary schools into housing for the elderly.

Increasing longevity has also brought the need for specialized housing for the elderly. New standards are being developed to make independent living possible for the aged and handicapped. Homes may have special features such as ramps, wide doors and safety features in bathrooms. Storage and equipment may be placed at more convenient locations.

LEISURE TIME

With the trend to a shorter work day and even a four-day work week, leisure time is increasing. As a result, furnishings and house designs are being influenced by activities such as entertaining, hobbies, and sports.

New apartments, too, generally meet the need for outdoor living areas. Many complexes offer recreation areas, clubhouses, and swimming pools. Fig. 1-26 reflects the desire for outdoor living areas. Good design in the arrangement of the balconies gives each tenant a private outdoor living area, even though surrounded by neighbors.

The furnishings in the room shown in Fig. 1-27, such as the hammock and kerosene lamp, show an interest in leisure time pursuits.

Can you think of other social and cultural conditions which may influence design?

Building Materials

The dwelling built by the Eskimos in the Arctic is an example of one of the most ingenious shelters ever devised. Using snow or ice, the only material at hand, they provided convenient shelter where most building materials are scarce because of the long winters.

The adobe house of the southwest shows how native material is used to solve the opposite problem—intense heat in the desert. Thick bricks of **adobe,** made of clay and straw, Fig. 1-28, keep the sun from penetrating the interior during the heat of the day. By evening the bricks have stored up heat and help keep the house warm as the temperature falls during the chilly night.

1-28. Adobe walls were usually covered with stucco to prevent erosion due to wind and rain.

Even in large modern metropolitan areas where there is a greater variety of materials to choose from, people are still limited to the things produced or used frequently in their part of the country. Although other materials might be shipped in, they may be so expensive only those people who are wealthy could afford to use them.

The discovery of a new material often contributes to other changes within a culture. For example, bronze replaced stone, then iron replaced bronze, but each brought about new ages in human history that endured for thousands of years. Dormant artistic talents were brought into play with the discovery of silk.

Recently, the development of new synthetic materials—such as plastic—has created a new opportunity for design. Plastics are light, flexible, may be molded, and come in a remarkable range of colors. They are as important today as other materials were in their time.

There are many features of house design which have resulted from the use of new materials. For example, because wood breaks under heavy loads, timber construction required the use of pitched or high-peak roofs to carry the weight of snow in cold areas. When steel beams became available, flat-roof construction in heavy snow areas became possible.

Steel and preformed concrete, along with new types of insulation and heating methods, have given a greater flexibility to house design. For example, large window areas and floor plans that open to the outdoors are now possible. The house in Fig. 1-29 is made of concrete. How did the material used influence the form of this house? The architects wanted to create a house that allowed for freedom and change. Do you think they were successful?

DESIGN HONESTY

The designer must respect the opportunities and limitations imposed by all materials, new and old. The object must express the qualities of the materials used. The object must not look like something it is not. This is known as **design**

Thomas McNulty and
Mary Otis Stevens, Architects
1-29. *Do you think this house would be comfortable in a cold climate?*

honesty. If a designer fails to be open-minded and uses new materials in old ways, poor design may result.

Let's examine the use of materials in the two cookie containers shown in Fig. 1-30. The sleek, modern cookie canister on the left is made of plastic, a relatively inexpensive material. It is a transparent gold color, which is attractive when the jar is empty and blends with the color of the baked goods when it is filled. When containers are transparent, it is easy to see what is stored inside. A set of these canisters stacks and stores easily, and the simple shape is easy to clean. The canister would not seem out of place in a traditional kitchen, and its clean, modern lines would fit a contemporary decor.

The cookie canister on the right is made of pottery glazed to look like iron. The handle is not part of the pot but is attached to the lid. What do you think of this design? What do you think of using pottery to masquerade as iron? Is the material honestly used?

The sofa in Fig. 1-31 was made of molded cellular foam. There was no precedent for this design. The designer took advantage of the exciting possibilities of a material, which in its liq-

1-30. *How might a pottery canister be designed to express qualities of the material?*

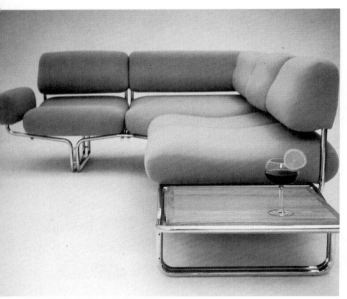

1-31. The legs on this furniture continue its fluid lines.

uid form, could be shaped for the human body. The fluid design expresses the material used in its construction.

Tools and Methods of Production

Tools also influence building. Early tools were often made of materials close at hand. Stones, skins, sticks, and bones were used by primitive people as their tools. These simple instruments limited the builder. Imagine trying to cut down a tree without an axe or saw.

Design is also influenced greatly by production methods. For centuries, skilled workers and designers were responsible for training **apprentices**—beginners in the trade who worked for them. The apprentices accepted this training as part or whole payment for their work because

they knew their future depended on how well they learned their trades. As a result, designs were handed down from one craftsperson to another, with minor changes resulting in a gradual evolution of styles.

MASS PRODUCTION

Today, most products are machine-made in large quantities. In general, skilled artists or designers are employed to design the object. Then the machine delivers as many duplicates of the original design as the manufacturer believes the market can absorb.

While **mass production** methods have influenced design in general, no aspect of twentieth-century life has been more affected by technological changes than the building industry. Construction techniques have altered building methods. Kitchens and bathrooms may be molded in one piece and installed as a unit, Fig. 1-32. It is no longer necessary that houses be built one at a time—now they may be mass produced. One real estate developer may purchase

1-32. A preassembled bathroom is being lowered by crane into this apartment building.

1-33. Prefabricated homes can be built very quickly.

land and build hundreds of houses all at one time. New designs adapted to this type of construction operation have been developed.

The summer home in Fig. 1-33. is an example of mass production in housing. This house was designed and **prefabricated** many miles from the building site. The ready-cut sections of the house were shipped by truck to the lake-

shore and erected in a few days by workers who are specialists in prefabs, as these ready-cut or pre-cut homes are called.

The mobile homes, Fig. 1-34, are "instant housing." Each home is completely constructed and perhaps already occupied when it is delivered to its new location.

Prefabrication and the ability to ship houses

1-34. Mobile homes usually come furnished as well.

1-35. Do these bowls have design honesty?

over long distances have helped to create uniform styles all over the country. Regional designs are no longer common.

JUDGING MACHINE-MADE OBJECTS

There is an essential difference in judging old and new styles.

The two bowls shown in Fig. 1-35 may serve to illustrate this difference. The pottery bowl on the right is handmade. Notice the many small variations on the surface and the slight differences in the design. You probably don't mind these little mistakes or variations. In fact, as you look at the old handmade bowl, you may think of the potter making it for a friend. Although it was made for common household use, it is a beautiful one-of-a-kind and prized as a work of art.

By contrast, look at the plastic bowl. It is smooth and flawless. In fact, if the person who bought it found the slightest imperfection, it might be returned for a refund.

You can see just from these two examples that there is an important design difference between old or handmade articles and modern,

machine-made items. In one, we prize the small imperfections; in the other, we seek perfection.

The Environment

As discussed earlier shelter is a basic physical need, and the environment determines the type of shelter. The environment can include many things, but the most important to housing is climate. The climate of the United States has a very wide range. It varies from that of the Arctic Zone in Alaska—which is swept by strong winds and has many months of darkness and snow—to that of the mild, tropical, rain forests of Hawaii. Temperatures have ranged from as low as −51°C (−60°F) in the Rocky Mountains to highs of 54°C (130°F) in Death Valley, California.

In such widely different areas, the influence of climate on house design is important. For example, in cold areas a house might be placed facing the sun on the side of a slope which protects it from the chilling wind.

Almost every basic principle of construction we know today was developed by builders long ago in their search for protection from the weather. The cold, snowy winters of the northeast have given us a style which was associated with that region: compact house plans, low ceilings, central chimneys, and small windows to contain heat; steep roofs to shed snow; and wood shingles to insulate against driving rain and snow. The hot, dry air of the southwest

1-36. You will need to make comparisons between traditional and contemporary forms when selecting and furnishing a home.

called for a plan faced on a garden for convenience, thick walls of adobe brick with outside doors to the rooms—usually on an inner court, a flat roof of timber and mud protected with clay tile, and an earth floor with only slight drainage around it. Today's ranch style house is based on this plan.

In the deep south houses built as recently as 50 years ago have high ceilings to allow the warm air to escape, many windows, and large covered porches called verandas. Today southern homes do not always include these features as a way to adapt to the climate. Why not?

Tradition

In early times most people seldom traveled very far from their own neighborhoods. Because of this, regional styles developed which showed differences in social and economic backgrounds. People were taught by their parents how objects were made and passed these skills along to their own children. As the years went by, these design ideas became **traditions,** and this reservoir of styles has guided and inspired new generations of designers.

Can you think of objects you are familiar with that are based on the traditional designs of some previous period? For example, dress design is often inspired by some earlier style. Many house designs also reflect the past. The Cape Cod house is one example.

Some forms are so traditional we seldom question them. For instance, it is necessary when burning a candle for the flame to be at the top. Then the electric lamp came into use. Although a light bulb was as efficient in one position as in another, almost all lamps took the traditional upright form so well established by the burning candle. This is what we mean when we talk about tradition in design—ideas of the past are adopted by new generations.

People may be influenced by tradition without realizing it. They become accustomed to certain shapes and are reluctant to accept new designs; there is a certain comfort in the old and familiar!

The effect of tradition on design is illustrated by the pitchers in Fig. 1-36. These pitchers are alike in many ways—they are simple in shape, useful, and easy to clean. They are, however, very different in design concept. The designer of the pitcher on the left did not follow tradition since this pitcher has a lip rather than the traditional handle. Because you are accustomed to having a handle on a pitcher, this pitcher may look strange to you. However, let's analyze the design. What advantages might it offer? It is one of a set and, because it has no handle, it will stack for easy storage. This is important in a small home where there may be a space problem. A lip is less likely to break than a handle. If a dishwasher is used, this pitcher will take up less room. Since it is a form that is easy to manufacture and ship, this might contribute to a lower cost. This pitcher was molded entirely in one piece, and the new type handle is an appropriate design for this technique. As far as basic function is concerned, the pitchers perform well—they pour easily. Do you think you could hold the lip of this pitcher as comfortably as you could the traditional handles? Personal needs and taste would determine which one you would select.

An old idea may have charm and be chosen for that reason.

The tendency to follow tradition in housing is very strong as people are often reluctant to change from accepted building designs. Often, the seller and the buyer may not know the background of the tradition they are following. For example, the house shown in Fig. 1-37A has shutters which close. For many years shutters were used for security, to reduce heat loss and to protect against storms. The house in B has boards nailed on to suggest shutters. They cannot be closed.

Outside Cultures

Another factor in design is the influence of outside cultures. The **culture** of a people consists of their beliefs, social habits, and ways of living. When isolated primitive villagers began to

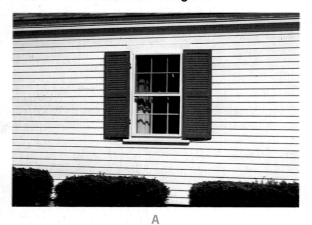

A

B

1-37. Can you think of a value these shutters might have other than usefulness?

travel, they were exposed to the cultures of other peoples. These cultures influenced their building designs and methods of construction. They took many products and ideas with them. They brought back some items which they used to decorate their homes.

Today our homes show the influence of other cultures. For instance Chinese styles in furniture and design have become very popular, Fig. 1-38. In the southwest, which is close to Mexico, Spanish styles in architecture and furniture are often imitated.

Maintenance

A well-designed object should be more than useful—it should be easy to care for and economical to repair. It should have lasting value in the event it must some day be sold. Since good design contributes to lasting value, designers are obliged for the sake of their reputations and the satisfaction of their customers to keep maintenance in mind. In many cases, the initial cost of good design is less than that of inferior design. Upkeep, likewise, may be less.

The houses shown in Fig. 1-39A and B, offer examples of contrasting materials with different problems of care and maintenance. The low brick house requires paint only on the window trim. Since all of the windows can be reached from a household ladder the owners might decide to paint the trim themselves and avoid the cost of professional help. The white Victorian house in B requires paint. Since it is a two-story house and has elaborate trim, platforms would have to be used by a painter to reach the high places. Most owners would have to hire professionals to paint this house.

The garden terrace in Fig. 1-40 is a good example of design planned to hold down care and maintenance. By defining the area with a stone wall, which blends with the rural setting, the natural grasses and weeds from the adjoining woodland are kept out. The patio area is paved with brick so only a small amount of lawn needs to be cared for.

In applying this principle to an entire house, you might find that materials or methods of construction may be employed to lower building costs and provide for easy care. However, the house should still be well designed. On the other hand, the materials used may result in higher maintenance costs but you might find this acceptable because you prefer the design or appearance.

Can you think of an item you selected that was not easy to care for, but you bought it because you liked it so much? People sometimes do this in furnishing a house, and this is not objectionable if the purchase is carefully consid-

1-38. Which decorating details in this kitchen are distinctly Chinese?

A   B

1-39. Maintenance can add to the cost of a house.

ered. For example, one person may select a piece of fine wood furniture even though it may require periodic oiling or waxing. Someone else may prefer plastic furniture that needs only to be dusted.

Laws And Restrictions

Laws and regulations have an important influence on housing. Many details in a house are determined by community laws and restrictions. For example, if 2 m (6 ft.) is the maximum height allowed for a fence, many in the community will be this height, giving the area a closed-in appearance. The use of only certain materials may be allowed by fire and safety laws. Restrictions on building size and height, and whether or not parking space is required, are only a few of the many common regulations.

Tax laws, too, affect housing. The city street in Fig. 1-41 is an example of the effect of unfair taxation. In this community, the houses were taxed according to street footage, and the corner house was taxed double—for each side of the corner. The owners reacted to this tax by tearing down every corner building in their area and leaving the land vacant. This speeded the decline of the neighborhood. However, taxation, if wisely applied, may also encourage neighborhood improvement.

Perhaps you would like to learn about the tax laws in your community. See if you can find out about changes in housing that may have resulted from tax laws or other regulations governing building. Your community may have set-back regulations which require that structures be built a specific distance from the sidewalk. Very often houses are aligned in straight rows to conform to building ordinances. Are people required to have garages? What are the rules concerning parking? Do you know of any community where people are required by law to build one style of house? Are there rules pertaining to the type of roof on a house?

Laws and restrictions also apply to items inside of houses. The design of the bathroom lights in Fig. 1-42 results in part from safety regulations. In most communities and according to federal housing regulations, bathroom lights must be permanently installed, with no switch or pull chain on the light itself. The light must be controlled by a wall switch that is not readily accessible from tub or shower. This is to make

Royal Berry Wills and Assoc.
1-40. Although surrounded by woodland, this yard is well-groomed.

it impossible for a person taking a bath or shower to reach a switch and receive an electric shock. Some codes specify grab-bars for safety. Note there is one beside the tub.

The Talent of the Designer

In the past, the type of shelter was also influenced by the builder-owners: their skills, their earnings or kind of occupation, and their desire for comfort and beauty. Because few people can

1-41. Are there laws in your community which might cause similar problems?

American Standard
1-42. What other features of this bathroom might be affected by laws?

afford to build a house themselves today, they often have to find one built by someone who has similar likes and values. The more talented the designer, the greater the beauty, livability, and freshness of the design.

The best designers are those who consider all aspects of a home—its function, the materials and methods used, the environment where it will be placed, its maintenance, valuable design traditions which may provide ideas, the laws affecting construction, and the needs of the people who are to live in it—before they are satisfied with the final result.

Some of the greatest changes in design result when talented designers try new ideas. One example is Frank Lloyd Wright, an outstanding architect who did much to develop the Modern style of architecture. (See p. 119.)

The room in Fig. 1-43 reflects the interests and taste of its designer. It shows how exciting color and form in interior design may greatly reduce the need for furniture. The mobile, which also adds color, gracefully fills a large space. Think about this room; how does it reflect this century and its social customs? See if you can find pictures of other rooms which reveal new ideas in architecture, interiors, and furnishings.

Acorn Structures
1-43. Does this room reflect your taste?

Part 1: How Homes Are Designed

Case Problem A

Write a detailed housing autobiography or story about several homes you have lived in or visited. Describe the rooms and buildings that you preferred and tell why you liked each one. Tell how they made you feel. For example, you might describe a kitchen that you remember. Tell about your reaction to the colors, the furniture, pots and pans on display, the fragrance of spices or food, plants on the window ledge—try to think of as many details as possible.

Describe the features that you liked best. Was it the color, the warm friendly atmosphere, the informal furniture, or possibly the view that was important to you? Write as though you are trying to make a young child understand exactly what you like.

Case Problem B

Begin a collection of pictures of homes that you like. Include exteriors, floor plans, interiors, furniture, equipment, accessories, and colors. Mount or file these in an orderly way so they may be used for future reference.

Case Problem C

Assume that the area in which you now live was your home in prehistoric times. Some of your neighbors in that distant past are about to build a house. Try to visualize the area as a wilderness, with none of our present-day conveniences in existence. What location will they select? Why? What type of house will they choose to build? Why? What materials will they need, and what tools must they make for use in construction?

ACTIVITIES

1. Do you know two or three people who come from different backgrounds? Can you cite any features of their homes which show the influence of family tradition?

2. Select a category such as sofas, stereos, refrigerators, lamps, TV sets. Then select advertisements showing designs which are not appropriate for the function of the item. Write a report, giving your reasons for your selections. Discuss in class.

3. Plan an exhibit that illustrates primitive housing. You might include simple models of the three ancient forms of housing. Collect pictures of primitive houses used today around the world. The *National Geographic* and other travel magazines are good sources.

4. Collect illustrations of modern tents and temporary houses. Some sporting goods stores have bulletins illustrating these, or pictures may be clipped from magazines. Also collect pictures of the tents, sleeping bags, and other equipment used by explorers, military services, and campers.

5. Pretend that you are living many centuries ago in a primitive house. Discuss family life:
- How would the duties of the homemaker compare with those of today? • What would children probably have to do to help in the house?

  Discuss these statements:
- The less people have to work with, the more they need to rely on nature. • The builders, their tools, the materials at hand, and the place where they build have determined the kinds of shelters constructed.

6. Collect songs and stories which tell of someone's longing for home or describing the great effort some person made to return home. Read excerpts and discuss in class.

7. If some members of the class have moved, ask them to discuss their feelings about leaving their former homes. Do you know someone who is an immigrant? Ask this person to discuss the features of a former home which is missed.

8. Survey students in your school. Ask them to describe their "ideal" home. Summarize your findings by making a chart on the bulletin board to show the type of home that is most popular. List the features most frequently mentioned.

9. Select a picture of a room from the text or from a magazine. Write a description of the person you think would be likely to live in it.

10. Study newspaper advertisements. Clip out or copy one using descriptions such as "For the Executive" or "Prestige Estate". Based on picture and descriptions do you think the realtor or owner is trying to take advantage of someone's self-esteem, or are the homes really superior?

11. Collect pictures of many types of houses. Mount them on sheets of paper. Pass the collection around your class. Ask each person to select the one he or she liked best and to explain the features that prompted the choice.

2 Elements
of Design

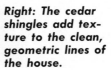

Far left: Notice how the roof lines of this house all seem to converge at a point in the sky, forming a triangle. (Red Cedar Shingle and Handsplit Shake Bureau)

Left: Although the house rambles over a large area, the soaring tower pulls the eye upward.

Right: The cedar shingles add texture to the clean, geometric lines of the house.

You may already have some very definite ideas about the style of furniture or architecture you like. No book can tell you what colors you will like, what sizes and shapes of rooms will appeal to you most, or what style of furniture will suit you. By your choice, you express your own personality in your own way. There are guides, however, to help you select designs that will suit your tastes and needs.

Good design means more than a certain style, for there have been good and bad designs in every style. There have been beautiful rooms in many forms. There are no ugly colors, but the result of combining colors can be ugly.

Terms To Know

analogous	monochromatic
color	neutral color
complementary	schemes
colors	primary colors
complementary	related color
styles	schemes
contrasting color	secondary colors
schemes	shades
density	space
form	tertiary colors
hue	texture
intensity	tints
line	value
mass	warmth

You are constantly using your senses in deciding what you like. However, design requires that you use your sense of sight more than any of your other senses. Around you are many visual experiences—some are pleasant, others unsatisfactory. Learning to recognize the elements of good design is learning to look at things in a new way—learning to really see what you are looking at. The elements of design are the essentials of every good design. These are space, form, line, texture, and color.

The sketches in this chapter illustrate some of the elements of design. They will help you to see how each element of design "works." Soon design to you will be not many parts but a total idea. Some of these elements are in all of the objects you see—houses, equipment, furniture, and clothing.

SPACE

Space, or the lack of it, is an important design element. It is, in general, the area with which the designer works. It can be a room or only part of a room, or an entire house. Space is changed by using the other elements of design, such as color.

● **Space may be filled, or it may be left to flow around or over objects,** such as the buildings in Fig. 2-1.

● **Space may be divided.** The stripe through the center of the rectangle in Fig. 2-2 cuts it in half, creating two separate spaces. A narrow rug through the center of a room would do the same thing. A straight sidewalk may cut a lawn in two. Long narrow hallways have the same effect in a house plan.

● **The apparent size of a space may be changed.** In Fig. 2-3, the two rectangles inside the one seem to create a new shape. As you

2-1. Open space around an object makes it stand out.

2-2. What sort of object might divide vertical space?

2-6. A pleasant, safe height.

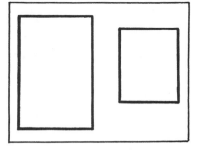

2-3. This division of space has created two islands.

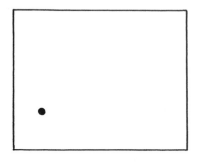

2-4. Too much space.

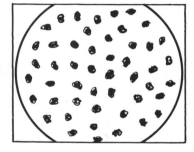

2-5. Too little space.

look at the two inside shapes, you tend to forget the outer one.

You get the same visual effect in a room by using two rugs. The effect is especially noticeable if the floor is of a neutral color, such as oak, and the rugs a bright, strong color. In effect, you make two areas out of one room, plus neutral space that is not noticed. In a very large room, this may be desirable.

The number of items placed within a space can make it appear larger or smaller. In Fig. 2-4, the little spot makes the rest of the area look large and vacant. In Fig. 2-5 you see many spots hemmed in by a tight, curved border. Too many small, cluttery objects in a room may make your gaze "scatter," destroying the design effect—as if the arrangement had not been planned. This decreases the apparent size of the room. You may feel distressed if you think there is not enough space in an area or in a room. You may have this same feeling about a room that is too full of furniture. Too little allowance for space gives the feeling of overcrowding.

- **The way space is arranged may affect your feelings.** The fence in Fig. 2-6 is high enough to shield you, but not so high as to make you feel caged. A small, protective space tends to make you feel snug and private. There is an example of this effect of space in every home—people generally have their favorite corner where they like to sit. Most people prefer to be near a wall.

In Fig. 2-7, the person is standing beside a very high wall. This often gives a trapped feel-

2-7. An over-powering height.

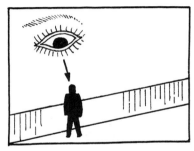

2-8. Not enough height.

2-9. Does this much open space make you feel lonely?

2-10. Some large spaces can be overpowering.

ing, especially if the wall surrounds a very small area. Elevators often make some people feel this way—the elevator shaft can be compared with a deep hole. A small room with a very high ceiling can have a similar effect.

A low wall or fence, as shown in Fig. 2-8, may make a person feel more exposed than if no fence were used. This is especially true if the low fence is around a small plot of land.

The tradition of open space is strong in the United States. However, as the sizes of lots have decreased, more and more people find they feel happier if they have an above-eye-level fence or screen planting to provide privacy. The effect is to extend the home outside its walls. Screened outdoor living areas are becoming more and more common. They are a response to a search for privacy and the need for greater use of existing space.

Too much empty space may give a lonely and inferior feeling. The person in Fig. 2-9 is alone in a vast room meant to hold many people. You may feel this way if you are alone in a house. People often arrange furniture in small clusters to give the effect of smaller areas and a feeling of intimacy or privacy.

A large space emphasized by massive structures may give a feeling of awe or reverence, such as the church entrance in Fig. 2-10. There is a feeling of luxury and space in a large room that has a very high ceiling. The feeling of loftiness is impressive.

FORM

Form, sometimes called shape, refers to solid objects. Form is the opposite of space, because forms fill space.

● **Form should fit the function planned for it.** Fig. 2-11 shows two garages, one satisfactory

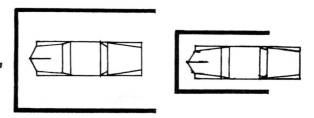

2-11. The smaller garage is too short for even a compact car.

and the other unsatisfactory. Yet they are both the same shape. To be desirable, form must fulfill the purpose for which it was planned.

● **Form may be two-dimensional or three-dimensional.** The background area in Fig. 2-12 appears to have length and width but no thickness. It could be a two-dimensional design on a rug or wall. If a form has thickness in addition to length and width, it would have three-dimensional volume as in the case of furniture. A painting can simulate three dimensions. Designers make use of this quality in scenic wallpapers.

Every designer uses a combination of two-dimensional and three-dimensional forms.

● **Variations in form may lead the eye and give direction.**

The objects in Fig. 2-13 increase in size from small to large. The eye tends to follow the line created by the top edge of the forms. A set of kitchen canisters arranged from large to small might also lead your eye from one end of the set to the other. If all your shoes are lined up in a row, your closet will appear wider.

A gradual change of form may be more pleasing than an abrupt change. The forms in Fig. 2-14 gradually change from low to high. Your gaze ripples up the slope. If there were one very little form and one big one, your gaze would shift back and forth. The effect would be "jumpy." When objects are related to each other, they complement one another. Window display artists are quick to use this principle. For this reason, an item may look much better in the store window than it does in your home. When you plan a decorative arrangement, try to think of all of the items together. Planting around a house helps soften the abrupt line at the foundation. It carries your eye up from the yard to the house in the same manner as the forms do in Fig. 2-14.

● **Form has mass and density. Mass** means weight or bulk. **Density** refers to the number of forms in a space. A high density of forms in a space can create the appearance of mass. The black rectangle in Fig. 2-15 sits firmly on the bottom line. Its form gives a feeling of stability or mass. Overstuffed chairs and couches usually create this same visual effect. They have a

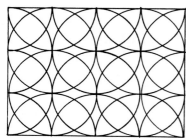

2-12. A two-dimensional design.

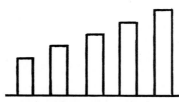

2-13. In which direction do your eyes move when you look at this picture?

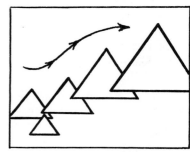

2-14. A gradual movement from bottom to top.

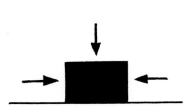

2-15. A form having mass.

2-16. Low density, no feeling of mass.

2-17. High density, considerable mass.

squarish look which generally lends an appearance of stability to a room. Long, low tables and chests may also have this quality because of their shape.

Mass or density may also be used to describe the number of dwellings packed in an area or the size of the object compared with its surroundings. In design, density refers to a feeling either of sparseness or abundance. One farm house, shown in Fig. 2-16, would be an example of low density. Many big skyscrapers grouped together as in Fig. 2-17 would be an example of high density.

The house shown in Fig. 2-18 does not give the feeling of mass because you see it in contrast with the distant countryside. However, it is a generous home with many outbuildings. Compare it with the townhouses in Fig. 2-19 which are smaller. They give a feeling of mass because they are relatively large compared with their setting and they are close together.

Good design requires careful placement of mass. Too many heavy pieces of furniture in a room can make the room appear crowded even though there is enough space. Incorrectly placed mass can also create the appearance of

Royal Berry Wills and Assoc.
2-18. Low density in comparison to background.

2-19. *High density in comparison to background.*

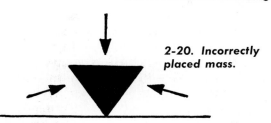

2-20. *Incorrectly placed mass.*

instability. The triangle in Fig. 2-20 looks as if it might fall over. The bottom is too small in proportion to the top. When you say something looks "top heavy," you are recognizing that quality in the object. A chair may be "tippy" because its legs are not far enough apart to support its mass. It, like the triangle, has a small base. A lamp that is too tall for its base is another example.

● **Related forms should be harmonious.** When related forms are extremely different, the effect is usually not satisfying. In Fig. 2-21 the 1870 Victorian house on the left is large with high ceilings. It has gables, a tall chimney and much of the outside is covered with jigsaw trim. Contrast this with the 1970 design shown in the center. It is characterized by low, long lines that flow smoothly. The 1770 colonial house on the right represents still another shape—square lines that give a feeling of solidity. Houses that are adjacent do not generally complement each other when there is a wide difference in shape. Things which have **complementary styles** look as if they belong together. The buildings in Fig. 2-22 are related in both shape and color.

The couch and table shown in Fig. 2-23 are also examples of forms that complement each other. The simple curving line of the couch is echoed in the shape of the table. An elaborate table would not be as complementary.

LINE

Line, another element of design, is a narrow, two-dimensional form which appears to have length but no width. It tends to cause your eyes to move from one end of it to the other. In the

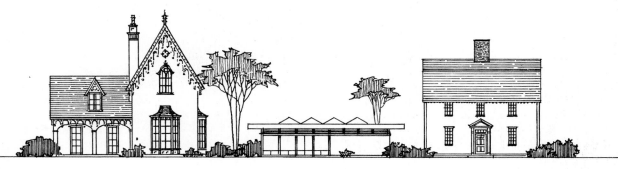

1 8 7 0   1 9 7 0   1 7 7 0

2-21. *These house designs are not complementary.*

2-22. These building designs complement one another.

the lines lead the eye beyond the edges of the composition.

Low sofas, bookshelves, or other objects which create horizontal lines carry the eye around a room. Tall windows and floor-to-ceiling draperies "point" up and down to make a room seem loftier. Stripes on furniture fabrics can create similar effects.

• **Lines may suggest different feelings.** Lines probably suggest different feelings to us because they remind us of things about ourselves. The horizontal line A in Fig. 2-26 may suggest rest or repose because that is the position human beings take while resting. The vertical line B may suggest action because that is the position we take for walking. The diagonal or zigzag line C indicates excitement and movement. That is the position we take for running.

design of an interior, it usually marks the edge of an object. Line is sometimes used to fool the eye and make an object appear a different shape than it really is.

• **Line may indicate direction.** In Fig. 2-24 the lines tend to pull the eye up and down. In Fig. 2-25 the eye goes across the space. For this reason, Fig. 2-25 tends to appear wider—

Add Interiors

2-23. The parts of a grouping should appear as if they belong together.

Zigzag lines can also remind us of lightning and windstorms, or breaking waves. The diagonally patterned rug in Fig. 2-27 adds excitement to the room.

When the lines of the furniture in a room are long and low and there is very little pattern in the upholstery, draperies, rugs, or wallpaper, the room appears more restful than it would if vertical lines and a great deal of pattern were used. If you wish to have a room seem quietly spacious, the longest piece of furniture should be on the longest wall so you tend to look past the edge of the furniture.

Small objects may be arranged to give the effect of continuous line. For example, the tops of all picture frames may be aligned so as to carry the eye around the room at that level.

To create excitement in decorating a game-room, you would use vertical along with diagonal or zigzag lines.

TEXTURE

Texture refers to the surface of objects. Fig. 2-28, part A, represents a smooth surface such as satin. Part B represents a rough surface such as carpeting or corduroy.

The surface or amount of roughness may affect the apparent color. Each little projection in

2-25. Lines can fool the eye.

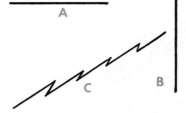

2-26. How do these lines make you feel?

a rough surface casts a shadow in certain light and makes the color seem darker. This is important to remember when you attempt to match colors in different textures. The identical color in two fabrics with different textures may not look the same in your home.

Texture is used to add variety and interest to a room. Through three-dimensional patterns creating shadows and reflected light, the lace-like pattern of the carved wood screen in Fig. 2-29 suggests formality. It might be used as a divider in a living room, and the bench, made of a single heavy plank, suggests a country kitchen or informal family room.

APPLYING SPACE, FORM, LINE AND TEXTURE

The use of space in the interior floor plan and the way a house relates to the outdoors

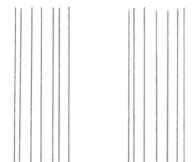

2-24. Lines indicate direction.

Armstrong Cork Company

2-27. How would a rug in a solid color change the appearance of this room?

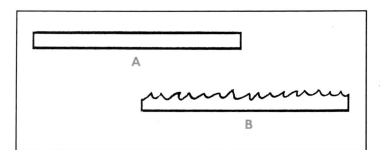

A

B

2-28. Texture adds variety and interest.

combine to make a home comfortable. Here are two practical problems that show how some of the elements of design may be applied.

Fig. 2-30A shows a typical small city yard. Rather than attempt a traditional planting, the owner removed the lawn portion and chose a more appropriate and contemporary solution, as shown in Fig. 2-30B. Let's analyze this yard in terms of the guidelines you have learned.

The rectangular pattern of the concrete blocks in the walk gives a feeling of stability. The concrete rectangles make a pleasant transition from the concrete sidewalk and pavements of the city to the garden. The same material has been used but in a more decorative manner.

The walk is slightly off-center so it does not split the yard—which is already small—and create the illusion of two even smaller, equal sections. The irregular walk carries the eye through the yard, adding interest and making the yard seem longer and appear as a whole.

A
B

Mary Bunting, R. Newton Mayall

2-30. How many uses of the elements of design can you find?

2-29. Textures can be combined.
Customwood Mfg. Co.

Imagine a straight walk instead of a zigzag. How would this change the design?

Do you get a feeling of more space in yard A or yard B? How do you feel about the combination of the small space and high fence? Since the fence is just above eye level, it assures privacy, protection, and a pleasant seclusion. A low fence would give a feeling of exposure.

The height variation in the plantings is gradual, hides the area under the steps, and helps

53

make a pleasant filler between the height of the fence and the height of the house. Do the horizontal rails in the fence in yard B pull the eye in specific directions? How does this affect the design? What about texture? The textures of the walk, the fence, and the bricks bordering the plantings are very different. How would the yard appear if all the textures were the same?

The complex of apartments for married college students in Fig. 2-31 shows a sensitive use of design. Three concrete towers make up the complex. Each building is different, yet all relate architecturally to each other and to their neighborhood. Walking through the complex, you find an interesting variety of paths and planted areas. For convenience and variety, bridges reach from building to building. Bright panels appear here and there to contrast with the texture of the concrete.

Jose Sert, Architect, Sert, Jackson and Assoc.
2-31. The use of similar materials, colors, and design make a complementary whole.

Fig. 2-32 shows the living room in a mobile home. Notice that the china cabinet, windows, and doorways are all the same height, creating a continuous line. How many different textures can you find in the picture? What is used to divide the living room space? Does the room create any special feelings?

COLOR

The word "magic" is often used to describe color. Color can play visual tricks and make the same objects seem different. The right color can make a high ceiling seem lower or a low one higher. Color can be used to make objects appear closer or farther away. It can help to make an object stand out and seem important. When the correct colors are chosen, the furniture styles of unrelated periods and origin may blend.

Color can be used in many ways to influence people. It may affect what they buy, how they feel, or how much work they do.

Here is a test for you to take and to give to your classmates and friends in order to learn about reactions to color. Make a copy of the following list. After each word write the color that comes to mind. Ask your test subjects to do the same.

Color Word List

snow	old age	crook
water	cold	danger
summer	happy	weak
Christmas	hot	stop
witches	king	go

Test as many people as you can. Compare the answers. What is your conclusion? Do some colors mean the same to almost everyone? If you find an unusual answer, ask the person to

Family Circle Magazine, Elyse Lewin and Vincent Lisanti

2-32. Can you find other examples of the elements of design in this room?

explain why the word is associated with the color named.

We know that color has great emotional appeal. Its use in the theater or on TV is only one example of how it can set a mood. A shadowed setting suggests an atmosphere of mystery. Bright, strong, warm colors like red, orange, and yellow give a vibrant, dynamic effect and suggest a celebration or excitement. Pastel colors such as pink, light blue, and pale green suggest a quiet, restful atmosphere.

Some color associations go back to the most primitive times. In early civilizations color was used in burial ceremonies. Perhaps the sight of life-giving blood led to the belief that the color red had some special power, which resulted in

the custom of coloring the bodies of the dead with red clay. This may have been part of an effort to give the dead eternal life.

Throughout the ages other meanings have been attached to colors and certain colors have developed very special significance in different countries. In the western world, brides wear white, but red is traditional for a bride in India. Can you think of a color that reminds you of someone you know or of something which happened to you?

How Color Happens

● **Color is in light—not in the object the light is shining upon.** For centuries color was considered to be a part of every object. In

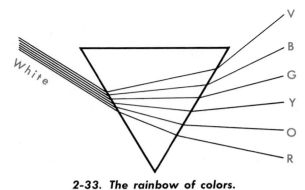

2-33. The rainbow of colors.

1666, Isaac Newton observed what happened when white sunlight passed through a prism. The white light broke up into the colors of the rainbow. He investigated further and found he could pass the colored light through another prism and gather all of the colors into white light again.

A prism bends the rays of light so that rays of different wave lengths are sorted out. White light, when it is passed through a prism as shown in Fig. 2-33, comes out in the form of a rainbow. The long red rays, which bend the least, are on one side; the short blue-violet rays, which bend the most, appear on the other side. The colors always form this pattern that Isaac Newton observed.

● **Color also depends upon the pigments or colorants in the surface of an object.** The surfaces of all objects contain pigments or colorants. These pigments absorb some of the light rays and reflect others. The reflected rays are the color that you see. For instance, when light strikes a red pillow, all of the rays in the light except the red rays are absorbed. The red rays bounce off, and you see the pillow as red. Most objects reflect some of the color in the light that hits them. If no light is reflected, the object is black. If all light is reflected, it is white.

● **Visible light rays are not all alike.** People sometimes select products under store lights and forget that the appearance may be different under the lights in their own homes. Fluorescent light, table lamp light (incandescent bulbs come in several colors), full sunlight, and daylight with clouds hiding the sun all differ.

Daylight or sunlight may be considered balanced for it contains about the same number of rays of each color. This gives what is called "true" color.

An ordinary white light bulb has more red or warm colors in it—it gives a yellowish cast to all of the objects seen under it.

Ordinary fluorescent light is more blue than red, giving a slightly cold cast to all of the objects it shines upon. Some street lamps have a very high number of blue rays. A person's skin and lips look purple when viewed under this light.

Any lamp shade other than pure white will affect the color of the light and, consequently, the colors in the room. For example, colors are distorted when the light shines through a red lamp shade.

The Language of Color

The following terms are generally used when discussing color. They are often confused, so be sure you understand their meanings.

Hue, intensity, value, tints, and shades are used to describe a color more accurately.

Hue is the name of a specific color. Each color on the outer circle of the color wheel in Fig. 2-34 is a hue—red is a hue, green is a hue, as are pink and chartreuse. New color names are introduced each season to promote fashions, such as "Irish Mist" or "Congo Pink". An advertiser may decide that a customer may be more inclined to purchase a dress if it is called "Peppermint Pink" rather than simply pink. Such promotional names come and go with the fashion seasons, but they are used to refer to the standard names on the color wheel, which do not change.

Intensity describes the degree of purity or strength of a color. It says how much a color has been grayed or changed by mixing the **complementary color** opposite it on the color wheel. Intense colors are clear and bright. Less intense colors are grayed and dull. Intense colors stimulate. They make objects appear larger and closer. They call attention to form. Colors of low intensity seem small and far away. Grayed or less intense colors create a calmer effect than highly intense or pure colors.

Value of a color depends on the amount of light it reflects. The hues shown on the color wheel are close to what are known as middle values. A value may be lightened or darkened without changing the color by varying its reflective properties through the addition of black or white. When mixed with a color, white lightens its value by making it more reflective. Similarly, black will darken its value by making it less reflective.

Tints are values above or lighter than the middle value and may be achieved by adding white to the color.

Shades are values below or darker than the middle value and may be accomplished by adding black to the color.

Colors vary in **warmth.** Red and the colors near it on the color wheel are the warmest. Blue and the colors near it are the coolest.

Using these terms correctly will give you color confidence. You will also gain knowledge and confidence by observing colors in nature, paintings, objects in museums, rooms arranged by experts, windows arranged by professionals, and the excellent color photography in some magazines.

The Color Wheel

The wheel is made up of the colors in the color rainbow arranged in a circle. It indicates sharply distinguished positions of colors in the

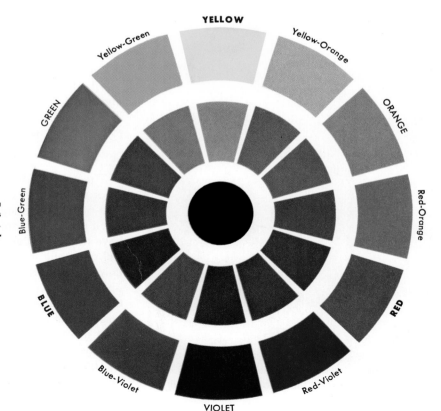

World Book Encyclopedia
c. 1972 Field Enterprises
Educational Corp.

2-34. The Prang System color wheel.

same order as they appear in a rainbow, Fig. 2-34. The colors of the color wheel have been used in the set of modern dishes shown in Fig. 2-35.

Primary, secondary, and tertiary are common names given to the twelve outer colors shown on the color wheel. Most of the colors in paint can be derived from the three **primary colors—** red, yellow, and blue, Table 2-A. Primary colors cannot be created by mixing other colors.

The three **secondary colors** are made by mixing equal parts of one primary with another. They appear on the color wheel between the colors used to make them. If only the primary and secondary colors were used, they would

Table 2-A.
MIXING COLORS

Primary Colors			
red			
yellow			
blue			

		Secondary Colors	
red + yellow	=	orange	
yellow + blue	=	green	
blue + red	=	violet	

			Tertiary Colors
red	+	violet	= red violet
red	+	orange	= red orange
yellow	+	green	= yellow green
yellow	+	orange	= yellow orange
blue	+	violet	= blue violet
blue	+	green	= blue green

make a six-color wheel—red, orange, yellow, green, blue, violet.

When colors next to each other on the wheel are mixed, a third group of colors is developed. The six additional colors that result are referred to as **tertiary colors.**

Color Schemes

The color wheel provides a basis for standard color schemes. A color wheel may be compared to a piano. You may have a very good piano, but if you don't know how to play, you will not have music. Hitting a few keys here and there will not result in a tune you like. Selecting a few colors here and there will probably be just as unsatisfactory. To learn to play music requires time and study. So it is with planning color harmonies that will be pleasing. One step in the right direction is to learn to use standard color schemes.

There are three kinds of color schemes: related, contrasting, and neutral. Note in Fig. 2-36 that each diagram has one or more dark areas.

2-35. These colors in their pure form are very intense.

A   B

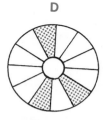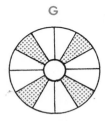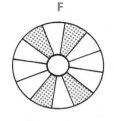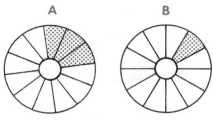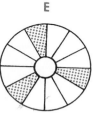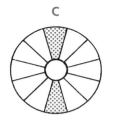

2-36. The different color schemes.

ANALOGOUS MONOCHROMATIC

RELATED COLORS

C   D   E   F   G

COMPLE- SPLIT TRIAD DOUBLE TETRAD
MENTARY COMPLEMENTARY   COMPLEMENTARY

CONTRASTING COLORS

If each diagram is turned on the color wheel, any combination of colors covered will be an example of the scheme indicated. For instance, the arrows on the complementary scheme are exactly opposite each other. Every time you turn the arrows to new colors, they will point to two opposite colors or to a different complementary color scheme, such as yellow and violet, red and green, or blue and orange.

Related color schemes are based on one color. There are two types of related color schemes—monochromatic and analogous.

The **monochromatic** color scheme is based on using tints and shades of one color on the wheel. For example, the scheme in Fig. 2-37 is based on brown and includes variations of brown from beige to rust.

The **analogous** scheme uses three colors that are next to each other on the color wheel. It combines one color with its related colors, Fig. 2-38. A scheme based on blue green, blue, and blue violet would also make an analogous scheme as would red violet used with red and violet. Related schemes based on single colors produce a quiet, restful effect.

Contrasting color schemes include complementary, split complementary, triad, double complementary, and tetrad. Contrasting color schemes are usually exciting and stimulating.

The room in Fig. 2-39 uses a contrasting color scheme. Large areas of beige unify the room and make it seem larger. Soft shades of the complementaries, orange and blue, have been chosen for accents. A room with large

59

Armstrong Cork Company
2-37. **Monochromatic color schemes can be restful.**

Family Circle Magazine
Elyse Lewin and Vincent Lisanti
2-38. Yellow, yellow-green, and yellow-orange are dominant in this room.

2-39. Complementary colors are opposite one another on the color wheel.

Family Circle Magazine, Elyse Lewin and Vincent Lisanti
2-40. Landscaping, too, can make use of the color wheel.

Interesting effects can be created by combining two color schemes. In Fig. 2-42 a hallway was converted into a dining-kitchen area for a small apartment. The designer achieved a neutral background and a bold double complementary scheme with the festive banners and accessories.

When you visit a museum, look at displays of Japanese prints, African masks, and English crewel work. These and many other art objects will suggest color schemes to you. They were all made by people who followed their own good taste, helped by examples of others carried down through the generations. However, if you have never worked with colors, it is helpful to have the suggestions of some of the accepted schemes.

Remember that one scheme is no better than another. In many instances, a color scheme may appear satisfying in one location and disappointing in another. To be successful, each combination must fit the place and purpose for which it is intended.

The Uses of Color

Color has been called the most important of all decorating tools. The colors you select may make a difference of many dollars in the cost of your home. Colors may also make a difference of many dollars of profit if the home must be sold. Here are a few examples of ways color can work for you.

quantities of strong pure orange and blue would have a completely different character; with this furniture it would appear garish. A true complementary color scheme is composed of colors directly opposite each other, as shown in Fig. 2-36C. The shading in D, E, F, and G shows variations of this idea. For example, a triad color scheme, E, consists of any three hues an equal distance apart on the color wheel. The flowers and grass in the garden in Fig. 2-40 form a split complementary.

Neutral color schemes are usually based on large areas of white, black, or other neutral colors such as pale beige or gray. For contrast, a small amount of a bright color is introduced. This generally gives a sophisticated effect. Some outstanding contemporary interiors have been decorated in neutral schemes. For example, a living room might have white walls, a gray floor, black rug, black and white furniture and, for contrast, bright red pillows on the chairs and sofa. For visual interest and variety, a combination of textures is used.

The soft tans in the furniture in Fig. 2-41 are the basis for a neutral color scheme. The same tones are repeated in the vinyl floor and on the walls. Note the variety of textures used in this room. What colors could be used for contrast?

Armstrong Cork Company
2-41. Orange adds warmth to the beige tones.

● **Color may save money.** Usually, people tend to tire more easily of bold, bright colors and may wish to change them. For this reason, colors you may tire of should be chosen for objects that can be redecorated easily or that do not represent significant and permanent investments. For example, a bright green vinyl tile floor will last a long time and might be relatively expensive to change if you tire of it. If you want a bright color, it might be well to use it in accessories or on a painted surface which could be easily redecorated. Repainting a room is fairly inexpensive and may be done by an amateur. However, it requires money and skill to tear out old floor covering and replace it with new.

It is also good to keep in mind that a potential buyer who does not like the pink you have chosen for large kitchen appliances will decide against purchasing your house due to the expense involved in changing the equipment. On the other hand, the cabinets painted pink will not present this problem because most buyers will realize these can be repainted at little cost. When you are planning color schemes, future changes should be considered.

It is especially important to think of future change in decorating a rented apartment. The bright-colored rug that looks just right in a small apartment may seem out of place in a larger apartment or house. Again, it might be better to introduce the bright color into the room with paint or some less costly item.

Color may earn you money in the event you must sell your property. Realtors generally agree that attractive, clean, and bright houses sell faster and for more money than houses that are dirty and dingy.

Color may save on utility bills. In many public buildings such as schools and hospitals, the wall colors are chosen on the basis of scientific readings indicating which colors will reflect the greatest amount of light. Choice of the proper paint colors can go a long way toward making the best use of light and reducing eyestrain. Studies have been made with light meters testing various colors and types of paints. Paint manufacturers have prepared charts rating the reflective qualities of their paints.

Color also affects the amount of heat that is absorbed or reflected from the sun. White or light colors reflect heat. Dark colors, especially black, absorb heat. The color chosen for roofs, terrace covers, awnings, and other surfaces may make the difference between comfort and discomfort, particularly in very hot or very cold areas. For example, a dark roof on a home in the southwest will absorb the heat from the sun, making the home more difficult to cool. A light-colored roof on a home in the northern states will reflect heat from the sun, making the house more difficult to heat.

Celanese House
2-42. A combination of two color schemes.

Armstrong Cork Company
2-43. The mottled tones in the tile do not show soil readily.

One of the best known ways to save money with color is by painting and refinishing furniture. For example, odd chairs or used furniture may be purchased at low cost and made to blend well with other furniture by the use of paint. By a skillful choice of color you can create furniture that is flexible and interchangeable. For instance, if the living room and dining room colors in a large apartment are harmonious, the furniture used in these two rooms may be combined later for one room in a larger home. For this reason many young people decorating an apartment may plan ahead and select styles and colors that will be equally appropriate when used later in a future home.

● **Color may save work.** Housekeeping is a constant challenge. Floors that are too light or too dark present a maintenance problem. However, floors of medium color value with some texture or pattern do not show dirt and dust as readily and are easier to keep attractive.

The floor in the entry hall in Fig. 2-43 is an example of a practical as well as attractive surface in an area that receives much traffic. The

Family Circle Magazine
Elyse Lewin and Vincent Lisanti
2-44. Would this bed stand out as much if it were covered to match the wall color?

varied tones of tan and the design of the tile make an effective background.

Industry has conducted many tests proving that people find work easier and make fewer mistakes in rooms that are well-lighted and decorated in restful colors.

Instead of many dust-catching small accessories which require constant cleaning and care, you may save work by using background color for decoration.

Can you think of other ways color is used to save work? What colors are used in gardening so you don't waste time looking for tools? Can color be used to make storage quicker and easier?

● **Color may suggest a time or place.** Certain colors are associated with geographic areas and historic periods. For example, bright, warm colors suggest a Mexican or Spanish motif. A person familiar with Early American design might be disturbed by the use of modern colors, which were not available at that time, in a colonial-style interior. To be effective, Louis XIV furniture should be complemented with colors that were popular in France during that period.

● **Color can create optical effects.** Bright, warm colors seem to come toward you. Furniture covered in bright red or yellow tends to

appear larger than it is. If the end wall in a long narrow room is painted in a warm color, the room tends to look shorter. A high ceiling can be made to appear lower by painting it a bright, warm color.

Pale, light colors have the opposite effect. Cool grays and light blues, for example, tend to recede. If they are used on a wall, it will tend to appear farther away. A small room will appear larger if walls, floor coverings, and furniture are different tones of the same light color.

Colors that are alike tend to conceal. For example, if you wish to make an ugly radiator or woodwork seem less important, paint it the same color as the walls. If you want some object to stand out, contrast it boldly with its background, Fig. 2-44.

Developing a Color Scheme

Your choice of a color scheme is usually influenced by the architectural features of the home, your possessions, your heritage, and how you live. Your emotions and ambitions may also affect your selections.

Note how different personalities were expressed when two different decorators furnished the same entry as shown in Fig. 2-45. Cool, closely related colors and sophisticated furniture

2-45. Which colors would you choose to decorate the area? How would they express your personality?

were selected for the entryway in A. Strong colors and contrast were used in the room in B. The wing chair with its ruffled skirt and the flowered paper seem warm and unsophisticated.

FEATURES TO CONSIDER

A number of features should be considered when developing a color scheme. An important consideration is the use of the room. Will the room be for quiet or more active pursuits? For instance, subtle, quiet colors would not be selected for a game room. Will the room receive hard wear? Colors that will not show dirt readily may be the choice.

Another consideration is the physical characteristics of the room. The room's exposure will influence the choice of colors. If it opens to the south or west, the value of the daylight will be warm, but if the windows are on the east or north, the light will be cooler. In general, in order to achieve a better balance of warmth or coolness, a southern or western exposure calls for cool colors while a northern or eastern calls for warm colors.

Also important is the type of electric lighting within the room. Incandescent bulbs give a warm light whereas fluorescent tubes are cool. Make color selections under light similar to that used in the room, and your selection will be more accurate.

What related areas are there to consider? Do doors open to expose pronounced color schemes in the adjacent rooms? For example, if there is a double door opening to a room featuring shades of brilliant yellow and red, this may limit the possible schemes in the room to be decorated. There should be a smooth transition from one room to another. One way to accomplish this is to use one or more of the colors that are used in the adjacent room. For instance, if an adjacent room features blues and greens, some of the blue tones might be used in the room to be decorated. Perhaps the same floor covering might extend from one room to the other to form a unity of color.

The mood of the room is another consideration. Decide on the mood you wish to develop. Do you want the effect to be active or subdued? Formal or informal? Sophisticated or unsophisticated? Your decision will have a great influence on your selection of a color scheme.

The style of the room is also important. Do architectural features suggest a particular style? White, rough-textured plaster walls might be appropriate for a Spanish decor.

You may have several favorite accessories or a prize collection that suggests a color. Blue and white china might look best against a pale yellow.

The availability of the colors you desire is another factor to consider. In general, almost any color is available in paint, since it can be mixed to order. Draperies, drapery fabrics, and curtains can usually be found in a wide range of colors. However, large pieces of upholstered furniture will probably come in a more limited color range. Some types of floor coverings are also available only in limited colors. The availability of the fabrics and furniture in the colors you desire may restrict the possible decorating schemes that you plan. For example, if you are determined to use a favorite color, you may have to compromise on your selection of furniture style or fabric.

Once you have evaluated these features, you are ready to start building a color scheme.

SELECTING THE COLORS

In order to develop a color scheme, you will first need to choose a dominant color. While it may not be the most obvious color in the room, it is the basis for your scheme. The dominant color may be your favorite color, or it may be the color of a prized accessory or piece of furniture. It may be a color that sets the mood you want to create. But remember that it should be a color you enjoy and are willing to live with.

There are several ways to select the additional colors. One common way is to use the color wheel, and select one of the standard color relationships. For example, refer to the color wheel in Fig. 2-34. Suppose you decide to use yellow as your dominant color and want a split complementary color scheme. Now look at Fig. 2-36D. When the one arrow points to yellow, the two complementary colors would be red violet and blue violet. These three colors form a ready-made combination. Look at the split complementary chart on p. 59 again. If you select blue-green, then the two colors that form a ready-made complementary combination are red and orange.

A painting, a piece of well-decorated china, a beautiful fabric, or a sample of wallpaper that you like might suggest a selection of harmonious colors. Look at the room in Fig. 2-46. Can you see how the colors in the throw rug on the couch inspired the rich color scheme of the room?

DETERMINING AREAS OF COLOR

Once you have selected a color scheme, you will need to determine the approximate area each of the colors will occupy.

Fig. 2-47 illustrates an empty room. Think of this room as it would appear if you walked into

Armstrong Cork Company

2-46. Which type of color scheme does this room represent?

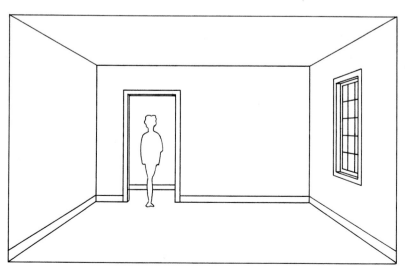

2-47. Begin with the background colors.

69

it. It is an empty cube with the four walls, the floor, and the ceiling forming the six sides of the cube. These six sides form the background of the room. The first step in planning a color scheme is to determine the background colors—the ones you will use for the walls, floor, and ceiling.

Professional decorators sometimes approach the problem in this manner: when you walk into a room you never see all of the room at one time. Your visual area includes three walls at a time. You see the wall in front of you and the one on each side. You do not see the wall behind you until you turn around. Also, the color in this large area will seldom look the same in every spot. There will be tints and shades due to lights and shadows.

Keep in mind the openings in the room such as doors, windows, and fireplaces. They affect the color inside of the room. For example, the wall will look different when the door stands open because the colors in the next room will show. A window at night adds a large area of black to the colors in the room.

Before selecting pieces of furniture or draperies to place in a room, you will need to imagine how all of the colors will look together. To do this, it is necessary to estimate the relative importance of each area of color. Each piece of furniture reduces the amount of background color—a tall piece of furniture against the wall covers part of the wall, and a large, low couch obscures the floor area it occupies.

A good way to estimate the size of the area each of the colors will cover is shown in Fig.

2-48. Chart A shows the relationships of the background areas of color. The floor and ceiling are the same size and the wall area is equal to the three walls. (Remember, you only see three walls at one time.) Chart B shows how these background color areas are reduced as furnishings and accessories are added. Part of the wall area, for example, is covered by furniture, pictures, mirrors, and draperies. There is no way to measure these areas. Make your own chart to estimate what you think will be the relative amount of the colors in any room you decorate.

When you have completed your chart, you will want to make a visual display of how the colors will actually look. To do this, you will need to collect samples of the colors and textures you plan to use. Don't try to use paint chips (little paper color samples) to represent all your colors. Remember that textures affect colors, so try to get samples of fabrics, upholstery, carpeting, and wood finishes, as well as paint chips.

Arrange the samples in the collage in the same relationship that they will have in the room. For example, if the couch is to stand on

2-48. The proportions of color areas.

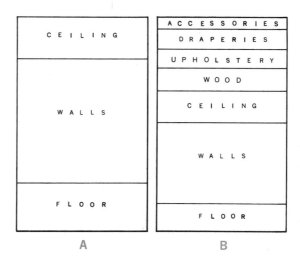

2-49. These samples have been sized in proportion to their use in the room.

the rug rather than directly on the wood floor, the color sample of the couch should be adjacent to the color sample of the rug. You can then judge the effect the colors have on each other.

Your chart, similar to Chart B, will show you the approximate quantity of each color area. If you determine that there will be about five times as much floor color as drapery color, then the rug sample should be five times as large as the sample of drapery fabric. In every case, think of the importance of the color to be displayed and the relative size of the area. The sample should be sized accordingly. Fig. 2-49 shows a collage prepared by a student.

Once you have the colors arranged, decide whether or not you like the combination. If not, then add or subtract colors until you find a combination that is pleasing to you.

Case Problem A

Plan a color scheme for an efficiency apartment for a nineteen-year old person who is employed as an accountant. The apartment is in an old building, so it has high ceilings, tall windows, and dark walnut-finish floors and woodwork. The walls and woodwork may be painted. The windows face west. The only piece of furniture the owner has is a sofa-bed in a simple design, upholstered in oyster white vinyl. Since the budget is limited, used or unpainted furniture may be selected. What color scheme would you select? Make up a collage showing samples of carpet, draperies, wood finishes, paint chips, and upholstery. Why did you select these colors and textures? If you were renting a similar apartment, would you use this color scheme? Why?

1. Look at the house plan in Fig. 2-50. It shows a living room with a stairway on the right near the front door (arrow pointing in). At the other end of the room a door leads from the dining room and another leads outdoors. Near the front of the living room are doors leading to the front hall on the right and the family room on the left. The family prefers to spend much more time in the family room than in the living room. On the basis of what you know about space, write a possible explanation for this.

2. Collect and mount pictures that illustrate contrasts in design. For example, you might picture two different rooms—one featuring quiet horizontal lines and the other expressing excitement with vertical or zigzag lines.

3. Find a picture of a room that has many small objects in it. Compare this with a picture of another room which has very few decorative objects. Which do you prefer? Why?

4. Make a collection of colored pictures showing room interiors. Label each one according to the type of color scheme it represents.

5. Select a color scheme that you like. Look through magazines and find several examples of rooms done in these colors. Compare the various rooms and decide which is the most successful. What are your reasons for your choice?

6. Ask a local paint store for a set of paint chips. Arrange these colors according to tints, tones, and shades. Get only a few samples to illustrate the range. Remember, tints are light because white has been added; tones have been darkened by the addition of black. Shades are grayed colors.

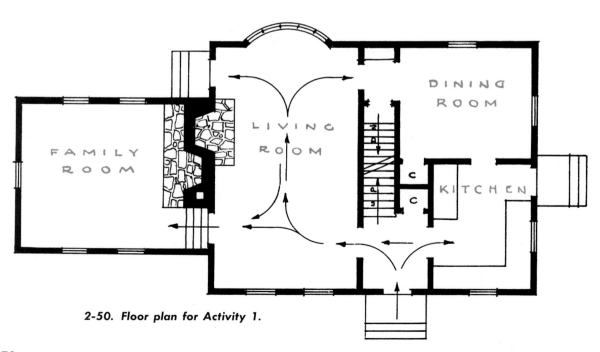

2-50. Floor plan for Activity 1.

7. Find examples of colors that vary in intensity. These are colors which have been grayed by the addition of the complementary color. Remember that the grayed color may be more subtle and interesting than one right out of the paint pot.

8. Study the use of color in packages containing soap and detergent powders. What colors predominate? Are certain colors used for certain types of cleaners? For example, is one particular color used for baby and hand soaps in contrast to another color for heavy-duty cleaning powders? How can these color associations be applied to uses in homes?

9. Interview someone who has been in the furniture business for many years. Ask the person to discuss color trends in furniture. Which colors retained their popularity longest?

10. Experiment with light and color. Use two or more kinds of light such as an incandescent lamp and a fluorescent desk lamp or use two lamps with different color bulbs. Separate the lamps by placing each in a large cardboard box cut away on one side so the light from only one lamp will shine upon each set of samples to be tested. Collect two identical groups of samples of colored paper and fabrics. Place the matching samples under each lamp and observe the effect of the lights on the colors.

11. When the class is studying color wheels, obtain a prism and let the sun shine through it to produce a rainbow. Notice the order of the colors—violet, indigo, blue, yellow, and red. If you have a color wheel in the class, compare the colors in sunlight through a prism with the colors on the wheel.

12. Make classroom displays to illustrate each of the standard color schemes—related, contrasting, and neutral. This can be done by combining paper, fabric, and decorative objects; or it can be done with paint or with paper samples.

13. Discuss some of your personal associations with color. For example, do you know someone you admire who wears a certain color often? Do you like that color partly because of the person? Can you think of some particular color which you associate with an unpleasant event?

14. Plan a "paper" color scheme for one of the rooms in your home. Use small pieces of paper to indicate the colors you would use for walls, ceiling, carpets, etc. What major purchases would you need to make to carry out your scheme? Discuss redoing furniture by removing color, painting, or antiquing. The plan should be based on a restricted budget which does not allow for any major expense.

15. Select a colored illustration of a room in the text. Assume you are an interior designer and that this room is in the home of a client. You are asked to submit a new color scheme. Recommend a new scheme and indicate the new colors by preparing color samples.

3 Principles
of Design

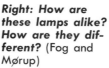

Far left: What is the first thing you notice when you look at this room? (GAF) Corporation)

Left: What shapes, colors, or textures are repeated in this area?

Right: How are these lamps alike? How are they different? (Fog and Mørup)

There can be no rigid rules for creating a design since the results would lack any freshness or individuality. Yet all good designs have several common qualities. Over the centuries, as a result of efforts to create beautiful objects, subtle rules or principles of good design have gradually evolved. They are: proportion and scale, balance, rhythm, emphasis, and unity and variety.

By applying these principles to the elements of design discussed in Chapter 2, pleasing results can be achieved.

First, we will look at each principle as it is applied to a simple object. Then we will apply

3-1. The top and bottom of this picture compete with one another.

3-2. The amount of ocean shown is out of proportion to the rest of the picture.

3-3. The main areas in the picture are given the correct amount of importance.

the principle to the more complicated problems of a house or garden.

PROPORTION AND SCALE

Proportion refers to the relationship of parts to each other and to the design as a whole.

In any object, the way parts relate to each other, whether good or bad, is called proportion. In Fig. 3-1 the picture is divided horizontally into two equal parts. Because the top and bottom compete with each other, the picture is disturbing. The areas in Fig. 3-2 are so out of

proportion that the picture has a clipped-off effect. Fig. 3-3 is more pleasing. The horizontal lines fill only about a third of the picture. The difference in the sizes of the main areas compels your eye to make a comparison. Since the areas are not too much alike or too different, the illustration is pleasing. This is the result of good proportion.

This principle might be applied to furniture itself or to the basic shapes of furniture in a room as compared with the whole room area. The size of the forms within a design might also be included; for example, the size of various shapes in the design of a printed pattern.

In Fig. 3-4, three simple bowls demonstrate a contrast in proportion. Compare the size of the base of each with the size of the bowl. Since the top and bottom of the bowl on the left are almost equal in depth, the proportion is awkward.

┌ Terms To Know ─────────────

asymmetrical	rhythm
balance	scale
balance	symmetrical balance
emphasis	unity
proportion	variety

3-4. Is any of these bowls out of proportion?

3-5. Which house is proportioned correctly?

The wide top and narrow base give a top-heavy effect. Do you think the bowls on the right are of more pleasing proportions? They have smaller bases in relation to their tops, and their silhouettes are more subtle. The bowl on the left is an example of one of the many perfectly useful but ordinary objects available today. The ones on the right are equally useful, but have simple classical lines.

Fig. 3-5A shows a seventeenth-century garrison house. This style was frequently used in the towns—the overhanging second story gave a little extra room by extending out over the narrow streets. Note the good proportions of the house with its low foundation and large chimney. The tops of the windows are just below the edge of the roof. Fig. 3-5B shows a contemporary interpretation of the garrison house. What do you

3-6. *This design is monotonous because the proportions are the same.*

are framed by the slender lines of the floors and the dividing partitions, creating an interesting relationship between the window and wall areas.

In many instances in the history of architecture, the principal differences in styles resulted from varying the relationship of the wall areas and windows. For example, a medieval house might have small windows spaced far apart, set in heavy masonry walls, while a contemporary house might feature large windows with only sufficient solid construction between to hold the roof in position. To achieve good proportion, regardless of the period or style of house, the openings and solid portions should not be equal.

You may wish to find other pictures of good and poor proportion to study. Think of the basic principle shown in Fig. 3-3 and apply it to the more complicated example of a room or house. For instance, in pictures of interiors you might consider the amount of floor area covered by

think of the proportions? Do you think the foundation is too high? The second story windows are up under the overhanging edge of the roof. Do you get a "cap-pulled-down-over-the-eyes" effect?

Let's apply the definition of proportion to the two apartment buildings in Figs. 3-6 and 3-7. How do the parts relate to the design as a whole in these two contrasting buildings?

In Fig. 3-6, the space between the bottom of one window and the top of the next is almost equal to the size of the window itself, making a monotonous design. In Fig. 3-7, large windows

3-7. The balcony rails divide the spaces unequally giving more pleasing proportions.

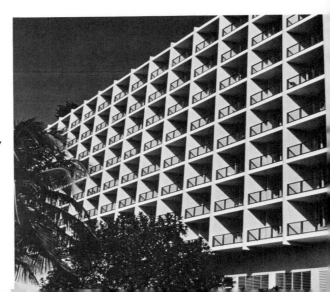

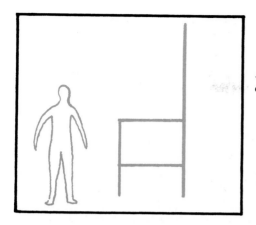

3-8. Scale tells about the relationship of the size of an object to the size of the human body.

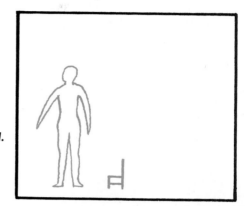

3-9. The chair is too small.

3-10. This chair is "in scale."

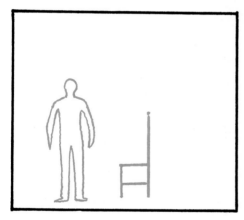

rugs in proportion to the area left uncovered. Or, you might study the size of lamps in relation to the tables on which they are placed.

Scale, too, can refer to the relationship of parts to each other and to the design as a whole. A design in good proportion is said to be in scale. But in addition, scale concerns the relation of the size of an object to the size of a human being.

Underlying any definition of scale in furniture or architecture is the measurement of the human figure. Furniture, rooms, or houses that appear too small or too large in relation to the human figure are out of scale.

This relationship can be illustrated with a chair. A chair seat is normally 450 mm (18 in.) above the floor. In Fig. 3-8 you see a chair with a seat that is 1200 mm (4 ft.) high and 900 mm (3 ft.) wide. Because the chair is much larger than the accepted size, it is described as being out of scale.

Fig. 3-9 shows a chair that is also out of scale. It is as much too small as the other is too large. The chair in Fig. 3-10 seems in scale because you think of objects in relation to human size and comfort. In a picture of the outside of

3-11. How tall would you say this building is?

a building, a human form is often included, as in Fig. 3-11. This helps the viewer judge the scale of the building.

Scale may also be used to describe the relationship of one object to another, in pattern, texture, proportion and dimension.

Fig. 3-12 and Fig. 3-13 show two harmonious room arrangements which feature very different scale. The neat pattern in the wall covering, fine handwork, filagree on the brass bed, small ruffles and small accessories in Fig. 3-12 all relate in size and combine to make an

Allied Chemical Corporation
3-12. The decorating in this room was done in small scale.

appealing room. In contrast the room in Fig. 3-13 features a bold scale. It is a room for two small boys. Bright colors and large patterns make the room bold in color as well as in scale.

BALANCE

Balance is composure or equilibrium. With formal or **symmetrical balance** matching objects are placed on each side of a central unit and featured at equal distances from it, as shown in Fig. 3-14. This type of balance in a room gives a quiet, formal effect. It suggests a feeling of repose because both sides of the composition or arrangement are of equal interest. The stability of the two similar objects is pleasing to the eyes.

If you drew a line through the center of the formal setting in Fig. 3-15 you would see that the two sides of the design are exactly alike. However, there is more to formal balance than just placing two items on either side of another object. The size of the items, the space around

3-13. Decorating in large scale.

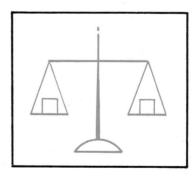

3-14. Symmetrical balance.

3-15. Formal balance.

Colonial Williamsburg
3-16. The chimneys, windows, shutters, and plantings are symmetrically balanced and give the house dignity.

3-17. Asymmetrical balance.

3-18. Informal balance.

them, as well as the contrast in color and texture contribute to this arrangement. Even so, it is easier for the beginner to plan a balanced grouping.

The house in Fig. 3-16 is a classic example of formal balance in exterior design. This comfortable dwelling erected in 1780 is a typical Virginia house plan with two rooms on each side of a central hall. Study the front of this house. Good balance in design provides a feeling of pleasantness and repose.

Informal balance is **asymmetrical.** This means the two halves of the arrangement are not the same, as shown in Fig. 3-17. It is more difficult for the untrained person to create satisfying informal arrangements. However, Modern and contemporary styles and functions often dictate the use of informal groupings.

When grouping different sized pictures on a wall, or combining several decorative objects, you need to use your eyes to judge the "weight" or importance of the items. This helps to achieve a satisfying balance of the objects. Warm, intense colors, dark values, and rough textures suggest heavy weight while pale, cool colors and soft, smooth textures suggest light weight. Note that in Fig. 3-17, the small, dark object seems heavier than the larger light object.

Informal arrangements may lack the quiet repose of more formal ones, but they may be more dramatic and exciting. Because objects are not alike or are not arranged symmetrically, however, does not mean they have been placed haphazardly in hit-and-miss array.

In an informal decorating scheme, large areas that are quiet often provide a contrast for areas that are smaller and more exciting. The small area may be an important accent in terms of color, design, texture, or other aspects. When you make comparisons and find harmonious relationships between areas, you are seeing balance in design.

Fig. 3-18 shows three different pieces of pewter in an informal arrangement. The flowing lines of the bittersweet branches hold the three dissimilar forms together in a balanced relationship which produces a satisfying result and appearance of ease. To move any of the elements would destroy its informal balance.

The small Cape Cod house in Fig. 3-19 features informal or asymmetrical balance in its exterior design. The door is off-center, there is a single bay window, one chimney, and a single sky-light.

Acorn Structures, Inc.
3-19. Informal balance is more casual.

3-20. A living room arranged asymmetrically.

The room setting in Fig. 3-20 provides another example of an informal arrangement. The pieces of furniture are different sizes and shapes. Just as your eyes traveled around the picture of the pewter grouping in Fig. 3-18, they also travel around this room. Notice the variety of small decorative objects. The sofa is at an angle to the patio doors. Chairs are placed casually opposite the sofa. Pillows are arranged at only one end. Food, toys, and books are placed for convenient use.

Because informality is the keynote of today, you may want to plan some attractive informal arrangements using table decorations or other decorative objects.

RHYTHM

Rhythm may be defined as a series of repeated accents spaced with regularity.

Rhythm may be produced by repeating certain lines, colors, or shapes. In design as in music, one group of accents followed by another, slightly varied, creates a rhythm which may be different and interesting.

The quilt pattern in Fig. 3-21 is an example of a rhythmic design. You may find rhythm in

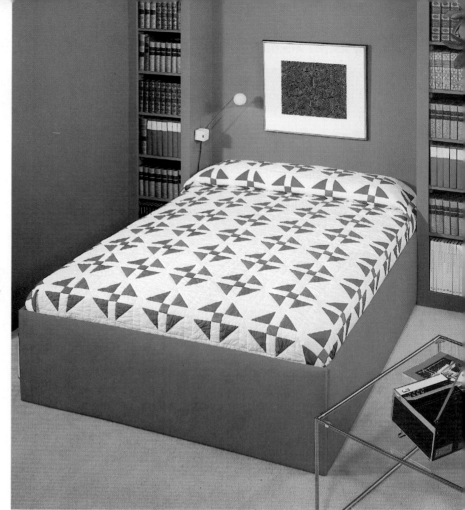

The Stearns and Foster Company

3-21. Repetition of the quilt pattern creates a kind of rhythm.

fence design, textile patterns, or the planting around a house. What other examples of rhythm in design can you think of?

The graceful awning treatment in Fig. 3-22 is a good example of an easy, rhythmic movement. A straight piece of canvas might have afforded shade, but this design does even more by providing the visual pleasure of an effective design.

Royston, Hanamoto, and Mayes, ASLA, California Redwood Association
3-22. Can you think of another awning design which would show rhythm?

85

3-23. Emphasis establishes what is important.

B

A

EMPHASIS

Emphasis shows dominance and subordination. Emphasis shows what is important. It causes one object or idea to stand out. In Fig. 3-23, the group of objects in A seem to "float." When they are grouped together as in B they hold your attention. What is the first thing you notice when you look at the mobile home living room in Fig. 3-24?

Emphasis implies order. When furniture or other objects appear in disorderly array, you

Family Circle Magazine, Elyse Lewin and Vinent Lisanti
3-24. Which object has been emphasized?

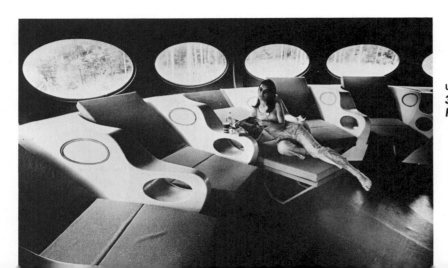

UPI
3-25. The outside of this home is shown on p. 12.

3-26. Too little variety can be monotonous, but too much is confusing.

cannot enjoy their design. A room that is carefully arranged allows you to see what is important. In an uncluttered room, objects not needed have been removed.

In Fig. 3-25 one design idea has been followed throughout. This living room is part of a space-age home. The outside of the home resembles a flying saucer. What design shape has been emphasized?

UNITY AND VARIETY

Unity occurs when parts are related by one idea. It is a consistency of style. **Variety** means combining different styles and materials to add

interest. Unity and variety should work together for a harmonious design.

Fig. 3-26 shows two pitchers. One has both unity and variety. The other has just variety. What do you think of the pottery pitcher? There is a confusion of ideas represented in this one small utensil. The front or spout is made to look like a flower sprinkler. A completely different design idea in the form of a nautical rope pattern is used around the outside. The top of the pot is decorated with a picture of a rooster.

The other pitcher features simplicity. No surface decoration has been used. The material chosen is a clear, heat-proof glass. Variety is introduced in the cover, which is plastic. Its simplicity makes it attractive and functional.

The sterling silver collection in Fig. 3-27 is another example of harmonious design. The shapes of the objects are all the same except for the sugar bowl and egg cup. Yet they, too, seem

Cohr
3-27. Notice how the candles continue the shape of their holders so together they make a unit.

Armstrong Cork Company
3-28. How is the triangle shape carried into the kitchen?

3-29. This house shows variety but no unity.

to blend. Why? Other than the variation in sizes, what gives variety to this collection? What would you think of putting a ruffled shade on the lamp to add variety?

The interior designer who arranged the room in Fig. 3-28 created an example of unity and variety. Notice how an Indian motif is repeated throughout the room. The triangle appears in the rug, pillows, drapery, upholstery fabric, and the candleholder above the fireplace. The triangular shape is complemented by the arched fireplace and doorway. A room completely filled with triangles would be monotonous. Notice the different textures. This room exhibits continuity because one idea is carried out, yet it is varied to provide interest.

What do you think of the house shown in Fig. 3-29? Four different materials are used on the front. Adding to the lack of unity are shutters that do not match, windows in odd sizes, and a mixture of styles.

Have you seen a house in your community which has a confusing variety of materials and styles used in its design? Builders sometimes dress up a house by trimming only the front, which results in a "false front" effect.

Perhaps you can think of some examples of lack of unity in design with which you are familiar. For example, a common mistake made in the decoration of a small house or apartment is the use of a different wallpaper and decorating style in each room. The lack of unity throughout makes a small home seem even smaller.

APPLYING PRINCIPLES OF DESIGN

In Fig. 3-30, two contrasting sets of saucers are used to show that good design should not be confused with formal and informal, traditional and modern. Good design based on the

six principles just discussed is not restricted to any one style.

The fine china saucers on the right are Royal Worcester and decorated in a traditional manner. The design of the surface pattern was intended for display in a table setting. The designer presumed they would be stored in a cupboard out of sight when not in use.

The second pair of saucers has been designed with a completely different objective. They are part of a modern table service for use in a small home or apartment with limited storage space. They may be stored conveniently on open shelves. These dishes will form a colorful display when stacked, since they are bright red. Principles of good design are timeless and applicable to formal or casual, traditional or modern objects.

In applying these principles of design to a house, it will be up to you to decide which style or type is more suited to your way of life. For some people, a traditional or formal house may seem best. For others, informal or contemporary is a more appealing choice. It cannot be said that one design is superior to another. However, you should strive to choose styles you like that use the principles of good design.

The small colonial house in Fig. 3-31 is a functional design, well suited to its location in a cold climate. The pitched roof with its heavy hand-split shakes is large in proportion to the house. Since we associate a roof with protection, this proportion suggests traditional comfort. The front, with an uneven number of windows

3-30. These saucers represent good design, although the material, pattern, and part of the function are completely different.

and an off-center door, is an example of informal balance. All of the details including the rough shingles, wooden siding, small-pane windows, and batten door are traditional colonial features which give a feeling of unity to the house. The huge chimney, characteristic of most seventeenth- and eighteenth-century houses, offers a point of emphasis. Viewed from a distance, the house seems anchored to its site by the big chimney. The windows on one side, interrupted by the door and a second spacing of windows, form a rhythmic pattern of openings.

The prize-winning modern house in Fig. 3-32 incorporates the principles of good design. Notice the pleasing proportions of the house. Observe how the width of each window relates to the window's height and how the total area of glass is related to the line of the roof. There is a balance between the strong horizontal lines in the roof and the terrace and the vertical lines in the windows and walls. The roof structure, designed to catch the prevailing breezes, creates a

rhythmic pattern of dark and light. A solid roof would have been heavy in appearance and would not have provided good ventilation. Although the broad plain where this house is located does not show in the picture, the long, horizontal lines of the house give emphasis to the wide expanse of the desert.

There is also unity in the use of native building materials. The floor is made of polished concrete dyed a deep red. The wood trim was left unfinished. The massive walls along three sides of the room, made of colorful native stone cast in concrete, form both inside and outside walls. On the outside, these materials blend with the sand, stones, and native desert plants in the foreground and make the cactus garden seem part of the house.

The owners have recognized the scale established by the massive stone walls of the house and have chosen appropriate furnishings. In Fig. 3-33, notice the length of the couch and the size of the table. They are large, simple shapes

3-31. An example of good traditional design.

Walter Pierce, Architect

3-32. An example of good Modern design.

3-33. Notice how the interior design of this house carries through the design ideas of the exterior.

Walter Pierce, Architect

3-34. This young boy admires a museum display of pottery made by his Indian ancestors.

in scale with the massive walls. The big, bold patterns of the rugs and wall hangings are more effective than small, intricate patterns would be.

This house is also a good example of unity and consistency in style. The interior expresses one theme—the use of southwestern Indian rugs, blankets, basketry, and ceramics, and native materials. This results in a harmonious interior.

SELECTING GOOD DESIGN

From the many choices and possibilities open to you, how can you select housing of good design? In order to judge, you should be familiar with examples of many styles. All good houses have certain characteristics in common which you can learn to recognize. It is similar to your taste in clothing. You probably know the difference between today's styles and those of the past, even though they are similar. You may also be able to recognize styles that are truly

contemporary. So it is in judging apartments and houses. After you have studied examples of good design, you will have better reasons for selecting homes that measure up to your standards—and you will probably be able to make a better investment in a home when you buy.

What guides should you follow to help you make a wise selection? Learn about the great styles in architecture and furniture design, such as those discussed in the next two chapters. Read books and magazines and visit museums, Fig. 3-34. Contemporary homes are displayed in popular magazines. You can also learn much about design by observing the houses around you.

3-35. Illustration for Case Problem A.

Case
Problem
A

Look at the mugs in Fig. 3-35 and decide how the principles of design apply to them. Which design do you think is best related to the shape of the mug? Are any of the designs well balanced? Could any of the mugs be used to illustrate a design which lacks rhythm? Which design lacks unity and continuity? Consider how each of the mugs will look when used to serve beverage. Do you think use and care were considered when the mugs were designed?

A C T I V I T I E S

1. Plan a bulletin board titled "Museum 2080". Select pictures of furniture and decorative items which you think will be popular "antiques" of the future, since they represent the best design of our time.

2. Select three different designs in a small object such as three vases, chairs, or record album covers. Write an opinion of each, based on the principles of design covered in this chapter.

3. Collect a group of household objects and have the class rate them as good, fair, and poor in terms of design. See if members of the class generally agree. Have your art teacher rate them so that you may compare answers.

4. Write a critique of the design of the house in Fig. 3-36 in terms of the principles discussed in this chapter.

(Continued)

3-36. Illustration for Activity 4.

A
C
T
I
V
I
T
I
E
S

5. Look through magazines and select items of household equipment that represent good and bad examples of each of the design principles discussed in this chapter.

6. Find pictures of either houses or interiors which are good examples of the principles of design and collect them in a notebook. Write near each picture why you chose it.

7. Select a room in your home and list the different materials used in the construction of the furnishings. For example, in your living room you may have a plastic TV set, a wool carpet, wood furniture, and nylon upholstery. Describe how the design of the items you list would vary if other materials were used in their construction.

8. Select a product such as a lamp, fabric, or a floor tile. Learn all you can about it. Consider both design and performance and plan an advertisement which points out its good features.

9. Visit several furniture stores. What materials other than wood and fabric are being used in the manufacture of furniture? Are the styles and designs suitable for the materials? Explain. Are new materials used to imitate old?

2 HOUSING STYLES IN THE UNITED STATES

4 Early Colonial
Styles

Far left: Do you know in which country log cabins originated?

Left: Why do you suppose that both this house and the log cabin have large chimneys?

Right: This architectural style is still popular today. From which country did it come?

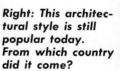

As you learned in Chapter 1, the design of housing is a reflection of time, place, and the occupant. Environment strongly affects the form housing takes. You may remember watching a motion picture when the projector was not running correctly. The film started off very slowly, then went faster and faster until the picture turned into a blur. The history of housing has been almost like that. Fig. 4-1 represents the relative length of time of the three major eras in economic development that influenced housing.

When North America was first settled, the agricultural pattern which had been followed for centuries in Europe was brought here. More

4-1. Modern housing developments have occurred over a very short period.

A — Agriculture – 8000 yrs.
B — Industrial Revolution – 200 yrs.
C — Automation – 40 yrs.

Terms To Know

apprentice system
Cape Cod house
clapboards
coquina
cornice
dormer window
Dutch door
ell
gables

gambrel roof
garrison house
half-houses
half-timbered
pitched roof
saltbox house
traditional
   construction

than nine-tenths of the people made their living from farming. Houses were far apart, families self-sufficient, and communication difficult. Housing during this period may be compared with the slowly running movie and, for many years, changed very little.

During the thousands of years of the agricultural era, people used their knowledge and skill to harness animal power. But the great majority of people had a low standard of living. Houses were small and often crowded since families then were larger than today's, and several generations of one family often lived under one roof. Space was devoted more often to sheltering animals than people. Only a very few people had fine houses and enjoyed leisure time. This long agricultural era was nearing its end when the first houses were built in the American Colonies.

THE FIRST COLONISTS

During the sixteenth century the Spaniards built churches, public buildings, roads, aqueducts, and housing in South America, Central America, and Mexico, in the manner of their homeland.

The first to settle as colonists in North America were the French and Spanish in Florida, the

4-2. This structure resembles a tent.

4-3. How is this shelter like the one in Fig. 1-8?

4-4. A house under construction. Poles were used for the frame.

French in Quebec, and the English in Virginia and New England. How far from home the first settlers must have felt as they watched the tiny ships leave them and head for home.

The settlers were faced with many problems as they attempted to build their homes: the never-ending task of finding food, caring for the sick, and guarding against Indian attacks. Also, they had only limited tools, materials, and equipment, which made building difficult.

No examples of the first dwellings have survived, but through written accounts and sketches made by the builders and through the findings of archaeologists, we have a fairly good idea of what they looked like.

Because of the European **apprentice system,** people of many trades were among the first settlers. Under the apprentice system, a person made a legal arrangement to work for another in order to learn that person's trade. Records show that masons, thatchers, lathers, and carpenters—to mention only a few—were among the first arrivals. **Traditional construction** methods, ways of building passed down from generation to generation, were part of their training. It is not surprising that later, when they constructed more permanent dwellings, they followed the building practices they knew, even though materials were limited. For example, they had no hinges and locks, no paint, no nails, and no glass. The structure of a house was often held together with wooden pegs. A number of early houses were lost because the owners burned them when they moved. Reproductions like those shown in Figs. 4-2 and 4-3 give us a fairly accurate picture of these early shelters.

TEMPORARY SHELTERS

The first settlers on the east coast of North America found abundant forests. They used poles to build houses like the one in Fig. 4-4. Rocks also were plentiful and were used to make the fireplace. The finished house is shown in Fig. 4-5.

4-5. Handmade shingles have been used to cover the frame. Why do you suppose the shingles overlap?

4-6. Can you guess how the legs were attached to this bench?

Furniture also had to be made from materials at hand. The bench shown in Fig. 4-6 is made of a log cut in half. Since fire was a constant danger in the small wooden houses, cooking was often done outdoors. Pots like the one in Fig. 4-7 were hung over an open fire.

After the first winter more permanent houses like the one shown in Fig. 4-8 were built. Corn and plants used to make medicine were grown in the dooryard.

PERMANENT HOUSES

The home in Fig. 4-9 was typical of the first houses constructed by English settlers in James-

4-7. To remove the pot from the fire, a pole was put through the handle and two people lifted it off.

4-8. Note how the cooking pot is suspended over the fire.

100

4-9. A copy of a house first built in Jamestown, Virginia.

conditions and to use materials available. The same was done by other settlers.

Although the history of housing extends over thousands of years, there have been few major changes until comparatively recent times. These changes are the result of our efforts to control heat, cold, and humidity through mechanical equipment and insulating materials, and to adapt the earlier forms to modern living.

Except possibly for the American Indian and the Eskimo, the people of continental North America are of immigrant background. They or their families have come from some other country. There has been an enriching combination of many cultures.

THE GROWTH OF TRADITIONAL STYLES

Houses have ancestors, just as people do. Floor plans and the design of a house tell a great deal about the period in which it was built and about the people who constructed it and

town. They copied the homes they knew—**half-timbered** Tudor houses, then common in rural England, Fig. 4-10. The house frame was constructed of wood and the spaces filled with masonry. It was traditional to use oak, so they followed this custom, although more easily worked wood was plentiful.

They also used the traditional method of filling the walls with bricks and covering them with plaster or clay. However, the first winter in their new home convinced them that this method was not suitable for the wild snowstorms, heavy rains, and extremes of heat and cold common in the areas where they had settled.

Wood was plentiful so the settlers soon adopted the system of covering the exterior of their houses with wood. The English thatch roof developed leaks in the harsher climate, so shingles were soon used. Generally, however, the settlers followed the familiar style of their homeland, modifying it only to meet the new climatic

4-10. This house, built in the seventeenth century in England, is still standing.

Table 4-A.
ARCHITECTURAL STYLES

Period or Style	Approximate Dates
Pilgrim	1640–1720
Georgian	1720–1790
Classical	1790–1830
Victorian	1830–1900
Modern	1900–

lived in it. The architectural styles of many nations have been modified under new conditions and with the use of new materials and new methods. But features of the early styles are still visible.

The people who had risked so much to find a new way of life would not accept for long the rude hovels that necessity forced upon them when they first arrived. As soon as possible, they built buildings of brick, stone, and timber.

On the following pages are illustrations of houses that were built by settlers from each of the major countries that explored and established colonies in North America. Later you will see how some characteristics of these houses appear in modern designs. Table 4-A shows the approximate dates of American architectural styles. Knowledge of the characteristics will serve as a foundation for judging today's homes and furnishings. Learning to recognize the source of design takes experience and training. When you become aware of a design, ask as many questions as possible. Where did it come from? How old is it? What is its family history?

THE PILGRIM PERIOD, 1640–1720

English Settlements

English settlements were widespread. The people represented many different groups. They varied from wealthy aristocrats to the poor people who had been sent out of the country to reduce the numbers on welfare.

During the Pilgrim period, many changes were occurring in North America. The isolated little settlements were growing into larger towns with more permanent and comfortable houses. Some roads were constructed, and trade by land and sea was growing.

The settlers began to take advantage of the abundant natural resources such as fish, wood, tobacco, indigo, and fur; and they put some of their profits into good houses. Since there were no schools, the children were trained at home. All members of the family had to work at home to produce the furniture, cloth, food, fuel, and other necessities.

The English who settled in New England were artisans and other middle-class people. The houses they built were simple and plain.

The house in Fig. 4-11 is typical of the many houses built by the English in the northeast, on rocky, forested land. Small, individual farms and modest houses were common. Because it originated on Cape Cod, Massachusetts, it was called the **Cape Cod house** and was to become the most popular style ever used in the United States. Even today, it is basic to the typical small house.

Originally, the house consisted of one room which was called a hall, or great room, and one or two small rooms. As families grew, an **ell,** or lean-to, was often added. Houses were frequently built with an end chimney like the one shown in Fig. 4-12. These were called **half-houses.** When an addition to the house was made, it was placed so the chimney would be in the center.

Almost all family life centered in the great room. Some family members slept there. Cooking was done in the large fireplace which often furnished the only light. Many tasks such as furniture making, weaving, and repair of clothing were performed near the fireside. The small house and floor plan shown in Fig. 4-13, illustrate the importance of the fireplace. The round hole shown in the brickwork of the fireplace is the oven. It was filled with hot coals from the fire. When the oven bricks became hot, the

4-11. The Cape Cod house.

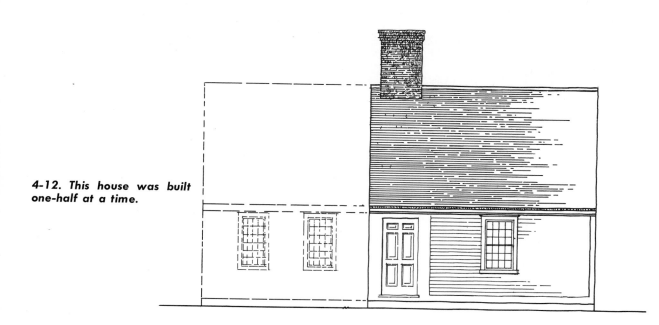

4-12. This house was built one-half at a time.

coals were raked out, and the food was placed in the oven to bake by the heat radiating from the bricks. The room labeled East Room on this plan was used for special occasions; it was the equivalent of today's living room.

The **gambrel roof,** Fig. 4-14, came into being because the simple, **pitched roof** (a roof at a steep angle) of the Cape Cod house left little usable space on the second floor. The roof slope restricted room areas, door locations, and furniture placement. To overcome this problem, the gambrel was developed. Instead of one slope or pitch from the cornice to the ridge, the gambrel had two: a steep slope from the **cor-**

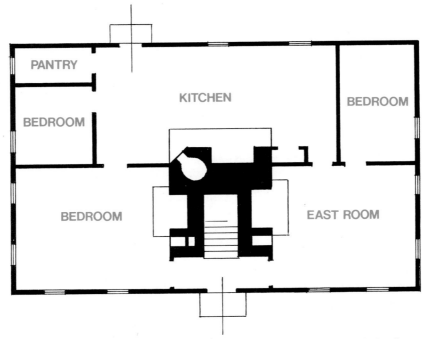

4-13. This home was built in 1690. One fireplace heated the entire house.

4-14. Why do you suppose a flat roof was not used instead of this gambrel?

4-15. The saltbox house.

nice, or overhang of the roof at the eaves, to the second floor ceiling line, and a flattened slope from this point to the top of the house. This made larger second-floor rooms possible.

When time and material permitted some colonists built houses which were a full two stories. The **saltbox house** in Fig. 4-15 began as a two-story, pitched roof house. The need for extra space prompted some owners to add one set of rooms along the back of the house and to bring the roof line down to cover this addition. Designers have adopted the name saltbox for this style because the long slope of the roof suggested the sloping cover on saltboxes, Fig. 4-16, which often hung on the wall of colonial kitchens.

The **garrison house,** Fig. 4-17, can be recognized by the overhanging second story, generally located along the front. This style was copied from the Elizabethan houses common in England at that time. The overhang was also used

on forts or "garrisons", Fig. 4-18, to prevent attackers from scaling the walls, and this is how the house got its name.

Almost all these early houses were covered with shingles or **clapboards,** narrow boards thicker at one edge to protect the walls from the weather. A huge chimney served a fireplace in each room, necessary for heat in the severe winter. Windows were small for two reasons: to save fuel by reducing heat loss, and because there was a high tax on window glass, Fig. 4-19. The huge wooden frame of the house was held together with wooden pegs.

The early English dwellings in the now restored town of Williamsburg, Virginia, Fig. 4-20,

4-16. A saltbox.

4-17. A garrison house.

represent the taste of a more worldly and so-phisticated group.

German and Dutch Settlements

Fig. 4-21 is an example of a house built by German immigrants who settled in Pennsylvania. They were religious, hard-working, middle-class business people and farmers. They treated servants as equals and made a place for them in the home. The elderly and unmarried family members remained at home. With such large family groups, they built houses of generous size.

The German work in wood and stone resulted in durable homes, many of which still survive. The smoke houses, ovens, barns and other outbuildings were so carefully made that they, too, are still standing. Their design tradition is much admired today.

4-18. A garrison at Fort Ticonderoga, N.Y.

4-19. How do our modern windows differ from these? Why?

4-21. This durable home is made of wood and stone.

The first houses built by the Dutch in New Amsterdam (now New York) and in towns and cities of the Hudson Valley were the largest in the colonies. Using stone and brick, materials similar to those they had used in Holland, they often built houses four or five stories high with ornamented brick work and intricate stepped **gables**—the vertical, triangular ends of a building, Fig. 4-22. The early roofs were steep, of straight pitch, with dormer windows also shown on the house in Fig. 4-22. A **dormer window** projects out from a sloping roof. An early Dutch

4-20. Notice the size of the chimney. How does its design show unity with the rest of the house?

4-22. The triangular portion of the side of this house is called a gable.

Besides providing material for a home, building with logs had another merit—it helped to clear land. This system was used for years by the pioneers of all nationalities as they pushed west and built in forested areas. It was so common that it became a part of American folklore and was looked upon as an American method of building. The fact that it was originally a Swedish tradition has been gradually forgotten.

Russian Settlements

The first buildings erected by the Russians in Alaska had fancy columns supporting the roof, cornices, and cupolas—small domed structures on top of the roof. The wooden trim copied the style that was fashionable in St. Petersburg, Russia, at the time. This style was confined to a

heritage is apparent in the house in Fig. 4-23. Characteristic of Dutch styles were metal gutters, small windows with sliding shutters, and the **Dutch door**—a door cut in half at the center so the top half could be opened separately.

Swedish Settlements

The Swedes used log construction since they had been using timber in their buildings for many years. They felled the trees, cut them into logs, and then laid them on one another horizontally. The logs were joined with notched corners. The joints were filled with clay, bark, or moss.

The log cabin, Fig. 4-24, was a primitive building, the walls of which were rarely longer than the length of a single log. Sometimes a cabin was divided into two rooms with an attic above, but more often there was only one room. In the earliest times the roof was of bark or thatch. Later, shingles were used.

4-23. This home was built by a Dutch settler in Newcastle, Delaware around 1700.

4-24. Log cabins originated in Sweden.

small area. Because of their remote location these houses had little effect on later building styles. No examples remain today.

French Settlements

The early French house in North America, Fig. 4-25, had a high steep roof common in Normandy. It had only a few small windows and wooden shutters which could be closed to protect against heavy snow and cold.

The houses the French built in New Orleans and other places in the south were raised to avoid floods and insects. The ornamental iron work was especially beautiful. Galleries and out-

Bolduc House, Ste. Genevieve, Mo.
4-25. An early French house.

St. Augustine and St. Johns County,
Chamber of Commerce
4-26. An early Spanish house in Florida.

110

4-27. A modern home which resembles a Spanish mission.

side stairs were common. For coolness and fire safety kitchens were often separate buildings.

Spanish Settlements

Spanish explorers first entered California and Florida in the early 1500's and were soon followed by missionaries. The house in Fig. 4-26, known as the oldest Spanish house in the United States, is built of **coquina,** a soft, porous limestone composed of shell and coral. Inside the house is a hand-hewn, beamed ceiling with whitewashed plaster walls and tile floors. The Spanish were both explorers and builders. Unlike the English, they did not drive the Indians out. Instead, they taught them Spanish building techniques. Spanish buildings often show the mark of Indian artistry. The home in Fig. 4-27 clearly shows its ancestry. It copies the style and details of the early Spanish mission buildings.

Case Problem A

Bring to class photographs or illustrations from other books and from magazines, which show the dwellings of the early explorers and settlers. For each illustration write a description of the area and its climate. Of what materials were the dwellings constructed?

ACTIVITIES

1. Go to your library and look up how people in other countries around the world used the materials at hand to build primitive shelters. Report your findings to the class.

2. Versions of the apprentice system are being used today. Discover what these are and write a brief report on them.

5 From The Georgian Period Through The Modern

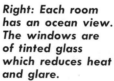

Far left: Not only its geometric design, but its function and the materials used to build it, reveal that this home is of the Modern period. (PPG Industries)

Left: Open to sun and sand, this home is keyed to outdoor activities. The basic materials are concrete and steel covered with reinforced fiberglas which resists the damaging effects of salt spray.

Right: Each room has an ocean view. The windows are of tinted glass which reduces heat and glare.

THE GEORGIAN PERIOD,
1720–1790

Although people of many different nationalities came to live in colonial America, the predominant architectural styles were English.

By 1720, life was easier. There was great contrast between the elegant town houses and the crude cabins in frontier settlements where life was still hard and dangerous.

Shipyards grew in many ports. Timber from the forests furnished lumber to build ships that were soon sailing around the world. Trade became important, and the shipowners and merchants became wealthy.

┌ Terms To Know ─────────────────────

classical   hip roof
Georgian   Modern
Gothic   Victorian
Greek Revival

5-2. A hip roof.

After fire destroyed much of London, the city required all new houses to be built of brick or stone. After a while, people liked the appearance of this building material so much that it was used in places that did not have fire prevention regulations. George Washington's Mount Vernon in Virginia, which is made of wood, was painted and sanded to look like the new fashionable stone.

Now formal design became important, as shown in Fig. 5-1. It became the fashion to have doorways in the center of the house. If there were two windows on one side of the door, two were placed on the other side for formal balance. A style of architecture called **Georgian** flourished in Williamsburg, as well as in New York, Boston, Philadelphia, and other cities in the east. The Georgian style was inspired by the architecture of England popular during the reigns of Kings George I, II, III.

The main characteristics of the Georgian house are formal balance, regularity of larger window forms and spacing, classical cornice and doorway details, the use of contrasting colors and materials such as red brick and white trim, and the hip roof. A **hip roof,** Fig. 5-2, slopes on all sides. As the slopes intersect at the outer corners, they form "hips". This hip roof style is similar in form to the pyramids of Egypt.

The large country estates of Virginia, Fig. 5-3, were certainly different from those of New England. The owners were aristocrats. They acquired large land holdings and had many servants. They had much time for leisure, travel, and study. They built homes following the style and practice of the landed gentry in England.

Tobacco, as well as indigo plants, rice, and later cotton, all thrived in the vast fertile fields of the south. These farms could be economically worked only in large units. Only people with large land holdings or plantations could get money from England, a fact which worked against the development of small farms. This resulted in a form of agriculture which greatly influenced the type of housing that was to develop in the south.

The baronial house in Fig. 5-3 was part of an impressive plantation. The owners had their own tannery, warehouses, grist mill, and

5-1. The Wythe House in Williamsburg, Virginia, is an example of Georgian architecture.

wharves where rich cargoes arrived from England. They also had thousands of acres of crops and numerous fine horses. Often as many as 200 to 500 people worked on one plantation.

The house plans in Figs. 4-13 and 5-3 are examples of how environment influences housing. Although the plans differ in scale, they are similar in several important ways. Each house was constructed by its owner from materials available on the land. No provision was made in either house for heat, with the exception of the

fireplace. Neither house had plumbing or lighting. Notice the lack of closets.

English architecture eventually penetrated all areas of the United States and influenced all other national styles.

During the last half of the 1700's, the French and Indian War, the Boston Massacre, and the American Revolution all occurred. It was a period of great contrasts. People like Daniel Boone were living on the frontier; and, at the same time, elegant houses and furniture were in

Stratford Hall Plantation, Westmoreland County, Virginia
5-3. Notice that the kitchen and office are separate from the main living area. Why?

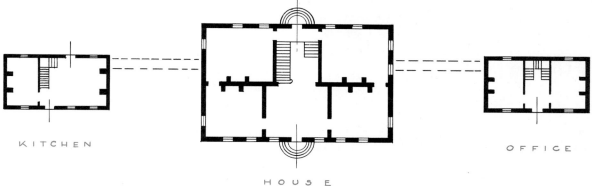

KITCHEN

HOUSE

OFFICE

demand. Banks, factories, and other business ventures grew.

Even though the country was in a state of turmoil and unrest, some of the people remained confident and continued in building fine houses and acquiring fine furniture.

When considering design, it is important to think of the economy of the times. In the first years of this country, everyone was more or less on the same footing. Wealthy and poor alike lived in the most primitive types of shelters. Gradually some people became wealthy. The rest of the population lived in frontier surroundings. Except for a few merchants and shopkeepers, there was virtually no middle class.

Until those of the Victorian era, the furniture and houses you usually see illustrated were only for the wealthy aristocracy. Today there are relatively few wealthy people and we have a very large middle class. Although Americans are concerned about the poor, the percentage of the total population who are poor at present is quite low as compared with the past.

Asian Influence

An important contribution in design heritage has come from the Far East. However, the first design details were not brought to the United States by Asian immigrants and traders. In the

5-5. How are these two tables similar?

5-4. A Japanese tea set.

early nineteenth century, sailing ships from the major ports of the east coast brought back cargoes of silk, ivory, and porcelain. These imports inspired designs for furniture and houses. The tea service shown in Fig. 5-4 is typical of the decorative items that were brought to America from places like China and Japan.

Chinese influence took two forms. Western versions of Chinese designs were used on wallpaper and furniture (See p. 328). Chinese-style lattice was used on staircases, fences, and in architecture. The straight leg form of Chinese furniture was also adopted.

The plain, simple lines of much modern arthitecture and furniture find their origin in Far

Helen Kowtaluk

5-6. Jefferson designed this home himself.

Eastern art. For example, the inexpensive plastic parsons table shown in Fig. 5-5 derives its lines from antique Chinese tables like the one shown beside it.

THE CLASSICAL PERIOD, 1790-1830

The American Revolution upset many of the old patterns—people who had been leaders due to their ties with England found they had lost influence. New trend-setting leaders—traders and merchants—arose. Cities with busy ports gained importance. The industrial era had arrived.

Some of the most significant examples of the **classical** style in architecture were designed by Thomas Jefferson, the first great American architect. His home, Monticello, Fig. 5-6, is a model of the classical simplicity of this style, which was based on the temple form found in Roman and Greek design. The latest form of this style was called **Greek Revival,** Fig. 5-7. In addition to rooms for eating, sleeping, cooking, and entertaining, rooms were also planned for such functions as dressing, study, or business.

THE VICTORIAN PERIOD, 1830–1900

During the **Victorian** era, named for Queen Victoria of England, railroads were built which linked together all parts of the country. Many factories were constructed and the new products shipped by railroad and steamship to the rapidly expanding population. The Industrial Revolution was fully under way. Profits from these enter-

5-7. Greek Revival architecture.

117

prises created a new social group of Americans who traveled to Europe and frequented fashionable hotels and museums. They brought home many ideas of splendor which they wished to build into their new homes, their fashions, and their standard of living.

The economy also gave rise to a large number of factory workers skilled in the operation of newly perfected machines. For the first time, quantity production made houses and furniture in the current fashion available to both the workers and those of greater wealth. Now, hundreds of people, working in factories, put together machine-made parts and glued on ornaments. Woodworking machinery made possible a large variety of ornament for both furniture and architecture.

Like all styles, the Victorian reflected social changes. Romanticism, or a revival of medieval forms, influenced all of the arts. The provincial architecture of medieval England, France, and Italy was used and abused by all designers. The obvious result was a sort of planned confusion! Row houses, apartments, and other multi-unit dwellings became common. Poor-quality houses were built near factories, and many present-day slums had their beginnings in these developments.

Although wood was frequently used in the construction of Victorian buildings, many brownstone houses were erected in eastern cities. Cast iron came into general use for the first time. Elaborate Corinthian capitals, columns, trellises, railings, window grills, and other ornaments of cast iron became features of the Victorian house.

Flexible floor plans were more common and rooms in the Victorian house were more informal. Irregular window arrangement and doors in a hit-and-miss pattern added to the popular, fanciful exterior.

Gothic design, featuring pointed arches and cut-out tracery similar to the window of a medieval church, was revived. This influence was

Victoria Society of Maine Women,
Roger D. Calderwood
5-8. Victoria Mansion, built in 1859.

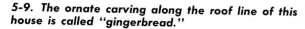

5-9. The ornate carving along the roof line of this house is called "gingerbread."

more evident in architecture than in furniture. The country became dotted with high-peaked Gothic roofs, festooned in lacy, cut-out wood trim called "gingerbread."

In general, all Victorian houses display some or all of the following details: picturesque broken lines, irregular mass, porches, balconies, bay windows, gables, dormers, high ceilings, tall windows, big chimneys, towers, and lavish ornament. But the end of the nineteenth century saw strong reactions to the prevailing Victorian style. A stronger preference for earlier styles was favored by some, and others departed from everything traditional.

Observe the differences in early and late Victorian styles, shown in Figs. 5-8 and 5-9. Victoria Mansion, shown in Fig. 5-8, is one of the finest examples of Victorian architecture. It was an inspiration to decorators, architects, and furniture manufacturers.

Victoria Mansion was designed by Henry Austin, an eclectic. The word "eclectic" means a designer who turns to a combination of many styles for inspiration. This home combines features of an Italian villa in the French style, with those of Greek, Roman, and Gothic.

Fig. 5-9 shows an example of an 1890 house of less elaborate design. This house is in the Gothic style and has an exterior of boards placed vertically, with joints covered with strips

of wood called "battens." The vertical boards increase the apparent height of the already tall house.

THE BEGINNING OF THE MODERN PERIOD

When the United States was recovering from the depression of the 1930's, the new Modern style was under way. Unlike the styles which came before, it could not be called American. It was an international style. Because of rapid communication and a mutual understanding of the challenges of contemporary life, it was accepted by the architects of many countries at once.

No one designer dominates modern design. Many designers are at work, and the range of choice in design is wide. The architects "Le Corbusier" (Charles E. Jeanneret-Gris) of France, Walter Gropius of Germany, and Frank Lloyd Wright of the United States were influential in establishing this style. Now there are many who are following in their footsteps.

Frank Lloyd Wright believed that a house should grow from the inside out and should be based on family needs. He used informal changes in floor levels and variations in ceiling

5-10. The Robie House was built in 1909 and was planned to fit a long, narrow lot.

heights. The Robie House shown in Fig. 5-10 is an example. It is the forerunner of the modern split level. Another characteristic of Wright's designs was continuity between house and site. He loved nature and considered the outdoors as part of the house. The idea of the "picture win-dow" evolved from this feature of his plans. He also developed the open plan. Many of his houses featured rooms which were functionally related spaces. He used common materials such as concrete blocks or natural rocks and pro-moted built-in furniture as cost saving features.

The first **Modern** houses were flat-roofed and were based on simple geometric forms. Their design is based on function and utility. Glass areas were often excessive. While the houses provided photographers with thrilling subject matter, they were often hard to furnish and uncomfortable to live in. The Modern was a rejection of the overdone styles of previous periods. All ornamentation was avoided and the results were stark, barren simplicity.

The designs that followed were more personal. In the house in Fig. 5-11, areas of privacy are screened from public view, and desirable indoor and outdoor living areas are combined. More color and variety in materials and a more informal plan were utilized without surrendering the principles of good design. Perhaps a trend is developing toward a national rather than international style. However, American houses will probably never be the same as those in some foreign countries because of differences in building materials, construction methods, and land use.

While environment and social changes have influenced the development of house designs, elements of national styles persist. People still use design details which show a national heritage. For example, the vacation house in Fig. 5-12 is in the style of a Swiss mountain chalet. A home is very complex and personal. Emotion or nostalgia plays a big part in its design.

Acorn Structures, Inc.
5-11. Sliding glass doors make the outdoors easily accessible.

Stanmar, Inc.
*5-12. **This house is in the style of a Swiss mountain chalet.***

Case Problem A

Residents of a community are planning a meeting with town officials in an effort to prevent the destruction of a building which has local historic significance. This building, situated on ample tree-shaded grounds, is to be demolished and the site used for a large commercial structure. Students in a nearby school plan to join in the effort to save the historic structure. How do you think they should proceed? What facts should they gather? Would it be a good idea to show "before" and "after" pictures of historic buildings that have been restored? Should they show pictures of poorly designed or unsightly commercial structures that have replaced historic buildings?

ACTIVITIES

1. Check your newspaper for announcements of tours of historic homes. Go on a tour. Select a famous house and find pictures of its interior. Read about the period in history when the house was built. Learn about the people who lived there and the events that occurred in the house. Pretend you live in the house. Give a report to your class so the class will feel they have visited there.

2. Make a list of the countries or world areas represented by the members of your class and their ancestors. Plan an exhibit of decorative articles from one or more of these countries. An exhibit is always more effective if appropriate backgrounds are planned. What colors, textiles, or pictures would be suitable with the items you will exhibit?

3. Select one or more countries. Find pictures of houses and home furnishings used there. Discuss how their design ideas could be applied to a modern home in your community.

4. Take a walk through your own neighborhood. Cover from 4–6 blocks. Count the number of houses you pass. How many of those houses are colonial designs? Make a list of those addresses. How many are Modern? Make a list of those. Of the colonial designs, try to decide which styles they are. What do your findings tell you about which styles are popular? Report your experiences to the class.

6 Homes Available Today

Far left: These row houses have been converted into city apartments.

Upper left: Traditional single-family homes are the most popular.

Lower left: A type of mobile home which can be taken apart, moved, and put together again.

Right: Do you know the difference between an apartment and a condominium?

In this chapter you will begin to apply what you have learned about housing styles and how they satisfy human needs. You will also learn about the kinds of homes which are available to you and your family. Each family must eventually decide which kind of home appeals the most, offers the most livability for the money to be spent, and is best suited to where they want to live.

THE DESIGN OF TODAY'S HOUSES

The large farm house, common until the 1900's, sheltered families and in-laws—cousins,

6-1. *This home, which used to house a single family, has 17 fireplaces. Today it is used as an apartment building.*

aunts, and other relations—as well as many visitors. The main home and outbuildings housed many who worked on the farm. The family home was almost the equivalent of a boarding house Fig. 6-1.

By contrast, the modern house is almost exclusively a two-generation home. In the average home you do not usually find grandparents or other relatives.

Some of the rooms featured in yesterday's houses are not considered practical for today's

living. For example, most houses had cellars and pantries for food storage. Now we use refrigerators, freezers, and storage cabinets. People used to sit on front porches. Now there may be a patio or a balcony. A recreation room or family room takes the place of the old-fashioned, formal parlor or living room.

Most early houses were divided into specialized rooms such as a dining room, kitchen, parlor, library, or music room. The modern house is more likely to have open space and multi-

included in earlier houses. Note that the space allotted for the garage is equal to two-thirds of the first floor.

Modern Use of Colonial Styles

Almost all the house styles you learned about in Chapter 5 are being used today. Of course each style has been modernized so it satisfies

purpose rooms. The dining area, living area, and kitchen, for example, may be included in one large more or less open space.

Another feature of early styles is that houses were often two or more stories high, which separated family activities. Bathroom and bedrooms were all upstairs. The modern house is more likely to be on one level or split levels. If two-storied, it usually has some kind of sleeping space and bathroom on the first floor as well as the second.

Fig. 6-2 shows the floor plan of a modern house. Although a fireplace is no longer always used for heat, cooking, or light, the one in this plan covers one wall of the living room. It will add a note of tradition and serve as a decorative feature. On the other hand, note that the kitchen is fully equipped with storage space and automatic equipment. A large family room offers space for informal hospitality and leisure activities, while a separate dining room is available for more formal occasions. The entire first floor suggests social and leisure-time activities.

A significant difference between this house and earlier houses is the amount of space used for storage and equipment—space which consumes about half of the area of today's average house. The tinted portion of Fig. 6-2 indicates storage space and equipment which was not

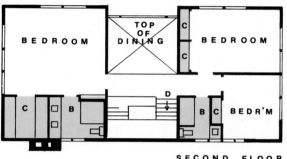

SECOND FLOOR

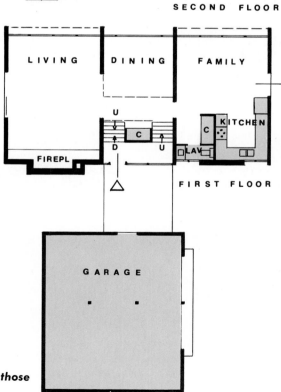

FIRST FLOOR

6-2. Today's home differs in some ways from those of the past.

127

Royal Berry Wills and Assoc.

6-3. A modern Cape Cod house.

A

B

6-4. The saltbox in traditional and modern forms.

the needs of today's families, but you will be able to recognize the basic designs. The examples given in the text refer only to basic shapes since each of these types occurs in many varieties.

THE CAPE COD HOUSE

In its three centuries of evolution, many social and economic changes have had an effect on the trim little Cape Cod house. Bathrooms and garages have been added, chimneys reduced in size, roof slopes flattened, windows enlarged, and the house itself raised to accommodate a basement or recreation room. This design is the traditional style most often constructed today—perhaps because of these changes. The basic reasons for its continued use, however, are economy of construction due to size, form, and materials; expandability; and, if appropriately designed, its attractiveness.

The lines of the twentieth-century Cape Cod in Fig. 6-3 are typical of this style. The architect followed the spirit of the style in adding the garage, which of course, was never a part of the original design.

THE SALTBOX

Many modern versions of this house feature a family room and kitchen in the one-story rear portion, which is very similar to its original function and purpose. In Fig. 6-4A you can see a traditional saltbox house. A modern adaptation of the style is in B—the long, vertical lines of the siding contrast with the sharp angles of the roof. In one section, a skylight serves as a window.

THE GARRISON HOUSE

The house in Fig. 6-5 is a present-day version of the garrison style. It is a good reproduc-

Royal Berry Wills and Assoc.
6-5. A modern garrison house.

George H. Sherwood, Architect
6-6. A modern Georgian house.

6-7. A modern house with a gambrel roof. Note the shape of the chimney.
Royal Berry Wills and Assoc.

6-8. A mansard roof is a form of the gambrel.

House in Williamsburg, Virginia, shown on page 114.

THE GAMBREL ROOF

The new house in Fig. 6-7 has a gambrel roof, making an attractive combination of old and new details. There are two dormer windows on the slope of the front roof. These give light and ventilation to the upstairs rooms.

THE MANSARD ROOF

The **mansard roof,** Fig. 6-8, a variation of the gambrel, was developed by a French architect by that name and was used commonly in France during the eighteenth century. It differed from the gambrel in that the roof pitched more steeply above the cornice and, wherever possible, continued around all sides of the structure.

THE SOUTHERN COLONIAL HOUSE

The **southern colonial** shown in Fig. 6-9 has the appealing solid, square-built features of Greek Revival houses. Actually, there were more houses of this type in New England, New York, Ohio, and Michigan in the early nineteenth century than there were in the south. However, the classic elegance of the exterior suggests a plantation home, and thus they are called southern colonial.

tion of the original colonial house. Its distinctive feature—the projecting second floor—has been retained. When modern real estate advertisements refer to a house as "colonial" they are usually describing this style.

THE GEORGIAN HOUSE

Fig. 6-6 shows a new, formal Georgian house, which features a hip roof. Sometimes a traditional style may be followed very closely— this house is very similar to the famous Wythe

6-9. Southern colonial homes are based on Greek Revival styles.

The roof of the house in Fig. 6-9 is not Greek Revival. What style is it?

Modern and Contemporary Styles

The Modern style, which began in the early 1900's is still in the process of development. **Contemporary** refers to a style that is just coming into being. Perhaps in a few years it may become accepted as part of the Modern style. Or it may be just a fad that fades away. Unusual or experimental designs are generally classified as contemporary.

Every successful house style is contemporary when it originates. People often look at styles of the past and consider them old-fashioned. They forget they were contemporary in their day. New materials and methods of construction will appear, and social and economic changes will occur. The house that people look upon today as the latest style will someday be old.

Unfortunately, the words Modern and contemporary are not always used to describe a house style. Sometimes the word modern is used in real estate advertisements because the house features the latest designs in bathroom or kitchen equipment. An advertiser may also use the word simply to mean "new," and thus it may be applied to any style. If the word is capitalized, however, it should refer only to the Modern style.

At first the design of the Modern house was accepted with reservation because it seemed cold and mechanical in its determination to be unlike any designs in the past. Such rigidity is gone now. The good Modern house of today features straightforward use of both new and old materials. It is a part of its **site,** or location, affording seclusion where desired and opening up into private gardens, pools, and terraces. Respect for climate is also kept in mind. The Modern plan often includes open areas, screened areas, centrally located kitchens, and accessibility to the outdoors.

The Modern house is an individualistic style but not to the point of being extreme. It reflects the strong preferences of the owner or the conviction of its designer that this house must be distinctive. Because it is different, it may cost more to build than a traditional style.

Of all the Modern styles, only two have characteristics that can be readily identified. These are the ranch house and the split level. The contemporary style includes the experimental designs.

THE RANCH HOUSE

The **ranch house,** shown in Fig. 6-10, is seldom what its name implies. It acquired that name because it resembled the rambling one-story house built by the early settlers of the western states. Most American styles originated in the east and moved west. The ranch house originated in the west and moved east. The original ranch house plan was suitable only for warm climates. Its open corridors, large windows, and light construction were not practical in colder sections of the country.

Today, with the use of modern heating methods, insulation, double-pane windows, and a great range of building materials, it is a style that can be adapted to all sections of the country. Frank Lloyd Wright was one of the architects who contributed to the development of the ranch style house. He made popular the open, flexible floor plan, and the large glass areas associated with this design.

Many people prefer this one-floor house with no stairs, which makes maintenance fairly easy. All rooms may have direct access to outdoor living areas, and furniture may be arranged many different ways.

One fault of the ranch house is that it occupies a fairly large area. This increases the cost of roof construction and foundation work. However, other styles also have special costs. If the lot size permits, the ranch house fits well into today's living.

THE SPLIT LEVEL HOUSE

The **split level house** design was brought about by the increasing cost of land and fewer good building sites. Originally, the split level was

6-10. The ranch house originated in the west.

reserved for a hillside lot with the low end of the lot holding the two-story portion and the high end the one-story part. This change in levels produced some dramatic and interesting plans. Soon builders began to copy the idea for houses on level lots.

Generally, in a split level, the living room and kitchen are at ground level. The garage, laundry, and utility rooms are a short flight below, and the bedrooms and bathrooms are a short flight above. The garage then is located in a semi-basement and the driveway usually slopes down to it.

The house shown in Fig. 6-11 has three levels built on a sloping lot. The garage and utility room are entered below the level of the front yard. The living room wing is halfway between

6-11. Originally, split level homes were designed for hillside lots.

Walter A. Jones, Architect

6-12. No two contemporary houses are alike.

the garage floor and the bedrooms, which are located over the garage. This style has many of the advantages of a two-story house but saves steps since only one-half flight of stairs must be climbed to go from one level to another.

THE CONTEMPORARY HOUSE

One important feature of contemporary style is evident in the house shown in Fig. 6-12, and that is uniqueness. For example, all Cape Cod

Howard M. Simpson
6-13. A vacation house in the form of a geodesic dome.

houses have a common form that is easily recognized. Contemporary houses may tend to "follow the leader" but no two designs are alike. Furthermore, new changes continue to appear as styles develop Fig. 6-13.

In general, a contemporary house forms a unit with its site. The successful design often relates the interior functions to outdoor areas. Areas within the house are less clearly defined than in traditional plans. That is, activities may be kept separate by furniture arrangement rather than divided by walls. The contemporary house is well-proportioned and of simple design, depending on form rather than ornamentation for its beauty.

The contemporary house may be composed of colors and materials which are beautiful as well as functional. The characteristics of the principal building materials—wood, brick, stone, stucco, and concrete—are respected and their natural appearance retained. Concrete, for example, is no longer regarded as an unattractive material to be hidden by brick but is part of the display. Rough stone walls contrast with such mechanically cut, smooth materials as plate glass and metal. Rather than planed smooth, wood sheathing may be left with saw marks for a textural effect.

What Roof Styles Can Tell You

The roof offers one of the most important variations in house styles. Sometimes the same floor plan may be used for a number of houses in large subdivisions while the roof shapes are changed to provide exterior variety. As you may have noted earlier, the style of a house is often distinguished by the shape of its roof. The mobile home in Fig. 6-14 is an attempt to satisfy consumer demands for traditional styling. What type roof does it have?

If you are house-hunting, knowledge of the types of roofs may help you to visualize what a house will be like inside. Fig. 6-15 shows some of the basic roof shapes used in the United States. Observe the characteristic shape of the house as well as the roof. For example, the salt-

6-14. Does this mobile home have design honesty? Is it well-proportioned?

box house would probably have two stories in front and one in back. This means that there are probably rooms on the first two floors in the front and an attic. The house is not tall enough where the roof slopes in the rear to permit two full floors.

The roof may be the only difference between a so-called modern or contemporary home and the traditional or colonial. Flat, vaulted, and shed roofs are generally considered more modern. A **vaulted roof** is one which is arched, part extending above the rest. However, even traditional roof styles appear in today's contemporary homes.

TYPES OF HOUSING AVAILABLE

In addition to a variety of styles, different forms of housing are also available. These include the development house, the prefabricated house, the custom-built house, the older or "used" house, the mobile home, the cooperative apartment, the condominium, and the rental apartment.

Single Family Housing

The Older or "Used" House

In most communities new houses represent a small portion of the number of houses offered

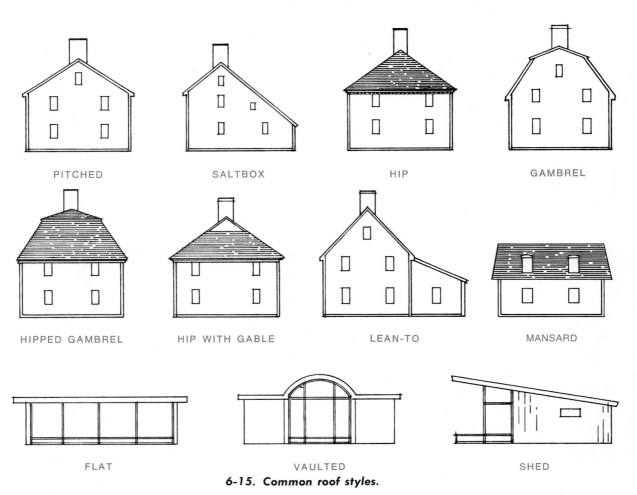

| PITCHED | SALTBOX | HIP | GAMBREL |

| HIPPED GAMBREL | HIP WITH GABLE | LEAN-TO | MANSARD |

| FLAT | VAULTED | SHED |

6-15. Common roof styles.

for sale. Most of the houses for sale have been occupied and are being re-sold. These houses may range in age from fairly new to antique.

The high cost of replacing existing buildings with new ones has convinced some owners that it is wise to maintain old property through repairs and alterations. The 1914 house shown in Fig. 6-16A was completely transformed into a striking contemporary as shown in Fig. 6-16B. The small double dormer was extended across the entire house. The exterior was finished in shingles. Extensive improvements which bring an old or lower priced house up to the neighborhood level may be a good investment.

Generally, a used home can be purchased for less than a new home of the same size and quality. However, the cost of repairs must be

A

Red Cedar Shingle and Hand Split Shake Bureau

6-16. Would you recognize A and B as the same house?

B

6-17. In most developments, the houses look alike.

THE DEVELOPMENT HOUSE

Developers buy large tracts of land and divide the land into house lots. They then build **development houses** on these lots. In most subdivisions, only a limited number of house plans are used because repeating one or two economical plans helps to control costs and streamline work, Fig. 6-17. The houses are often widely advertised, and there may be a sales office at the site. Often one or two furnished houses are on display. The developer may offer financing or assistance in obtaining the financing.

Because developers try to keep prices down the houses may not be well-designed. Development houses include only basic landscaping. For the first few years, a new development may appear very bare and unfinished. Buyers in a new development take some chance since they

figured in the price to be sure that the price represents good value.

In an effort to preserve old neighborhoods, some large cities offer the houses for sale for a very small sum. The owners must then agree to make repairs and changes within a certain amount of time.

PPG Industries

6-18. A modular home being delivered to its lot.

cannot be sure how the area will eventually look.

Since only a few house designs are used in a development, each owner may achieve individuality through planting, exterior paint and decoration, and interior decoration.

THE PREFABRICATED HOUSE

Prefabrication is a fairly new industry and accounts for about 5% of the housing being built today. A prefabricated home is produced off-site, indoors, using ordinary building materials and construction. There are three major types of manufactured homes, the pre-cut package, the two-dimensional system (panels), and the three-dimensional (modular) system.

The pre-cut package delivers the assorted parts to the site where about 90% of the work is completed. The two-dimensional system delivers assembled flat sections, but erection, plumbing, heating, wiring and all interior finishing still remain to be done. The three-dimensional or modular system normally delivers a finished product with only minimal assembly and some minor finishing required, Fig. 6-18.

The prefabrication industry is a leader in the field of good design in low-cost housing. While an individual constructing an inexpensive house usually cannot afford to spend money on careful design, firms producing many inexpensive houses can afford to pay for the services of an architect.

THE CUSTOM-BUILT HOUSE

Few people can afford a custom-built home today. However, these homes are like the dress designs which appear in high fashion magazines, for they set the styles and standards. New designs, materials, and equipment are tried in these homes, which benefit all buyers. The home illustrated in Figs. 6-19A and 6-19B is an expensive, custom-built house. A study of custom houses may result in new ideas for all housing.

A **custom-built** house is designed by an architect who draws the plans and writes the specifications. The **specifications** give a detailed description of the material to be used and spell out details regarding the construction.

6-19A. Custom-built homes set the styles and standards which other homes follow.

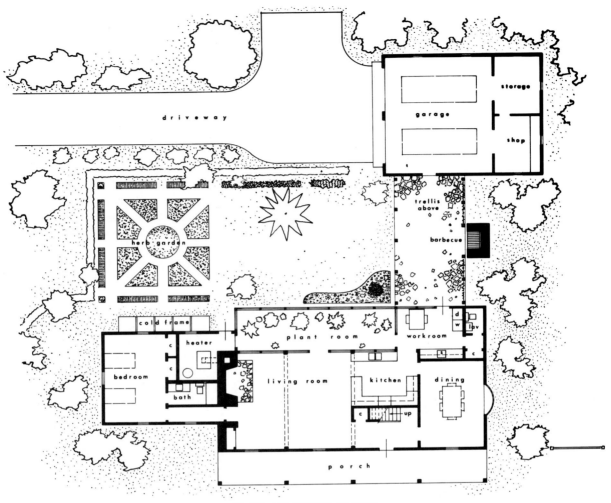

PLAN OF FIRST FLOOR

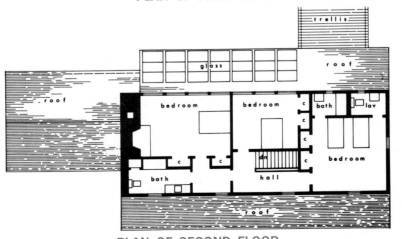

6-19B. The floor plan of the home in Fig. 6-19A.

PLAN OF SECOND FLOOR

6-20. A double-width mobile home.

If the custom-built house is to be satisfactory, the owners must be able to describe their ideas and needs so the architect can include them in the design. The prospective owners should be able to read plans and visualize the finished house in order to avoid disappointment. They should be able to judge the value of the house before it is built—while it is still on paper. Can you tell why?

The house in Fig. 6-19A and B was designed to meet the needs of the owners. Since they are interested in gardening, the plan includes a cold frame, a plant room, and an herb garden. The workroom can be shared by husband and wife. The bedroom and bath on the first floor are for an older member of the family who cannot climb stairs.

THE MOBILE HOME

The **mobile home** is described as a movable dwelling made to be towed on its own chassis to a location where it may be connected to utilities. Usually it is a house without permanent foundation although it is used for year-round living. It may be designed so that it can be compressed in size when towed and then expanded at the site. Also, separate units may be joined to create larger living areas. For example, Fig. 6-20 shows a sales model which is made up of two long units that have been joined side to side to form a double-width area.

New mobile homes are sold fully equipped with major appliances and furniture, draperies, lamps, and carpeting included in the purchase price. The owners may add their choice of many extra features including air conditioning and washer and dryer.

The furniture in the model home shown in Fig. 6-21 is not included in the price but has been selected for both good looks and low cost. The interior offers design suggestions which could apply to any small home.

Some areas have special parks for mobile homes. These often include recreational facilities and services that are not available in many other single-family neighborhoods.

Possible restrictions must also be taken into account. Some mobile home parks are open only to those who purchase homes from the owners. Others exclude children. It is well to check in advance the restrictions that may apply.

An extensive series of federal guidelines and standards regarding mobile homes has been is-

141

6-21. *The interior of a mobile home may be attractively decorated.*

6-22. *A contemporary apartment complex.*

142

sued by the U.S. Department of Housing and Urban Development (HUD). These guidelines establish requirements on all equipment and installations, including plumbing, heating, electrical systems, and fire safety. Each model must be approved before construction. The rules establish requirements for safety. For example, the design of windows is specified if the window might be used for an emergency exit.

Consumers should look for a data plate on mobile homes that are for sale. It should state that the home has been designed to comply with the Federal Mobile Home Construction and Safety Standards in force at the time of manufacture. Consumers should do comparison shopping, read warranties and find out what regulations apply in their state.

Multiple-Family Housing

RENTAL APARTMENTS

Many of the new apartments built in recent years are a reflection of our times. Singles, newly married couples, and a large number of older individuals may need this type of housing. Further, the mobility of our society has created a need for readily available rental units.

The buildings in Fig. 6-22 are high-rise apartments in a large complex, popular in many cities. These huge buildings offer most of the facilities of a small town such as parking, stores, business offices, and recreation.

Townhouse apartments, shown in Fig. 6-23, offer some of the privacy of a single house. Each unit has its own separate entrance and a private back yard, and are more common in suburban locations. Because the units are grouped together and a large area planned at

one time, good land use practices can be followed. In this development large areas of land were used for a golf course, recreation hall, swimming pool, and a small shopping center.

Small apartment communities are being built for the elderly. Many of these are only one story high to give the area a residential character. They may feature large flower gardens and patios, a large recreation hall, a low-cost restaurant, a nursing home, and a nearby hospital. Many come equipped with an intercom system so the tenant may summon help if needed. The units are rented exclusively to people 65 and over. The buildings are usually located near a public bus line and good shopping facilities. Some specialized apartments for the elderly are designed so that the daily cleaning in each apartment is handled by staff members.

THE COOPERATIVE APARTMENT

The **cooperative apartment** or co-op is a form of home ownership and not a design. It combines the advantages, financial and otherwise, of house ownership with the convenience and freedom from care of apartment rental, Fig. 6-24.

6-23. These townhouses share common walls.

The cooperative form of ownership began in the 1920's. The management is run as a corporation. The buyers purchase an apartment and receive stock in the corporation which runs the building, just as they would if they purchased stock from a broker. The amount of stock depends on the value of the apartment purchased. Along with the stock, the buyers get a lease giving them possession of the apartment.

A co-op has a major advantage over other apartments since the owners have a voice in how it is run. The owner cannot be evicted, and there are no restrictions on redecorating. Unlike any other home, the owner has a voice in selecting neighbors. If a family wants to purchase an apartment in the building, the corporation puts it to a vote; if the residents vote against them, the apartment is not sold.

The major disadvantage of the cooperative apartment is that it is a joint venture, and each resident must respect the judgment and decisions of the group. If, as a group, they fail to use good judgment or to make wise decisions, the dissenting individual must still go along with them.

THE CONDOMINIUM

In some respects a **condominium** is like a cooperative—it is a multi-family building, and individuals own their own apartments. The major difference between a cooperative and a condominium is in the form of ownership. In a condominium each individual owns the unit and a share of the common ground. He or she may sell the unit without the approval of the other owners.

The ownership of land, driveways, and other areas are owned in common by all of the tenants. There is usually a home owner's association which governs the use of the common areas. Each person has a vote in the proportion to the value of the unit or units owned.

A condominium may be a single apartment building, or it may consist of a condominium complex that includes apartments, townhouses, club house, swimming pool, and perhaps even a golf course, Fig. 6-25.

THE DUPLEX

A **duplex** is a house for two families. Often the owners of a duplex live in one half of the house and rent out the second half, as the family in Fig. 6-26 has done. The rental income helps them pay the cost of the house.

A duplex can be compared to a townhouse as it may have its own yard and separate entrance. Although a duplex may offer more privacy than a townhouse, it does not offer the recreational facilities of a complex.

6-24. Cooperative apartments are owned, not rented.

6-25. This condominium resembles a vacation resort.

6-26. Each half of this duplex has its own front and rear entrances.

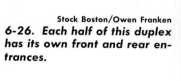

Mark Browning needs to earn money for college expenses so he has a job working for a realtor in a large city. The realtor handles apartment rentals in many
types of buildings. Mark's job is to show apartments to possible tenants. If he does
well, he may be employed by the firm another year. He decides to familiarize himself with all of the types of apartments available in his city so that he will be able to
discuss them with people who are seeking housing. If you had a job similar to this
in your area, what types of apartments would you have to show? What would you
say about each?

Find the "homes for sale" section of a newspaper. Clip six apartment ads and
mount them on sheets of paper. Under each one, list its selling points.

1. Prepare a bulletin board showing the types of housing common in your neighborhood, such as new and older homes and types of apartments.

2. Visit a model mobile home on display. Evaluate it according to your family's needs by
making lists of its good and bad points.

3. Find a picture of a house style described in this chapter. Play the role of a realtor
who has it for sale and describe it to a prospective buyer.

4. List the house styles discussed in this section and find a magazine or newspaper picture of each. Have the builders been true to the original style or have they changed it?
How?

3 HOW A HOUSE IS MADE

7 Housing and the Environment

Far left: If you lived here, which rooms would you place facing this view? All photographs these two pages, M. K. Weigel)

Upper left: Allowing this land to remain naturally forested protects our air and water as well as providing beauty.

Lower left: Careful landscaping of this land lets it blend with the wooded background.

Right: Would you like to live in the western mountains? an eastern city? the South? the Middle West?

WORKING WITH NATURE

Environment is everything which surrounds us—air, water, soil, trees and other plants, buildings, streets, even sounds. While we react to our surroundings with all of our senses, we speak mainly of what we see, hear, and feel.

Ecology is the study of the relationship between people and the environment. To live in ecological harmony people must maintain a balance among themselves and other creatures and their natural surroundings.

Consumer Responsibility

Natural resources must be protected and

Terms To Know

aesthetic codes	master plan
area plan	orientation
building code	redevelopment
cross-ventilated	plan
depreciating	topography
ecology	unplanned change
environment	urban renewal
exposure	urban sprawl
ghetto	variance
impervious paving	zoning

used wisely. Care must be taken to preserve the healthfulness and beauty of land, water, and air. In a fairly short time, energy conservation and pollution have become topics of world-wide concern. People have had to realize that individuals can no longer think only in terms of their own comfort and pleasure.

Many decisions related to housing affect the environment. For example, burning leaves instead of composting them pollutes the air and wastes a valuable soil enricher. The improper use of chemicals, paints, and insecticides around the home may pollute both air and water.

The use of materials in house construction may affect the supply of natural products. For example, certain types of forests may be depleted by over-cutting. Efforts in forest improvement have resulted in new building materials. Some are composed of wood chips and sawdust, which not too long ago were considered waste products, Fig. 7-1. Older buildings are being renovated to save natural materials.

Thought must now be given to the selection of home equipment that is the most efficient while causing the least pollution. Chapter 9 will discuss energy use and conservation in the home.

Whether people build their own homes, buy them ready-built, or rent them, they must be able to make wise consumer decisions. They must be able to decide if a house or apartment takes advantage of what the environment has to offer or if it works against the environment. The first thing to consider is placement of the house on the land.

Use of the Land

The way land is used may cause undesirable changes in the environment. Often, old buildings are allowed to deteriorate. Rather than repairing the old existing houses, people build new ones

Reynolds Metals Company and
Bay State Builders

7-1. This house is made completely of recycled materials.

Massachusetts Audubon Society
7-2. None of the natural qualities of this area were preserved.

Buyers of so-called "bargain" land often find that they have made a costly mistake. Since the land shown in Fig. 7-3 is subject to periodic flooding, it should never have been used to build on. Such wetlands form an essential part of our environment, and must be preserved.

Some communities are preserving natural beauty by restricting the use of outdoor advertising and controlling the use of land. This results in the elimination of what has been called visual pollution.

THE HOME AND ITS SITE

The site of a home is the space of ground on which it sits and which surrounds it. The site is the home's natural environment.

in new locations. Thus land is wasted. When housing developments remove good agricultural land from production, the food supply may be affected. When marshland is filled to create house lots, the ecological balance of a large area may be upset. Improper land use may reduce open spaces or parklands unnecessarily and may destroy wildlife.

The aerial view of a housing development in Fig. 7-2 is an example of poor land use. Hundreds of look-alike houses on small lots and bare streets afford little privacy. Most of the open spaces have been eliminated by the builder.

As communities grow, new approaches to land use need to be explored. A high-rise apartment, for example, may house the same number of people as a subdivision but leaves more open space. Houses built in clusters also make better use of land by leaving more open space.

Massachusetts Audubon Society
7-3. A poor choice for a building site.

7-5. When space for parking is limited, products such as this may solve the problem without damaging the environment.

7-4. It will be many years before enough trees and shrubs grow to beautify this land.

7-6. Landscaping helps a home blend with its environment.

Topography

Topography refers to the contour of the land. For example, is the site low and flat or rolling and rocky? If it is available, flat, well-drained land free of rocks is generally the easiest and most inexpensive to build on. If the lot contains solid rock, it will require blasting before the house can be built.

Steep sites may mean hazardous driveways and walks. Low land with poor drainage may cause sewerage problems and result in wet basements. Unstable, eroding, or shifting land should be avoided.

Lots created by filling should also be avoided since filled land is seldom able to carry the weight of construction without settling. Filled land often results in a site without plants and trees, Fig. 7-4. Unless adequate topsoil is provided, it will be difficult and expensive to landscape.

Landscaping

Landscaping also affects a home's environment. The type of walks, parking areas, and driveways may increase the runoff of water after storms. If many people build huge areas of **impervious paving**—paving made of material that water cannot penetrate, such as concrete or asphalt—the runoff may be so great that floods occur. Large trees and other plants surrounded by solid paving may lack moisture and die. Too much paving may also reduce the underground supplies of water and affect the amount and quality of drinking water.

The unique paving blocks shown in Fig. 7-5 are an example of a product that does not damage the environment. Grass grows through the blocks so that people may drive and park cars and trucks on a beautiful lawn. The design of the blocks also allows for natural drainage. The oxygen-producing grass provides a healthful alternative to concrete and asphalt.

Landscaping can improve the appearance of a home and can improve its interior environment. Fig. 7-6 shows a house with and without shrubs and trees. How will the addition of the tree affect the glassed-in breezeway in this house? How does the addition of landscaping add to the attractiveness of the low-cost city apartments in Fig. 7-7?

Boston Housing Authority
7-7. How would this area look without the shrubs and trees?

153

7-8. This home has patio windows and a balcony overlooking the beach.

ORIENTATION

To make the best use of a site one should take advantage of the direction the house or apartment will face. This is called its **orientation.** An ideal orientation does the following:

- It enables the occupants to enjoy the advantages of sunshine. In the north, where winters are cold, sun exposure is important.

- It should take advantage of pleasant breezes. The ideal is to have a building **cross-ventilated.** This means air can travel in one side of the home and out the other. Cross-ventilation is important to summer cooling. However, the site should also be protected by trees or natural elevations to avoid the full force of strong, cold,

or hot winds. In desert, coastal, open-plain, or mountain country, additional windbreak protection is needed.

- It lets the natural beauty of the site be seen and enjoyed. If a site offers a pleasant view, like the one shown in Fig. 7-8, it is important to make the most of it. If this means that large windows will be exposed to hot or cold winds, additional insulation or other architectural adjustments may be needed.

Exposure

Exposure is the position of the house with respect to its orientation and the weather. Many buyers do not think about exposure until they have built or purchased the house. Then they discover the living room is either too hot or too dark, or perhaps cold winds hit large picture windows facing north. It is very easy to change a plan while it is on paper. It is difficult, if not impossible, to make major changes once the house is built.

The principles of good exposure apply to both a high-rise apartment and a one-family house. An apartment balcony facing west will be unprotected from afternoon sun. On the north side, the balcony might interfere with natural light, making the apartment interior dark.

Fig. 7-9 illustrates why the design and placement of windows are important. It shows how the house may be designed to take advantage of the sun during the winter months when it is needed. By properly designing the roof or by selecting an awning to provide shade, the direct rays of the sun can be screened during the summer months. Although the roof projection is sufficient to shield the windows from the sun during the summer, it does not keep out the rays during the winter when the sun is low in the sky. A double-pane window or a storm window reduces the loss of heat from the house during cold weather.

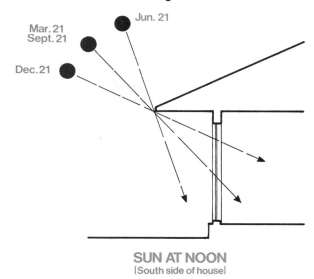

SUN AT NOON
(South side of house)

7-9. The angles of the sun throughout the year.

The house shown in Fig. 7-10 is located in a temperate climate, where hot summers and cold winters may usually be expected. In this illustration you can see what an architect has done to achieve a comfortable indoor temperature the

Tech Built Homes, Inc.
7-10. Good orientation and exposure can add to the comfort of a house.

155

year round, without the use of any special equipment. A generous roof overhang shields the second floor windows from the summer midday sun. The large tree shades a great portion of the front of the house. A lattice at each end provides semi-shade for main living areas. Generous windows assure good cross ventilation. In winter, the tree loses its leaves and the house receives the benefit of the sun's rays. When the sun is low in the sky, the shadow from the roof overhang is greatly reduced. The densely wooded area at the far side of the house breaks the force of cold winter winds from that direction. The walls and roof are insulated. The house has insulated glass windows, an efficient heating system, and air conditioning.

The Size and Shape of the Lot

The size and shape of a lot may present limitations which will seriously affect fuel costs as well as the pleasure of living on the site.

First, the size of the lot and the placement of the house must meet community regulations. For instance, most communities have zoning laws which specify the distance a house must be from the adjoining property lines. The lot should be large enough to meet these requirements and also permit good orientation. Lots that are narrow and deep or irregularly shaped may make placement more difficult.

Suppose a couple looks at lots in the subdivision shown in Fig. 7-11. The house plan shown has already been chosen. Which lot should the owners choose? In many such subdivisions, houses are placed so that they will face the street. In almost every case, the living room is in front.

This couple would like to have the house face south in order to enjoy sunshine in the living room, dining room, and garage, which would also be used as a hobby workshop. If these rooms face south, the porch will face west and will be hot in the afternoon during the summer but pleasant in the evening when used most. Sunshine would be pleasant in the morning in the kitchen. However, in the area where

this house is to be built, cold, unpleasant winds come from the north in the winter. The owners hope to plant trees on the north side of the house to cut the winds and provide a shady area that can be easily reached from the porch. The owners do not want the bedroom on the east side since the morning sun would wake them too early. The bedroom—which they would also like to be cooler than the rest of the house—a closet, a bath with extra heat provided, and the storage wall in the garage will be on the north side of the house.

The house plan poses a problem. The garage is to be entered from the side. This means the lot must be wide enough to provide a drive and turning area on the right side. The owners want sunshine in the hobby and work area of the garage and do not want the open doors to face the street. If the doors are left open in nice weather, everything on the inside will be exposed to the street.

The requirements seem simple. Let's look at the subdivision again and see how many lots fit their requirements. Consider the lots that face south. Numbers 1 through 6 are long and narrow. They do not provide the area needed for a side driveway. Lots 7, 8, and 9 are wider, but 7 is on a corner. The owners would have to decide whether they would like the porch on the street side. Lots 10 through 15 all face south and are large enough. However, no one can predict what might happen east of Lot 15, since it is on the edge of the development. Lots 16 and 17 are wide, but Lot 17 also abuts the end of the subdivision. Lot 18 is interesting because it is wide and meets the requirements of the plan. However, this lot has three back yards adjoining it. Only a few lots in this large subdivision of over one hundred can meet the couple's requirements.

Making the Most of the View

Ideally, a home should be placed on its site so any enjoyable view can be seen from as many rooms as possible. The futuristic village facing the sea on the coast of France, Fig. 7-12,

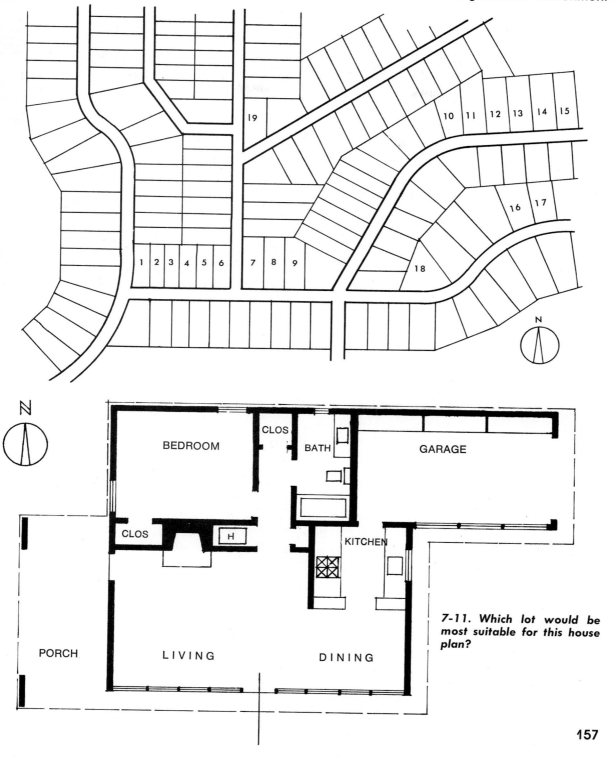

7-11. Which lot would be most suitable for this house plan?

157

7-12. Notice how the buildings curve to fit the contours of the land.

7-13. Even limited spaces can provide a pleasant view.

looks like the stage set for a contemporary play. The unusual design ignores tradition. Each dwelling has many windows and balconies taking advantage of the ocean view.

However, you cannot always have a desirable view from every window. Creating your own view is one way to overcome this kind of disadvantage in a site. If there is no pleasing, open view, you might want to create your own scenery, such as a garden or courtyard, or a decorative, shrubbed wall, fence or hedge.

Fig. 7-13 shows a private walled garden that gives the owner a pleasant view. The floor-to-ceiling windows bring the outdoors inside and add spaciousness to the interior. Open space in the garden reduces the cost and effort of maintaining shrubbery and, at the same time, helps create a spacious effect.

In some cases there may be no solution to the problem of view. Yard space may not be available or the addition may be too costly. In this event, the window may be screened off from the unattractive view or may be covered with a translucent wall or sheer drapery, which would cover the view completely but let in daylight.

HOMES DESIGNED FOR SELF-SUFFICIENCY

The portions of the house shown in Fig. 7-14A, B, and C were designed by a group of scientists to demonstrate the benefits that come from cooperation with nature. The builders hope to show that people living on small lots in northern climates can be more self-sufficient, and that it is possible for a family to raise all of their own vegetables and fish on a year-round basis.

7-14. A home that cooperates with nature.

A

B

C

159

Integral Urban House, Berkeley,
California/Pat Goudvis
*7-15. A city home which helps teach
people to work with the environment.*

The large black cylinder shown in A is one of several tanks used to raise fish. The solar-heated and wind-powered greenhouse is shown in B and C. When the fish tanks are cleaned the nutrient-rich water is used to water the plants. The greenhouse is built partially underground in order to take advantage of the earth's natural insulation. The roof panels close at night to conserve heat.

A renovated city house and garden are shown in Fig. 7-15. They are used for a college course in which city people are taught to work with nature. Solar water heaters, a solar oven, a means to convert sewage to clean fertilizer, a greenhouse, and a garden all help provide food and fuel with a minimum of pollution.

Not one inch is wasted in the small outdoor area. Animal pens hold enough rabbits and chickens to supply four residents with fresh meat and eggs. Beehives providing honey are set on platforms above a pond for raising fish. Waste water from the Japanese bathtub in the house flows into the pond to supply nutrients for the growth of algae on which the fish feed. Other household water irrigates the garden. Even the fencing around the yard is put to use supporting vines and fruit trees. Compost bins for collecting organic wastes from the house, garden, and animal pens are everywhere.

WHERE DO YOU WANT TO LIVE?

People live in one of three general areas: city, country, or suburbs. If you like small towns and opportunities for being outdoors, you may prefer rural life, Fig. 7-16. If you enjoy a wide range of cultural activities and like being around lots of people, you may want to live in the city. If you think you'd prefer a combination of both, the suburbs may have what you're looking for. Table 7-A shows the major advantages and disadvantages of each area.

The Urban Environment

Since more than 90% of the population now lives in urban-suburban areas, such as that in Fig. 7-17, the city environment must be considered in more detail.

A drive from Maine to Virginia on the east coast, from Pittsburgh to Detroit in the midwest, or in the Los Angeles area of southern California is a ride through one city after another. Only a marker indicates where one stops and another begins. Compact downtown areas have become less populated while business has spread out along the highways to create new fields of congestion. Today's city is a part of a constantly changing business world, characterized by large-scale, specialized production and complicated transportation systems for both people and products.

New developments may result in major changes in the years ahead—within city structures. Each of these may affect the value of homes. Real estate values have gone up and down as the demand for property in an area has increased or diminished.

Unplanned change generally occurs gradually. Fire may destroy an old section, or parts of the city may deteriorate through neglect or

7-16. A country road in Tennessee.

Table 7-A.
SOME ADVANTAGES AND DISADVANTAGES OF CITY, COUNTRY, AND SUBURBS

Area	Advantages	Disadvantages
City	• Widest range of housing prices • Largest selection of services and goods • Greatest number of entertainment and cultural opportunities • Greatest variety of jobs available at widest range of salaries • Greatest opportunities for meeting a variety of people from different social, economic, cultural, and ethnic backgrounds	• Large areas of substandard housing • Highest crime rates • Fewest outdoor facilities, such as parks and gardens; fewest play areas for children • Highest levels of pollution, dirt, and noise due to industry, automobiles, and inadequate cleanup services • Overcrowded, transient; many areas lack sense of community and help create feelings of loneliness
Suburbs	• Most people own their own homes • Many open areas and parks; many play areas for children • Within reasonable distances of city jobs and attractions • Widest range of housing types available, from apartments to semi-farms	• Becoming heavily populated; poor housing design common • Dependence on cars creates heavy traffic and energy waste
Country	• Cheapest land available • Strong sense of belonging and neighborliness • Least pollution, noise, and dirt • Plenty of open space and greatest opportunity to be outdoors • Opportunity to produce low-cost food and fuel.	• Fewest entertainment and cultural opportunities • Fewest community services and facilities • Least variety of services and goods • Fewest job opportunities

change in city regulations. Areas in cities may change slowly from residential to industrial. The outside appearance of the houses may not change but alterations may occur inside. For example a house may be converted to office or business use or turned into a private school or nursing home. Changing traffic patterns may mean that new highways and parking areas are required and that buildings must be removed to provide space for them. In Fig. 7-18 you can see what happens to property when an owner resists the change to commercial use.

Another and more subtle change may be in the quality of individual use. Owners or renters may not keep houses in good repair due to low income, long periods of unemployment, ill health, or indifference.

Population may spurt in one region, with no

Aerial Photos of New England
7-17. An aerial view of the Chicago Loop.

increase in the amount of land available. This results in great competition for good building sites. One-family houses may be converted to apartments or rooming houses. Although the appearance of an area may not change very rapidly, the value of the land may increase based on demand. With this increase, a rise in taxes is certain. This generally leads to the replacement of some buildings with those of greater earning power.

When some city dwellers see the area beginning to deteriorate, they may move into better

7-18. Now this person's home overlooks a parking lot.

163

7-19. Land developers plan shopping centers, industrial sites, and residential areas.

for museums, art galleries, and other cultural centers are included in the best city plans.

Unfortunately, in many cities, before such plans can be carried out, much has to be undone which is often costly in time and money. Efforts are sometimes delayed and hampered by legal restrictions.

The **area plan** is another approach used in many cities. It is often called a **redevelopment** or **urban renewal** plan. It is usually for the purpose of rescuing an area which is in a state of decline. For example, a neighborhood which is going down in value and is unattractive in appearance may be torn down. Before this can be accomplished, homes must be found for the residents, and facilities provided for businesses in a new area. Funds must be obtained to provide low-cost schools, hospitals, and sanitation facilities.

The apartments in Fig. 7-20A, B, and C were built by the Federal Housing Authority to renew an area which had declined. Fig. 7-20A shows the area before redevelopment. In B a new form of housing, modular units, are being used to create the homes. Each new apartment is two stories high. The first floor has a living room, kitchen, dining area, storage space, and hall. The second floor consists of a hall, two bedrooms, a full bathroom, and storage closets. The top unit is designed to project over the bottom module one foot, front and back. The upper and lower units are bolted together. After the units are in place, the roof, which is finished with a gravel aggregate, is added.

Fig. 7-20C shows the completed project. Final exterior decorating is done at the site. The finished apartments face a terraced courtyard.

sections. Their exit speeds the decline. People who move to the suburbs often find problems created by rush and lack of planning. Isolated buildings without adequate utility services or quickie developments have been labeled **urban sprawl.**

Cities which use planned change may follow a **master plan** to guide both private developers, Fig. 7-19, and government agencies in construction projects. The plan may include provisions for traffic control, public transportation, schools, parks and recreational grounds, or other facilities.

City planners recognize the need to create an attractive urban environment by eliminating undesirable features and encouraging those that will please the eye, such as small parks, playgrounds, and natural beauty areas. Provisions

A

B

Guerdon Industries, Inc.

7-20. These apartments are constructed of modular units.

C

7-21. Many buildings are worth saving and can be made into attractive homes.

Trees and other plantings have been added, along with sidewalks.

In some areas residents themselves are rescuing fading neighborhoods. Increasing costs for new houses have made restoring older structures worthwhile. Often older buildings are in convenient intown locations which means the new owner can save on commuting costs as well. The neglected millworker houses shown in Fig. 7-21 were recycled by private individuals. Like many older houses their generous size made conversion to apartments practical. Now they are attractive homes.

Choosing a Location

Usually the best way to start house-hunting is by looking at the surroundings. When you buy a house, a site to build a house, or when you rent an apartment, you also buy or rent the neighborhood and community. A home in an area you do not like is not a bargain at any price.

Unless a house is way below standard, its location is the greatest single factor affecting its value. Location affects the amount of money that can be borrowed to purchase a property, and also influences future tax costs, insurance, and transportation charges. In addition, you must consider peace of mind. The family will be unhappy if the house proves to be poorly located. A modest home in a suitable area is a better investment than a more expensive one in the wrong location.

Most authorities agree that when a person selects a location, certain area features should be considered. Some of these features may not be among your own requirements, but you should be aware of them. Remember, if you ever wish to sell your home, they may be requirements of the new buyer.

THE TYPE OF NEIGHBORHOOD

The word "neighborhood" suggests a group of people having common interests. The term is applied also to areas where the land and its history are associated; for example, the Nob Hill neighborhood in San Francisco or Beacon Hill in Boston.

New houses of similar design or structure may make a neighborhood. The people who buy in a development of two-story houses may have similar tastes since they have all chosen this style.

A new suburban business district may be connected to apartment compounds serving young married couples. A new college campus also attracts home developments. Naturally, near a campus, teachers and administrators tend to build. The word neighborhood also suggests a physically defined area. In many instances these areas are separated from the rest of the community by barriers such as a highway, a river, or a canyon. Other areas may be "social islands" also called **ghettos**, because of racial, ethnic, religious, or economic differences. They have acquired a character which sets them apart.

• **A neighborhood should contain certain conveniences or be within easy access of them.** Years ago, when transportation was limited, the small compact neighborhood was essential. It included shopping and places of employment, schools, churches, fire and police protection, as well as other essential facilities. With the automobile, air travel, and fast public transportation, homes were built farther and farther from church, shopping, and schools. Daily commuting to work over long distances is now common. Daily traffic jams are the result. And now a new problem has arisen. Energy shortages make driving long distances both expensive and wasteful. More and more people may find it necessary to live and work in the same neighborhood once again.

Today's city planners realize that coordinated community development is needed. The proposed apartment center shown in Fig. 7-22 is an imaginative example of a complete neighborhood. The plan shows the location of retail shops, commercial services, a day care center, community center, offices, and a restaurant. Provision is made for underground parking.

7-22. In complexes of the future, people may live and work in the same set of buildings.

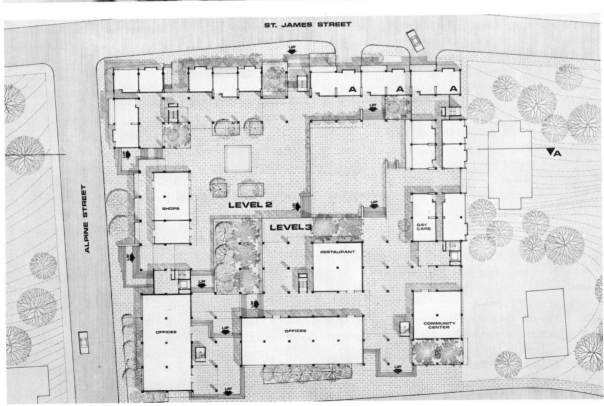

Apartments with a view of the courtyard occupy the floors above the noise of traffic.

This building represents fine planning for social needs. It is designed so that the roof of one apartment forms a small private yard for its neighbor. The yards are arranged in clusters with covered areas which may be used as play space for small children on stormy days. The play areas may be viewed from any of the apartments in the group. By taking turns watching the children, parents may have free time to use the community center, to visit the restaurant, or to shop.

- **The condition of the neighborhood affects the value of the home.** Although a home may be kept in good repair, its market value increases or decreases with neighborhood values. Changes in the valuation of a home are gradual. These gradual changes may be anticipated before they become serious and the owner may be able to sell well in advance of a decline. Of course, you should avoid choosing a home in an area where values are already **depreciating,** or going down.

Before you buy a home, determine what the pattern of growth has been in the area. Talk to people who have lived there a long time. See if you can learn of people who may have bought homes and sold them to be used for another purpose, such as a place of business. Inquire about houses that are being razed to make way for stores or apartments, or houses in the process of being renovated.

Another way to predict the character of change in a suburban area is to study carefully the distribution of neighborhood types within the city. As a city expands, neighborhoods often tend to move outward, following the main traffic arteries without much change in character. For example, it is more likely that a neighborhood of expensive residences will progress onward and outward without change than develop into an area of small lots and inexpensive houses. Also, a street that has proved its worth as a commercial artery is likely to attract more businesses.

Good residential areas seldom "jump over" an industrial area. However, expanding industry may absorb a residential district. Look for natural barriers or attractions that may direct growth. A river, hill, or swampland may cause a city to grow in a certain direction—over, around, or away from the obstacle.

- **The size of your neighborhood is the distance you travel in an average day.** An elderly person who doesn't drive may choose to live in a compact neighborhood where almost all of the essential facilities are within walking distance. A downtown apartment near churches, shops, doctors, and friends would be ideal in this case. Many people like having public transportation, such as a bus or train, nearby. A young, working couple without children might select a location with access to a super highway within 32 to 48 km (20 to 30 mi.) of the downtown area where they work. Their neighborhood would be much larger.

NEIGHBORS

Some people prefer living near others of their own age group or those having the same interests or social and economic lifestyles. For instance, families with young children usually prefer areas where their children will have playmates. Other people prefer a variety of neighbors. Whatever your preferences, you must be sure the location meets your needs.

It can also be important to be among friendly people who are willing to help one another or a new neighbor. Talk to people in the community and learn to know them a little before you make a decision.

AESTHETIC AND CULTURAL FEATURES

Keep your personal feelings in mind when choosing a location. For example, if the view from a picture window is the rear of a supermarket, you may become dissatisfied. This may also be true if the neighbors do not maintain their yards.

Is the area pleasing to the eye? If you are building a new home, consider how the type of house you have in mind will relate to the homes already in the area.

● **Community pride is a stamp people put on their environment.** It says, "This is the kind of people we are." It is hard to define but easy to see. If your term paper is neat, if you have spelled words correctly, and spent time doing a good job, your paper says you take pride in your work. Neighborhood pride shows in yards that are clean, houses that are neat and in good repair, and in a community that is well managed.

Property may be very reasonable in an area where improvements are just beginning to appear. Sometimes a section of a city will decline and then, because of its architecture or some other factor, be rediscovered and restored to attractivness.

A run-down house can generally be improved and, if the neighborhood is good, the improvement may be justified as an investment. If the neighborhood is not good, both your investment and satisfaction are endangered.

● **The location of churches and schools must also be considered.** If your church plays an important part in your life, you may want it nearby. Parents with school-age children will probably want a school within walking distance or one with a safe bus service. Fig. 7-23. The facilities and reputation of schools are so important that property values tend to be high in communities with top-rated schools.

UTILITIES AND SERVICES

Most people generally take for granted the presence of water mains and sewers, trash collections, and street maintenance. Therefore many a new home-owner is shocked to find these services are poor or even nonexistent. Especially in rural areas, lots may not have water mains, sewers, or utilities. The seller or landlord may not point out the lack of these services.

The number of dwellings has increased so rapidly in some areas that the public services and utilities have been strained. Even in established neighborhoods, it is often necessary to increase electric power or telephone service or the size of sewers and water mains to satisfy new demands. Some of these demands cannot be anticipated.

Before buying, you should determine what additional costs you are likely to have to pay in the near future. For example, if there is no public sanitary sewer, you must pay for your own

Boston Housing Authority

7-23. Some communities provide day care centers for families with children.

septic tank and leaching field. If there is no gas service, you must use bottled gas. If there is no electric service close by, you may have to pay for utility poles and power lines to bring it to your house.

• **Sometimes the owner of the lot must pay for the street and sidewalks.** The cost of new streets is usually paid for by the town as a whole. If a street must be widened to accommodate increased traffic in an existing neighborhood, the property owners usually pay for the improvement.

In northern areas roads and streets must be kept clear of snow in winter to insure adequate fire and police protection and to keep accidents to a minimum. Even though the expense of this service adds to the cost of city government, it must be considered money well spent. Many country homes have long driveways or private roads. In winter these must be plowed at the owner's expense.

Wide, curving streets that carry only local traffic are most desirable. Curved streets discourage high speeds and are less likely to become main traffic arteries. They also offer more variety in the way houses may be situated on the lots, thus creating more attractive neighborhoods. Streets should be well-lit and kept in repair. In rural areas roads should be paved and give easy access to main highways.

• **The ideal public water supply is one with the mains in place, high-quality water, good pressure, and reasonable rates.** If water mains have not already been placed in an area, the owner may be charged for them.

Water supplies in some areas may be threatened by sewage and other pollutants. In areas hit by drought, residents may not be able to use water for such things as watering lawns during dry, hot weather.

• **Sewerage may be a serious problem if the public system is inadequate.** Some states have few requirements regarding sewage disposal. Many health problems have developed because regulations were lacking or not enforced. Where an area has grown too fast, the existing sewers may be inadequate, and flooded basements may result during heavy rains. If there is a septic tank, check its age and capacity.

• **The area should have well-trained police and firemen.** Your home will be safer, and you will have more peace of mind knowing you can receive assistance in an emergency. Also, insurance companies charge lower rates in communities that provide good protective services.

• **Medical needs may dictate locating within range of a certain hospital or clinic.** This is often important for older couples and for young couples who plan to have children.

• **In urban areas where there is little space for recreation, community playgrounds and recreation areas are an asset.** As in the case of a school, buyers may want a playground to be near but not next door.

The playground shown in Fig. 7-24 is an example of one which students created out of a parking lot. In addition to its attractiveness the flower garden mural encourages children to invent many new games.

Certain sports and hobbies may be important to a family. Good facilities for these may influence choice of housing, Fig. 7-25.

NUISANCES

Many nuisances can make an area unpleasant and reduce the value of property. Certain entertainment centers may cause local hazards as can heavy or dangerous industry.

• **A home must be safe.** In modern times safety has come to include new things. Technology has brought benefits and new hazards. It means safe disposal of waste material to avoid contamination of our natural resources. Fire, noise, and air pollution are serious problems in some places. The people in Fig. 7-26 are threatened by the technology of heavy airport and automobile traffic. Styles of homes change continually to meet the need for shelter and safety.

• **Excess noise is a nuisance.** In some areas noise may be so intense that the location should

7-24. Children, too, can help make their environment a pleasant place.

be rejected. For example, the site may be close to industrial activity or to an airport, which makes it impossible to screen out the sound. Because noise is so undesirable, houses in locations with high noise levels must be priced very low if they are to be sold.

In most areas, normal traffic sounds may be diminished by plantings or fences or the way the house is positioned on the lot. Good sound proofing materials are available to decrease interior sounds. Rooms that should be quiet may be placed away from the street.

TRANSPORTATION AND SHOPPING

Few people are free to live in any location that suits their fancy. Your place of employment usually determines the general area in which you must live. Unless you have a home business, a farm, or a live-in job, you should decide on the maximum time and amount of money you are willing to spend going to and from work. For some, the distance they can walk

(perhaps only a few blocks) will be as far as they wish to go. Others may be willing to spend forty or fifty minutes each night and morning.

The distance to other essential facilities is also important. You must consider what you want in your neighborhood and set your own limitations in terms of miles, blocks, or time, for outside activities.

One way to begin is to record the distance members of your family travel in the course of a month. Include trips to churches, schools, shopping, and the homes of friends. The distance you travel in daily visits is most important.

Parking is also a consideration. If an apartment house does not provide it, parking may be an added expense and constant problem. Some communities forbid overnight parking on the streets.

Some people want to be located where they can walk to a small store for emergency needs. Others say the store should be near but not too near; they want convenience, but do not want the confusion and traffic nuisance of business in their immediate area. The development of huge shopping centers has made people willing to drive some distance to shop. Energy shortages may change this.

LAWS AND REGULATIONS

Many communities do not have master plans, but almost all have regulations to govern and direct growth. These may take the form of rulings known as zoning regulations, building codes, aesthetic codes, and tax policies.

Zoning

The purpose of **zoning** is to regulate the use of land. Regulations vary widely from town to town and limit the type of building which may be erected.

Zoning regulations may influence:
- minimum lot sizes
- the distance a house may be placed from porperty lines
- whether single or multiple family residences may be built
- height of buildings
- parking areas
- amount of land left for open spaces
- districts set aside as "green belts" where no building is permitted
- overcrowding
- entrance of businesses into residential areas
- provision of streets, water, sewerage, and electricity in newly developed areas
- area population growth

Zoning must be based on sound plans and must be enforced in order to be effective. Most towns have maps indicating zoning. These maps are usually on display in the town or city hall. Realtors often have copies available to show buyers.

The most restricted zoning specifies large lots and single-family residences. However, there may be some areas where smaller lot sizes are permitted.

The next classification is usually general residence where several types of residential build-

7-25. These residents enjoy their community's swimming pool.

Massachusetts Audubon Society

7-26. Air and noise pollution can threaten the health of these residents.

7-27. Even small things, such as storage of garbage cans, can help protect the environment.

ings may be erected. Apartment houses, two-family dwellings, and homes combined with an office or business are usually allowed in this district.

Business and industrial districts form other types of zones. These may be divided into several sub-sections. For example, light industry which creates no sound or odor may be allowed in certain areas that do not permit heavy industry. Zoning laws may change. This is usually accomplished by a vote of the townspeople. Also, town officials may, under certain circumstances, grant an exception, or **variance,** to an individual.

Building Codes

Another form of planning aid is the **building code.** Building codes regulate:
- type and quality of materials
- form of construction
- the provisions for health, safety, and sanitation
- use of flammable materials
- fire exits
- type and installation of plumbing
- electrical work
- type and installation of heating systems

Aesthetic Codes

Some cities have **aesthetic codes** concerning the appearance of buildings. These often apply to new construction in historic zones where styles which are not in keeping with the period

of the district are forbidden. A town may regulate the colors that may be used. Some districts under federal control forbid all types of building in order to protect a natural resource or attraction such as a seashore, a mountain area, or a historic site. Steps are being taken at present to ensure that new construction does not damage historic sites along major highways.

In an attempt to beautify their areas, a number of cities have passed laws governing appearance. For example, one community prohibits storing rubbish containers in the open. Fig. 7-27 shows one homeowner's solution—a wood enclosure was built to store the containers. The top was left open for ventilation.

Some communities have outlawed all outdoor advertising. Another has limited the materials and colors that may be used on any building in its business district. Many communities have review boards that must approve plans—including design, materials, and landscaping—before a building can be constructed. Some have established high standards in the design of new public buildings.

Taxes

Taxes indirectly influence the environment of a community. If, in any one area, taxes are extremely high, new structures such as one-family houses may not be built. Good buildings are sometimes reduced in size or torn down in order to decrease the property's taxable value. Existing buildings may be neglected or even abandoned. Very high taxes cause homes to change ownership frequently.

Older people on fixed or declining incomes may find that they cannot afford to stay in high-tax areas. Younger people can seldom afford high tax rates and, consequently, builders find it difficult to sell new homes to this group in high-tax neighborhoods. This slows down building activity.

An area may be chosen by a family on the basis of tax consideration alone. For example, some areas in highly industrial towns or suburbs have low residential taxes because of the taxes paid by the industries. The residents are willing to live close to industry and benefit from the tax advantage.

Remember, zoning laws, building codes, and all other related rules and regulations are steps that have been taken to help insure more orderly growth. In the end, however, the best protection comes from having good neighbors. People who have high standards, who want attractive homes, and who keep them in good repair thus create good neighborhoods.

Case Problem A

Make a study of housing and site locations in your area. Real estate firms, the Chamber of Commerce, historical societies, the library, and your local newspaper are good sources of information for this project.

Is industry concentrated in one area? Why or why not? Where are new industries located? Why?

Where do people generally move when they leave the central area?

Determine the general trend of growth in your area. Are some neighborhoods growing faster than others? Are any neighborhoods beginning to show signs of decline?

Where are most of the new houses being built?

Which areas provide the most attractive sites for new houses?

Do the new, growing residential areas have strict zoning codes?

What neighborhoods offer the best living conditions for a growing family? A retired couple? A single?

Pretend you are going to build the house shown in Fig. 7-28. The second floor, not shown on the plan, has two bedrooms; each bedroom has windows on three sides. What site requirements would you have for this house? Select the site in your city that you would like for this house. Why did you select this site? Does it meet all of your requirements for this house? Why or why not?

Would it be easier to begin with a site and design a house to fit it? Why?

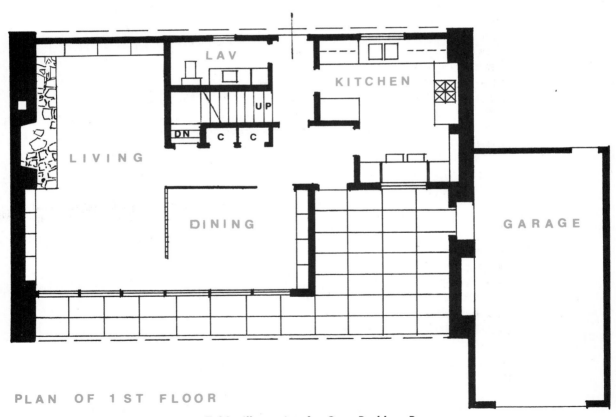

PLAN OF 1ST FLOOR

7-28. Illustration for Case Problem B.

ACTIVITIES

1. Find out what anti-pollution laws are in effect in your community. In a large city, the Board of Health will have copies of the laws affecting health and safety. In a small community, someone in the town hall can tell you where you can obtain this information. Perhaps your teacher will invite someone who is an expert in this field to discuss the effectiveness of the laws.

2. Visit the water department in your community and find out what treatment, if any, is required for your drinking water.

3. Find out through reading and interviews what the major sources of pollution are in your community. What additional controls do you think are necessary to stop this pollution? Discuss in class.

4. You might like to make a collection of all the information you can find on ways to improve the environment as it relates to your home. For example, we know that excessive noise is a pollutant since it has adverse effects on the nervous systems of both man and animals. How can excessive noise be reduced? Make up a bulletin board of your ideas.

5. Note the effect of widening a through street, making it a heavy traffic route with frequent signal lights. How many homes have become rundown in appearance or replaced by businesses such as small restaurants, service stations, insurance agents? Do property values increase? Find three or four examples to answer this question.

6. Read about the redevelopment of a near-by area. Have any businesspeople and home owners been affected by the changes that resulted from the enterprise? What did they think about it?

7. Make a pollution rating sheet. You might include such items as bad odors, smoke, smog, soot, bad drainage, refuse and litter on streets and lawns, inadequate garbage removal, and polluted lakes and streams. Rate your own community. Also rate another area you know well such as a nearby town. How do the ratings of the two areas compare?

8. Start a class scrapbook. Have class members contribute newspaper and magazine articles concerning environmental problems. The articles might be arranged according to catagories and indexed.

9. Learn about terrariums. A terrarium is a self-maintaining eco-system. Plan and build one for your classroom.

10. Write to the United States Department of Interior, Washington, D.C. 20240. Ask for a list of agencies and organizations active in environmental affairs. Write to selected agencies and request up-to-date information related to the environment and housing. Develop a classroom reference shelf.

11. Read a science fiction account of an orbiting space station for people. Do some research on how a livable environment will be created in real space stations. Report on both to the class.

12. Select a neighborhood where you can determine whether values are going up or down. List all of the sources for your information. What do you think accounts for the changes in value?

13. Sketch a rough plan of your present home. Indicate on the plan its orientation and exposure. From which direction do prevailing winds blow? Which rooms get the most sunlight?

Try to learn the size and shape of the lot. Add that to your plan. Indicate where any trees or bushes are located. How do they affect your home environment?

8 The Structure of a House

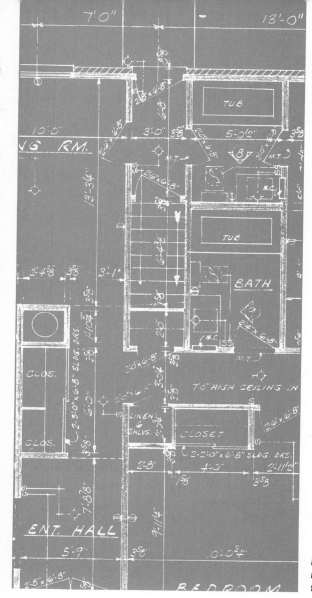

Far left: Why do you suppose learning how a house is made will help you if you rent an apartment?

Left: A blueprint tells a builder which things go where in a house. (William Spence)

Right: Every detail must be accounted for.

Knowing how a house is built can help you in many ways. If you are buying a ready-built house, this knowledge may help you to communicate with real estate agents and to judge the houses you look at. It may also help you to understand what is involved in remodeling. If you are building a new house, it may help you to read the blueprints, to communicate with the builder, and to understand the steps in the construction process. If you are renting a house or apartment it will help you to tell how well the building is constructed and maintained.

Terms To Know

anchor bolts	fanlight	jalousie window	riser
apron	fill	jalousie door	roofing felt
balcony	fill-type insulation	jambs	roof pitch
batten doors	finish flooring	joists	rough boarding
bay window	finish grade	lath	R value
beam	fire stop	lights	sash
blanket insulation	fittings	load-bearing wall	screen doors
blueprint	flashing	louvers	section
breezeway	floor framing	louvered doors	septic tank
bridging	floor plan	mantel	sidelights
cap	floor slab	mullion	siding
casement	flue	muntins	sill
cesspool	flush doors	Palladian window	skylight
chimney	folding door	paneled doors	storm window
circuit breakers	footing	patio	studs
circuits	foundation wall	pediment	subfloor
columns	frame	picket fence	termite guard
cornice	French door	piping	terrace
crawl space	fuses	pivoted window	thermostat
damper	fuse box	plaster	threshold
detail	glazed doors	plates	throat
disposal field	glazing	plumbing	transom
double-hung	ground drain	plumbing code	tread
downspout	gutter	portico	valley
drain tile	hangers	post lamp	wall framing
dry wall	head	rafters	window sill
dry well	header	rail fence	
electric meter	hearth	recovery rate	
elevations	insulation	ridge	

HOW TO READ A BLUEPRINT

A **blueprint** is a reproduction of a drawing of a floor plan. The **floor plan** shows the layout of the rooms as they would appear if the roof were removed and you looked down into the house. Floor plans show only length and width, so you cannot tell how high the rooms will be. Frequently, the electrical system is also shown on the floor plan. When a special part of a floor plan is difficult to draw at a small scale, it is drawn separately to a larger scale. This drawing is known as a **detail.** A blueprint may be either white lines on a blue background or blue lines on white.

Several sets of prints are usually required for the construction of an average house. In making application for a building permit, the owner files one set of blueprints and the contractor uses two or more on the job. Plumbing, heating, and electrical tradespeople require a set each.

If you are building a home, a blueprint will help you to understand the plans and to visualize how the proposed house will look when it is completed.

Since there is only a limited amount of space

on a blueprint, it is impossible to write in all the information needed, so symbols are used. A list of the more common symbols appears in Fig. 8-1. A blueprint showing the first floor plan of a house appears in Fig. 8-2.

In the past, architects and members of the building trades have worked with customary measurement in design, manufacturing, and construction. The change to metric is likely to be slow, and many kinds of building materials are not available yet in metric sizes. Since the building trades prefer working with millimeters, even large sizes are given in millimeters throughout this text.

THE BASIC STRUCTURE

If you were to make an imaginary vertical cut through a finished house and carefully remove the portion closest to you, you would find that much of the material used in the construction of the house might be seen along the cut. Furthermore, by carefully examining this exposed material, you could learn a lot about how the house was put together. This cut, called a **section,** can be seen in Fig. 8-3 (page 184). It shows many parts of a typical house. Some of these parts may be used to evaluate the quality of construction. Others are not visible in a finished house. But if you observe a house during different phases of its construction, you will probably be able to see all of the parts discussed here.

This house is a one-story wood-frame structure with a basement and an attic. If you are evaluating a house that uses different construction methods such as a prefabricated model or a contemporary design, some of the construction methods discussed here may not apply.

The Foundation

For a house with a basement, the dimensions are staked out on the lot on which the house is to be built. Then the earth is excavated down to the proper level. Once the excavation is dug, the **footing** is poured. This is a continuous concrete base running around the edges of the foundation, generally 300 mm (1 ft.) deep and 600 mm (2 ft.) wide. Footings are also poured to serve as a base for columns which support the floors. Note the placement of footings in Fig. 8-3. The type and size of footing should be suitable for soil conditions. In cold climates, the footings should be far enough below ground level (about 1200 mm or 4 ft.) to be protected from frost action.

Footings should be placed on solid undisturbed soil, which will not settle and cause cracks to form in the house.

To reduce the danger of water damage, it is customary to place **drain tile** around the footings and, in some cases, under the concrete floor. The tile collects any water and directs it to nearby drains. This protects the foundation from water damage and keeps water from finding its way under the basement floor. If the water in the area should rise above the level of the floor, the floor will be lifted up by the pressure of the water and the house will float like a boat.

The **foundation wall** is a poured concrete or concrete block wall about 250 to 300 mm (10 to 12 in.) thick. Generally, the foundation walls should extend above the grass level so that the frame structure will be well above the surface of the lot and protected from soil moisture. If the house will not have a basement but only a **crawl space** between it and the ground, the space should be high enough for a person to crawl under the house for maintenance care.

The **sill** is a continuous piece of wood. It provides a base on which to build wood floors and walls. The sill is anchored to the foundation with **anchor bolts**—galvanized steel bolts placed in the concrete with their threaded ends up. The sill is then bolted to the concrete wall, and the frame structure is built directly onto the sill. This construction helps to hold the house down during high winds and storms.

It is advisable to apply waterproofing in areas where dampness can be anticipated. The waterproofing material is applied on the outer face of the concrete wall from the line just below the final ground level down to and including the top of the footing. If the wall is built of concrete

ARCHITECTURAL

PLUMBING

ELECTRICAL

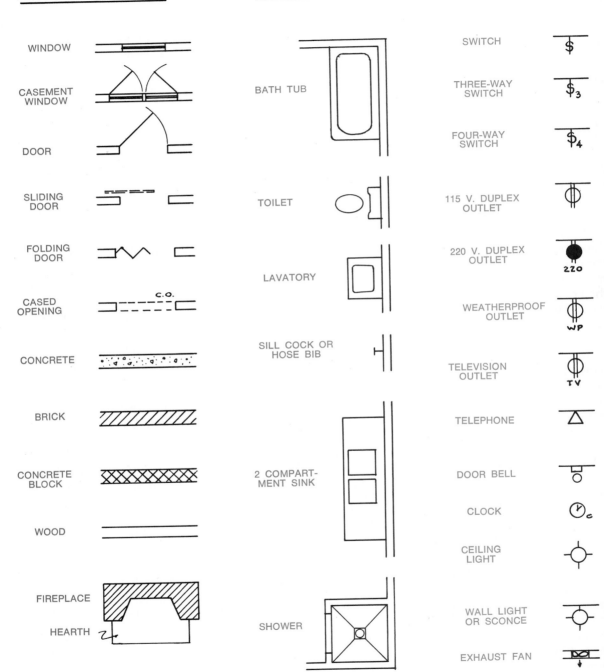

8-1. Common blueprint symbols.

WINDOW

CASEMENT WINDOW

DOOR

SLIDING DOOR

FOLDING DOOR

CASED OPENING

CONCRETE

BRICK

CONCRETE BLOCK

WOOD

FIREPLACE

HEARTH

BATH TUB

TOILET

LAVATORY

SILL COCK OR HOSE BIB

2 COMPART-MENT SINK

SHOWER

SWITCH

THREE-WAY SWITCH

FOUR-WAY SWITCH

115 V. DUPLEX OUTLET

220 V. DUPLEX OUTLET

WEATHERPROOF OUTLET

TELEVISION OUTLET

TELEPHONE

DOOR BELL

CLOCK

CEILING LIGHT

WALL LIGHT OR SCONCE

EXHAUST FAN

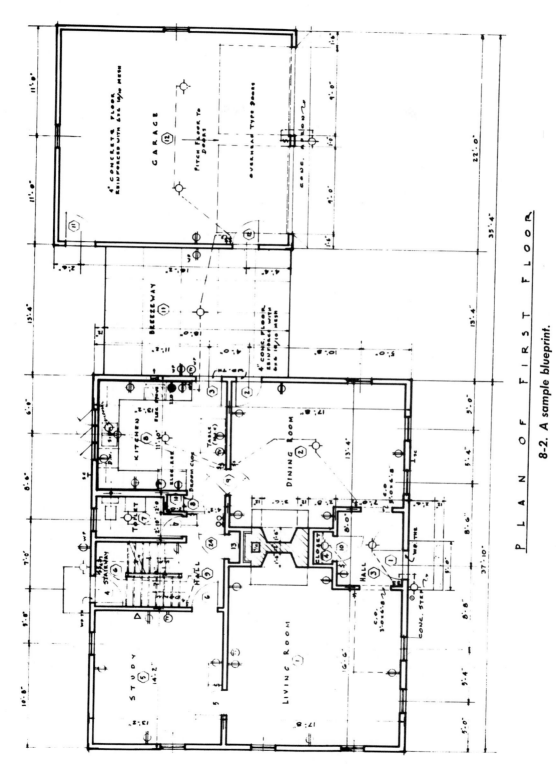

PLAN OF FIRST FLOOR

8-2. A sample blueprint.

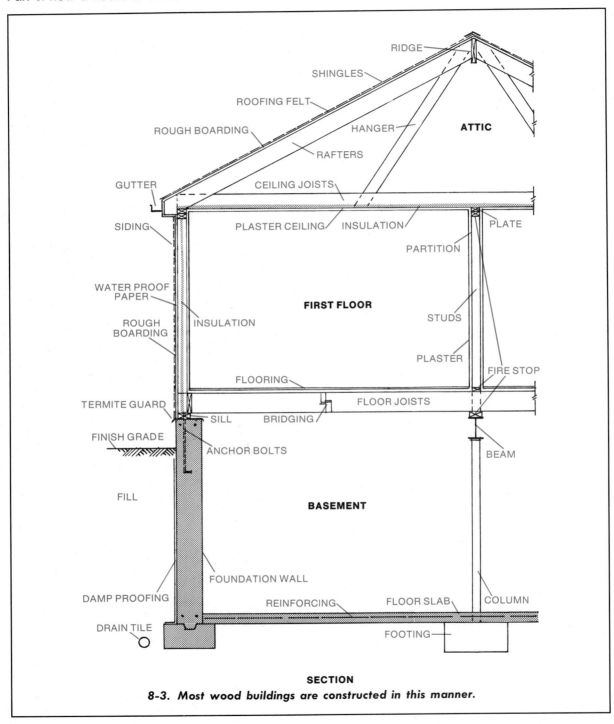

SECTION

8-3. Most wood buildings are constructed in this manner.

8-4. Mixing concrete at a building site.

blocks, the outer surface should be covered with a coat of cement plaster on which the waterproofing material is applied.

In areas where termites, wood-eating insects, are common, a **termite guard** should be installed. Termites can cause extensive damage to wood structures. To safeguard against termites, no wooden part of any building should touch the ground. To discourage termites, the copper termite guard should be placed on top of the concrete foundation wall just below the wood sill, extending beyond the face of the wall. Chemicals may also be applied to certain wooden parts of the house such as the sill for added protection. However, they are not effective for more than a few years.

The basement floor or **floor slab** consists of concrete poured on well-compacted earth and reinforced with a steel mesh. The concrete should be troweled to a smooth, level finish, Fig. 8-4.

The **chimney** consists of two parts: a **flue,** which is a vertical shaft through which smoke and hot gasses are carried to open air; and the walls, generally of brick, which surround the flue. The flue is usually lined with a preformed terracotta clay lining which, because of its smooth surface, allows the hot gasses to rise with a minimum of friction, and adds fire protection. The chimney top must be far enough above the top of the roof to allow the gasses to escape freely. If the chimney is too low, downdrafts of air may force the gasses back down the chimney and into the house.

The top of the chimney is called the **cap.** It is advisable to build a stainless steel screen into the top of the chimney to prevent updrafts from carrying sparks out onto the roof and also to keep out leaves, birds, and small animals.

The Frame

THE FIRST FLOOR

The **floor framing** consists of the columns, beams, sills, plates, joists, and subfloor. When they are properly put together on the foundation, they form a level, anchored base for the rest of the house. The floor **joists** support the flooring. They are small timbers placed parallel from wall to wall.

The joists are often supported at intervals by a **beam**—a horizontal piece of wood or steel.

The beam, in turn, is supported by columns or posts resting on separate footings beneath the basement floor. The **columns** are usually hollow steel pipes, with a steel plate welded to the top and bottom. For additional strength, pipe columns are often filled with concrete.

The **subfloor,** or rough flooring, is made of tongue-and-groove boards or plywood well nailed to the joists, Fig. 8-5. One edge of each board has a groove cut in it. The opposite edge has a tongue or extension which fits the groove of the adjoining board. This provides a tight-fitting joint. The subfloor is nailed to the top of the floor joists to hold them in line. Fig. 8-6 shows plywood subflooring being nailed to the floor joists.

After the rough flooring is nailed to the joists, the **bridging** is installed. Bridging consists of wood braces criss-crossed between the joists and nailed to them tightly. Bridging distributes the load from one point over several joists, making them all work together. If floors squeak, it often means that bridging is either not nailed tightly or is missing entirely.

The **wall framing** supports ceilings, upper floors, and the roof and serves as a nailing base for wall finishes. It includes the vertical studs and the horizontal plates as well as headers for doors and windows. Fig. 8-7 shows wall framing under construction. **Studs,** Fig. 8-3, are vertical timbers usually spaced 400 mm (16 in.) from center to center.

To prevent the possibility of fire going up inside the walls from the basement, **fire stops** must be used. They consist of solid blocks nailed between the joists and against the lower ends of the studs, to close the opening. Fire stops may also be used between the studs and directly above the joists. Even if the basement has a plaster ceiling, the fire stops are important. The fire could be above the ceiling between the joists, and could easily travel up the walls if stops were not used.

Plates consist of two lapped pieces spiked together. They are nailed on top of the studs to keep the studs in a straight line.

The **header,** or lintel, is a timber long enough to span the door or window opening at the top and deep enough to support the load of an upper floor.

THE CEILING AND ROOF

Ceiling joists support ceiling finishes and often act as floor joists for second and attic floors. They also hold the bottom ends of the roof rafters together. Fig. 8-6 gives a view of the ceiling joists.

If the ceiling joists are too long, they may be supported from the roof structure by hangers at each joist. **Hangers,** shown in Fig. 8-3, serve a function similar to the columns in the basement, but instead of supporting the joists from below they carry them from above.

The **ridge** is a horizontal length of wood that spans the peak of the roof. It supports very little

8-5. Tongue-and-groove boards.

American Plywood Association
8-6. Nailing subflooring to the joists.

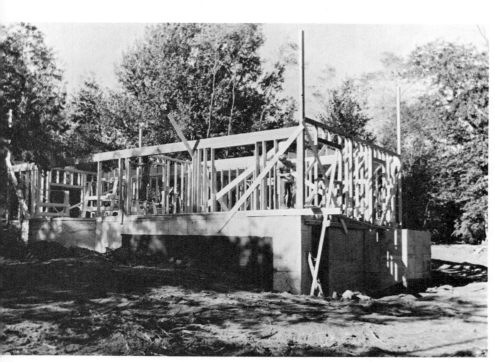

8-7. Wall framing.

187

8-8. Clapboards overlap to shed moisture.

weight, but its purpose is to make it easier for the builder to frame the roof.

The **rafters** form the roof and extend from the plate at the top of the studs to the ridge. The slope of the rafters establishes the **roof pitch.** In general, the steeper the slope of a shingled roof, the less likely it is to leak. The gable is the triangular wall section at the end of a pitched roof house. A **valley** is an angle formed by the meeting of two roof slopes. For example, in an L-shaped house, the corner where the roofs of the two house sections meet is the valley.

FINISHING THE EXTERIOR
Walls

THE ROUGH FINISH

Rough boarding, also called sheathing, is applied to the outside face of the roof and walls. It consists of 20 mm ($\frac{3}{4}$ in.) tongue-and-groove boards or 15 mm ($\frac{5}{8}$ in.) plywood nailed to every rafter and stud. The rough boarding helps to brace the frame against the wind by joining the rafters and studs together.

To make the house more weathertight, a layer of heavy waterproof paper is usually applied to the outside face of the rough wall boarding. This helps to reduce heat loss by clos-

ing most of the small cracks and holes in the rough boarding.

FINAL FINISH

Exterior walls should include the amount of fire resistance needed in that location. For example, in an area where a fire is likely to jump from one house to another walls and roof should be fire resistant.

Many materials are available for exterior wall coverings. The choice depends on the architectural effect desired and on the budget. The principal materials used are **siding** (wood or aluminum clapboards), asphalt shingles, wood shingles, asbestos-cement sheets, vertical wood boarding, horizontal wood boarding, and waterproof plywood.

Wood clapboards are the most popular. They're attractive, easy to fit on the job, good insulators, and easy to patch if alterations are necessary, Fig. 8-8.

Siding such as vertical and horizontal wood boarding has some of the advantages of wood clapboards. However, it is less weatherproof because it does not overlap. An exception is the vertically scored plywood simulating vertical siding shown in Fig. 8-9. This siding is available in large sheets with few joints all of which fit tightly or are protected by metal strips.

Aluminum is inexpensive. Because it's factory finished it requires no paint. Because of its reflective qualities, it helps to lower heating and cooling costs. Its maintenance cost is low.

Plywood siding, like the other wood sidings available, is economical and strong. It comes in interesting textures and is a good insulator. Only exterior grade plywood should be used for siding, as it is laminated with a weatherproof glue.

The Roof

Roofing materials must be durable and weatherproof. As soon as the roof is covered with the rough boarding, it should be also covered with a heavy waterproof building paper known as **roofing felt.** When properly applied, the roofing felt will keep out the rain and allow

8-9. This siding is plywood with grooves cut into it to resemble boards.

Acorn Structures, Inc.

the house to dry so that the interior finish may be installed.

Asphalt shingles are the most widely used roofing material because of their fire-resistant qualities, appearance, and low cost. In general, the heavier the shingle, the longer its life will be. In a hurricane area, the heaviest shingles should be used, and the ends should be cemented down.

Wood shingles may cost from 50 to 100% more than asphalt, but they are attractive in appearance and longer-lasting, Fig. 8-10. Asbestos shingles are durable, fireproof, and suffer little from the weather.

Slate and tile are usually chosen for their

Red Cedar Shingle and Handsplit Shake Bureau

8-10. To remodel this house, shingles are applied over an old roof.

8-11. Design details on a Cape Cod house.

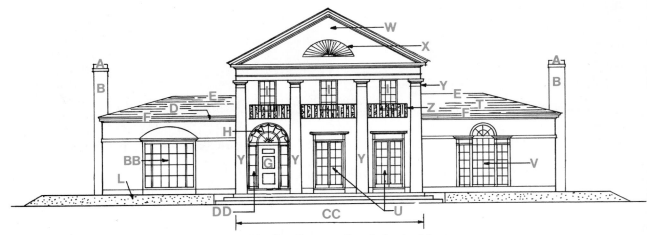

8-12. Design details on a Greek Revival house.

ELEVATION DETAILS

A Chimney cap	K Picture window	U French door
B Chimney	L Terrace	V Palladian window
C Dormer window	M Gable	W Pediment
D Cornice	N Rain leader or downspout	X Louvers
E Ridge	O Rail fence	Y Columns
F Gutter	P Post lamp	Z Balcony
G Door	Q Porch	AA Transom
H Fanlight	R Picket fence	BB Bay window
I Double-hung window	S Step or stair	CC Portico
J Casement window	T Roof	DD Sidelight

special design qualities. They are fireproof and very durable roofing materials. However, they tend to break if installed in an area where water can back up under them and then freeze. Installation is costly and requires a skilled craftsperson. Slate and tile are heavy, so the house must be designed with rafters that are strong enough to carry them.

Metal roofing made of lead, zinc, copper, or aluminum is fireproof, but it provides little insulation. It is noisy in heavy rain, hail, or sleet. Usually, metal is used on curved roofs that require forming and soldering. It may also be used on flat roofs that have too little slope for shingles, slate, or tile.

Glass is used in skylights and for roofing on sunrooms. Its major advantage is that it admits the sun. However, it breaks easily and offers little insulation. Plastic may be used in roof areas where light is desired. Plastic is low in cost, but it, too, is a poor insulator. Its durability has not been tested by years of use, as have some of the older roofing materials.

When a roof is flat, several layers of building paper may be applied with a special compound and then covered with gravel or marble chips. Since light-colored roofs reflect heat, white marble chips are sometimes used in climates where cooling a house is desirable.

Design Features

There are several other house features that should be noted. Figs. 8-11 and 8-12 show the front views of two houses. These views are called **elevations.** The elevations show many exterior details. Some of these details are discussed below.

Louvers (X) may be set in a wall opening to ventilate an area that is too small for a window such as a storage area under a roof. They keep out the weather, birds, and animals but allow air to circulate.

Columns (Y) may be used either for decorative purposes or to support overhead construction. The design of exterior columns should be in keeping with the design of the house. A **por-**tico (CC) is an open space or entrance covered with a roof supported by columns.

A **cornice** (D) may be highly decorative but should be in keeping with the architecture of the house.

A **pediment** (W) is a broad triangular form above a door or window, or it may be used as a decorative detail on the front of a house. It often occurs in Greek Revival or Federal style houses. The pediment in Fig. 8-12 covers the entire portico.

Shutters were first used to cover windows. Now they may provide security or be used for decorative purposes. Dummy shutters may be used on the exterior to make small windows appear larger and to give a colonial effect to the design of the house.

For a discussion of most of the window styles shown in Figs. 8-11 and 8-12, see p. 202.

The popularity of outdoor living has made outdoor recreation areas adjacent to the house almost a necessity. A **patio** is a recreational area that adjoins a house. It is often paved or made of concrete and may or may not have a roof. It is adapted especially to outdoor dining. A porch is a covered structure. If it adjoins the garage, it is called a **breezeway** (Q). A **balcony** is a porch or a projecting platform with a railing around it, on a level higher than the ground floor. It may or may not have a roof. Many apartments have balconies.

Several types of fences are available, but the two most popular are the picket fence and the rail fence. The **picket fence** (R) is made of small vertical sticks held together by horizontal bars at the bottom and near the top. Since the sticks are usually sharp at the top, a picket fence should never be built directly under a window that might be used as an emergency exit. A **rail fence** (O) is made of horizontal boards or bars supported by vertical posts. It is fairly inexpensive to build and maintain but must be painted to protect it from the weather. Wire fences are also available.

A **post lamp,** (P) is a light at the top of a vertical post, similar to a street light. It may be either gas or electric and is used to light driveways, parking areas, and patios.

A **terrace** is raised level ground, often with one or more sloping sides or a retaining wall.

Other Construction Details

Flashing is a protective barrier that keeps water from seeping into joints. It is used at a joint between dissimilar materials, at the intersection of different planes even though the materials are alike, or at a joint between materials likely to expand or contract in different ways. Flashing may be of metal such as copper, zinc, lead, galvanized iron, tin, or copperbearing steel; it may be a heavy impregnated felt; or it may be a combination of felt and metal.

When it is desired to raise the level of the ground around the house or to eliminate holes which often result from excavations, sand and gravel are usually used as **fill.** Fill should not contain any materials likely to rot and cause too much settling such as peat, loam, sod, or tree stumps. It should not consist of clay since moisture or dryness will cause too much expansion or contraction. Since even the best fill is bound to settle, new construction should not be placed on top of it. Wood scraps and tree stumps included in the fill encourage the development of termites.

Fill placed in the excavation around new construction is usually referred to as back fill. The **finish grade,** or final level of earth outside the house foundation, should be kept below the top of the concrete. This will keep ground moisture from coming in contact with any of the wood construction and eventually causing wood to rot.

Rainwater falling from a sloping roof to the ground will erode the soil and damage the planting close to the house unless it is collected by a gutter. The **gutter** is a horizontal open trough, generally at the eaves or edges of the house roof, which catches the rainwater that drains off the roof.

Connected to the gutter is a vertical pipe called a **downspout,** or rain leader, which carries the water down to the ground. At the bottom, the downspout is connected to the **ground drain,** a terracotta or cast iron pipe. This runs underground to a **dry well,** a pit filled with crushed stone or coarse gravel. Since the dry well is normally free of water, it acts as a receiver for the sudden flow of rain, which is finally absorbed by the surrounding earth.

FINISHING THE INTERIOR
Insulation

The purpose of **insulation** is to reduce the passage of heat through the walls and roof. If the insulation is installed properly, the house will feel warmer in winter and cooler in summer. The effectiveness of insulation depends on its R value. The **R value** of an insulation stands for resistance to heat flow; the higher the R value, the better the insulation. As a rule, an R value of 30 or more is needed in northern areas. Quality insulation bears the label of the National Association of Home Builders.

Heat loss can also be reduced by the use of building materials which are poor conductors. Wood is an excellent insulator as are many types of wallboard. If one surface of the insulating material is bright, heat loss can be reduced. Bright surfaces are good heat reflectors and poor absorbers. If the insulating material has a bright surface facing the interior of the house, it will help keep the house warm. If the bright surface faces the outside, it reflects the sun's rays and helps keep the house cool.

Two basic types of insulating materials may be used—blanket and fill-type insulation.

Blanket insulation is composed of porous material such as wood or glass fibers between two coverings. It is inserted in the air spaces between studs, joists, and rafters and stops the movement of air and resulting heat loss. Blanket insulation combined with metal foil makes an effective insulating material.

Fill-type insulation is used in existing houses to completely fill inner spaces. This is the oldest type of insulation used. Spaces between the walls of early houses were filled with dry moss and straw, which served as insulation. Today,

Amspec, Inc.

8-13. Insulation and sheathing are installed in one unit.

fill-type insulation is usually blown between the walls. However, it has a disadvantage—it tends to settle. When part of a wall is warm and part cold, condensation may occur and moisture may be trapped in the insulating fill. This causes paint to blister and wood to rot.

New products continue to be developed. The tongue-and-groove plastic foam sheathing in Fig. 8-13 permits the builder to sheathe the house quickly so that inside work may proceed at an early stage in the construction, even in bad weather. The foam is also an insulator. This material saves time, cuts costs, and provides continuous sidewall coverage.

Electric Wiring

State and local rules generally require that house wiring installations meet high safety standards.

Electric power enters the house from the utility line in the street through the main supply line. The main supply line from the street to the house may be through overhead wires or an underground conduit. Underground service is more desirable because there are no poles and lines above ground. Therefore there is less chance of storm damage, which may interrupt power.

The main supply line enters the house through an **electric meter,** which measures the amount of current used. A service entrance, also called a panel box or **fuse box,** distributes the electricity to the home wiring system.

The home wiring system is divided into **circuits,** which carry a specified amount of electricity. There is usually a separate circuit for each heavy-duty appliance and other circuits for lights and small appliances. The number of circuits depends on the lighting system, the number of electric outlets needed, and the number of appliances to be used. It is important to have an ample number of circuits. If spare circuits are included in the original wiring, the family can add new appliances in the future without costly rewiring.

The fuse box is equipped with safety devices. A main switch can be used to disconnect the house wiring system from the main supply line. **Fuses** or **circuit breakers** in the panel box control each circuit in the house. Each circuit carries a specific amount of electricity. If too many appliances are used on one circuit, it becomes overloaded. The wires may overheat and cause a fire. The fuse or circuit breaker is a protective device. When a circuit is overloaded, the fuse melts and cuts off the power before the wires are damaged. The circuit breaker serves the same purpose—it breaks the circuit automatically if the line is overloaded. When this happens, the cause should be determined and corrected. Power can be restored by replacing the fuse or returning the breaker to position. However, if the cause of overloading is not corrected, power to the circuit will be continually cut off.

To make use of appliances, ample outlets should be planned for all areas of the house. Conveniently placed outlets eliminate the use of unsightly extension cords stretched to reach distant lamps or appliances. In general, outlets should be spaced 1500 to 1800 mm (5 to 6 ft.) apart and never more than 3000 mm (10 ft.) apart. Some building codes specify the location of outlets. For example, they may have to be located 300 to 400 mm (12 to 16 in.) above the floor. Thus, when floors are washed, water cannot splash into the outlet at that height. Most codes require that wall switches be outside of the bathroom, or far enough from tub or shower so that someone taking a shower cannot reach the switch and receive a shock.

Safety covers should be placed on outlets when small children live in the home. These prevent a small child from putting a paper clip, hair pin, or other small piece of metal into the outlet and receiving a shock.

Weatherproof outlets, designed to keep out moisture, may be installed outdoors so that tools or appliances may be used in the yard or on the patio.

HOME LIGHTING NEEDS

Good home lighting should provide the correct amount of light for safe work and recreation, and it should complement the decorating.

The correct amount and source of light helps to prevent eyestrain and reduce accidents. Well lighted stairs and entranceways help to prevent falls and make safe exit possible. The three-way switch makes it possible to turn lights on or off at two entrances and should be provided to make it unnecessary to walk through a dark room, garage, or yard. Night lights contribute to safety and may comfort a small child.

Control of all lights by a switch in the bedroom or hall is a useful safety device. In case of emergency, all of the lights in the house and yard may be turned on at one time.

Statistics show that intruders avoid well-lighted areas. For this reason, light-sensitive switches, which will turn the house lights on automatically when a certain degree of darkness is reached, may be desired. Lights may also be attached to time clocks, set to come on and go off at predetermined times.

Proper lights add to the usefulness, safety, and beauty of outdoor areas. An outdoor lamp extends the hours that a yard or patio may be enjoyed.

Plumbing

The term **plumbing** refers to the system used to carry water into and out of the house. The entire plumbing system must be planned and constructed according to rules and regulations established by state and local boards of health to protect all members of the community from disease. These rules are called the **plumbing code.**

Water may be supplied by a publicly maintained system having as its source driven wells, lakes, or rivers. To make the water safe to drink, it goes through a purification process that destroys disease-producing microorganisms. The water is generally stored in a reservoir, and it either flows by gravity or is pumped.

In some areas water contains minerals such as calcium and magnesium salts, which make it "hard." These minerals create problems in plumbing systems by building up a coating inside water pipes. As a result, the pipes must be replaced periodically. A water softener may be installed to reduce water hardness. (See Chapter 14.)

PIPES AND FITTINGS

Fittings control the flow of water. They include faucets, valves, drains, a stopcock for shutting off the flow of water at or near the point of entrance, and a draincock for letting water out of the system in the event of repairs.

Faucets are usually made of solid brass or chrome-plated brass. However, other finishes such as satin-finish pewter, or even gold- or silver-plate may be had.

Piping may be made of copper, brass, cast or wrought iron, steel, or plastic. Copper and brass are generally used for water pipes. They will not rust and, unless exposed to acid, will not corrode much.

Cast iron is used for soil and vent pipes, which carry off wastes and odors from plumbing fixtures. Wrought iron is satisfactory for use as water or gas pipes since it is durable, rusts slowly, and may be adapted easily to any cast fittings.

Plastic has proved to be a satisfactory material for water pipes. Besides being resistant to rust and corrosion, plastic has another advantage—economy of installation. By snaking it between studs and joists and around obstructions, a plumber may install plastic piping in less time than would be required for metal piping. Occasionally in alteration and repair work, plastic piping may be pulled through existing but abandoned piping of a larger diameter, thereby avoiding the expense of removing and replacing plaster or other interior finish.

FIXTURES

Porcelain enamel on cast iron is used for bathtubs, lavatories, and sinks. It comes in a wide variety of colors to fit any decorating scheme. It is easy to clean, but it chips easily. Scouring powder and drainpipe cleaner should not be used on porcelain.

China fixtures are made of clay fired at a high temperature. China is resistant to ordinary acids and cleansers and is used for toilet bowls, reservoir tanks, and sinks. It, too, is available in a wide color and style range. China is heavy, but will break if dropped or given a heavy blow.

Stainless steel is used for sinks. It is durable and rust-resistant. It water spots but the marks are less conspicuous on the satin finish.

Prefabricated plastic tub-shower units are now being manufactured. Since the entire unit is essentially in one piece, the house must be specifically designed to take its dimensions. For this reason, these units are more likely to be used in new houses or apartments. They are easy to install, making costly on-the-job trim and finishing unnecessary. They are easy to clean and maintain, Fig. 8-14.

Special fixtures can be installed. The bathroom in Fig. 8-15 has a fixture called a bidet (pronounced *bee-dày*). It is for localized bathing after use of the toilet. The sink in Fig. 8-16 is at a child's height to make it easier for small children to use.

WATER HEATERS

A water heater consists of a tank to hold the water, and a burner or unit underneath the tank to provide heat. Water may be heated by electricity or gas. Four percent of the energy we use goes for heating water.

The size of the water heater you need depends on the size of your family and your activi-

Formica Corporation

8-14. Prefabricated units are easier to clean because they have no seams in which dirt can lodge.

8-15. Notice also the smaller size tub.

American Standard, Inc.

American Standard, Inc.
8-16. The mirrors and diagonal designs make this room seem larger.

ties. Normally, if you have an automatic clothes washer and a dishwasher, you will need a larger water heater than a family that does not have these appliances. Generally, a 190 L (50 gal.) water heater is recommended if automatic appliances are used.

In addition to the capacity of the water heater, you will want to know its recovery rate. The **recovery rate** indicates the average amount of water that will be heated in the tank in one hour. When buying a water heater, be sure you select one that gives an ample supply of hot water for peak demand. Since a water heater is a long-term investment, try to anticipate your needs for at least the next ten years.

Check with your local gas or electric company to see if it might be more economical to rent a water heater than to buy one.

SEWAGE DISPOSAL

Disposal of waste or sewage is done by connecting the fixtures in the house to a system of underground piping. This piping in turn is connected to a public sanitary sewer, a septic tank and leaching field, or a cesspool.

Sewage is carried to a public sewer system through cast iron piping for a distance of at least 1500 mm (5 ft.) from the building, and then terracotta piping. Sewer pipes and water pipes should be kept as far apart as reasonable to prevent leaks in the sewers from contaminating the water supply.

If there is no public sewer system, the sewage is disposed of through a **septic tank.** The tank is a large concrete box, generally buried underground. In it, the solids settle and after a time decompose. The liquids overflow into a system of terracotta pipe with open joints laid underground. This is called the **disposal,** or leaching, field. The liquids gradually seep out the pipe joints into the soil. After several years of use, the septic tank must be cleaned and the residue removed.

A **cesspool** may also be used to dispose of sewage. The cesspool collects sewage and lets it gradually seep into the surrounding earth.In some areas local health regulations prohibit the use of cesspools because they may overflow and contaminate soil and nearby water supplies.

Septic tanks and cesspools may develop problems under certain conditions. Gutters and swimming pools connected to them will cause overloading. High-foaming detergents and other cleaning products may interfere with the bacteriological action. Mechanical waste disposers fill them up very quickly so they must be cleaned frequently.

Heating Systems

In order to control heat loss from within a home and to achieve modern standards of comfort a number of heating systems have evolved. These include warm air, steam, hot water, and radiant heat. Fireplaces and stoves are also used both for atmosphere and economy. In addition to heating systems there are many other variables such as the fuels and types of equipment used. These are discussed in more detail in Chapter 9.

Because of construction methods and materials used, each house has special needs. For instance heating oil and gas are stored in large tanks. Local building codes regulate the size and location of these storage tanks. It is important to select a size which will hold the quantities sold locally and which will meet the needs of the household. Electric heat requires a well-insulated house. The elements must be placed carefully to avoid fire hazards. Solar heating requires special collecting units installed in roofs or windows and a reservoir to store the heat. Therefore the selection and installation of a heating system should be based on competent advice. Designers of quality systems will guarantee performance. For example, they will guarantee that the system will provide a temperature of at least 21°C (70°F) at the lowest recorded temperature in your area. A heating system should not be selected or designed by an amateur.

The cost of operating any heating system is determined by the level of heat required, the climate, the effectiveness of insulation, and the type of fuel used.

HEAT CONTROL

Regardless of the type of heating system used, the flow of heat into a room must be controlled. This is accomplished by an automatic, temperature-activated switch known as a thermostat. The **thermostat** turns the heating system on when the room temperature drops below the level set by the resident and turns it off when room temperature rises to the desired level. Usually, it is electrically operated.

In all systems, the thermostat should be located where there is normal circulation of air. It is placed on an inside wall and about 900 to 1200 mm (3 to 4 ft.) above the floor.

FIREPLACES

A fireplace may be compared to a box without a front and with a hole in the top. A fire is built in the fireplace and the smoke goes out of the hole at the top, called the **throat.** The floor, or **hearth,** extends out in front as a precaution against flying sparks. The **mantel** is the facing around the fireplace, including the shelf above it. It forms a decorative frame around the fireplace opening.

The size of the fireplace determines the size of the chimney. If you plan to build a house with a fireplace, keep in mind that the chimney will have to be larger than normal, adding to the cost of the house. Every fireplace must have its own flue. Otherwise, smoke from one fireplace may be carried to another by drafts.

At the bottom of the chimney, just above the fireplace, there must be an adjustable cast iron **damper.** This closes the opening and prevents heat in the house from escaping up the chimney when the fireplace is not in use.

Styles range from the traditional brick to modern stainless steel. Contemporary freestanding fireplaces can be installed even in mobile homes. Since they do not require a heavy chimney, they are less costly to install. Freestanding fireplaces come in unusual shapes and brilliant colors. The fireplace divider wall shown in Fig. 8-17 opens into two rooms. The raised hearth extends to form a platform which may be used as a seat.

Franklin stoves have become popular alternatives to fireplaces. There are some special safety precautions that should be observed when installing a stove. There must be adequate clearance between stove and floors, walls, and ceiling, and the stove must be placed on a fireproof base, such as metal, covered asbestos, brick or concrete. The chimney must be clean and sound, and there must be enough air for combustion. Always follow the local building code and manufacturer's directions. For the advantages and disadvantages of stove and fireplace heat see p. 223.

Windows

STRUCTURE

A window performs a variety of functions, the most important of which is to let in daylight.

Tech Built Homes, Inc.

8-17. People on both sides of this fireplace can enjoy the fire.

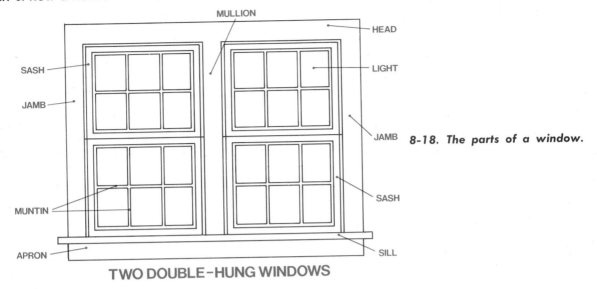

8-18. *The parts of a window.*

Also, it is opened for ventilation, and it is closed to reduce heat loss and to keep out weather. It is also used as a decorative feature on both the inside and outside of the house.

The three essential parts of a window are the sash, the frame, and the lights, Fig. 8-18.

The **sash** is the framework which surrounds the glass. Sometimes a window is divided into smaller panes by bars called **muntins** which hold the small pieces of glass within the sash.

The **frame** is the part of the window built into the wall to receive the sash. It consists of the vertical sides or **jambs,** the top or **head,** and the bottom or **sill.** The **apron** is beneath the sill. If the frame is designed to accommodate more than one sash placed side by side, the vertical divider is called a **mullion.**

Wood is most commonly used for window frames. It must be painted, and it may be treated to protect it from moisture. Generally, the wood is treated with a preservative when the sash and frame are manufactured.

Aluminum window frames are lightweight and come in a variety of factory finishes and de-

signs. Because their light weight makes them easy to install and remove, they are popular. In humid southern climates, ceramic tile may be used with aluminum frames to prevent moisture damage, Fig. 8-19.

The panes of glass in a window are known as **lights.** If a window has one piece of glass, it is described as single light, and if it has more than one it has divided lights. The placement of glass in a window is called **glazing.**

The thickness of glass determines its strength. A lightweight glass may be used in small windows, but a heavy plate glass is required for a large picture window.

Insulating glass consists of two sheets of glass separated by a sealed air space, which provides the insulation. Besides reducing heat loss from the room, it eliminates accumulation of moisture on the inside face of the glass.

Tempered plate glass is made to be extra strong by reheating it and then suddenly cooling it. Because of its strength, it is used for sliding glass doors.

Solar control glass is plate glass tinted in a

variety of colors to reduce heat from the sun's rays. This keeps the inside air cooler and results in lower air-conditioning costs.

Patterned glass, sometimes called obscure glass, is textured on the surface by ribs, flutes, or other irregularities. It allows light to pass through, but you can't see through it. It's used for bathroom windows.

A single thickness of glass is a poor heat insulator and may cause discomfort in cold weather. The heat loss may be reduced by installing a second window or **storm window.** The air space created between the two windows provides insulation. In the spring, the storm windows are generally replaced by screens. The storm windows may be difficult to remove or install if they are large and heavy or in a high location. Combination storm windows and screens have been developed that are light in weight and easily interchanged. Many can be changed from the inside of the house rather than from the outside.

Loss of heat may also be prevented by covering the windows with sheet plastic. It is light and inexpensive, but it may detract from the appearance of the house. Some types greatly reduce the amount of outdoor light entering the house. Air movement is desirable for health and comfort and is necessary for the operation of certain heating units. However, to prevent drafts weather stripping may be used.

STYLES

The style of the windows should fit in with the architecture of the house. A wide variety of window styles and designs is available. Fig. 8-20 shows some of the more common types of windows used in houses today.

The three principal types of windows are the sliding, the hinged, and the fixed or picture window.

The most widely used sliding window is the **double-hung.** It consists of two sashes, either or both of which may be raised and lowered in vertical tracks. A relatively new variety is the gliding window with a sash that slides on horizontal tracks. Both the double-hung and gliding sash have a common fault—the window can never be more than half open.

The hinged window, also called a **casement,** has hinges on one side of the sash so the win-

Lorenne and Edwin Weigel

8-19. Ceramic tile may also be used to surface ledges which hold plants.

dow may be fully opened. The projected or awning casement has hinges at top or bottom. Closely related is the **jalousie window,** which consists of a series of horizontal, adjustable louvers, or slats, made of glass or metal. When open, the bottom edge of each louver moves outward, allowing complete air circulation. When closed, the bottom edge rests snugly against the outer face of the louver below. Another variation is the **pivoted window**—the sash may be rotated about center pins at the top and bottom.

While these are the basic types most frequently used, there are other popular shapes and styles. See Figs. 8-11 and 8-12, p. 190.

The **bay** or bow **window** is generally a group of windows or a curved sash that projects beyond the face of the exterior wall. The projection may be angular or rounded.

A dormer window is a small window that is set vertically in a sloping roof (see p. 108).

A **Palladian window** is a combination of an arched center window with rectangular windows on each side.

A **skylight** is a window installed in the roof, Fig. 8-21.

A **French door** is actually a window which extends to the floor and opens in the same manner as a door. It may be used as a door

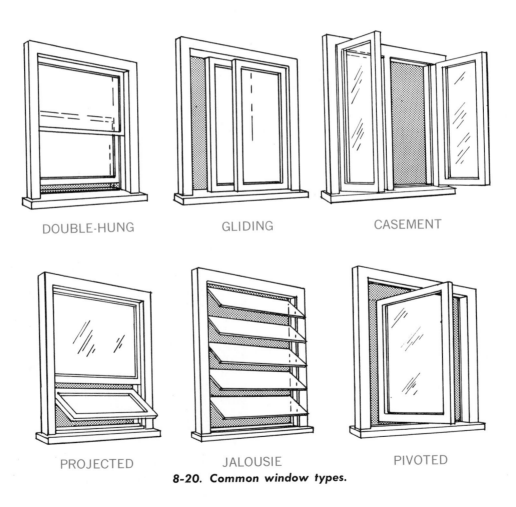

DOUBLE-HUNG   GLIDING   CASEMENT

PROJECTED   JALOUSIE   PIVOTED

8-20. Common window types.

8-21. Skylights must be made of insulating or solar control glass to prevent heat loss.

and usually opens onto a porch, patio, or balcony.

A **fanlight** is a semi-circular window which is usually located over a door. It is normally a fixed window, and the shape of the panes suggests a fan.

Sidelights are small windows along the side of a door. They admit daylight into an entrance hall and give the person inside a view of anyone at the door. Their major disadvantage is that they may be broken by an intruder who can then reach inside and unlock the door.

The house shown in Fig. 8-22 is fitted with many different window types. What you learned about design applies to all parts of the house. This house design would be more harmonious if all of the windows featured panes of glass of similar proportion and style.

Doors

STRUCTURE

The door generally fits into a **frame** consisting of a **head** and **jambs.** Exterior entrances also have a **threshold** at the bottom.

Doors are either solid or hollow. For exterior use, a solid door is recommended. Because of the difference in indoor and outdoor temperatures, the hollow door may fill with moisture and warp. In cold weather, the moisture may freeze and seriously damage the door. Hollow doors are lighter in weight than solid doors and are generally used for interiors only. Although they are less expensive, they are also less sound-resistant.

Most doors today are generally made of Douglas fir or ponderosa pine. The manufacturer treats ponderosa pine with a chemical pre-

8-22. The design of this house shows little unity.

servative to make it moisture-repellent and rot-resistant.

Weather stripping, plastic covering, or a second or storm door help prevent heat loss through doors. To give greater protection against heat loss many outer doors are placed in small hallways or entryways.

If there is an entry hall in the house with no source of daylight, the entrance door should have a small window to provide light.

Exterior doors are normally hinged so that they swing inward. Enough space should be allowed for the door to swing freely. Interior doors should be hinged in the direction of natural entry. Whenever possible, they should swing against a blank wall, and one door should not be obstructed by another swinging door. Doors should never be hinged to swing into a hallway. Can you give the reason for this?

Doors to basement furnace rooms, storage rooms, and attached garages should be heavy enough to restrain fire. In a house which has a basement heating plant it is desirable to have an outside access door in case of fire.

STYLES

The decorative design of exterior doors should always be in keeping with the architecture of the house. Doors are available in a wide range of designs, some of which are shown in Fig. 8-23.

Flush doors (B) are perfectly flat on both sides and are usually available with a hardwood veneer suitable for staining or varnishing. They are either solid or hollow. When ordering a flush door, be sure to specify to the dealer where it is to be used, inside or out.

Paneled doors (A) are built of vertical pieces called stiles and horizontal pieces called rails. The set-in thinner sheets of wood are called panels. The doors are described according to the number of panels in the design such as three-panel, six-panel, or eight-panel.

Louvered doors (C) have thin slats of wood with open spaces between to permit ventilation. The slats are tilted so no one can look through the openings. Louvered doors are desirable where air circulation is needed but where soundproofing is not required.

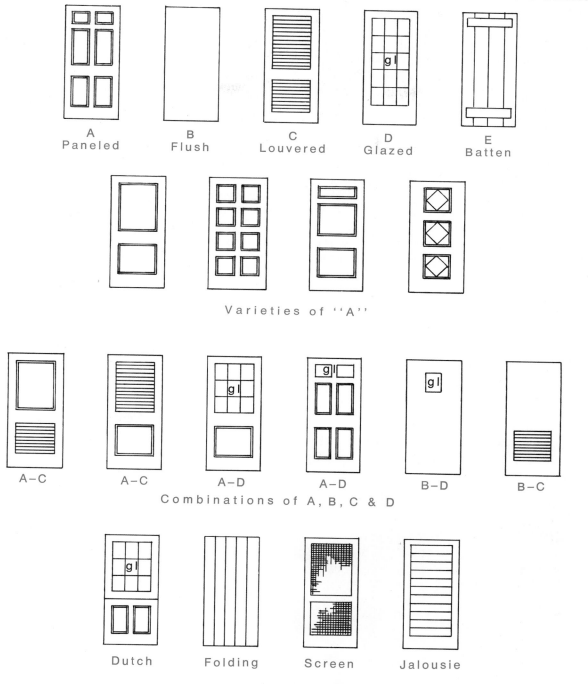

A	B	C	D	E
Paneled	Flush	Louvered	Glazed	Batten

Varieties of "A"

| A–C | A–C | A–D | A–D | B–D | B–C |

Combinations of A, B, C & D

| Dutch | Folding | Screen | Jalousie |

Miscellaneous

8-23. Common door types.

Glazed doors (D) have one or more windows inserted for light.

Batten doors (E) are generally of rough construction and are often used in cellars or barns. Vertical boards are nailed together at the top, bottom, and center with horizontal boards called battens. A refined version, attractively finished, may be used on houses of rustic or country design.

A Dutch door is really two doors, one above the other. The upper portion, which is usually glazed, may be opened for ventilation while the lower portion is kept closed. Both portions may be fastened together and opened and closed as one door. The main problem with the Dutch door is that, in spite of weather stripping, rain may penetrate the joint between the upper and lower portions.

A **folding door** consists of narrow sections hinged together and gliding on an overhead track. The sections fold against each other accordion-fashion at the sides of the door opening. Since they cannot be locked effectively, their use is generally limited to closets. They require much less floor space for opening than a swinging door.

A **jalousie door** has a series of adjustable louvers made of glass or metal.

Screen doors have wood or metal frames. The screening may be of aluminum or copper mesh. The door swings outward and usually closes automatically by the action of a spring-type device.

A **transom** is a small horizontal opening above a door. When used above an outside door, it frequently has glass in it.

Stairways

A step consists of a riser and a tread. The **riser** is the vertical part of the step and the **tread** is the horizontal part you walk on. For a short stairway, it is safer to have either one riser or three since records show that people fall more frequently where there are only two steps. If the sizes of the risers or the treads are not uniform on a stairway, people may stumble. Stairways should have a handrail when possible.

Winding stairways are attractive. However, because they make a turn, they have V-shaped treads that are narrow at one end, Fig. 8-24. Straight stairways with platforms at the turns are safer.

Walls

STRUCTURE

In wood construction, an interior wall or partition usually consists of studs spaced at intervals with a finish applied to both sides. If it supports the floors or roof above, it is known as a **load-bearing wall.** This is important to keep in mind when remodeling and especially when changing the size or shape of a room. A load-bearing interior wall should never be removed unless a beam is used to take its place to support the upper structure.

Peoria Journal Star
8-24. *In a curving stair, such as this, the treads must be tapered at the point of the curve.*

206

Table 8-A.
INTERIOR WALL COVERINGS

Material	Characteristics	Advantages and Disadvantages
Brick	Warm earthy look; forms interesting patterns	Resists fire; durable; low upkeep; poor insulator for its thickness
Concrete	Massive appearance; looks institutional; colorless	Durable; low upkeep; fireproof; can be painted; poor insulator
Plaster	Smooth, no joints; can be given texture	Durable; can be finished in many ways; may crack
Plastic (panels, tiles, sheets)	A variety of textures and colors	Durable; easy to clean; easy to install; moisture resistant; new types not wear-tested
Tile (glazed, clay)	A variety of sizes, shapes, and colors	Easy to clean; durable; reflects noise; resists water and stains; requires strong base such as cement or plaster
Wallboard (plaster board, pressed wood, gypsum)	Smooth finish; joints must be taped	Durable; moderate cost; can be finished many ways; fire resistant
Solid wood (panels)	Natural wood color and grain	Durable; easily maintained; costly
Veneered plywood (panels)	Provides the beauty of natural wood color and grain	Less costly than solid panels; less wasteful of rare woods

FINISHING

A wide variety of wall materials is available today. The consumer needs to decide what qualities the wall should have for a particular room and should be aware of the advantages and disadvantages of the different materials. For example, color, texture, pattern, ease of maintenance, sound absorption, ease of installation, or cost might be qualities to consider.

One of the best materials for interior wall and ceiling finishes is plaster on lath. **Plaster** is a hard, white finish made of lime or gypsum, sand, and water. The **lath** is nailed to the studs and can be made of various materials including gypsum board, fiberboard and metal. Metal is the best—it is smooth, hard, and fire-resistant and provides a firm base for the plaster. However, it is expensive.

Since plaster on lath is costly, various types of gypsum wallboard may be nailed directly to the studs instead. This is generally referred to as **dry-wall** construction. The joints between the outer layers of wallboard are concealed with tape, and the surface is painted or papered.

After the wall finish is applied, a **cornice** is added. This is the trim around the top of the room where the ceiling and wall join.

Table 8-A shows the most common wall ma-

8-25. *This hardwood floor is formed of parquet tiles.*

terials. Paint and other decorative finishes are discussed in Chapter 15.

Floors

Hard surface flooring is more expensive to install but lasts indefinitely. Resilient flooring is easy to clean and can be changed.

Wood is the most popular floor material, Fig. 8-25. Both hardwoods and softwoods are used for finish flooring. The hardwoods are generally more durable and attractive.

Wood **finish flooring** is usually made in strips. It is tongue-and-groove along the edges and at the ends so that each piece is held in place by its neighbor. It is fastened to the sub-flooring by nails.

Since there are many types of flooring it is important to consider the qualities of each. For example, the cost and amount of labor required for installation, appearance, insulating qualities for both heat and sound, durability, and ease of maintenance must be evaluated, Fig. 8-26.

Different rooms require different floors. For example, the requirements for a bathroom and a living room may be quite different. There may be architectural limitations as well. For instance, a stone or brick floor is very heavy and a room where these are used requires special framing to carry the additional weight.

Tables 8-B and 8-C show the characteristics of the most common floor materials.

Azrock Floor Products
8-26. This homeowner saves installation costs by laying the vinyl asbestos floor herself.

Table 8-B.
HARD FLOOR COVERINGS

Material	Characteristics	Advantages and Disadvantages
Concrete	Lacks color and texture	Low cost; can be painted; durable; hard; noisy, cold; may crack; stains unless sealed
Stone	Interesting texture and colors; natural earthy look	Very durable; hard; noisy, expensive; cold; heavy
Brick and ceramic tile (unglazed)	Varied patterns; earthy colors in brick, many colors in tile	Durable; moisture resistant; easy maintenance; may crack; brick is heavy
Wood	Beautiful natural grain and colors; hardwoods are more durable.	Takes variety of finishes; shows wear; does not resist water

Table 8-C.
RESILIENT FLOOR COVERINGS

Material	Characteristics	Advantages and Disadvantages
Asphalt tile	Many subdued colors	Resists moisture (good for basements); easy care; durable
Cork	Rich, natural brown colors	Quiet; difficult to care for; absorbs dirt; dented by furniture; may fade
Linoleum	Almost unlimited range of patterns and colors	Easy care but requires waxing; moderate cost; sound absorbent
Rubber tile	Many clear colors	Easy care; may be damaged by grease and dented by furniture
Vinyl-asbestos tile	Wide range of colors and patterns	Very durable; easy to install; resists grease
Vinyl sheets and tiles	Wide variety of colors; simulates marble; lustrous surface	Easy to install; easy care; fairly expensive

Manuel and Carla Rodriquez live in the northeastern part of the country. They intend to build a new house and are interested in quality construction. When the builder gave Manuel and Carla an estimate for the cost of construction of the house, they were disappointed to find it was far above the amount they wanted to pay. Below is a list of some of the features included in the estimate. In order to reduce the cost of the house and still retain the quality of construction, which of these features may be eliminated? What is your reason for each suggestion?

Case Problem A

• Full basement with poured concrete walls, 100 mm (4 in.) reinforced concrete floor, waterproofing, drain tile, and termite guard. The basement will be divided into a recreation room and a utility room.
   • Year-round automatic air conditioning.
   • Sill with anchor bolts.
   • A fireplace in the living room and one in the recreation room.
   • Floor construction to include bridging.
   • Wiring system to include an adequate supply of outlets for automatic appliances and lighting.
   • Mahogany paneling in living and dining rooms.
   • Brick kitchen floor and clay tile wall above kitchen counters.
   • Wood shingles on the roof.
   • A 190 L (50 gal.) water heater with 166 L (44 gal.) recovery rate.
   • All copper plumbing with color-coordinated fixtures.

ACTIVITIES

1. Visit a house under construction. Make a list of all the structural parts you recognize.
2. Identify the structural parts of the house under construction in Fig. 8-27.
3. In old magazines, find pictures of four different window styles as shown in Fig. 8-21. Find one example of a style described on pp. 202-203. Clip the pictures and mount them for a decorating notebook.
4. In old magazines, find pictures of six different door styles as shown in Fig. 8-23. Clip the pictures and mount them for a decorating notebook.
5. Make a rough sketch of a room plan to resemble a blueprint. On your plan include ten of the symbols shown in Fig. 8-1.

8-27. Illustration for Activity 2.

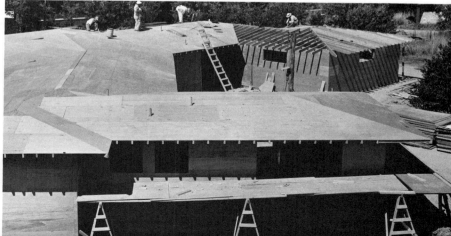

 Natural Resources:
Their Use and
Conservation

Far left: This dune house is built overlooking the ocean. (William Morgan, Architect/CPS Photo)

Left: The windows are recessed to provide small patio areas.

Right: A thick layer of sod acts as insulation and helps reduce heating and air conditioning costs.

SOURCES OF POWER

The scarcity of fuel has become a world-wide problem. Scientists and engineers are doing their best to develop new fuels and efficient equipment, such as a new furnace designed to take not one fuel but four! The furnace switches from one fuel to another automatically. This al-

lows the consumer to select the cheapest or most plentiful fuel and provides insurance against shortages. Unfortunately the system is costly.

Environmental damage, cost, safety, pollution, adaptation of equipment, and fuel storage are some of the problems which must be solved

213

regarding natural resources. Consumers must conserve resources and carefully evaluate products which have not been proved before making a choice. Would you want to live in the earth houses shown in Fig. 9-1 or on p. 212? Earth houses save energy because the soil acts as insulation. What do you think the disadvantages might be?

The possible sources of energy range from traditional fuels—such as wood, coal, oil, gas, and electricity—to the many alternate sources of energy now being pursued through research. The choice of fuel depends on many factors such as local supply, cost, and estimates of future availability.

So many potential fuels exist it seems there should be new energy available in the next decades. Some of the future fuels have already arrived. Converters depending on solar energy are commercially available, and nuclear reactors using uranium fuel are now producing some of the electricity we use. However, we will need to practice conservation and make changes in our life styles while the new sources are being developed.

Wind

Wind has been used to grind grain and pump water since ancient times. Windmills like the one in Fig. 9-2 were used to pump water for many years. Small-scale windpower projects work well. Now there are plans for large-scale windmill installations. However, converting and storing of wind energy presents problems. Although the wind is free, it is often the wrong strength—too heavy or too light.

Wood

Until about 1850, wood was the only source of fuel. Although wood alone could not supply enough fuel to serve modern needs, it is becoming more popular as a second source of home heating. One cord (about one large wagon load) of wood can produce the same amount of heat as 760 L (200 gal.) of oil. Unfortunately, heat escapes from wood fires along

with the smoke. The advantages of using wood for fuel are that users can replace the trees by planting new ones, and wood smoke is not as polluting as that of other fuels.

Coal

Coal is plentiful but presents environmental hazards, such as air pollution. Also, coal mining can be dangerous to the miners. But these drawbacks can be lessened. The United States has large coal reserves, and it is anticipated that coal production and use will increase significantly.

Oil

Oil is commonly used as a fuel in many parts of the country. The future cost of oil will be influenced by the fact that a large portion of oil used by the United States is imported. Reserves are very limited.

Gas

Three types of gas are used for heating: natural, butane, and propane. Natural gas comes from wells and is piped to the consumer. Butane and propane are forms of liquid petroleum (LP gas). They are sold in pressurized tanks. In the tank, the gas is in a liquid state, but it burns as a vapor. Gas is also a limited resource.

Electricity

Electricity must be generated by other sources of power. The water rushing over large dams helps produce electricity in some areas. In most

William Morgan. Architect
9-1. An aerial view of an earth form house located in central Florida.

places, however, electricity is generated by burning oil and other fuels. The shortage of these fuels has affected the cost of electricity.

Electricity is measured in watts. A **watt** is the number of amperes of electricity times the number of volts.

$$W = A \times V$$

The number of watts available in a house wiring system depends on the amperage of the power cable entering the house and the volts it carries. For example, in a house which is provided with 100-ampere service at 230 volts, there will be 23 000 watts of total service available ($100 \times 230 = 23\,000$).

Fuses regulate the amperage traveling along circuits inside the house. A 120 volt circuit, which is all that is needed for lights and small appliances, may have a 15-ampere fuse. Together they supply 1800 watts ($120 \times 15 = 1800$). This circuit could light eighteen 100-watt lightbulbs or run an appliance which requires 1800 watts.

Nuclear Energy

Reactors using uranium fuel now produce about 10% of the electricity used in the United

9-2. Farms like this one still depend on wind power.

States. A new type of reactor called the breeder, which produces more fuel than it uses, is being brought into use. The use of nuclear power is controversial. Some people feel that the radioactivity produced by nuclear reactors makes them unsafe.

Nuclear fusion, a different type of nuclear reaction, is now being considered as a power source. Fusion makes use of non-radioactive fuels and its wastes are non-radioactive as well. Fusion is also fairly clean in contrast to the pollution caused by burning fossil fuels. Another advantage of fusion is that it depends on fuels which are abundant. For example, one method of fusion uses deuterium, which is present in seawater, and there is enough to provide power for the earth for a billion years. Unfortunately, many problems must be solved before this source of energy becomes available.

Solar Energy

Few alternative energy sources are as appealing as the sun. It is clean, free, and plentiful. Two days of sunlight falling on the earth contains as much energy as the total of all the fossil fuel in the world.

Practical solar heating systems are now available. All solar systems use some type of collector. Because the sun reaches us only during the day, a reservoir to store the heat is also needed.

Those who favor solar power estimate that energy costs can be reduced about 50% by insulation, and another 25% by using solar energy, leaving only a total of 25% to come from other heat sources. However converting existing buildings to solar may be costly and, in some locations, impossible.

Prototype I in Fig 9-3 is a home in New Mexico which depends entirely on wind and sun for its sources of energy. The windmill pumps water and runs an electric generator, while solar collectors in the foreground provide energy for both heating and air cooling. The house, which is the dome-shaped structure, is built of prefabricated, insulated steel panels.

Solar One, Fig. 9-4, is an experimental house that will provide information for residential dwellings in the future. Eighty percent of its heat and electricity comes from sunlight, the rest is furnished by the local utility company.

The solar house shown in Fig. 9-5 is designed to conserve energy in many ways. The chimney is inside the building so the heat loss is minimized. Note the small projecting back entry. It protects the living area from a loss of heat when the door is opened. There is maximum insulation in walls, roof and floors. Double insulating glass is used throughout, and windows and doors are tightly weatherstripped. There are few windows on the north side and large picture windows on the south. The roof overhang protects the house from summer sun. The rooms are arranged so the heat within the house can be zoned. On the north and northwest sides, trees reduce heat loss from prevailing cold winds.

In the cut-away view of the house you can see the collector plates on the roof. The heat absorbed by these plates is transferred to water circulated from the storage tank in the basement. Enough hot water can be stored in the tank to heat the house for several days. During long periods of cloudiness an oil-fired furnace provides the necessary extra heat.

The experimental building in Fig. 9-6 does not look like a solar house, since it has no big collector on the roof. It has newly developed windows fitted with heat mirrors, consisting of specially treated sheets of plastic which reflect escaping heat back into the building. A venetian blind silvered on top reflects incoming sunlight up to the ceiling, and a thin ceiling tile with a chemical core stores several day's heat.

Alternate Fuels

Alternate fuels range from common garbage and waste, which some communities use to produce energy, to more exotic tidal power and ocean thermal power which obtain energy from the tides and temperature differences in the

The National Ass'n of Architectural
Metals Manufacturers

9-3. Prototype I gets all its power from sun and wind.

9-4. Rooftop cells provide the power for both heat and light in this experimental home.

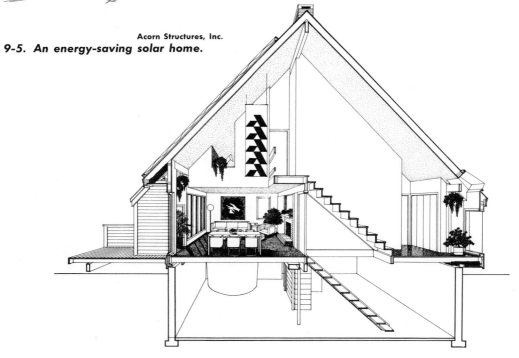

Acorn Structures, Inc.

*9-5. **An energy-saving solar home.***

9-6. A solar house being built by the Massachusetts Institute of Technology.

ocean. In a few locations, such as Hawaii, the natural steam and hot water in the earth is piped into buildings.

In the future there may be energy "plantations" where fast-growing trees, shrubs, or plants (including kelp or seaweed) are converted to power. Intensive care can produce a new crop of hardwood trees every six years. Plants which produce sugar might be harvested for

ethyl alcohol, a substitute for oil in some cases. These would be converted in large refineries.

WATER

Water, unlike energy, is not consumed—it is used and reused. The natural cycle of rain-to ground water-to evaporation-to rain is illustrated in Fig. 9-7. Waterways must be protected to insure adequate clean water. Generally rain and

Massachusetts Audubon Society
9-7. Earth's water cycle.

snow should be allowed to enter the ground naturally in order to build up ground water supplies. Proper drainage which will conserve water should be planned for all buildings.

Modern households use enormous quantities of water. We can conserve water by fixing leaky faucets, using appliances only at full capacity, and by using other means to dispose of those wastes and substances which upset the natural balance in waterways. What one person does, such as failing to turn off an unnecessary light, or allowing a faucet to drip may not seem significant, but when thousands use electricity and water carelessly, brownouts and water shortages may result.

ACHIEVING A COMFORTABLE TEMPERATURE

In order to understand home heating requirements we need to understand our body's heat requirements. What should an indoor temperature be for you to feel comfortable? The most important fact to remember is that your body is a heat-generating furnace. Your fuel is the food you eat, and the temperature you maintain is normally 37°C (98.6°F).

Your body is always losing heat and never gaining it except under unusual conditions. When you lose heat rapidly, you feel cool. When you lose heat slowly, you feel warm. Heat is always on the move in one direction, transferring itself to a cooler substance in an attempt to arrive at a balance. But cold never transfers itself to a warm substance.

As your body loses heat, it also loses moisture through evaporation. The air about you contains moisture in varying degrees of saturation, which is called **humidity.** In much of the southwestern portion of our country, there is relatively little humidity. In the southeast, the humidity is generally high. The amount of humidity affects the rate of moisture evaporation from your body, which has a lot to do with how you feel. Rapid evaporation aided by low humidity tends to make both low and high temperatures pleasant to live with. The low rate of evaporation which

accompanies high humidity causes some discomfort in low temperatures and a great deal in high temperatures.

Air movement can speed up the evaporation of moisture from your body and make you feel more comfortable. An example of this can be found in the islands of the Caribbean. Although the climate is warm and humid all year, the constant tradewinds make the temperature comfortable.

How Heat Travels

The transfer of heat from a body of higher temperature to one of lower temperature by contact is called **conduction.** For example, when you step on a cold floor in your bare feet, you feel the heat leave your feet through conduction. When you touch a piece of ice, you can feel heat leave your hand. The ice becomes warmer and starts to melt. The heat of your body is transferred to the colder ice by conduction.

The transfer of heat by means of air flow is called **convection.** For example, when you stand in front of a fan, you usually feel cool. The stronger the wind, the cooler you feel. But the wind itself is not cooling; it is merely speeding up the transfer of heat away from you. If you were to face the wind blowing across hot desert sands, you would feel the warmth from the sands being transferred to you. Have you noticed your breath on a cold day? The air was warm and moist when it left your lungs. After coming in contact with cold air, its temperature fell rapidly, and the vapor condensed into tiny visible droplets. This shows the pattern or extent of convection. The most common way to provide heat in a house is through convection. Air which has been warmed by a furnace is circulated through each room. In air conditioning or cooling a house, the circulating cool air absorbs the warmth of everything it touches.

The transmission of heat by means of rays traveling in straight lines from the source is called **radiation.** Rays of light and heat are similar in that either may be intercepted by a shadow-casting object. For example, if you sit in front of an open fire, you feel warm. However, if you hold a book between your face and the fire, your sensation of warmth is reduced by what is known as a heat shadow or screen. The classic example of radiation is the sun. Its heat does not come to you through physical contact nor is it blown upon you. The only way you can control the sensation of warmth the direct sun's rays give is to put yourself in a shadow.

To achieve physical comfort you should consider temperature, humidity, and air movement. The house you live in, if care is taken to adapt its design to all natural conditions, should contribute much to your comfort.

Types of Heating Systems

THE WARM AIR SYSTEM

While it is true that air is warmed in all heating systems, the term **warm air system** refers to a specific method of heating. Air is warmed by the furnace—either by gas, oil, or electricity—and is sent to the rooms through metal ducts. It circulates through the rooms and returns to the furnace through another system of ducts. It is reheated, and then redistributed. A filter cleans the air before it is circulated.

In a forced warm air system, the warm air is propelled through the ducts by blowers. In a warm air gravity system, warm air rises and finds its way upward through the ducts and into the rooms without the help of a blower. After it has cooled it becomes heavier and drops to the floor of the room and into the return ducts by the action of gravity.

There are several advantages to a warm air system. If properly sized, the same ducts can be used to carry warm air in winter and cool air in summer. In cold areas, where heated air tends to be dry, a humidifier may be added to the furnace, and humid air distributed evenly through the same ductwork. In case of a power failure, a severe drop in room temperature will not cause the heating system to freeze. It is the fastest method of raising room temperature.

The warm air system has a few disadvan-

tages. Valuable space is needed for duct work. Without a humidifier, the heated air may dry out skin, furniture, and paintings. The circulating air may stir up dust which may aggravate allergies. The warm air gravity system cannot be installed in a house that does not have basement space for the furnace.

THE STEAM SYSTEM

In a **steam system,** water is heated in a boiler, generating steam. The steam is forced by its own pressure through pipes to the rooms to be heated. As the steam cools it changes to water, which returns through pipes to the boiler for re-heating. Special valves and pumps are needed. The advantage of steam heat is that it raises room temperature quickly. However, it is less able to maintain even temperature. Also, pipes may freeze in severe weather.

THE HOT WATER SYSTEM

In a forced **hot water system,** the water is heated in a boiler, circulated through pipes to radiators by a pump, and then returned to the boiler for re-heating and re-circulating. Because the water is forced through the pipes, the boiler need not be located in a basement, but can be put in a utility room.

A hot water gravity system is similar to the warm air gravity system. Warm water rises and cool water drops by gravity because it is heavier. In a gravity system, the boiler must be in the basement so that it is lower than any of the radiators. Hot water heat is the most uniform. It is also economical.

RADIANT HEAT

Radiant heat is a method of heating by means of concealed heating elements, either hot water piping or electric wiring. The heating elements may be buried in a concrete floor, concealed in ceiling plaster, or hidden in baseboard units. The advantage of this system is the complete absence of radiators, which tend to interfere with decorating plans. It has a disadvantage in that walls or floors must be taken apart to make repairs. Because repairs are such a prob-

9-8. *This fireplace provides heat as well as a cozy atmosphere.*

lem, the system should be designed by competent heating engineers. Also, if heat loss in the room is great, the floors may be uncomfortably hot. Electric systems lose efficiency as they get older.

FIREPLACES AND COAL- OR WOOD-BURNING STOVES

The fireplace is a popular decoration in many homes, Fig. 9-8. Now more and more people are beginning to depend on it as an extra source of heat.

The fireplace chimney may also be used for a coal- or wood-burning stove, or the fireplace can be converted to accommodate one of the more heat efficient free-standing fireplaces called **Franklin stoves,** Fig. 9-9. By being placed well into the room, the Franklin stove radiates heat in all directions. American foundries are producing stoves in record numbers, and several foreign models are also widely available.

Surveys show that fireplaces or stoves are among the most wanted features in a home. A fireplace is cheerful and decorative, uses low-

Vermont Castings, Inc.

9-9. These stoves must be placed on fireproof bases and be a safe distance from the walls.

cost, renewable fuel or material otherwise wasted such as newspaper logs and wood scraps, and requires no electricity, which makes it helpful during power failures. However, there are disadvantages. Fireplaces are expensive to build, cause cold drafts, require attention and maintenance, waste heat (90% goes up the chimney), cause some air pollution, create a fire hazard, and can lead to enviromental damage if too many trees are cut for firewood.

Stoves have the advantages of fireplaces, but not all of their disadvantages. They do not cause drafts, require less attention (new models hold heat 12 or more hours), use less fuel (about 20% of the wood required for the same amount of heat from a fireplace), and if properly installed create less fire hazard.

Cooling and Ventilating

Along with cooling, clean air and a suitable level of humidity are also desirable for health and comfort. Controlled humidity and filtered air also help to preserve the furniture and fabrics in a home.

In order to be comfortable, your internal heat should not be retained—you must be cooler outside than in. If the temperature of the air around you was equal to your body temperature and continued day and night, you would be very uncomfortable. Temperatures from 21°C to 24°C (70°F to 75°F) are desirable for most people, although, properly dressed, most people can be comfortable at lower temperatures.

While a home may be cooled by an air conditioner, steps should be taken to reduce the amount of sunlight and heat entering a house, Fig. 9-10. If the home has large window areas exposed to sunlight all day, it will be warmer than a house with windows shaded by trees, plantings, roof overhang, or awnings.

Every room should have windows which may be opened for ventilation. The design of the

UPI

9-10. The roof on this house remains stationary while the rest rotates to find the sun or avoid it.

home and the construction materials used also affect the amount of cooling that may be needed.

Fans may be used to drive hot air out of a home and allow cool air to enter. They increase comfort by keeping the air moving. Attic exhaust fans can reduce the amount of heat in a house by removing it as it builds up near the roof. At night, the air close to the ground is coolest so if only basement or first floor windows are opened and an attic fan used, cool air will be pulled into the house.

Certain rooms in a home should be ventilated for health as much as comfort. These are the bathrooms, the kitchen, the laundry area or utility room, and the garage. The basement or utility room, which houses the furnace and water heater, must have air brought into it for safety. Without an adequate supply of fresh air, the flame may be extinguished. Crawl spaces under houses, attics, and garages should also be ventilated.

An air conditioner, whether a window unit or a central system, consists of two sections—one in the house and one outdoors—connected to each other. The air conditioner cools, removes excess moisture, filters, and circulates the air.

The two parts of a room air conditioner are contained in one unit, with the outside section projecting from the wall or window. Room air conditioners are available in different sizes, some large enough to cool an entire small home.

Central air conditioning can be built into a new home or installed in some older homes by adding it to the heating system. The home may need additional insulation to help the air conditioning system operate more efficiently and economically.

THE UTILITY METER

Meters are installed by utility companies or communities to measure the use of water, gas, and electricity, Fig. 9-11. The occupant is charged according to the amount registered from one reading to the next.

9-11. An electric meter.

Fig. 9-12 shows a water bill. Note that the "previous" reading is subtracted from the "present" reading and the customer is billed for the difference. The card with the dials is left when the customer is away. It must be marked to match the meter readings and mailed. Note the top circle on the card. The 2 is marked, in the next circle the 3 is marked, and so on, for a total of 23,850 cubic feet of water. This is the reading also shown on the bill.

Similar meters measure gas and electricity. They are usually located on the outside of the building. In an apartment house each tenant has a separate meter.

ENERGY CONSERVATION THROUGH DESIGN AND CONSTRUCTION

Energy conservation can be built into housing. Measures taken to reduce heating costs also help reduce the costs of cooling.

● Insulation should be used on walls, ceilings, heating ducts, and around windows and doors. Closets, storage, and furnace rooms placed on the cold side of the house help reduce heat loss. It is important to seal all spots

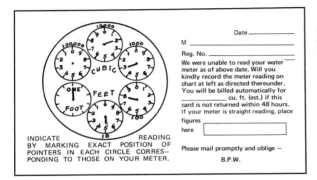

TOWN OF ANDOVER
WATER DEPARTMENT

| DATE | METER READINGS IN CUBIC FEET | | | | | AMOUNT PAST DUE | AMOUNT THIS PERIOD | PAY THIS AMOUNT |
	PRESENT READING	PREVIOUS READING	ESTIMATED READING	USE IN CUBIC FEET				
JUL 31 78	23,850	19,870		3,980	W		28.26	
					S		15.92	44.18

W = WATER   S = SEWER SERVICE CHARGE
Demand _____

Name _____   1,445   Interest _____
Address _____   TOTAL _____

6   0345   SEMI-ANNUAL CHARGES
BILLS PAYABLE WITHIN 30 DAYS
Bills Unpaid Subject To $1.00 Demand and 10% Interest.

Bills payable at Tax Office - 20 Main St. - Retain Original.
Make checks payable to Town of Andover - Return Copy.

INDICATE _____ READING
BY MARKING EXACT POSITION OF
POINTERS IN EACH CIRCLE CORRES—
PONDING TO THOSE ON YOUR METER.

Date _____
M _____
Reg. No. _____
We were unable to read your water
meter as of above date. Will you
kindly record the meter reading on
chart at left as directed thereunder.
You will be billed automatically for
_____ cu. ft. (est.) if this
card is not returned within 48 hours.
If your meter is straight reading, place
figures
here _____

Please mail promptly and oblige —
B.P.W.

9-12. The card is left with the customer to fill out. The bill is sent following the reading.

where loss may occur. For example, water heaters are large users of energy. Insulating them as shown in Fig. 9-13 can result in savings.

• If large windows are used in cold climates they should have a southern exposure and should be double-glazed. Storm windows and storm doors also help prevent heat loss as does weatherstripping used on all windows and exterior doors.

Homes in warm climates can be kept cooler with bronze reflective glass in the windows, Fig. 9-14. This type of glass allows only 26% of the sun's heat to enter, compared to 65% for clear double-paned glass.

• Heating, humidifying, and cooling equipment should be selected for efficiency. Most systems should be installed by an expert. Equipment should be placed so it contributes to savings in fuel. For example, a refrigerator

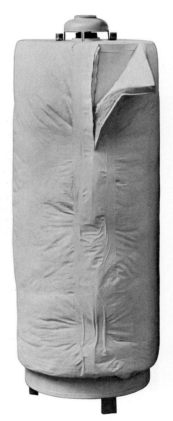

Johns-Manville
9-13. Insulation for water heaters can be purchased.

placed beside a radiator or stove will have to work harder. Inadequate materials and shoddy workmanship result in increased heating and cooling costs.

• The smaller the roof the less the heat loss. Compact two story houses are best in cold climates since there is less roof in proportion to the total floor area, which means less heat loss.

• A covered veranda, or porch, in hot humid areas provides welcome shade, Fig. 9-14.

• Ceiling height can influence room temperature. In warm climates high ceilings collect rising room heat which can be pulled by exhaust fans to the outside.

• A plan which includes a vestibule or entryway saves air conditioning costs in hot climates and reduces heat loss in cold areas. The entryway does not allow cooled or heated air to escape each time the door is opened.

• The smaller the wall area the more easily

PPG Industries

9-14. Bronze reflective glass helps cool homes in warm climates.

9-15. Central chimneys lose less heat.

a house may be heated or cooled mechanically. This means round houses are most efficient, square are next, and rambling L-shaped and T-shaped least efficient.

• Good house plans contribute to energy conservation. If activities are zoned, heat or cooling may also be zoned. Some areas of the house may be closed off when not in use or during severe hot or cold weather. In northern areas family rooms and living rooms should be placed where they get afternoon sun.

The modern New England Cape Cod house in Fig. 9-15 and the small 18th century Virginia house in Fig. 9-16 illustrate designs which have evolved to fit the climate. A central chimney in the Cape Cod saves heat since it warms surrounding rooms. End chimneys are favored in southern areas. They provide heat for the few months when it is needed and allow for a central hallway which affords ventilation.

• Many small details may effect savings. For example, the choice of color for the roof should be based on temperature needs. A white roof reflects heat, dark colors absorb heat.

● Whenever possible equipment which uses the least energy should be used. For example, install windows you can open since natural ventilation is free.

● Sometimes simple tricks will increase comfort and save fuel. For example, building paper or newspapers placed under rugs will help reduce heat loss through the floor. Enclosing the foundation around the house by banking it with dirt or leaves may also reduce drafts on the floor.

CHOOSING ENERGY-EFFICIENT APPLIANCES

There are two ways of saving energy with appliances. One is not to use them. Learn to get along without air conditioning for example. Use only those appliances which are absolutely necessary.

The second method is to choose appliances which use the least amount of energy. A fan costs far less than air conditioning to purchase and run. Avoid self-cleaning ovens, automatic ice makers, and self-defrosting refrigerators. These extra features require more energy.

9-16. End chimneys take less floor space.

Part 3: How a House Is Made

Each appliance usually has a small metal plate which gives the number of watts required to operate it. Occasionally this information will be on a label, and it may show only the volts and amperes required. In that case, you will need to calculate the watts by multiplying the volts times the amperes. Read the plates on some of the appliances at school or at home.

The wattage required for electric furnaces, ranges, dryers, heaters, irons, and other appliances with heating elements is high. Air conditioning equipment also places a heavy drain on electrical power.

Large appliances are now given an **energy efficiency rating** (EER). This measures how efficiently the unit uses electricity. The higher the EER, the better—it should be between 7 and 12.

Watch for news of energy saving products on the market. Many devices are appearing which promise to reduce electric consumption. For example, a new energy security lock turns off lights when the door is locked from the outside. Timers are available which turn water heaters on and off to take advantage of lower rates.

When new products appear on the market it is wise to deal with established merchants who are trained in the field and to take advantage of the expert advice available from government agencies and from utility companies. More information on buying appliances may be found in Chapter 14.

ACTIVITIES

1. If you were buying a house in your community, what fuel would you use for heating? Why? Would you use the same fuel for cooking? Why?

2. Discuss the advantages and disadvantages of air conditioning other than cooling the air. Are new homes and apartments in your community air conditioned? Why or why not?

3. Obtain up-to-date rates from utility and fuel companies for gas, electricity, oil, and any other fuels used in your community. Ask your parents to discuss changes that have occurred in the rates in recent years.

4. Have members of your class find out their family fuel bill for the proceeding year. Make a chart which does not identify any person. Show the amount by type of fuel for each family. What other facts should be included in the chart in order for you to judge the importance of the numbers?

5. Those who argue against the conservation and preservation of old buildings say jobs will be lost if new buildings are not built and that fewer natural resources will be needed to save existing buildings so stores will lose sales. Make a list of the arguments pro and con on this subject.

6. Discuss the cost of moving food long distances and the energy that might be saved by growing food near home.

7. Investigate and report on ways to conserve energy with the proper use of home appliances.

8. Start a campaign at home to conserve water. Make a list of the steps you would advise your family to take.

9. Enlist your family and friends in a recycling program. Perhaps you can persuade people at your school to recycle some items if they are not already doing this. Find out about collection points in your community.

10. List one appliance in your home which you could do without if power use were restricted. Name several tasks which you now do by machine, but which you could do by hand. List five electrical appliances in order from most essential to least essential.

11. Assume that your utility company makes off-peak use of electricity so economical that your family and you want to take advantage of it. This could mean that the rates are substantially lower in the early morning and late at night. List the ways you might plan household work to take advantage of the rate. For example, you might prepare several meals at night and serve them later during the hours when costs are higher. You might plan a candlelight meal during peak hours.

Evaluating the
Basic Home

Far left: Because of good design this older home may be a worthwhile investment.

Left: Will this gingerbread trim require the work of professional painters? Would the windows be easy for intruders to open?

Right: Why do you suppose the height of the chimney would be an important consideration?

JUDGING THE STRUCTURE

Since most people purchase houses that are already built, they seldom have an opportunity to watch the construction. If you are seriously interested in a certain house, it is wise to have a builder inspect it and advise you of any bad construction and the cost of necessary repairs. If the structure requires repairs or remodeling, that cost must be added to the purchase price of the house.

While you are considering many houses, however, there are some trouble spots you can detect yourself. Table 10-A tells you some things to look for. Many of these same items must be

Table 10-A.
FINDING TROUBLESPOTS

Things To Check	What To Look For	What It Means	What To Do About It
Basement	Signs of moisture on columns, walls, floor; rust around lower edges of furnace; a newly painted basement floor and the house being sold during the dry season	A leaky or flooding basement; the basement could not be used as living space, for storage, or as a workshop	Ask in the neighborhood if there's a problem with underground leaks; repairing leaks from underground water is expensive and often impossible
		Condensation	Install dehumidifier
		Inadequate drainage	Install drainage tile
		Water penetrating the wall	Damp proof the exterior wall; expensive
		Mortar has crumbled in a brick wall	Rake out the joints and repoint
		Frost action or settlement of footing	No satisfactory correction except rebuilding which is expensive
	Cracks	Shrinkage during drying	Not serious; can be patched
		Floating of slab due to water pressure	Install sump pump to reduce pressure
		Inadequate reinforcement; unequal settlement of earth under slab	Remove slab and replace; expensive
	A direct exit from basement to outdoors		
	Signs of insects, such as cockroaches	Infestation may be serious	Some insects may be difficult or impossible to exterminate
	Are windows in good condition?		
	Is drainage adequate? Look for signs of water buildup around the floor drain	Any freak flooding or water spills could not be quickly drained away and may cause damage	

FINDING TROUBLESPOTS

Things To Check	What To Look For	What It Means	What To Do About It
Plumbing	Look for any exposed water pipes: determine if the pipes are copper, iron, or steel	Copper pipes will last a long time; the others will corrode; brass fittings may be used on copper but will corrode on other pipes	Since most pipes are concealed in walls and floors they are expensive to replace. Contact a plumbing expert
	Flush the toilets; be sure the tanks fill properly	Fittings may have to be replaced	Obtain estimate of repairs
	Turn on the faucets: is there plenty of pressure? when you turn off the faucets, is there a loud noise in the pipes?	The water pump may need repair; there may be air in the pipes indicating possible leaks; the pipes may be corroded or too small	Get advice of plumber
Sewage disposal	Ask if there is a septic tank and how often it must be cleaned		Find out the cost of maintenance
	Ask if a cesspool is used	Cesspools are not acceptable to most state and local boards of health	May have to be replaced with a septic tank; expensive
Heating plant	Ask its age; if over ten years old it may not give too many more years service; is the furnace cracked or rusty?	The furnace may not produce enough heat or may quit working during a period of intense cold	Learn the name of the company which has serviced the furnace and discuss its condition; you may have to replace it
Water heater	Be sure the size is adequate for your family	Clothes washers and dishwashers require at least a 190 L (50 gal.) tank	
	Check for leaks and water on the floor around the unit	Most leaks are not repairable	Replace the water heater
Wiring	The age of the wiring: when was it installed? A 3-wire, 220 volt, 100-ampere capacity main circuit is usually adequate for most homes	Even if the wiring is still sound, an older home may not have circuits adequate for large modern appliances	Total the wattage of all the appliances, equipment, and lights you will be using and compare it to the wattage supplied by the house wiring;

(Continued on page 236)

Table 10-A. (Continued)
FINDING TROUBLESPOTS

Things to Check	What To Look For	What It Means	What To Do About It
Wiring (continued)	Signs of inadequate wiring are: • double or triple plugs in an outlet • extension cords • the need to disconnect one appliance before another can be plugged in or used • dimming of lights when a major appliance goes on • wall switches which are hard to find		circuits may have to be added or the house rewired. Have an electrician give you a firm bid for any repairs or additions
Insulation	Check under the attic floor and between the rafters for insulation; try to learn its R value; check exterior walls by removing an electric plate to see if insulation shows	If there is none in the attic, it's very possible that there is none in the rest of the house; cold climates require an R value of at least 30	Insulation must be installed; get infra-red photo to locate heat loss areas. (Utility companies and government agencies may provide this service)
Attic ventilation	Signs of water caused by condensation; leaks	Condensation due to lack of ventilation	Install screened louvers; add attic fan
Floors	Spots which squeak when you walk on them; any that bounce when you jump lightly up and down	A structural defect or settling of the house; framing not adequate; settling	Consult expert; repairs might be expensive
		Rot; insect damage; concealed fire damage	Consult expert; repairs might be expensive
Walls	Any cracks in walls or ceilings; does the plaster feel loose when you push against it? do doors swing easily? are windows difficult to open?	A structural defect or settling of the house	Correct defects; patch cracks
		Lath loosened from joists, plaster fails to stick	Remove loose plaster, repair loose joists, replaster

FINDING TROUBLESPOTS

Things to Check	What To Look For	What It Means	What To Do About It
Walls (continued)	Stains on inside or outside walls	Leaks from plumbing, rainwater, or condensation; gutters or flashing may be missing	Correct source of leak; repair and repaint; missing flashing can be expensive to repair
Window and door sills	Rot; cracked wood, dampness	Condensation, wet insulation, leaks in pipes	Consult expert; replace insulation or repair leaks; replace damaged wood; expensive
Outside walls	Peeling or blistering paint	Paint may have to be removed and new paint applied; it also may mean there are leaks in the flashing, through rotted window sills	Scrape or sand and repaint; if due to leaks, repair leaks
		Flashing may be missing	Consult expert; expensive to repair
Chimney	Height	Low chimney causes down-drafts	Add to height of chimney
	Size of flues	Illegal to add new equipment	Build new chimney; expensive
Exposed wood around the foundation	Termites; mud tunnels, dust or tiny holes in the wood; see Fig. 10-1 (page 238)	Termites may have seriously damaged the structure	Find an exterminating company which will give you a free inspection; get a written estimate for any repairs; ask experts at any US Department of Agriculture Field Station for advice; ask the seller to give you a written guarantee before you purchase the house
Roof	Ask its age	It may have to be replaced	Ask a roofing company to tell you the approximate life expectancy
	Does it have many jogs and valleys? check for water spots on the ceilings	These places may leak	

237

inspected in a used home, a mobile home, a condominium, or even a rental apartment. Although you may easily move from an apartment, it may mean breaking your lease, and a defect such as a leaky roof might cause damage to your belongings in the meantime.

If you consider remodeling a used home, you should decide whether the features you do not like can be easily changed or if it will involve too much work and high costs. Some of the features may be impossible to change. For example, a tall Victorian house will remain essentially that style, no matter how it is modernized.

SHOPPING FOR A HOME

Look at as many places as you can before you make a final choice. Be critical but not fault-finding. Judge by a reasonable standard but judge with care. Do not overlook price. Extra space, extra plumbing, complicated roof lines, and fancy windows, doors, and hardware add to the cost without adding to the basic value.

If you're looking for a house you may want to use a realtor. Unlike merchandise sold in a store, where everything may be seen in one department, the realtor's stock may be scattered over many miles. To avoid a waste of time, many realtors have on file photographs and descriptions of the property listed by them. To look at these may be of help to you in judging the general character of the market as to both quality and price.

As you investigate, you will find that many houses and sites must be eliminated because they fail to meet your needs. The challenge is to find a house and site that are satisfactory and will also fit within your budget.

It is often wise to select a realtor who is located in the area where you hope to live. She or he will be familiar with local conditions and will be able to answer questions about neighborhood changes, local costs, local facilities, and the advantages and drawbacks of the area.

To decide on the amount of money you can safely spend is the second step. You will find more about housing costs in Chapter 16. The price range that suits you may eliminate certain desirable locations since there may be no houses in these areas that are within your limit. After you select a neighborhood that you believe

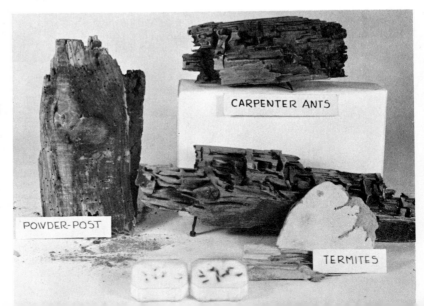

10-1. *These pests destroy the wood structure of a house.*

CARPENTER ANTS

POWDER-POST

TERMITES

10-2. Before buying a house, make careful comparisons.

will best suit your needs, and after you determine the price you can afford, the next step will be to look at specific houses.

Should You Buy an Old or a New House?

Old and new homes have advantages and disadvantages that need to be considered before a final decision is made.

House A in Fig. 10-2 is older but the design is pleasing and suitable to its location in California. Shrubs and trees add to its appeal. From this photo two possible problems can be seen: the room off the columned entry may be dark because of the extended roof; and the roof tiles may be expensive to replace. House B is brand new. It should require no repairs for a long time. However, the garrison design has not been carefully proportioned and there is no landscaping. Even if trees are planted immediately, it will be a number of years before they provide shade.

In general, an older house will offer more space since the room sizes were determined at a time when labor and material costs were lower. In selecting a house that has been lived in, the buyer can judge to some extent how the house will stand up under use since defects such as cracks and leaks will have had time to develop.

The quality of construction in older houses may be superior to that found in houses built today. An older house may have a design which you find appealing. The historic houses shown in Part Two were built by strong-minded people, and each is highly individual. Today, relatively few houses are designed for individuals to their order. Most are planned for developers who build them in quantity to be sold to the buyer who has little choice as to design. Some neighborhoods are monotonous since many of the houses are alike.

The new house is often in a new neighborhood with other new houses of equal quality. Old neighborhoods are seldom uniformly good. For example, a huge house in an old neighborhood may be an eyesore because the owner cannot afford to paint it and keep it in good repair.

Storage space is often lacking in older houses

Table 10-B.
WHAT TO LOOK FOR WHEN YOU RENT

☐ How much is the rent each month?
☐ Must you place a security deposit? Will you be paid interest on the deposit?
☐ Can the rent be increased before the end of the lease?
☐ Which items are not included in the rent: utilities? parking? swimming pool? TV antenna?
☐ Can you sublet? What are the provisions?
☐ Whom do you contact for maintenance? Is there an emergency phone number?
☐ Are laundry facilities available?
☐ Are public areas clean, well-lighted, and well-maintained: lobby? elevators? hallways? parking area? laundry room?
☐ Is the apartment well-maintained? Does the plumbing work properly? Does the stove work? Is it clean? Is the heating system in good working order? Are windows broken? Is the plaster cracked? Is the paint peeling?
☐ Will the electrical wiring accommodate any large appliances you intend to bring with you? Are there enough outlets?
☐ Are there any signs of insects, mice, or rats?
☐ If there is a fireplace, is it usable?
☐ Will the landlord repaint in a color you choose? If not, are you allowed to paint at your own expense?
☐ Is ventilation adequate? Do windows let in enough light?
☐ Is there enough storage space? Is there extra storage somewhere else in the building?
☐ Does the front door have a double lock? A security chain? A peep hole?
☐ Can you hear your neighbors? Are there lease restrictions about noise?
☐ Does the renter control the heat?

since the first builder may have used cupboards, chests, wardrobes, and other pieces of storage furniture. Now families often do not own these large pieces since built-in storage areas make them unnecessary in many houses.

There are advantages to both new and old houses. Only by comparing specific houses for sale and considering personal preferences can you say which is the best buy for you.

The same requirements apply to an apartment or a mobile home as to a house, except the size, variety of rooms, and outdoor areas will be much more limited. Each has special characteristics which should be considered.

Selecting a Rental Apartment or a Condominium

When looking for an apartment to rent, do your own investigating *before* you sign the lease or contract. What are your requirements? It helps to make a list of the features you might want. Table 10-B is a list of those items which should not be overlooked. Some are discussed in more detail in the following pages.

If possible, visit one or more apartments and see how many of your requirements could be met by each. Remember, you may not be able to find all of the features you want in one apartment. You will have to determine which of your requirements are the most essential.

Your next step will be to determine the area where you wish to live.

If you have friends in the area, they may know of apartment vacancies. When an apartment is available, a "For Rent" sign may be displayed on the building. Also, vacancies are advertised in local newspapers. Occasionally, there may be an advertisement by individuals seeking roommates to help share the rent.

Realtors who specialize in both rentals and sales have lists of vacancies and perhaps lists of apartments that will be vacant in the future. Although condominiums are often advertised in newspapers, many are also avaliable through realtors.

Very large apartment buildings or complexes have their own business offices. Whenever new buildings are opened, there may be model apartments on view. Prospective tenants often rent or buy the apartments before the building is completed.

In some college communities, the school may maintain a referral service or have a list of approved apartments.

FEATURES TO KEEP IN MIND

The managements of many new apartments have copies of their floor plans. They know one of the most common questions tenants ask is, "Will my furniture fit?" Prospective tenants or buyers can take a floor plan home and try out different arrangements.

The apartment should be attractive, clean, and well-lighted. The design and colors should harmonize with your furniture. A good apartment is designed to accommodate the major pieces of furniture the tenant is likely to own. Does the apartment lend itself to inexpensive furnishings if that is what you have to buy? Young people often must select inexpensive furniture for a first apartment, but they should not waste their money buying items they cannot use later.

If you haven't purchased furniture yet, be sure the apartment is free of features which would require special pieces. If you are just starting out, a place which would be suitable for inexpensive furniture like the wicker in Fig. 10-3 might be best.

When looking at an apartment, think of your hobbies and activities and be sure you will have space for them. If you enjoy having parties for large groups, determine whether the rooms are large enough to accommodate the number of guests you may wish to entertain. If you like to paint, is there room for an easel? If you like to keep houseplants, are the windows located so that the plants will have enough light?

An apartment should offer privacy, Fig. 10-4. Some apartments limit the noise occupants can make so the comfort of everyone is protected. Does the bedroom of one apartment share the

10-3. Wicker can give a room a fresh, airy look.

10-4. The sloping walls of this apartment house are designed to screen the outdoor areas from one another and from the street.

There is no standard ceiling height, but one that is too low will give a cramped effect. Also, tall pieces of furniture may not fit.

Sometimes an apartment may be reasonable in price because it has a drawback. Perhaps it is old and needs redecorating. If you can turn the drawback into an asset, you may get more value for your money. For instance, when older houses are converted into apartments, large rooms with high ceilings may be cut into several areas. This makes the high ceilings out of proportion to the small room size. It may present a decorating problem but may also allow for unusual decorative effects.

When you visit an apartment, there should be no cans of rubbish in evidence—this is a sure clue to sloppy management. Halls, stairs, and

same wall as the living room of another? If so, those in the first apartment may hear a TV or stereo when they're trying to sleep.

Ample storage space is desirable. If possible, there should be one good closet in each bedroom. In older apartments, storage may open off living areas. Additional clean, dry storage space for each tenant should also be available in the basement or general storage area. Be sure the space can be locked and that the area is clean and well-lighted. Remember, an apartment may lack detail such as built-in storage. However, the minimum apartment may be furnished more attractively than a larger and possibly more expensive apartment. The closet in Fig. 10-5 opens off a living room. The challenge was to keep the living room looking presentable when the closet was open. Used for storing a stereo, linens, and many small items, this closet was turned into a decorative asset. The walls and doors were covered in matching wallpaper. Two decorated window shades were used to conceal the shelves. The whole closet or the top or the bottom halves may be closed by pulling the shades down.

10-5. Storage areas can be attractively covered.

laundry should be clean and attractive. If possible, talk to other tenants about the care of the building.

The kitchen should have good ventilation with no signs of grease or dirt in the ventilating ducts. A greasy duct is a frequent cause of fire. Easy-to-clean counters and ample cabinet storage are also important. Most apartments are equipped with a range and a refrigerator. Some may also have a garbage disposer and a dishwasher. Equipment should be clean and in good working order. Plumbing fixtures should be clean and quiet in operation. There should be ample hot water. (Turn the faucet on and see how long it takes for the hot water to come.)

Selecting A Mobile Home

If you plan to buy a new mobile home, floor plans will be given you by the salesperson. For a used home you will have to make your own.

In most mobile homes the wall colors have been provided and the rooms are often small or long and narrow and generally come with the floor covering and some furniture, Fig. 10-6. Mobile homes also have built-in storage units which may not be adequate for everyone.

Be sure the park where the home is located has all the facilities you require, such as a coin laundry, and that it is well-maintained. If the homes are placed too close together it may interfere with privacy and increase the amount of noise.

SAFETY AND SECURITY

Safety and security are important considerations in selecting a home. Poor safety and security practices and unsafe conditions can make a home a dangerous place. Many deaths and injuries could be avoided if proper care were taken to eliminate the most common household hazards—fires, accidents, and the chance a burglar will pick the home as a target.

Fire

Fire safety can be increased by an understanding of how fire behaves. Locating a home where there is good public fire protection service, the use of fire resistant building materials, observation of fire safety standards for lighting and heating, the use of protective devices, and the observance of fire-wise personal habits all help to reduce the danger of loss by fire.

It is important to understand how fire behaves in order to select a fire-safe home and keep it safe. There are four stages in almost every fire.

In the first stage invisible gases are being generated. In a **smoldering** fire there is little or no smoke, flame, or appreciable heat. For example, a short circuit in the wall, an oily rag smoldering in the basement, or a hot iron left sitting on a cloth-covered ironing board might not be noticed at this stage. In the second stage, smoldering continues and some smoke is apparent. Flame and heat are still not present. Some toxic gases may be generated. In the third stage flame is apparent, there is little heat, but it will follow fast. In the final stage there is high, uncontrolled heat which generates poisonous gases and forces the air containing these gases to expand rapidly. This stage is very dangerous, especially for those on upper floors.

Except in the case of an explosion all fires start small. Some may smolder for a long time. For this reason a **smoke detector,** Fig. 10-7, is a valuable safety device, since it warns that a fire is present while it is in the first stage and can be easily controlled.

Since heat and gases rise, the most dangerous spot in a building is the top floor. **Combustion gases** are the gases generated by a fire. They can cause death even before a flame exists because people smother for lack of oxygen. Bedrooms are usually located on upper floors, and chances of survival in them may be poor. Since people's senses are dulled when asleep, they may die without even being aware of a fire.

THE LOCATION OF A HOME

An efficient public fire department and adequate water supplies are important factors in the safety of a home. Before purchasing a home or

Woman's Day Magazine, Darwin Davidson Photographer

10-6. Picture A shows the mobile home rooms as they were purchased, with paneling and wall-to-wall carpeting installed. Picture B shows the same rooms: the carpeting has been retained but the paneling has been partially covered, and the new decorating colors make the room light and cheerful.

B

10-7. Smoke detectors are useful and inexpensive safety devices.

renting an apartment locate the nearest fire station and find out how long it takes the fire fighters to respond. Find the nearest fire hydrant. The distance to the nearest hydrant is so important it affects the cost of homeowner's insurance.

Fire Safe Design ,

The use of fire resistant materials in construction is a major factor in fire safety. All competent fire prevention authorities have lists of tested and approved materials which home builders may obtain.

Tenants should be satisfied that a building meets safety standards before renting an apartment. For example, the building should be equipped with sprinklers and be constructed of fireproof materials, such as steel, concrete, or brick. There should be evidence of good housekeeping. Cluttered hallways and storage areas can breed fires. Fire escapes and safety exits must be easy to reach and in usable condition. If you are in doubt the local fire chief can state whether fire safety requirements have been met.

The danger of kitchen fires can be reduced by good kitchen design. Curtains, shelves, and doors that are too close to a range can be dangerous. Learning proper cooking techniques, selecting safe appliances and equipment and using them correctly, keeping ducts free of grease, and prompt disposal of rubbish all help minimize the possibility of kitchen fires.

Deficiencies in construction, design, and installation account for twice as many mobile home fires as those of other dwellings. According to the National Fire Protection Association, heating, cooking, and electrical equipment together cause nearly 85% of mobile home fires. Because of the fire hazards in mobile homes new federal guidelines and standards have been issued by the U.S. Department of Housing and Urban Development. The federal standards seek to establish performance requirements on all equipment and installations. They set tighter and more consistent guidelines for the installation of plumbing, heating, electrical systems, and fire safety. Manufacturers of mobile homes must submit building plans for each model to HUD for approval before construction can begin. Each mobile home must have a data plate attached which shows compliance.

These guidelines provide valuable information for consumers, but the main burden of protection still falls on the consumers themselves. This means that those considering a mobile home should do comparison shopping, read warranties, and carefully study all the various aspects of purchasing a mobile home.

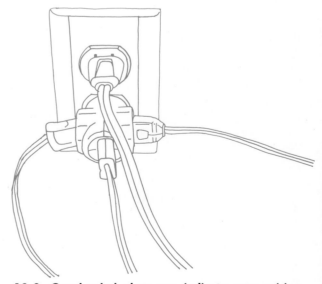

10-8. Overloaded plugs can indicate poor wiring and too few sockets.

SAFE HEATING AND ELECTRICAL WIRING

The possibility of fire may be reduced by good wiring and a safe heating plant. Unless you plan to do extensive remodeling, it would be unwise to purchase or rent a home which did not have both, Fig. 10-8.

There should be adequate space in the home for safe installation of heating appliances and fuel storage. This means room for the appliances themselves and sufficient additional space to properly service the equipment. Heating plants should be designed and installed by experts. Operating instructions should be followed carefully.

Stoves that allow poisonous gas to escape or that are in disrepair may cause serious illness or death. It is important to keep heating equipment in good repair and to read all labels of possibly dangerous materials and to follow recommended safety procedures. Electrical wiring should be designed and installed in accordance with the provisions of the National Electrical Code. The work should be done by a licensed electrician.

If a circuit is overloaded, do not plan to put in a larger fuse which will allow the additional electricity to flow through. This is dangerous since the wires in the overloaded circuit will be damaged. Damaged wires can start a fire in the walls. A fuse or circuit breaker should be the weakest link in the chain—it should burn out before the wires are damaged.

Learn where the fuse box is and how to replace the fuses or return the circuit breaker. If you are not sure the fuse is the correct size, consult an electrician.

Theft

There is no way for a home to be completely burglar-proof. Residential burglary has been increasing at an incredible rate. However, architectural design and security systems can help.

SECURITY FOR SINGLE-FAMILY HOMES

Be sure doors and windows are sturdy. It may be advisable to replace some. First floor

10-9. Grilles can protect street level windows.

louvered windows and large glass doors are security risks. All windows should be secured with locks. Outer doors can be fitted with peepholes and double locks.

Grilles and gratings can make forced entry difficult. Note the city home shown in Fig. 10-9. It has a high iron fence and an iron grille is on the window.

Skylights and ventilators on the roof may be used by a burglar to gain entry unless they are protected.

Inexpensive devices, such as the appliance timer in Fig. 10-10 are available. This timer automatically turns lights on and off in your absence making it appear as if you are home. You may wish to invest in such a device.

Most people who take suitable precautions do not need expensive electronic equipment. Nevertheless, there are situations where a security system may be a good investment: (1) if you are in a remote location with no near neighbors; (2) if there are many thefts in your area; (3) if you are often away from home; (4) if you have many valuable items that need protection, and insurance is expensive or hard to get. Information about several types of systems is in Chapter 14.

10-10. *An automatic appliance timer.*

10-12. *These tenants must install their own safety locks.*

10-11. *This call system requires visitors to contact individual apartments before being admitted to the building.*

SECURITY FOR MULTIPLE-FAMILY HOMES

Since tenants may be limited in the changes they can make to improve security it is important to evaluate a building before renting. Here are some guidelines.

There should be a way to identify visitors before you admit them into the building, Fig. 10-11. There should be adequate lighting on every floor—not just in the lobby. It is mandatory in some cities that all elevators be equipped with mirrors to reveal any person already in an elevator. Mirrors should be in all elevators and placed at the corners of all hallways to reveal hidden intruders.

Outdoor and indoor parking areas and walks should be in good condition and well lighted.

The color of the building and the size and location of shrubbery should be designed to make it difficult for prowlers to hide. The laundry room, an area where assaults frequently occur, should be locked and every tenant given a key.

Tenants have the right to install additional locks and security devices. This should be part of the lease agreement.

Because of the concern about security the presence of security guards and check-in gates are commonplace features of large apartments. Some have only one entrance and that under guard. In others, tenants gain entrance by inserting a special plastic card into an electronic slot which activates the gate. Tenants should be certain that these complicated systems and the limited number of exits designed to keep out intruders do not make it difficult to get out in case of fire.

In apartments with individual outside entrances like the one shown in Fig. 10-12, the need for making apartments secure is primarily the responsibility of each tenant.

Case Problem A

Study the room in Fig. 10-6. Plan a scheme for this room that reflects your taste using the same furniture. Assume that the furniture is in good condition. Your budget is limited to minor changes. For example, you may add new wallpaper or wall color, new slipcovers and draperies, new accessories, but no major pieces of furniture. Describe the changes you would make if this were to be your living room. You may use color chips, fabric samples, other pictures or write a detailed description of your suggestions.

Case Problem B

Howard is a factory worker with a good job and enough saved for a down payment on a house. Because he is handy at home repairs he is considering an older home, which he will remodel. However, he can't afford to make major changes.

The house he is most interested in has a large basement, three bedrooms, one bath, a one-car garage, and a fully landscaped yard. Although the house is large for one person, Howard believes he will marry someday and the house will accommodate a growing family. Over the next five years he intends to turn a closet into a second bathroom, half of the basement into a game room, and give the kitchen a rustic country look by installing new appliances and a brick floor.

On his last visit to look at the house, Howard noticed the following items. Make a list of the items and write what you think they mean and what Howard might do about them.

- The wood in the kitchen window sill is soft and cracked and feels damp.
- The present owner has used double plugs in the wall outlets in the living room.
- The floor in the kitchen squeaks when you walk past the refrigerator.
- There is a large stain on the ceiling of one of the bedrooms, but the present owner says he'll repaint the room before the sale.
- There is some condensation on the basement walls but no sign of cracks or standing water.
- The closet he intends to turn into a bathroom is only 4 m (10 ft.) from the existing bathroom.

1. Make a list of the leisure activities you would like to carry out in your home. Beside each, list the equipment needed. For example, playing records: storage for player and 100 records; sewing: storage for sewing machine, table, small chest of drawers.

2. Send for or pick up catalogs for home entertainment equipment. Plan the storage that would be required if you could select the equipment that appeals to you.

3. Visit someone who has a home workshop which is equipped to take care of ordinary home repairs. Describe the space used and the storage arrangements.

4. Important safety precautions are given in this chapter. You might compile a safety check list by rooms or areas which applies to your school or to your home. For example, you might head your list "stairway," then state that there should be light switches at both the top and bottom of the stairway. Or you might list closets and add that there should be a light bulb in each so no one is tempted to use a match to find some item in the closet. Also you might state that the bulb be well removed from any flammable material such as clothes or a papered wall. Detailed lists help people think of all possible hazards.

5. Collect information on home fire safety. You might contact insurance firms, utility companies, and firms selling safety and security equipment for current literature. Share this information with your classmates.

6. Make a safety tour of your home to find possible fire and safety hazards. How can these hazards be eliminated? Collect news articles about home fires. Discuss the stories in class. How can situations described in these news items be avoided in your home?

7. Visit two model apartments. Make a list of the features you liked and disliked in each. Write a brief criticism of them.

8. Obtain a rental application form and a copy of the standard lease form used in your community. Study both forms. Discuss the information asked for on the application form. Why does the owner want to know such things as the tenant's previous landlord, credit references, bank account numbers, length of stay at previous address, and detailed information about the tenant's automobile?

After reading the lease be sure you can answer important questions like: Who pays for utilities? Who is responsible if a sink needs repair? Are there restrictions regarding noise?

9. Visit a new apartment building and observe the arrangement of service and public areas. Do the apartments have balconies for outdoor living? Recreation facilities? Is there a park nearby? Compare the facilities with other apartments you have visited.

10. Contact people who have moved from a house to an apartment; ask them what their reactions are to the change. Ask them to compare the two types of housing.

11. Do some research at your local library on the damage pests, such as termites, can do to a building and report to the class.

12. Do some research at your local library on house and apartment pests, such as cockroaches, and report to the class.

PART 4 DESIGNING INTERIORS

11 Floor Plans

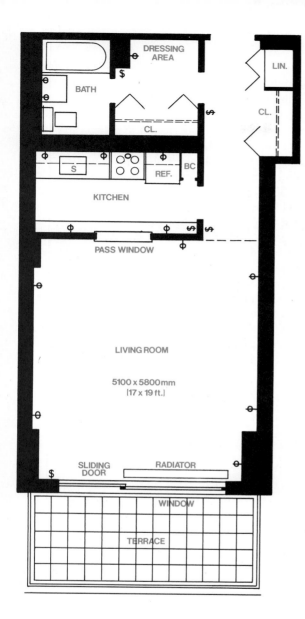

DRESSING AREA

LIN.

BATH

CL.

CL.

KITCHEN

S

REF.

BC

PASS WINDOW

LIVING ROOM

5100 x 5800mm
[17 x 19 ft.]

SLIDING DOOR

RADIATOR

WINDOW

TERRACE

Far left: Any kind of home you select must meet your space requirements.

Left: Learning to make your own floor plan can save you inconvenience later on.

Right: How much space do you suppose is required for movement around this area? (Family Circle Magazine/ Elyse Lewin and Vincent Lisanti)

MAKING A FLOOR PLAN

The plan of a house before it is built is shown on the blueprint. When you buy a used home or rent an apartment, you will not have a blueprint. Instead you must make your own floor plan.

The first step in making a floor plan is to measure the room. Be sure you are accurate—use a stiff folding rule or a flexible metal tape. You will need the following room measurements:
   ● width and length of the room, from wall to wall

Terms To Know

public area	territoriality
quiet area	traffic lanes
scale drawing	work-play area
social area	zones
template	

• location and width of doors, windows, and other openings

• distance of window sills from floor

• height of windows and doors

• exact location of electric outlets and switches, plumbing fixtures, drains, and lights

• exact location and size of special features, such as chimneys, closets, radiators, registers, door jambs, alcoves, and window seats

After you take the measurements, make a sketch of the room, showing its features. Draw the plan to scale. On a **scale drawing** a certain number of millimeters or inches equals a given number of millimeters or feet. Fig. 11-1 shows a sketch of a bedroom, including the measurements.

Once you have taken the measurements and made a sketch, make a final drawing to scale. Architects and builders generally use scales of 1:50 (1 mm = 50 mm) or $\frac{1}{4}$ in. = 1 ft. You will find it easier to make a scale drawing if you use graph paper with 5 or 10 mm or $\frac{1}{2}$ or 1 in. squares printed on it. You can also make your own grid. To measure you merely count the required number of squares.

In the scale drawing, include all of the features such as doors, windows, lights, and electrical outlets along with any special features. Indicate the direction in which doors open so that you can allow enough space for the swing. Fig. 11-2 is a scale drawing of the bedroom

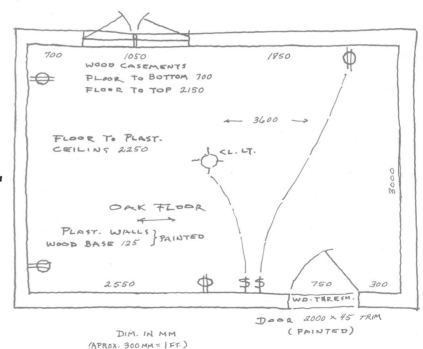

11-1. A rough sketch of a bedroom floor plan.

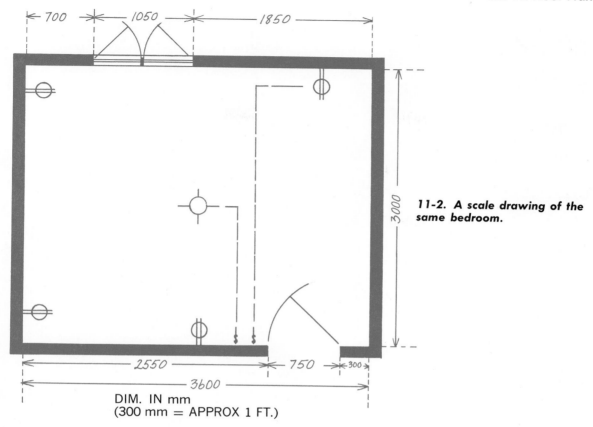

700 · 1050 · 1850

3000

11-2. A scale drawing of the same bedroom.

2550 · 750 · 300

3600

DIM. IN mm
(300 mm = APPROX 1 FT.)

shown in Fig. 11-1. Note that all measurements are included in the scale drawing, too.

One of the drawbacks of a floor plan is that it does not show the height of furniture or room features such as windows. You must make an elevation of one wall, showing the features of the wall.

THE USE OF SPACE

Before you build, buy, or rent, study several plans, pretending you are living in each place. If you decide after you have studied it that a floor plan has serious shortcomings, you should make another choice.

In studying any plan, look carefully to see if it provides for different types of activities. **Traffic lanes** are routes of travel from one room to another and through an area within the house. Those used most often should be direct, efficient, and without obstacles. For example, you should find it convenient to walk from the garage to the kitchen with heavy packages of groceries. **Zones** are the areas of use in a home. The three principal zones are social, quiet, and work. Outside, there are the same three areas of use. Look at Fig. 11-3. Notice the outdoor areas are separated from each other by landscaping, fences, or part of the house itself. Also outside is a fourth zone which, because of its exposure to the street, is called public. Each

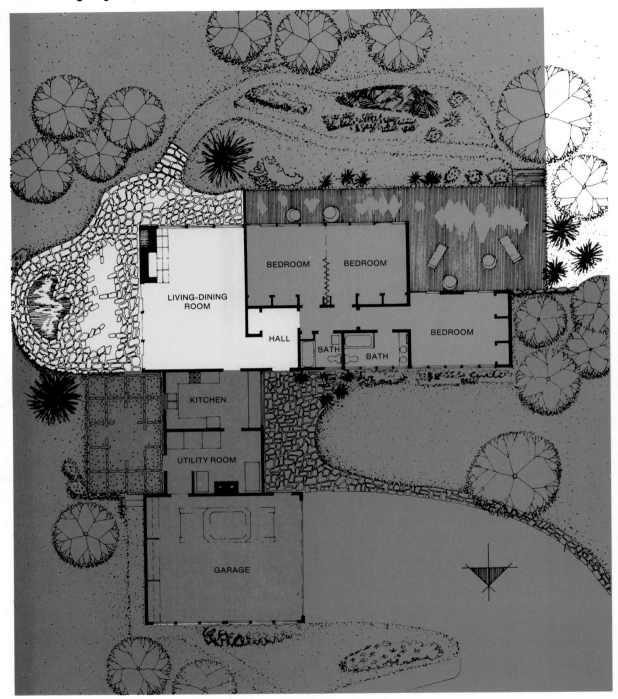

11-3. The principal zones in a house.

area of use should be properly related to the other areas, as well as to the home site and to the sun.

Public Area

Look at Fig. 11-3 again. The green tinted area in the foreground is the **public area.** This is the view you will see as you face the house from the street. It consists of walks, the entrance to the house, the driveway, and the garage. Do the landscaping and the shape of the house afford privacy? Are service spaces such as the garage well screened from the street?

Work-play and Social Areas

The red tinted area in Fig. 11-3 shows the **work-play area**—the garage, laundry or utility room, kitchen, and a small patio for outdoor activities. Note that outdoor activity here is screened from the street, but is within sight of the kitchen and laundry or utility room. This enables a parent to watch children at play while working in the area.

The **social area,** tinted yellow, includes the main entrance, the dining and living rooms, and the surrounding patio. This is where you may entertain your friends and have family cookouts.

The work-play and social areas are shown furnished in Fig. 11-4.

Begin with the entrance. If well designed, the main entrance will express hospitality. What would you think if you were a guest waiting at the door? Is it wide enough to appear inviting? Generally, 900 mm (36 in.) is a desirable width for an exterior door. Is the entrance sheltered from the weather, Fig. 11-5? The house in Fig. 11-3 has an entrance hall to use in greeting or saying farewell, and a coat closet. There is space for guests to remove their coats without bumping into each other.

The living-dining area to the left of the hall has several features to consider. This room serves two functions. The dining table and chairs are placed at the end near the kitchen. At the far end is the living room furniture. A light, movable screen could be used to separate

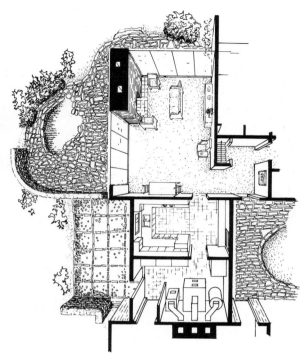

11-4. The work-play and social areas furnished.

the two functions and could be folded up when one large room is required.

The fireplace in the far corner of the living room is completely removed from lanes of traffic. This means that people do not have to pass it to get to another room. Usually, the size of the living room should be in proportion to the number of bedrooms, since that indicates the number of people who will be living in the house.

Furniture may be grouped informally around the fireplace so that family and guests may enjoy its warmth without distraction. The long wall opposite the fireplace gives ample space to display a favorite picture or mirror and to arrange large and small furniture without crowding. Through the glass wall and glass door to the left of the fireplace you can see the attractive outdoor social area.

Tech Built Homes, Inc.

11-5. Would someone standing in front of this door be sheltered from rain or snow?

In the corner of the dining area near the entrance hall is the doorway to the kitchen. As you go through it you find a "U"-shaped kitchen. A window over the sink permits a view of the outside work-play area and the children. A low counter on the wall opposite the sink may be used as a desk, a serving table, or for informal dining. Notice that dishes could be stored in the kitchen cupboards or under the counter. A window above the low counter affords a view of the street, the driveway, and the front entrance. The homemaker in this kitchen is not separated from family or guests while working. Since people walking through the kitchen do not cross the cooking area, work is not interrupted.

Adjacent to the kitchen is the utility room containing a furnace, a water heater, an inciner-ator, a washer, and dryer. There are two doors—one to the garage and the other to the outdoors. There may be a great deal of activity and traffic in a utility room so the size must be adequate.

Beyond the utility room is the garage, with a storage wall along the back for garden tools and housekeeping appliances. It is important that the garage be wide enough to permit car doors to be opened without hitting the wall of the garage or the side of the adjacent car.

Quiet Area

Finally, toward the rear of the house you will enter the **quiet area** shown by the blue tinted area in Fig. 11-3. This includes the bedrooms and bathrooms along with a sun deck and back yard. Here you may relax, undisturbed by activity in any of the other zones. The drawing in Fig. 11-6 shows you how this area will look when furnished. Three bedrooms, two baths, a corridor, and a sundeck make up this area in which quiet and seclusion are important. These rooms and the adjacent yard must be away from the noise of street traffic and separated from the activities of the rest of the house.

The corridor is relatively small, but provides access to any one of five rooms.

Each of the bathrooms has a combined shower and tub. Would you rather have a shower without a tub in one of the bathrooms? Why? The lavatory basins in the large bathroom are set in a counter with a storage space below, a large mirror above, and a cabinet to the left. The floors and walls are ceramic tile. The windows in the bathrooms and at the end of the bedroom along the street are six feet above the floor, to assure privacy.

Just as in the other rooms, wall space in the bedrooms is important for furniture placement. Does every bedroom have sufficient space for twin beds? Can the beds be placed against a

wall rather than under a window which might be drafty? Is there space for other furniture such as chests of drawers, dressing tables, a TV set, or a desk? In this plan, the windows along the rear of the two adjoining bedrooms are large, and doors lead from each bedroom to the porch overlooking the private yard. These two bedrooms may be made into one large room by simply folding back a moving partition; this is an interesting feature but it has a fault. What might this be?

Even though a house is air conditioned, cross ventilation is to be desired, particularly in bedrooms. In most parts of the country there are prevailing winds, and a house may be placed on the lot to take advantage of them.

It is well to have closets that can be opened full width. This may be accomplished either by folding doors or by pairs of doors. One advantage of the latter is that they can be louvered for ventilation.

This house is only one example. What have you learned that might help you in a real experience? Table 11-A is a checklist of desirable features on any floor plan.

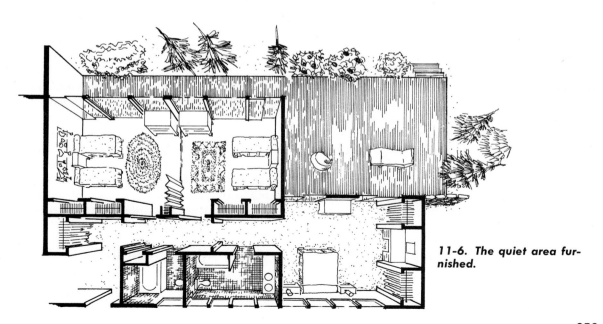

11-6. The quiet area furnished.

Table 11-A.
CHECKLIST FOR A FLOOR PLAN

Entrance
- [ ] Sheltered doorway
- [ ] Few steps to climb
- [ ] Good access to rest of home
- [ ] Space for removal of coats

Bedroom
- [ ] Quiet location
- [ ] Privacy for older children and adults
- [ ] Good ventilation
- [ ] Space for beds and bedmaking
- [ ] Conveniently located bathrooms
- [ ] Adequate closet and storage space
- [ ] A place for older children to do homework

Living room
- [ ] Space away from traffic areas
- [ ] Adequate space for furniture
- [ ] Wall space for pictures, etc.
- [ ] Pleasant view
- [ ] Adequate size for family needs
- [ ] Cross ventilation
- [ ] Screening from the street or passersby for privacy

Dining room
- [ ] Easy access to kitchen
- [ ] Adequate space for family seating
- [ ] Pleasant view

Kitchen
- [ ] Plenty of counter space
- [ ] Adequate storage for foods, dishes and cooking utensils
- [ ] Easy access to dining area and rest of home
- [ ] Space for informal meals
- [ ] View of children's play area
- [ ] Space for convenient arrangement of large appliances

Other areas
- [ ] Space for workshop or tool storage
- [ ] Indoor play area for children
- [ ] Garage of adequate size for cars and storage

JUDGING SPACE REQUIREMENTS

After you have found a floor plan you like, you must decide whether it has enough space to meet your needs. Unless you are an experienced decorator, it is difficult to judge space by merely looking at a room. Low, wide windows and light colors may make a room appear larger than it really is. A room with high ceilings and high, narrow windows may appear to be smaller than it is. The best way to judge space is to measure the room, draw a floor plan to scale, and then measure your furniture to determine if it will fit.

There are other reasons why you may want a floor plan of a room. It can help you to select the best possible furniture arrangement. If you are planning to add furniture to a present room, a floor plan can help you to determine the sizes to buy and whether the pieces you have selected will fit properly. If you are planning to rearrange furniture, the floor plan may enable you to work out several arrangements and then decide on the best one. If you are planning a new room or want to remodel an existing one, a floor plan is a necessity.

Measuring Furniture and Making Templates

After you have made a floor plan using a grid, you will need to measure the furniture you

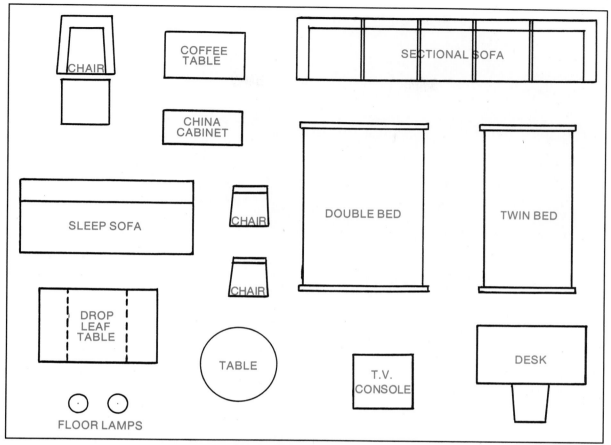

11-7. Furniture templates.

plan to use in each room. To do this, measure the length and depth of each piece at the longest and deepest points. For example, if you are measuring a sofa that has a curved back, measure it to the deepest point of the curve so that you will allow enough space. Do not just measure the depth of the seat. Measure the sofa from the front edge to the back edge. If the back or legs slant, be sure to add any extra space needed for the slant. If you are measuring a table that can be expanded with leaves, measure it with the leaves in place so that you will allow enough space for its maximum size.

When developing a furniture arrangement on a floor plan, small squares, rectangles, and other shapes called templates are used to represent the actual furniture in the room. A **template** is a piece of paper cut to the size and shape of the real furniture and in the same scale as the floor plan. Fig. 11-7 shows templates for different pieces of furniture.

Draw each piece of furniture and mark the name and dimensions on each for identification. Cut them out and place them on your floor plan. You can move the templates around to develop the best possible furniture arrangement.

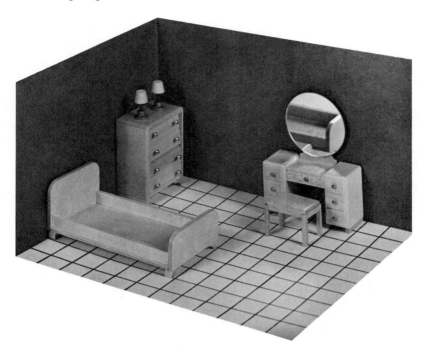

11-8. A model bedroom.

11-9. Although the template covers the same floor space as the model, remember the model is three-dimensional.

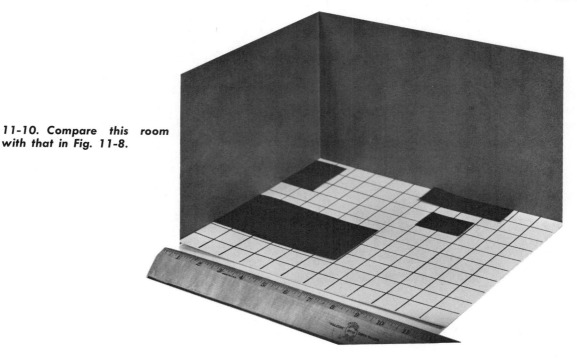

11-10. Compare this room with that in Fig. 11-8.

By using the templates, you will be spared unnecessary moving of heavy pieces of furniture.

As an example, let's measure the furniture shown in the model of a bedroom in Fig. 11-8. There are 10 squares in the width and 12 squares in the length of the room. Each square represents a space 300 mm × 300 mm (1 ft. × 1 ft.). Model furniture which has been made to this scale represents the furniture in the real room. When using templates it is easy to forget that the real objects are three-dimensional. These models let you see how much space each piece of furniture really occupies.

In Fig. 11-9, the model of the bed is being removed and replaced with a template covering the floor space occupied by the bed. The real bed is 1800 mm (6 ft.) long and 900 mm (3 ft.) wide, which means it covers a space on the floor plan six squares long and three squares wide. In Fig. 11-10 templates are used to represent the furniture in the bedroom. If you were not satisfied with the arrangement you would

move the templates until you had the best possible one.

Space Needed for Movement

It is easier to determine the amount of space required for furniture than for people, since furniture is not in motion. Because people move about, they require different amounts of space for varying activities.

In Fig. 11-11, the scale model of a person is shown seated in a straight chair. The average straight chair is a little over 350 mm (14 in.) deep. With the figure in the chair, however, the space requirement increases to almost three squares or 900 mm (3 ft.) from the back of the chair to the person's toes. The chair, plus the seated figure, requires a space 900 mm (3 ft.) one way by 600 mm (2 ft.) the other.

How does this requirement apply to the diagram of the bedroom in Fig. 11-12? If there is knee space under the dressing table (located to the right of the window), there will be room for a second person to pass. However, if the chair is pulled out to allow room for knees in front of the dressing table, there will at best be only 300 mm (1 ft.) of space left for another person to pass the end of the bed and go to the chest. Try walking through 300 mm (1 ft.) of space; use a

ruler and place two chairs 300 mm (1 ft.) apart. Is there room between them for a good passageway? If only one person occupies this room, however, it may not be a problem.

Look at the space available in front of the chest of drawers between the window and the bed. A chest with drawers closed extends into the room about 500 mm (20 in.). Now look at Fig. 11-13. Notice what happens to the space when the drawers in the chest are pulled out. When a person stands in front of the chest and opens a drawer only part way, an additional 900 mm (3 ft.) of space is needed. In the room illustrated in Fig. 11-12, there is a clear area of 1200 mm (4 ft.). The chest is well placed—there is ample space in front of it.

Decide whether you think there is room

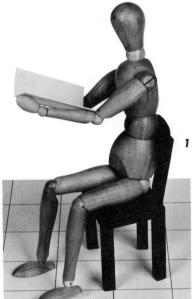

11-11. The space required for a straight chair.

11-12. Note the space required in the floor plan for a straight chair.

11-13. When someone pulls out a drawer, more space is required.

11-14. The shaded areas indicate the minimum space required for movement when using these pieces of furniture.

CHEST

DRESSING TABLE

CHAIR

BED

BOOK CASE

enough around the bed. Is there room to bend over the bed when you make it? You can make a bed when one side is against a wall, but it is much easier when you can move around it. Would you be satisfied with the space in the room in Fig. 11-12?

Fig. 11-14 shows the area required for the furniture and for one person to move about in the room. Notice how very little space there is to spare.

Suppose the person who used this room decided it would be nice to have a lounge chair

265

and floor lamp in the room. What would this do to the space left for traffic?

Fig. 11-15 shows the space required for a comfortable chair fully extended. Compare this with the space needed for the straight chair in Fig. 11-11. It is almost double! From the toes of the model to the edge of the back of the chair is 1800 mm (6 ft.). If the lounge chair were added to this room it would be impossible to move about. Fig. 11-16 shows what would happen if a lounge chair were placed in the only available space. It would be almost impossible to open the door. Is there a place for some other furniture that isn't so large, such as a wall desk?

The bedroom in Fig. 11-12 is comfortable when furnished with basic pieces, but there is no space for large extra furniture. Because of high construction costs, the bedrooms in many new houses and apartments are small. For this reason you need to plan carefully. Furniture especially designed for smaller rooms is appropriate. If this bedroom were to be shared, different furniture might make it more usable for two persons.

The same consideration should be given to the space requirements of other rooms in your home. How much space is needed for a conversational grouping? People should not be so close to one another that they stumble when they get up to move about; nor should they be so far apart that they must shout to carry on a conversation.

The same space tests used for the dressing table apply to a dining room. There should be space for the table, plus the 750 mm (30 in.) or more needed for a person seated in a straight chair. You should allow sufficient space for someone to pass behind the chair to serve food, or to remove dishes from the table. This requires about 1350 mm (54 in.) from the edge of the table to the wall or to another piece of furniture.

With practice you can learn to judge room sizes. Some people can look at an empty room and accurately visualize furniture and people in the space. This is good space perception. You can learn to measure areas with your eyes. Interior designers and architects make accurate estimates due to training and practice. However, the best way to insure that the room arrangement you plan will be comfortable for you and your guests is to use a scale drawing and templates.

Attention to Privacy

The word **territoriality** describes the need people have to control some space. It is closely related to privacy. There is a limit to the amount of crowding each person will tolerate. When someone comes too close, annoyance is felt. Each person has his or her own "space bubble". The size of this bubble varies from situation to situation. For example, people seem to tolerate more crowding on a subway or bus than in a classroom. Expressions, such as "stop breathing down my neck," vividly reflect the intense dislike people have to crowding.

It is known that overcrowding in a home may cause family strain. For example, conflicts may occur over the use of radio and television, sleep may be interrupted, and members of the family

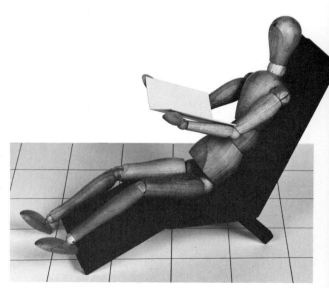

11-15. A model of a lounge chair.

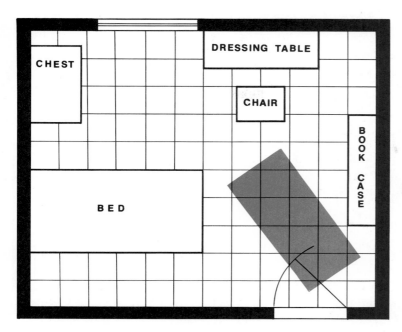

11-16. Would there be room in this bedroom for a lounge chair?

who might like to pursue constructive hobbies may be unable to do so for lack of space, Fig. 11-17. Family unity may break down because members go elsewhere. Even a small space, such as the desk in Fig. 11-18, may help give a person a sense of privacy and individuality.

Even when people are aware of poor planning it may not be possible to change living space because of cost, or because it is rented space. But rearranged furniture may be one way to improve a room's function. For example,

11-17. By listening to his stereo through earphones, this student shows consideration for others who may not want to hear the music.

E.I. Du Pont De Nemours & Company

11-18. Having a space you can call your own is important.

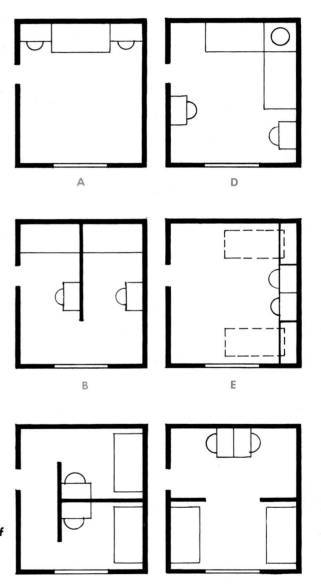

A   D

B   E

C   F

study the bedroom arrangements in Fig. 11-19. This is an average size room shared by two teenagers. Note how various arrangements of the beds and desks might affect privacy for sleep or study, and the amount of space for other activities or furniture.

Bunk beds are used in A. Since one bed is above the other this frees floor space, but places

11-19. Which arrangement makes the best use of space?

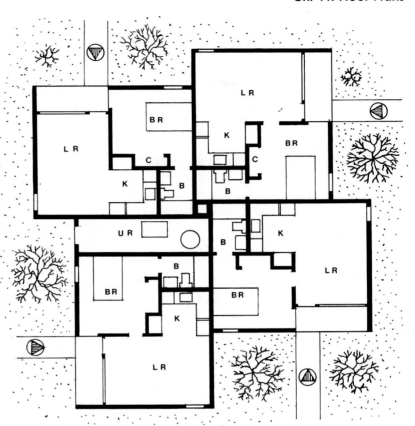

11-20. Would you want your bedroom next to a kitchen?

the sleepers close to each other. Privacy has been greatly increased in B by the addition of a partial wall. In C an additional dividing wall has been added, creating two small rooms. The window, however, cannot be fully enjoyed. In D both beds and desks are partially separated; however the useable floor space seen in E and A is lacking. The plan in E calls for built-in fold-up beds. Do you think this is a good idea? If the family moves they would have to leave the beds behind since they are part of the house. In F the two study areas are very close to each other as are the beds. In this plan activities are separated, rather than people.

High building costs in new housing have led to reduction in physical space. In order to make some rooms appear more spacious builders have used low dividers or partial screens to cut the view. These areas afford the occupants only a false privacy. Poorly constructed buildings may have walls so thin one can hear activities of other people in adjoining areas. Fig. 11-20 is the floor plan of an apartment building. Each apartment has a private entrance. What do you think of the bedroom placements. Would noise be a problem?

Provision for various amounts of privacy is one of the features which separate good floor plans from poor ones. The plan in Fig. 11-21 is that of a real house. It is an example of poor design since it provides little privacy for its occupants. People in the two front bedrooms must

KITCHEN

BEDROOM

11-21. How many disadvantages to this floor plan can you find?

DINING ROOM

BATH

DN →

BEDROOM

LIVING ROOM

BEDROOM

walk through the living room and dining room to reach the bathroom. There are several other poor features. Can you name them?

Space for Storage

How much space is needed for adequate storage? The answer to this question varies. Some people need a maximum of storage space. Others may not collect things and therefore need less storage space. The most accurate way for you to determine what is right for you is to inventory the items you wish to store, measure them, and determine the amount of drawer, shelf, and hanging area needed. For example, add up the number of feet of book shelves you need to hold your books. Measure the amount of pole space required to hang your clothes.

Fig. 11-22 shows a child's room designed for storage of books and toys which would not take up play space from the center of the room.

Builders generally provide closet space in each of the major areas in a house. In most newer houses and apartments, there is an ample closet in the entranceway. It may be equipped with special storage shelves or racks for outdoor clothing. There may be space in the dining room to store silver, linen, and china. Sometimes this storage has specialized drawers designed for silver and linen.

Storage space in kitchens is discussed in Chapter 12.

There should be one closet in the bedroom and, if possible, a closet for out-of-season garments and luggage. Additional storage in attic, basement, and garage may also be provided. In apartments, extra space such as a storage locker is often provided in a special area set aside for this purpose. In the well-planned home, wall space is usually included in each room for furniture with storage space such as a chest, hutch, or bookcase. When building, a family should decide whether to put money into built-in storage or into movable storage pieces, such as chests, that may be taken with them if they sell the house.

The house that has ample closets equipped with racks, drawers, lights, mirrors, and other conveniences is usually well designed.

11-22. Storage of children's playthings is an important consideration in planning their living space.

Draw the floor plan of a room in your home to scale. Make templates of the existing furniture in the room and place them in position. Select a new piece of furniture for this room. You might study pictures in your file for suggestions. Choose a piece that you would enjoy owning now and would want to keep for a future home of your own. If you cannot find a picture make a sketch or write a description. Make a template indicating the approximate size of the piece you would like to own.

Case Problem A

Move the templates around to try several different furniture arrangements. Pictures in your collection may offer suggestions for new arrangements. Can you improve on the present arrangement? Is there sufficient space for you to walk around comfortably? Draw the furniture arrangement that you like, including the location of the new piece that you would like to add to the room. Is there space for the furniture presently in the room if you make this addition?

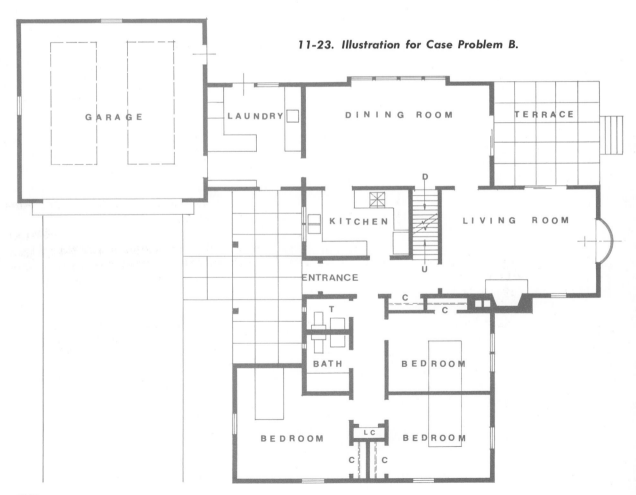

11-23. Illustration for Case Problem B.

Case
Problem
B

Pretend that you are a real estate agent. A couple with a 13-year-old girl and a 16-year-old boy have just moved into town and are planning to build a house. They have tentatively selected the plan shown in Fig. 11-23. They have asked you to locate an appropriate site for the house and have also asked you to evaluate the house plan.

• Study the house plan. What would be your specifications for a site for this house? Note the garage entrance and the main entrance in relation to the bedrooms and the living room. If this living room faces the front of the lot, where must the driveway be? Would you want to have the main entrance at the rear of the lot? Include your suggestions for landscaping that would allow for three areas discussed in this chapter: work-play area, social area, and quiet area. Give reasons for your site specifications.

• Write an evaluation of the house plan. Study the lanes of traffic. Can people move freely through the rooms and from one area to another? Will the traffic lane in the kitchen interfere with meal preparation? Is there room for the teenagers to entertain their friends? Is there good storage space? Is there enough wall space for additional storage units such as bookcases and cabinets?

• Since the house is still in the planning stage, this would be a good time to make desirable changes. What changes would you suggest for this plan to improve its livability for this family of four?

A
C
T
I
V
I
T
I
E
S

• Ask your home economics teacher to discuss space requirements for outdoor parties and buffet suppers. Plan a party you would like to give.

• Interview a physical education instructor or a nursery school teacher. Find out what outdoor play equipment is recommended for two- to six-year-old children for use in a yard similar to the one shown in Fig. 11-3. Ask about the safety and the educational value of the various kinds of equipment.

• Describe a family you know, but do not give their names. Give as many facts about them as you can which you believe would influence their choice in housing. For example, the number of children, the number of adults, the age of each member, their hobbies, their special interests, their geographic location, and their income. Look at the floor plan in Fig. 11-23. Discuss in terms of the family you have described.

• Conduct an opinion survey. Ask several adults to look at the floor plans in Figs. 11-20 and 11-23. Ask them to tell you what they like or dislike about the plans. Record their answers and report to the class.

• Look at some typical floor plans of farm and city houses in other countries. Sketch or describe the examples you have found. How do they differ from American houses? Can you explain the reasons for the differences?

12 Planning Kitchen, Bath, and Laundry

Far left: This compact apartment kitchen was formerly a butler's pantry. (Celanese House)

Upper left: How would you decorate this dressing room and bath? (Family Circle Magazine/Elyse Lewin and Vincent Lisanti)

Lower left: The laundry area can be used for other activities, such as sewing. (Family Circle Magazine/ Elyse Lewin and Vincent Lisanti)

Right: Would you prefer a separate dining area, such as the one in this mobile home? (Family Circle Magazine/Elyse Lewin and Vincent Lisanti)

Kitchen planning reached its height during the 1930's when energy-saving kitchens based on careful research were developed. All pieces of equipment were in a step-saving arrangement. The most efficient floor plans with only one door were adopted. In order to save steps, the size of the kitchen was kept as small as possible. Emphasis was placed on sanitation as well as efficiency. Kitchens were often all-white with a minimum of decoration and detail. Long lists of the most desirable dimensions for each part of the kitchen have been developed. Today's kitchen planners do not ignore the need for efficient and economical plans. However, they also

12-1. A kitchen designed on the open plan.

Armstrong Cork Company

recognize the desire for pleasant, attractive open areas where activities other than cooking may take place. The kitchen of today is often the center of family activity.

In addition to the emphasis on family activities, several architectural developments have changed the basic, efficient unit that evolved during the 1930's. For example, today's kitchens may have large areas of glass. A large picture window may overlook a play area so that adults may observe small children. Glass areas

may connect the kitchen with a garden, balcony, or greenhouse.

Another influence on kitchen design was the development of the open plan. The kitchen shown in Fig. 12-1 is an example of an open kitchen. There is no wall between the kitchen and living area. The person preparing meals in this kitchen is not isolated since it is near the family and entertainment center.

Each family must decide what type of plan will best suit their pattern of living and their

Terms To Know

---Terms To Know-------------------

built–in range	one–wall kitchen
corridor kitchen	U–shaped kitchen
eye–level console	work centers
free–standing range	work triangle
L–shaped kitchen	

budget. Because built-in mechanical equipment is standard in almost all of today's homes, the kitchen in the average home is usually the most expensive room. The cost of the equipment and the labor required for its installation generally increase the cost of the kitchen above that of the other areas.

A kitchen must meet FHA (Federal Housing Authority) minimum standards, required for an FHA loan. Your builder or kitchen installer should be familiar with these. And while you may not be buying under an FHA loan, a future buyer may want to do so.

THINGS TO CONSIDER

Whether you are building a new one or selecting an existing one, you must decide on the kind of kitchen suitable to your way of life. If, for example, you will be living in an apartment, your choices may be very limited, and you may have to compromise, Fig. 12-2A. However, it is wise to know in advance what your needs are so you can plan for them.

● **The kind of cooking you will do.** When kitchen designers plan large commercial kitchens, they "walk through" sample menus. Every step of the preparation process is planned on paper, and every ingredient and utensil required for the food to be prepared is listed. This is the reason the kitchen in a drive-in that sells hamburgers is not the same as the one in a gourmet restaurant. The equipment, utensils, and storage in each are designed to accommodate the work that will take place there.

Do you enjoy experimenting with exotic recipes? You would need storage space for gourmet foods and specialized equipment. Do you rely on convenience foods? You would need extra storage space for packaged foods and space for a large freezer. Whatever special food preparation needs you have, think them through so that you can plan a kitchen around them.

● **The activities which will take place in the kitchen.** Some homeowners want space in the kitchen for sewing and doing laundry, and

Sue Scott

12-2A. This apartment kitchen in an old house has limited storage. The renter added shelves beneath the sink.

Kitchen Compact/Frank Thomas Adv.
12-2B. A kitchen office.

the rear door of a house or the door opening into the garage, Fig. 12-3. In an apartment it should be located so that food and grocery items do not have to be carried through rooms where guests may be seated, or where activities of others in the family will be interrupted.

Ideally the kitchen should be located so that there is access to the front door, bathroom, and bedrooms without going through the living areas.

If possible, it should be located so that the children's play area may be observed from the kitchen windows.

The kitchen should be adjacent to the dining area as well as the receiving door. If possible, a counter pass-through to the dining room should be included to make serving more convenient.

● **The orientation you prefer.** Whether the family wishes to have the kitchen face east for morning sun, or west to enjoy the afternoon sun may influence the way in which a house is situated on the lot. In cold areas the kitchen, which

for a telephone, writing materials, and cookbooks, Fig. 12-2B. A television set may be included in the kitchen. One or more easy chairs and even a couch may be in the family-room end of a large multi-purpose kitchen. Perhaps you want a fireplace. This might limit the location of the kitchen since it would have to be built next to the chimney. Or it might add greatly to the expense if another chimney would have to be installed.

Does your kitchen always seem to become the center of activity where guests gather at parties? You might want to plan a kitchen designed for your guests' comfort and enjoyment.

● **A convenient location.** Since the kitchen is a much-used room, a poorly located kitchen might make a homemaker's chores unnecessarily difficult.

The kitchen should be located near a service door where deliveries are received. This may be

Poggenpohl
12-3. This kitchen is near a back entrance.

278

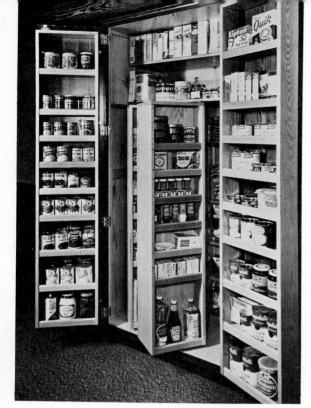

Wood Mode Cabinetry

12-4. A pantry with fold-out shelving.

kitchen such as the elegant window treatment in Fig. 12-1.

● **The type and amount of ventilation required for kitchen equipment established by local building codes.** Before you build or remodel learn what the codes say.

A good over-the-range exhaust hood will draw off heat, smoke, steam, and cooking odors. A range should never be placed under a window. Window curtains could catch fire. Too, the drafts might extinguish a pilot light or flame. A window over a range would also be difficult to keep clean.

● **Adequate storage.** If the home is situated far from a shopping area so that buying in quantity is advisable, a separate storeroom may be practical. In a large kitchen, some of the space might be turned into a pantry, a closet, or other storage space. Fig. 12-4 shows a pantry unit available in kitchen cabinets. Fig. 12-5 shows storage space in an under-the-counter unit.

In some homes space for storage may be provided in the garage. Any area used for stor-

has additional heat due to cooking activities, may be a good room to locate on the north or coldest side of the house.

● **The door and window openings in a room which affect both the traffic pattern and the location of furniture and equipment.** Many experts rate kitchens according to the number of windows and doors. The fewer openings, the greater the possible efficiency. Due to advanced mechanical ventilation and good artificial light, some people suggest eliminating windows and using only one door. Others prefer many windows and a plan so open that counters are free-standing islands. Most families choose a plan between these two extremes. Three doors seem a reasonable maximum.

Very few homes sell readily if ample window space has not been provided. The window area can lead to effective decorative accents in the

Poggenpohl

12-5. Roll-out shelves make finding items easier.

age should not be subject to excessive heat, nor should the temperature go below freezing.

If the kitchen is used for dining as well as food preparation, it would be wise to provide for storage of dishes, silver, and table linen. Many kitchen cabinet manufacturers have specialized storage cabinets available for silver and linen.

- **If you are building a house, the style and number of cabinets desired.** These must be decided on before the kitchen layouts are final. Although most cabinets are made in standard sizes, not all manufacturers make the same kinds of corner and specialized storage cabinets, which could affect your floor plan. Be sure to select a brand that has the features you want. Since it is desirable that the cabinets match, it is best to use only one brand of kitchen cabinets.

If you are remodeling an existing kitchen, do not overlook the possibility of using the existing cabinets. Many older styles are sturdily constructed and have excellent storage potential. The outside can be refinished, painted, or antiqued. Fig. 12-6 shows cabinets which have had fabric panels added. The paint color and fabric can be changed again when the owners wish to redecorate.

The use of storage aids can make the shelf space more efficient. You might have to replace the sink and counter top, but this would be a small expense compared to replacing the cabinets, too.

- **The size of major appliances you already own.** You must be sure they will fit the space available. Since major appliances are expensive and their resale value is not high, you will want to use those you have.

WORK CENTERS

The basic requirements for storage, food preparation, and cleanup are the same in any kitchen. A knowledge of the standards which have been developed will be helpful in evaluating plans and in planning your own kitchen.

In most kitchens, work revolves around three major pieces of equipment—range, sink, and refrigerator-freezer—called **work centers.**

The work centers organize a kitchen in a logical way. Here, similar tasks requiring similar ingredients and related utensils take place. All the items needed for these activities are usually stored here.

The most efficient arrangement for the work centers permits the homemaker to proceed from one center to the next without retracing steps. This arrangement results in what is called the **work triangle,** Fig. 12-7.

In the illustration food is brought in through a door on the left and stored in the refrigerator-freezer. Next it is cleaned and prepared at the sink, then it is cooked at the range and taken to the dining room, which is on the right. Leftovers are returned to the refrigerator, which completes the triangle. In the standard work triangle, the sink is placed at the point of the triangle between the refrigerator and the range.

Kitchen experts generally agree that the three sides of the work triangle should measure no more than a total of 6600 mm (22 ft.). A larger triangle is inefficient because it requires too much walking.

Fig. 12-8 shows a kitchen with a compact work triangle. The refrigerator and stove are placed at an angle which helps save steps. Typical of many new kitchens, the oven and stove top are two separate appliances.

The Refrigerator–freezer Center

This is also called the mixing and food preparation area. Since this is where fresh and frozen food is stored, it should be located near a door leading to the garage or outdoors.

Ideally, there should be at least 500 mm (18 in.) of counter area located on the opening side of the refrigerator-freezer so bundles may be conveniently unwrapped and the contents sorted.

12-6. When the owners redecorate, these fabric panels can be easily changed.

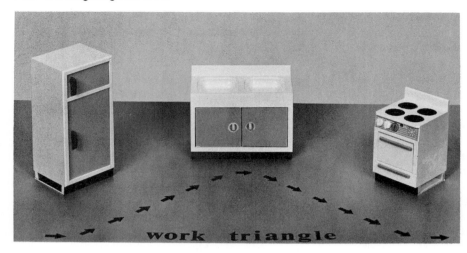

12-7. The work triangle.

E.I. Du Pont De Nemours & Company
12-8. A step-saving kitchen.

282

To plan the storage and organization of this center, consider first of all the items that are normally used to store refrigerated and frozen foods. Here you would want freezer containers, foil wrap, freezer tape, waxed paper, plastic bags, and storage containers.

The area between the refrigerator and sink is usually the most convenient for mixing and preparing food. Think of the items that you would normally use. It will help you to analyze the type of food you prepare. Do you like to experiment with recipes that require elaborate preparation? Do you prefer convenience foods? Each would require different storage space. You probably would use this area for making such foods

Poggenpohl

12-10. Multi-use units help make a kitchen more efficient.

as cakes, breads, casseroles, puddings, salads, and cookies.

What utensils would you use in the preparation of these foods? Here you would store items such as measuring equipment, mixing bowls and spoons, mixer and beaters, blender, baking pans, casseroles, and paper towels. Among the foods stored here, in addition to the refrigerated and frozen foods, would be prepared mixes, flour, sugar, spices, and convenience foods.

Two of the specialized cabinets available for this area include a "file" drawer for storing baking pans and lids, Fig. 12-9 and a bread drawer with a work shelf lid, Fig. 12-10.

The Sink Center

The sink center is also known as the clean-up center. Food preparation which requires water is done here. Washing hands, preparing beverages, cleaning vegetables and fruit, and washing dishes are only a few of the operations that will be carried on at the sink center. If there is a

Mutschler, Div. of Modernfold
Ind., an American Standard Co.

12-9. Lids and pans stored on edge are easier to find and take out.

283

E.I. Du Pont De Nemours & Company
12-11. A window makes a sink area more pleasant.

garbage disposer or a dishwasher in the kitchen, it is located here.

Although the sink is frequently located beneath a window, Fig. 12-11, this is not essential. For example, if the view is attractive, you may prefer to have the eating area near the window.

Counter space is needed on each side of the sink so that soiled dishes may be scraped and stacked on one side and washed dishes dried on the other. Ideally, there should be about 900 mm (3 ft.) of counter space on each side of the sink, in addition to the counter space adjacent to the refrigerator and range, Fig. 12-12.

Here you would want to store detergents, scouring powder, dish cloths, and dish towels. Storage for dishes is also handy in this area since they can be put away as they are dried. In addition, you might want to store equipment for making beverages such as a coffeepot and tea-

pot. You would need utensils such as knives, a vegetable brush, measuring cups and spoons, and pots and pans.

Foods that require water in preparation such as soups, dehydrated foods, macaroni products, and potatoes should be stored here. Can you think of other foods you would store in this center?

The Range Center

The range center is also known as the cooking and serving area. The range center should, if possible, be located on an outside wall to make it easier to provide an exhaust system that will remove heat and cooking odors. This can

E.I. Du Pont De Nemours & Company
12-12. This sink and counter are molded of one piece so they're easier to clean.

be done with a wall fan or with an exhaust hood over the range, Fig. 12-13.

Ideally, there should be at least 600 mm (2 ft.) of counter next to the range center. If possible, part of the counter should be made of a heatproof material such as stainless steel so that hot pans may be set directly on it without damaging it.

To organize this center, think of all the foods and utensils you would use at the range. What seasonings would you need? What serving equipment would you use?

Here you should store foods such as canned vegetables, stews, and sauces, frying fats and oils, salt and pepper, and spices. It's possible that you would use a certain ingredient such as salt in more than one place. To save time, you might want to have a container at each center, one at the mixing center and one near the range.

In this center, you would store all utensils you use in stirring, measuring, tasting, basting,

and all of the other operations that go on at the range. After the food is cooked, you would need pot holders, a tray, a trivet, serving spoons and forks, and serving bowls. What other food and equipment would you want to store here?

Other Appliance Centers

A separate freezer may create the need for an additional storage center.

A wide variety of attractively designed portable appliances makes cooking possible wherever an electric outlet is available. For example, an electric broiler-fry pan allows you to prepare food in the kitchen, on the dining room table, or on the patio. Microwave ovens are of a size that will fit on a counter top.

Some efficiency apartments are equipped with a one-piece kitchen, shown in Fig. 12-14. All of the work centers are combined, with the sink, range, and refrigerator in one unit. These compact units may be placed behind doors or shuttered openings. They require very little

E.I. Du Pont De Nemours & Company
12-13. A ceramic cooktop with a built-in exhaust hood.

Crane Co.
12-14. A very compact one-piece kitchen.

space and are inconspicuous. However, they do not provide enough storage or work space for someone who plans to do a lot of cooking.

BASIC KITCHEN SHAPES

The three work centers are generally combined into one of four basic kitchen shapes or layouts. All other kitchen plans are variations of one of these four basic plans.

The One–wall Kitchen

The **one-wall kitchen** is often used in apartments, or where there is a minimum amount of space. Fig. 12-15 is a model of a very simple one-wall kitchen. The outside door would be on the right of the illustration and the dining room on the left. This kitchen arrangement calls for

creativity since countertops and storage are in short supply. Overhead cupboards could be added if space permitted. In this example, they would probably be placed over the two counters and the sink, assuming there is no window. If there is a window, some other storage space would probably be planned such as a closet. Fold-down tables or a mobile cart might be used to add extra counter space when needed for

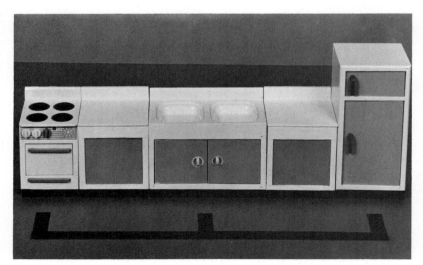

12-15. The one-wall kitchen.

Family Circle Magazine
Elyse Lewin and Vincent Lisanti
12-16. This one-wall mobile home kitchen leaves ample space for dining.

entertaining. If additional counters were added, the distance the homemaker would have to walk would also be increased.

The advantages of the one-wall kitchen are that it requires a minimum of space and that the work can flow in a straight line. In a one-room or studio apartment, the kitchen may be closed off by folding or sliding doors, and the rest of the room may function as a living room or bedroom when meals are not being prepared.

The space-saving design of the one-wall kitchen makes it a popular choice for mobile homes, Fig. 12-16.

The major disadvantages of the one-wall kitchen are the lack of storage space and its length, which may require much walking.

The Corridor Kitchen

The **corridor kitchen** is a variation of the one-wall. The appliances are on two walls with an aisle between, Fig. 12-17. Notice how this arrangement shortens the distance to be walked. As you can see, the work triangle is a very compact one. In the floor plan the sink is on the window wall opposite the range and refrig-

erator. If space permits, counters may be added to one or both sides of the kitchen without greatly increasing the distance to be walked. Both ends of the kitchen may be open, or one end may be a wall.

An advantage of the corridor kitchen is that it may be located between two rooms. It may, for example, open at one end to a screened porch or terrace and at the other end to a dining room or breakfast area and be equally convenient to both. Fig. 12-18 shows a corridor kitchen. The near end opens into an entrance hall while the far end opens into the dining room.

A disadvantage of the corridor kitchen is that it frequently becomes a hallway. If the room is narrow, people coming and going through the kitchen may interrupt the preparation of a meal.

The L-shaped Kitchen

Fig. 12-19 shows the **L-shaped kitchen** plan. Notice the convenient work triangle. The work area in this plan is not a passageway, and the open plan permits a dining area, Fig. 12-20. Because it is open, two people may work conveniently in this kitchen. Notice the size of the

287

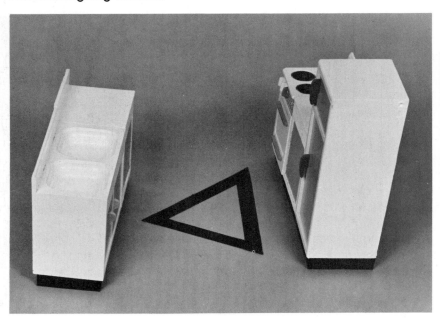

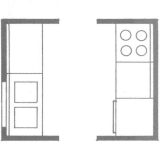

12-17. The corridor kitchen.

12-18. This corridor kitchen is formed by a free-standing sink instead of an opposing wall.

General Electric

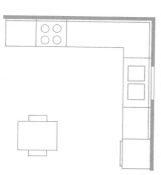

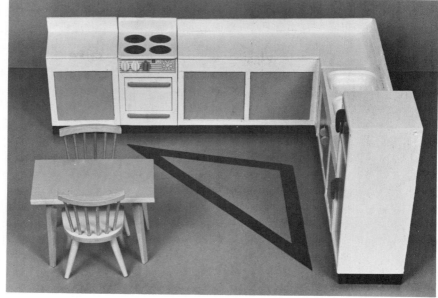

12-19. An L-shaped kitchen.

12-20. A free-standing counter could also be installed where the table is now in this L-shaped kitchen.
General Electric

Janell Gauwitz

12-21. The stools added to this counter make a handy snack area.

work triangle. It is only slightly larger than the triangle in the corridor plan, yet three base cabinets have been added. In terms of convenience, the experts consider this plan an improvement over both the one-wall and corridor arrangements.

In some kitchens a counter called an island is installed in this open area. It may include a second sink, cooktop, work space, or specialized equipment such as a built-in grill or a chopping

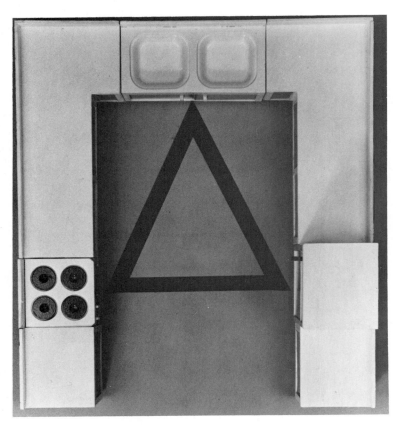

12-22. A U-shaped kitchen.

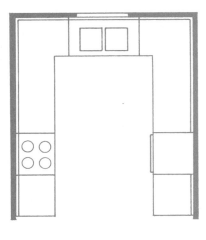

block. This space may also be used as a counter area for breakfast and quick snacks; stools instead of chairs may be used, Fig. 12-21.

The U-shaped Kitchen

Fig. 12-22 is a view looking down into a **U-shaped kitchen.** Notice that three more base cabinets have been added to this kitchen, giving this plan the most counter space of any of the examples shown. Observe, however, that the

work triangle has not been greatly increased by this substantial addition of storage space.

Generally, this U-shape is considered the most efficient arrangement of all. The sink in this plan is at the point of the work triangle and within easy reach of the other centers, Fig. 12-23. If the sink is placed on an outside wall, a picture window over it may afford a view of a play area, garden, or outside dining area. This is a favorite arrangement with many kitchen

Mutschler, Div. of Modernfold
Ind., an American Standard Co.
12-23. A U-shaped kitchen is considered the most efficient.

designers. The end of the U usually opens to a dining area.

The storage space in a U-shaped kitchen may be increased by making the U wider or longer. However, this increases walking distance. The floor space between the two opposite walls of cabinets in the U must be at least 1500 mm (5 ft.). If it is less, there is insufficient room to open doors and drawers, or to bend over to reach into bottom shelves.

PLANNING YOUR OWN KITCHEN

Authorities agree that certain general guidelines apply to all kitchens.

The basic types of kitchens may be modified to suit almost any room. The work triangle should not be so large that it causes unnecessary walking, or so small that the kitchen is cramped. It is generally most convenient when the three sides of the work space are approximately equal and there is good counter space beside each major appliance. Look first for traffic lanes between doors. It is desirable to keep all through traffic outside the work triangle.

A kitchen which has a minimum of 3000 to 4200 mm (10 to 14 linear ft.) of base cabinet storage, and 3000 mm (10 linear ft.) of wall cabinet space is generally recommended. The counter area should be continuous whenever possible.

Don't crowd appliances into corners with little or no work space around them.

The kitchen should be large enough for people to pass one another. There should also be enough clearance for stooping and for opening oven and cabinet doors and drawers. Allow at least 1500 mm (5 ft.) of space between opposite counters in a corridor or U-shaped kitchen.

Allow space for a chair or stool so you may sit down to perform some tasks.

If you are building or remodeling, make provision for the addition of new equipment, if possible. For example, you may not need or cannot afford a dishwasher or laundry equipment, but you may wish to add them in the future. Per-

haps a future owner might want to include them, and your lack of foresight in providing necessary space could make it more difficult to sell your house.

Measuring the Kitchen

If you are remodeling an existing kitchen or wondering if an apartment kitchen will meet your needs, you will need to measure it before you can begin to draw a floor plan. This is one room where every millimeter counts, so be sure you are accurate. Don't use a cloth measuring tape—a stiff folding rule or flexible metal tape is better.

FLOOR SPACE

Follow the instructions in Chapter 11 for measuring a room. In addition to the measurements specified, you will need to measure width, depth, and height of appliances which you plan to use, such as the refrigerator-freezer, range, and dishwasher. You will also need the width, depth, and height of any cabinets.

Construction features often limit the changes you can make without large expenditures of money. For example, the location of a gas line or a 220-volt outlet will determine the location of the range. Water pipes and drain will fix the sink location.

When measuring a kitchen, designers and installers usually make a rough sketch of the room and note all of the dimensions on the sketch, making notes of the features of the room. When making a sketch, be sure to total the measurements of each side. Then compare opposite walls to check the accuracy of your work. Unless the two opposite walls are different lengths, the totals should be the same.

If you are building a new home that is not completed, use the blueprint but keep in mind that the final dimensions may be slightly different.

STORAGE SPACE

It is also important to measure the many small items which require different kinds of storage space, varying widely in height, depth, and width. For example, if you have a mixer or a tall coffeemaker, measure it to determine where it can be stored.

Compare the two pairs of glasses shown in Fig. 12-24A and B. Fine glasses should not be stored in a small space because it would be easy to accidentally hit one against the other. On the other hand, if every shelf in the kitchen is the same height, you will waste space. The small glasses require neither the shelf area nor the height of those in A. This is why adjustable shelves give the most efficient storage. This is only one example. The same principle can be applied to almost every item in the kitchen.

When determining storage space, it is wise to be flexible. Experiment to find the best method of storing items in the space available. For instance, there is no rule that says towels must be folded in a certain manner. If large towels are folded in thirds instead of halves, they take the same amount of linear space as smaller ones.

Many grocery items come in different package sizes. Shelves for these items should be adjustable since the best buys in food and household items change constantly. Decide which size is likely to prove most economical for you. A large package of some item is not a bargain if it becomes stale before you can use it. At the same time, it can be costly to buy small boxes of certain items just to save on shelf space.

Once you determine the storage space you need, relate it to the storage available in the kitchen cabinets you plan to use.

Fig. 12-25 shows the shelf and counter space available in a standard kitchen cabinet.

Top shelf (A). Since this will be difficult to reach, store little-used items here. Do you have a bowl, platter, or tureen that you use only once

A

B

12-24. Different items require different storage space.

or twice a year, perhaps at Christmas or Thanksgiving or on special occasions? Store it in this area if it fits. Space that is easy to reach and needed every day should not be wasted on seldom-used items.

The space between the top of the wall cabinets and the ceiling is usually filled in with a short wall so the tops of the cabinets do not show. This may be installed flush with the cabinet fronts or extend beyond them.

Middle and bottom shelves (B). These shelves should be adjustable. They may also be equipped with step-up shelves for small items such as spice containers. These items will be easier to reach because they will be at different levels.

Counter top (C). Will tall, portable appliances fit in the space between the counter and the wall cabinet? Remember, you will not only use this area as work space but you may also want to keep frequently used items such as a blender or toaster on the counter.

There should be at least 400 mm (16 in.) clearance between the counter top and wall cabinets for comfortable work space on the counter. This will also allow for the use and perhaps storage of equipment such as a mixer and a blender. If undercounter lighting is to be used to illuminate the counter area, allow 450 mm (18 in.) space between wall cabinets and counter top. Counter tops are generally 25 mm (1 in.) deeper than the base cabinets.

Base cabinets (D). Storage in this area requires careful planning, or items will be lost in the deep corners. Pull-out shelves, bins, or turntables, Fig. 12-26, make this space more useful. If shelves do not pull out, a tray is a good substitute. A little time spent in organizing this area may save you much time later. Plan to put tall items in back where they will show. Stand food packages which are alike in single file one behind the other so you will know that the last package in back contains the same product as the one in front. Space should be allotted so that food packages may be rotated—those in back should be moved to the front and used, while newly purchased ones should be put in back. Decide what utensils you will store in the base cabinets. Also decide how many drawers

12-25. *Standard kitchen cabinets.*

12-26. Types of pull-out units.

you will need for cutlery, flatware, gadgets, and other small items.

In planning your storage space, you may want to consider the specialized cabinets available. However, these add to the cost of the kitchen.

You may prefer to use some of the storage aids shown in Fig. 12-27. They can usually be purchased in department stores and help to make kitchen storage convenient and more efficient.

Selecting Equipment

COUNTER TOPS

The counter top is usually made to order in sections, depending on the plan of the kitchen. They are available in laminated or vinyl plastic; ceramic, metal, or vinyl tile; stainless steel; or wood.

If you select a plastic or tile counter top, you may want to consider using an inset of stainless steel or glass ceramic near the range to provide a heat-proof counter for hot pans. You may also want to consider an inset of a small wood counter top for use as a cutting and chopping

block. Those who enjoy making pastry and candy may wish to have a small area of marble.

SINKS

Sinks come in white or colored porcelain or in stainless steel, with single, double, or triple bowls. Frequently, homemakers who have dishwashers feel that they do not need a double-bowl sink. However, it is useful in washing large pots and pans that do not fit into the dishwasher. If you prefer a single-bowl sink, be sure to get one that is large enough to hold a dishpan and that allows you to rinse the dishes to the side of the pan.

Cabinet sinks are available from most cabinet manufacturers. If you prefer, you may purchase a sink that is set into the counter top. See Fig. 12-12. This gives you more flexibility in selecting base cabinets to go under the sink.

APPLIANCES

Ranges are available in many shapes and sizes. A **free-standing range** does not have to be installed in a cabinet and can be easily replaced with a range that is the same size or

295

Rubbermaid
12-27. Kitchen storage aids.

smaller. A **built-in range** must be installed in cabinets specially designed for this purpose. Built-ins come in many styles, including a separate oven and cooktop. An **eye-level console** includes the cooktop and oven in one unit. Most ranges can be fitted with an exhaust hood.

When you select a refrigerator-freezer, look ahead and anticipate your needs, especially if you plan to surround the refrigerator by cabinets. If you would want to change to a larger size in a few years, it would involve expensive cabinet changes.

Refrigerator-freezers are available with door hinges on either the right side or left side.

Getting the Most for the Space

How can you use a drawing to get the most efficient arrangement of appliances and cabinets? How do you find the best possible work triangle?

Fig. 12-28A shows the placement of the appliances in a kitchen before it was remodeled. The sink was beneath the window and the range against the outside wall. The refrigerator and utility cabinet were against the wall between the two doors. A kitchen table and six chairs took up the corner between the range and the door. Note that the work triangle—refrigerator to sink to range—was interrupted by the traffic lane between the two doors. The only space available for preparing and mixing food was on the range or on the kitchen table. A utility cabinet and space under the sink provided the only storage.

Before designing a new plan for this kitchen, let's analyze the requirements of the family that will use it. There are five people in the family—mother, father, and three children in school. Although the family has a small dining area in the living-dining room, they like to eat in the kitchen. Since the range they have is fairly new, they have decided to continue using it. However, they plan to buy a new refrigerator which will provide needed food storage. Generally, the children are responsible for washing the dishes after meals.

What basic kitchen shape would be most efficient for this room? Because of the traffic lane between the two doors, it would be wise not to include this area as part of the work triangle. This leaves three walls available for the work triangle. Since the three walls form a U-shape that is unbroken by doors, the U-shaped kitchen was selected.

The next step is to place the work centers. The family wants to be able to look out of the window while working at the sink, so the new

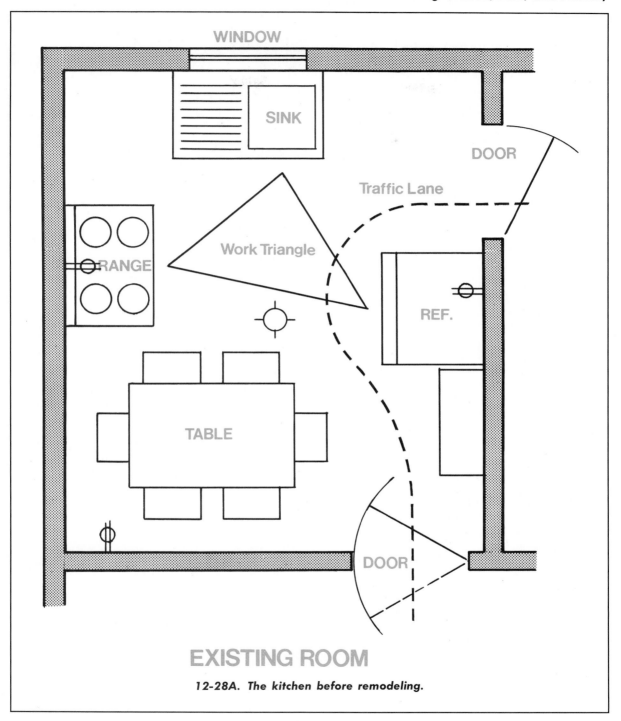

WINDOW

SINK

DOOR

Traffic Lane

Work Triangle

RANGE

REF.

TABLE

DOOR

EXISTING ROOM

12-28A. The kitchen before remodeling.

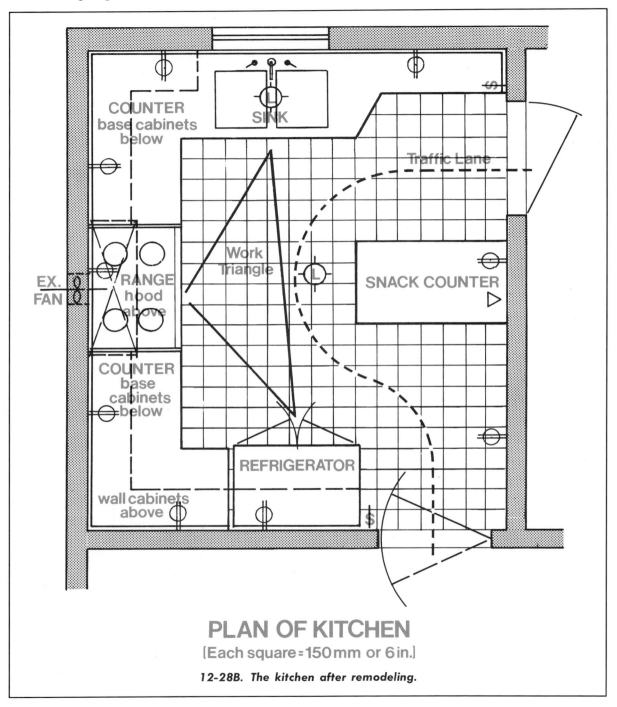

COUNTER
base cabinets
below

SINK

Traffic Lane

Work
Triangle

EX.
FAN

RANGE
hood
above

SNACK COUNTER

COUNTER
base
cabinets
below

wall cabinets
above

REFRIGERATOR

PLAN OF KITCHEN
(Each square = 150 mm or 6 in.)

12-28B. The kitchen after remodeling.

sink will be placed beneath the window. This is the most economical arrangement since the water connections and drains are already in that area. The range will remain in its present position, but a hood and exhaust fan will be installed over it. This can be accomplished with minimum expense since the range is against an outside wall. The refrigerator will be placed against the wall opposite the sink. A low snack counter will be placed next to the wall between the two doors. Stack-type stools will be stored under the counter when they are not in use. The counter will also provide a sit-down work area. The telephone will be located on the wall above the snack counter.

There is one problem in this kitchen—the door on the right-hand wall. The space from the door jamb to the window wall measures only 380 mm (15 in.). If regular base cabinets were used next to the door, they would block the doorway because they are 600 mm (24 in.) deep. To solve this problem, wall cabinets, which are only 300 mm (12 in.) deep, will be used as base cabinets for 900 mm (3 ft.) along the window wall from the doorway. This will allow enough space for people to walk through the doorway and into the kitchen.

Base cabinets were selected to fill the spaces between the appliances. The double-bowl sink will be in a base cabinet which provides storage space underneath. Next to the sink, a swing-away corner cabinet will offer efficient corner storage. The range will be placed next to this cabinet. To the left of the range will be a 450 mm (18 in.) cabinet with four drawers. A lazy-susan cabinet will be used in the corner next to the refrigerator. A counter top will be installed on the base cabinets. Wall cabinets will be placed over the base cabinets and over the refrigerator.

Fig. 12-28B shows the completed layout for the remodeled kitchen. Note that the continuous counter is broken only by the appliances, giving ample space for food preparation and mixing. The work triangle is efficient; most important, it is not interrupted by the traffic lane between the two doors.

Notice that the drawing shows the swing of all the doors, including that of the refrigerator. This is important when planning any room because enough space must be allowed for doors to open.

Ample electrical outlets are provided for any small appliances that the homemaker may wish to use. There will be a light in the ceiling just above the sink, one in the hood above the range, and a light in the center of the ceiling. Although not shown on the plan, the counters will be lighted by fluorescent lights installed under the wall cabinets.

Would you be satisfied with this kitchen arrangement? Can you think of any way to improve it? How would you change this kitchen arrangement for your own family?

This is just one of many possible floor plans that could be used in this kitchen. Fig. 12-29 shows another arrangement. The appliances are placed in the same locations as in the floor plan. However, instead of a corner cabinet next to the sink, the corner space is reached through the door next to the sink. Instead of a snack counter, a base cabinet with a maple chopping block was selected. The base cabinet is on wheels so that it can be rolled wherever it is needed. It also provides additional storage space.

Installing a Kitchen

To prevent costly mistakes, check and recheck your kitchen plan before work begins and equipment is ordered. Remember, if you do not like the way your furniture is arranged in the living room or bedroom, you can rearrange it. However, once the equipment and cabinets are installed in a kitchen, their location is fixed in that position. Since rearranging the "furniture" in a kitchen can only be done at great expense, it is essential to think through the details carefully.

Have a kitchen remodeler or builder go over

your plan. The remodeler will probably want to take the measurements of the kitchen as a double check. The remodeler will also determine whether the plumbing and wiring can be installed according to your plan and may have some suggestions for improving your plan, too. If you want any structural changes, such as removing a wall, consult a remodeler or builder to determine if the alterations are possible.

Once you have settled on a plan, be sure to get an estimate of the cost before you authorize work to start. Be sure also that the remodeler or builder secures the necessary building permit.

Decorating a Kitchen

Professional interior designers now plan the decoration and colors to be used in kitchens as well as in other rooms in the home. The wide circulation of home planning and building magazines picturing attractive kitchens has created a new demand for beauty as well as efficiency. As long as a kitchen is easy to clean, it can be decorated in many ways.

In decorating a kitchen, keep in mind the elements and principles of design discussed in Chapters 2 and 3.

COLOR

The color of the kitchen should be planned so that future changes may be made without great expense. Bright and unusual colors should be reserved for areas that can be converted at relatively little cost, Fig. 12-30.

Generally, when planning a kitchen color

Armstrong Cork Company
12-29. The same kitchen with a different look.

12-30. *The appliances and cabinets are a neutral color, but the wall coverings and linens are bright and highly decorative.*

12-31. Kitchens can be decorated in as many varieties as the rest of a home.

scheme, begin by selecting the color and finish of the cabinets you plan to use. Next decide on your general color scheme and the style or mood of the kitchen. Then select the colors for the counter tops, flooring, and appliances. Try to think of the appliances as broad surfaces in good proportion and simple design that will provide a background. Remember, it will probably be years before these items are replaced, so be sure you choose colors that you will want to live with for a long time. Then select harmonious textures and colors in wall and decorative treatments.

Color in equipment surfaces produces variety, and a flowered or plaid range may some day be available. Patterned surfaces are already available on refrigerators through the use of interchangeable door panels. Color trends influence kitchen decoration. It is easier and less expensive to update a kitchen when fashion colors are used in easy to change drapery, utensils and other accessories, rather than in expensive major equipment.

The kitchen in Fig. 12-31 shows the owners' interest in the regional arts of the southwest. The warm natural wood cabinets, yellow appliances, and stone patterned floor covering are accented with an interesting and colorful collection of pottery, tools, and fabrics. Properly vented stoves mean the kitchen is as clean as other rooms and as suitable for displaying a collection.

FLOOR COVERINGS

At one time, kitchen floor coverings were selected for durability, comfort, and ease-of-care. Then the role of the kitchen in family living expanded and emphasis was placed on appearance as well as livability. Today, new and improved flooring materials are so durable and easy to care for that decorative qualities are now regarded as most important.

A wide variety of floor coverings are now available. All come in many patterns and colors, and in many price ranges. Floor and wall surfaces are discussed in Chapter 15.

LIGHTING

Plan the lighting for your kitchen as you draw your layout so that the electrical wiring may be put where needed. If you wait until the kitchen is completed, you may be faced with costly electrical work that could have been done at a lower cost if properly planned for.

How much light do you need? In the well-planned, modern kitchen where a number of activities take place, different combinations and amounts of light are desirable. The size and number of bulbs needed to achieve this light level will depend upon the color of the nearby surfaces which reflect light and on the amount of natural light available. You might need one or two 100-watt bulbs. Generally, fluorescent lighting under the wall cabinets is the most practical way to light the counter work areas.

In addition to the light chosen for each of the work areas, there should be general illumination. The whole kitchen should be well-lighted. The lights should be placed so you do not work in your own shadow.

Since kitchens serve as entertainment centers as well as places to work, luminous panels, attractive ceiling fixtures, or other lights which will create a comfortable and pleasant atmosphere should be considered.

Remember that light affects color, so keep your kitchen colors in mind when selecting lights. The color of the lights selected will also affect the appearance of food prepared in the kitchen.

DINING AREAS
In the Kitchen

The kitchen may provide the only eating area available, Fig. 12-32, or there may be space in the kitchen as well as an adjoining dining room. Whether you can have a snack area in addition to a formal dining area depends, of course, on the size of the kitchen and the construction features.

Fig. 12-33 shows the only eating space available in a small apartment. Meals may be served in an attractive setting even though space and money are limited. The neutral color scheme makes the room appear larger. Would you have guessed that this dining area was once a closet off the kitchen?

Fig. 12-34 shows a more formal dining area in a kitchen. Dark colors and clean modern lines provide a sophisticated atmosphere.

Stock Boston/Owen Franken

12-32. A nearby window and a cheerful tablecloth make this kitchen dining area pleasant and home-like.

303

Celanese House
12-33. A sophisticated dining area that was once a closet.

In the Dining Room

As a rule, the dining room should be located next to the kitchen for easy serving. Some families prefer an adjacent formal dining room where all meals are to be served, Fig. 12-35. Most formal dining rooms are separate rooms. The dining room shown in Fig. 12-36 is one of easy going informality. Dining and other activities occur in one open area.

In Other Areas

Depending on the family living pattern, other areas of the home may be used for dining.

Some families may prefer to serve food in areas far removed from the kitchen. In this case, the kitchen should be located so that food and dishes do not have to be carried through rooms where other activities would be inter-

rupted. These families would probably select very specialized floor plans.

Serving food outdoors on a patio, porch, or balcony, especially during summer months, is very popular. Fig. 12-37 shows a more surprising dining location. This bedroom-dining room would be ideal for a family of three generations. An older person or an invalid might prefer or even require meals at different hours than the rest of the family.

PLANNING A HOME LAUNDRY
Location

In the past the laundry area was generally located in the basement. Today, however, automatic equipment makes it possible to have the laundry area anywhere in the house. Frequently, a utility room off the kitchen serves as a laundry. Laundry equipment may also be placed in the kitchen, a hallway, or in the bathroom.

In short, any location may be used that makes it convenient for the homemaker to work at other tasks while the laundry is being done.

Poggenpohl
12-34. This dining area has a pleasant mixture of modern and traditional pieces.

12-35. A formal dining room.

Another advantage to these locations is that the homemaker will not have to carry heavy basket-loads of clothes to and from the basement.

Whether you have a utility room for your laundry with space to spare, or a small hallway or other nook with very little space, planning can make your laundry job easier and more pleasant.

In selecting a location for the laundry, keep in mind these three basic requirements:

- plumbing, including drains and a good supply of hot water
- a 220-volt electrical outlet for an electric dryer or a gas line for a gas dryer
- location near an outside wall for the exhaust system for the dryer

Generally, it is more economical to locate the laundry in an area where the plumbing is concentrated such as in or near the kitchen or bathroom. This reduces the amount of piping

Acorn Structures, Inc.
12-36. An informal dining room.

Heywood Wakefield, Harold J. Siesel Co.
12-37. A dining spot in a bedroom.

needed. A laundry in the bathroom may be a step-saver, too, since this is the area where most soiled garments and linens are collected.

In addition to location, the size of the family, the cost of installing laundry equipment, and the amount the family can afford to spend also need to be considered. If space permits, it is wise to make provision for a complete laundry. Even if you do not have a dryer, allow space for it so that you may add it in the future, if you wish.

Fig. 12-38 shows a laundry area in a mobile home. It is placed in a closet just off the kitchen. Beside it is a well planned storage cupboard. The kitchen and laundry should always be separated in some way so that soiled clothes are not handled in the same area where food is prepared.

Arranging the Equipment

In determining the minimum space required, include the equipment selected and space to work, and make provision for future equipment.

Time and effort can be saved if laundry equipment is arranged to permit an orderly flow of work.

The first step in laundering is collecting and sorting. This may be done in specially designed containers that are divided so laundry may be easily sorted as it accumulates. Fig. 12-39 shows a laundry center with sorting bins to the right. Clothes requiring no special care are gathered in the mobile hamper. Others that require special handling such as permanent press and knits are sorted into baskets. The laundry may also be collected in one container and sorted just before it is washed. In a two-story house with a basement laundry, steps may be saved by having a clothes chute from the bedroom area. This would empty into a laundry bin in the basement.

Washing also involves spot treating so a sink and counter are generally needed. Storage space is also needed for supplies.

A wide assortment of washers is available, from a standard washing machine to an automatic one.

Drying may be done on a line either outdoors or inside the house, or in an automatic dryer. If drying is done outdoors, it is convenient to have the laundry located near the rear door. A basket or cart will be needed for transporting the wet laundry. See Chapter 14 on buying appliances.

Wash-and-wear fabrics and most synthetics should be placed on a hanger as soon as they are removed from the dryer, so a rack or line will be needed in the laundry area, Fig. 12-40.

Family Circle Magazine
Elyse Lewin and Vincent Lisanti
12-38. This laundry can be closed off when not in use.

Family Circle Magazine
Elyse Lewin and Vincent Lisanti

12-39. A very compact laundry center.

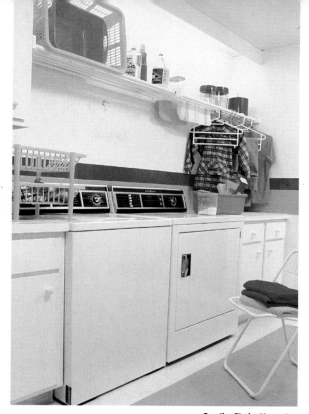

Family Circle Magazine
Elyse Lewin and Vincent Lisanti

12-40. Clothes may be hung on the rack over the appliances.

Line space is also useful for the final drying of blankets that must be taken from the automatic dryer while still damp.

Counter space is needed for folding dried clothes and also for drying some which must be shaped and dried on a flat surface.

The next step in laundering is ironing. Essential equipment includes an iron, an ironing board, a rack to hang ironed clothes, and counter space for folding and stacking ironed items. An ironing board may be built-in to save space when it is not in use, although many homemakers prefer a board that may be moved about. In a laundry room, storage for the ironing board is not necessary—it may be conveniently left open. However, if the laundry is in another room such as the kitchen, storage space is needed for the ironing board. Sleeve

boards and various padded shapes are helpful, especially for one who sews. Space should be allowed for storing these items.

It may save space in the house to expand the laundry room to accommodate other projects. For example, the laundry room may become a family workroom. Handicrafts, writing, typing, and flower arranging are only a few of the projects which might share the facilities in a laundry area. Fig. 12-41 shows a complete textile hobby center—supplies needed for home dying of yarns, a sewing machine, sewing supplies, patterns, books, and ample work space—in the laundry room.

You may find that you do not have enough space for a full laundry center. However, you can still have the convenience of an automatic washer and dryer. Try to locate them as con-

Poggenpohl

12-41. A sewing center in the laundry room.

veniently as possible, and be sure to shop around for models that best fit your needs. For example, where the space is wide enough for only one appliance, either a washer or dryer, a stack unit might be the answer, Fig. 12-42. This unit features a washer on the bottom with the dryer stacked on top of the washer. Another space-saver is a small, portable dryer which plugs into any standard electric outlet and requires no special wiring or venting.

PLANNING THE BATHROOM

For years bathrooms were planned with only utility in mind. The three basic fixtures—toilet, lavatory, and tub—a small window, and washable surfaces were the major requirements.

Family Circle Magazine
Elyse Lewin and Vincent Lisanti

12-42. These two appliances need only the floor space for one.

Today the bathroom is as colorful and carefully decorated as any other room. The room illustrated in Fig. 12-43 is typical of the new luxury bathroom. Note the bright towels, collector's items, and plants.

A small bathroom may be as attractive as a large one. That shown in Fig. 12-44 is in a mobile home. Mobile homes often feature very efficient space saving plans. The proper choice of fabrics and colors makes the small space as attractive as larger, more luxurious rooms.

Things To Consider

The bathroom should be located so it may be reached without going through or being visible from any living area.

Because the fixtures and utilities are built-in, the bathroom is costly. For this reason it is important to plan carefully and to consider future needs. Once the fixtures and the utilities serving them are in place it can be expensive to make changes. Even small accessories such as grab bars, soap dishes, and paper holders which are

12-43. A luxury bathroom with two sinks and a bidet.

built-in are difficult to change. Some points to remember:

- The more compact the plumbing the less it is likely to cost.
- The size and arrangement of the bathroom must meet local building codes. Some are very strict about waste disposal.
- There should be adequate storage space for medical supplies, cosmetics, towels, paper goods, and linens. If a laundry is included there should be space for laundry items.
- Durable, easy-to-clean materials should be used throughout, Fig. 12-45. All surfaces should be water resistant.
- There should be good light and ventilation. Windows should be located to provide privacy or be fitted with patterned glass.
- It may be desirable to provide extra heat and mechanical ventilation, such as an infra-red lamp combined with a fan.
- Insulation or interior walls surrounding the bath may help muffle the sounds of water.
- Door placement should provide privacy. The toilet fixtures should not be visible when the door is left ajar.

New bathrooms are characterized by interesting and individualized decoration. Since changes are expensive it is important to select colors carefully. It is generally wise to select fixtures that are neutral in color, such as those in Fig. 12-45.

Family Circle Magazine
Elyse Lewin and Vincent Lisanti
12-44. This mobile home bathroom, although small, is colorful and attractive.

Family Circle Magazine
Elyse Lewin and Vincent Lisanti
12-45. This bathtub is molded of one piece and is easy to clean.

Case
Problem
A

Rob and Debbie Washington have been married two years. They have no children but plan to start a family. Rob is a carpenter and Debbie is a department manager in a store. They have purchased a large, old, two-story house which they plan to remodel, doing most of the work themselves. The first major remodeling is the kitchen, shown in Fig. 12-46.

The house has a big dining room, but they would like an eating area in the kitchen that will seat at least six people. They plan to buy a double-door refrigerator-freezer, a dishwasher, a garbage disposer, a built-in oven and a cooktop with an exhaust hood. If possible, they would like two built-in ovens, either next to each other or one above the other. Rob hopes someday to go into business for himself as a remodeler, and he wants the house to be an example of his work.

Like most remodeling projects, this kitchen presents a challenge. Each wall is interrupted by a structural feature, either a window or a door. The wall on the right has a door which leads to the dining room, and it also has a chimney which juts out into the room. The other door leads to the back hall and outdoors. The windows create a problem. The cooktop should be located on the outside wall so the exhaust hood can be vented to the outside. However, a range should not be placed beneath a window, so this limits the location of the cooktop to the areas on either side of the windows.

Draw this floor plan on graph paper and design a kitchen for Rob and Debbie. Visit an appliance store to get the dimensions of the appliances. What shape kitchen would best fit this room? Why? Where would you place the eating area? Why?

Draw your final floor plan with the work triangle. Is your work triangle efficient? Is there enough counter space and storage at each work center?

Case Problem B

Use the floor plan shown in Fig. 12-46. Pretend that you and your family are now moving into this house, and you are going to remodel the kitchen. Draw the floor plan on graph paper and design the kitchen to fit your family's needs. Indicate the work triangle.

ACTIVITIES

1. Find a photograph of a kitchen in a magazine or newspaper. Redraw the plan to show how you would improve the storage.

2. Make a study of decorative storage containers. Collect illustrations of some of the many kinds that are available.

3. Discuss how new appliances might result in changes in the type of food a family purchases.

4. Discuss the idea of "social climbing" in kitchen design—neighbors trying to outdo each other in acquiring the latest gadget. Consider and discuss what your own values are in the selection of equipment.

5. Plan a bulletin board showing the three major work centers in a kitchen. List the food and equipment you would store in each.

(Continued)

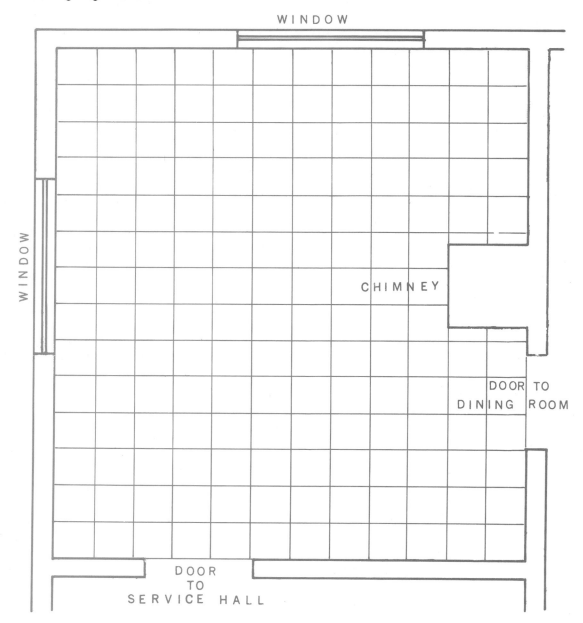

Each square equals 300 mm or 1 ft.

C A S E   P R O B L E M   K I T C H E N

12-46. Illustration for Case Problem A.

6. Assemble a "portable" kitchen. Collect pictures of appliances that may take the place of the traditional refrigerator such as small counter refrigerators, insulated storage chests, and ice-making machines. Also collect pictures of appliances that would substitute for the range. These might include a grill, coffeemaker, frying pan, broiler, and other electric appliances.

7. Ask your teacher to invite a panel of homemakers to share their preferences in kitchen design with you. Ask them to explain why they like or dislike the details they mention. Write a brief summary of the most desired design features. Do you agree or disagree with their choices?

8. Obtain a sample of vinyl floor covering or ceramic tile and develop a unified kitchen decor around it.

9. Prepare a home survey questionnaire covering the type of laundry equipment used by the families of the members of the class. Determine their problems and satisfactions with the equipment chosen.

10. Compare the advantages of owning your own laundry equipment with those of using a coin-operated laundromat. From your local utility company, obtain the costs of operating a washer and a dryer, including the cost of heating water for the washer. How does this compare with the cost of using a coin-operated laundromat? What else should you consider, besides just the cost of operating the equipment?

11. Find pictures to illustrate each of the four major types of kitchens—the one-wall, corridor, L-shape and U-shape. Collect other pictures that are variations of these. Mount the pictures for bulletin board display.

12. Secure a brochure on kitchens from a kitchen dealer and evaluate two layouts.
• How do the work centers relate to each other?
• List the amount of cabinet and counter space.
• Is the homemaker isolated while working in the kitchen?
• List the equipment included.
• Which plan would you consider best?

13. Obtain color cards from a fixture salesroom which show the range of colors available in bathroom fixtures. Plan a color scheme using the color you like best.

14. Discuss the cleaning problems of various surfaces that have been used in bathrooms that you are familiar with.

15. Special kitchens have been designed for persons suffering from a disability. The "Heart Kitchen," for example, designed after careful research, provides the best possible work heights for a person with a heart disability. Each counter in the kitchen is designed according to the work performed there.

Special kitchens designed for patients in wheelchairs include a low sink under which the chair can roll and easy-to-reach counter space. Other special equipment has been designed for the blind, featuring, for example, notched temperature indicators on oven thermostat controls.

Learn about these kitchens. Try to arrange a visit to see one of these kitchens or one designed for the aged. Report on your findings.

13 Furniture Design

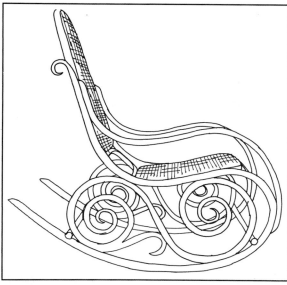

Far left: Do you know why this furniture design is considered contemporary? (Fog and Mørup)

Upper left: This rocking chair is a Victorian design.

Lower left: Many periods have their own style of "country" furniture. (Buckstaff)

Right: Clothing styles influence furniture styles. Why would this table and chairs be unsuitable for someone wearing hoop skirts? (Royal Systems)

THE INFLUENCE OF LIFESTYLE

Design is a reflection of its time and tells us many things about the people of the period.

The two chairs illustrated in Figs. 13-1 and 13-2 show how different the life of the owner of the seventeenth-century chair must have been from that of the owner of the contemporary chair.

The seventeenth-century chair of oak and ash was made to last. The design was inspired by chairs the colonial artisan remembered seeing in England. This chair was made for an individual customer and not for display in the shop win-

Asko
13-1. A contemporary chair.

that would not be regarded as the owner's exclusive property but would be shared with others. The form suggests a retreat from a busy, noisy world.

The mahogany secretary in Fig. 13-3 was made around 1760. The graceful top contains space for account books. A prosperous Boston or New York merchant—probably a man since few women were involved in business—sat at this desk in his home from which he ran his business. How do we know this? It was expensive when it was new. Therefore we may assume its owner to have been a person of means. How do we know he ran his business from his home? First, it doesn't look like a piece of furniture to be used in a warehouse or some other work-room. Second, although the top is designed for account books, the bottom is designed to hold linens. Linen suggests food and drink. In those days most business was conducted by a small, elite group of people. They were friends as well as business associates. Meetings to discuss business ventures took place in the home. Since travel was difficult and slow,

dow of a distant furniture store. Since its owner was the head of the household, this was known as the "great chair"—the rest of the family used stools or benches. Because it was a symbol of authority, it was cherished and passed down through succeeding generations.

Now consider the equally well-designed chair of today and see what it may tell us about its owner. First of all, it was purchased from a furniture store and, secondly, the designer did not know who the purchaser might be. It is a chair

Terms To Know

Bauhaus
cabriole
Chinese
  Chippendale
Duncan Phyfe
Federal
fiddleback
gateleg tables
Hepplewhite
highboy
Jacobean
machine-made look

modules
Queen Anne
reeding
reproductions
Sheraton
shieldback
traditionalists
transitional pieces
trends
turning
veneer
William and Mary

Richard W. Withington, Inc.
13-2. A seventeenth century chair.

people visited for longer periods and were often served food by their host.

Now look at the twentieth-century piece of furniture in Fig. 13-4. It is also a well-designed piece. What does it tell you? It is fitted with television, panel tape recorder, touch-a-matic memory bank telephone, 10 digit calculator, digital clock and memo directory. There is even an electric pencil sharpener! The unit is not a desk but is designed to accompany one. Its equipment and sleek lines suggest use in an office rather than a home. The person who uses it would probably do business by phone or mail and could keep in touch with world events simply by turning on the TV. Each of these examples illustrates an important point: there is no question as to whether one design is better than

Cee Jay Photo/Evelyn Radcliffe

13-4. A contemporary desk unit.

the other. Both are good design, representative of their time, place, and function.

DESIGNS WHICH LAST

The bulk of the furniture on the market today is copied from styles of earlier periods. The truly contemporary furniture, which is new and original in design, represents only a small part of the furniture sold. As time goes by, some of these contemporary styles in turn will be copied and become a part of tradition.

Good design is not limited to one period. Many pieces of ugly furniture were produced in the past, and there is a vast quantity of poorly designed contemporary furniture. Someone may say, "But you see very few pieces of ugly furniture in museums and many pieces of ugly new furniture, so design must have been better in the past." There is a good reason for this—ugliness is not cherished. Beautiful things survive because their beauty protects them. Over the years unusual and beautiful pieces of furniture, china, and glass have been saved because someone said, "Be careful with that; I like it." In each generation, its merit was recognized, and it survived.

The first cabinetmakers in America made furniture similar to the styles of Europe. People kept favorite pieces which had belonged to their parents or grandparents. The fact that period furniture has always been popular accounts for the many reproductions that are sold today.

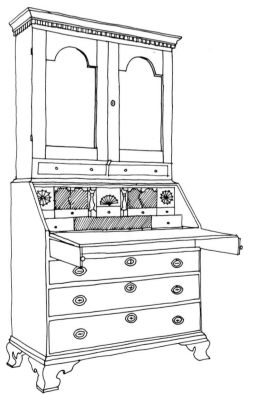

13-3. An eighteenth century secretary.

13-5. Notice the graceful curve over the doorway in this drawing.

"Today Victorian ends and Modern begins." There are no exact dates—each change was very gradual. To remember approximate dates and the sequence of changes is enough. It is more important to learn to think of furniture in terms of its setting in history, the people who used it, and the houses it occupied. When you learn to do this, it is easier to put each design into place in your mind. To refresh your memory as to the social and economic changes of the time and the exteriors of the houses, refer back to Chapters 4 and 5.

• **Learn to look at overall form, scale, and proportion,** just as you would in house or room design. For example, study the shape of a chair

The hobby of collecting antiques as we know it is relatively new. But people have always saved things they liked, and one of the main reasons an object is cherished is its good design. This can be the test of a piece of furniture today. Say to yourself, "Will I like this well enough to keep for many years?" The faddish, poorly designed pieces may not stand this test. What you are really asking is, "Will the piece of furniture age well?"

WHAT TO LOOK FOR

• **Try to gain a feeling for the period of time you are studying.** Do not try to memorize long lists of dates. At no time did someone say,

13-6. Notice how the curve on this highboy resembles that on the doorway in Fig. 13-5.

leg from top to bottom. Look at the chair back and the details of the carving or decoration. The eighteenth-century doorway in Fig. 13-5 was designed for a house many miles from the workshop where the highboy shown in Fig. 13-6 was made. Although one design is for the exterior of a house and the other for a piece of furniture and the makers were unknown to each other, the design motifs are very similar. When you learn to recognize the periods, the whole world of design will have new meaning to you.

● **All periods have gone through certain stages; each period begins simply, becomes more ornate, and finally very elaborate.** People tire of the overdone designs and a new cycle begins. Regardless of style, similar groups (simple, decorated, ornate) are apt to look well together. For example, simple early New England pine may blend well with equally simple modern or contemporary pieces.

● **Antique or period furniture, like new furniture, can be divided into other categories— fine, formal furniture and accessories, and country or informal furnishings.** Fine pieces of all periods go together, and simple informal pieces also have a common bond. For example, a good Queen Anne chair may look at home beside a modern sofa upholstered in formal fabric.

Look at examples of furniture; decide whether they are formal or informal. See if you can decide if a piece could be considered ornate, somewhat ornate, or simple.

● **It is important to remember that styles of one period overlap another.** There is seldom a sharp break. The pieces featuring designs of two periods are referred to as **transitional pieces.** When you study different periods you can detect **trends,** which indicate the general direction of change as one period blends into another.

● **Do not confuse design with cost.** We are not talking about cheap furniture and expensive furniture. It may take no more material and time to build a beautiful piece than it does to make something that is not attractive. Furniture

Table 13-A.
FURNITURE STYLES

Period or Style	Approximate Dates
Pilgrim period (Jacobean and William and Mary)	1640–1720
Queen Anne	1720–1755
Chippendale	1755–1790

Classical
    Adam
    Hepplewhite
    Sheraton
    Federal
    Duncan Phyfe
    Empire (French)
	
	1758–1792
	1780–1805
	1790–1805
	1790–1810
	1790–1825
	1810–1830

Victorian	1830–1900
Modern	1900–

that has good design does not necessarily cost more than ugly pieces. However, good design, because it has resale value, may in the long run prove cheaper.

● **The history of American furniture may be divided into six great periods of design,** Table 13-A. "Colonial" and "Early American" are used to describe country furniture of the three early periods—Pilgrim, Queen Anne, and Chippendale. Modern reproductions, Fig. 13-7, based on the designs of these early periods are also referred to as Colonial and Early American designs.

There are other regional styles such as French Provincial, Spanish, Pennsylvania Dutch, and Shaker that you may want to read about on your own.

All of the examples of antique furniture illustrated in this section are of museum quality. You may go to museums and study the furniture, fabrics, and accessories on exhibit. Inspect the arrangements on display in good retail

The Bartley Collection, Ltd.

13-7. The chair is a reproduction of one from the Queen Anne period.

stores. When you visit homes, notice how furniture, fabrics and colors have been combined.

THE PILGRIM PERIOD, 1640–1720
Jacobean

The style in the rooms in Figs. 13-8 and 13-9 is **Jacobean.** Although settlers came from several countries before 1700, English influence predominated. Styles developed in England in the 1600's continued to be produced for some time after they had gone out of fashion overseas because there were the only styles the craftspeople knew. But distance and poor communication with the style centers of Europe, the new materials found here, and frontier conditions gradually contributed to an individual style.

The interior in Fig. 13-8 shows the heavy structural timbers which the builder made no effort to disguise. This was characteristic of the period. This honest, simple type of building

Richard Merrill, Photographer
13-8. Furnishings were simple and rustic in these early homes.

The Metropolitan Museum of Art, New York
13-9. Although these furnishings are simple, notice the heavy carving on the chest, which was all done by hand.

would not reappear in America until seen in some of the functional homes of the twentieth century. The popular notion that interiors were all plain and dark is not true. Furniture was likely to be richly carved and often colored.

Museum of Fine Arts, Boston
13-10. A chest decorated with spindle jewels.

"Jewels" made of half-round spindles painted black were applied to decorate various kinds of wood furniture, Fig. 13-10. Far from being dark, dreary, and cell-like, these rooms showed a great deal of ornamentation; they gave an image of hopeful, happy living. Inside these early homes, the walls were whitewashed. The fabric colors were soft browns, yellows, reds, and greens—colors made by using natural dyes. Houses were built around huge chimneys; the beams, joists, rafters, and cornerposts were left exposed.

Since the houses were small, every room was used as a bedroom. The furniture in the room shown in Fig. 13-9, which dates 1640, is an example of the rectangular lines which characterized this period. Notice that although the room is simple and almost bare in appearance, there is evidence of a love for decoration. In spite of the long hours of work needed to provide shelter, food, and clothing, someone found time to carve carefully an intricate pattern over the surface of the chest; little turned posts were made to decorate the baby's cradle.

A Bible, like the one on the chest, was often the only book. The small iron device hanging near the bed is called a Betty lamp. It and the rushlight on the chest provided the only light except that from the open fire.

The chest was made in 1685. It shows how the early cabinetmakers in America used their own ideas—no chests like this are found in England. Rich overall pattern and rectangular shape characterize the style. Chests were prized by homemakers. Usually made of oak, the chests were the most common article in the homes of that day. The chest served as a trunk, seat, table, and even a bed. It might be the only piece of furniture the family would have for awhile.

The hutch table in Fig. 13-11 can be called a "country piece." Often furniture had to be made with little time and few tools. It was generally made of lumber cut on the owner's land. The hutch table is simple, honest, and una-

13-11. The top of this table tips back and the base is used as a chair.

dorned; nevertheless, it shows careful work. It also indicates the cleverness that made it possible for survival in a wilderness. The top tips to form a chair with a big back. When used as a chair near the fire, the back would cut off drafts in a poorly heated house.

These examples just suggest the type of furniture in the very first homes. There were no closets or cupboards. Chests and boxes were the only storage space. Stools and benches were

The Metropolitan Museum of Art, New York
13-12. Already designs are growing more elaborate. Notice the carved paneling and the delicately decorated furniture.

more common than chairs. Oak, a very hard wood, was formed with only the most primitive tools. It is surprising that such beautiful designs were produced.

Very little of this period furniture has survived. The pieces we do see were probably made in America. The early colonists brought very little furniture with them, since ships were tiny and crowded. Furniture from the Pilgrim period is seldom reproduced today. It is a matter of historical interest to us—it helps us see how later designs evolved.

William and Mary

The interior in Fig. 13-12 illustrates the great changes that occurred in America in a relatively short time. This room contains pieces made only about fifty years after those in Fig. 13-8.

Some homes provided more physical comfort. **William and Mary** rooms were paneled and had larger windows. The wood beams were concealed with plaster ceilings, and more elaborate furniture came into fashion.

A new lightness in the scale of the furniture appeared; finer materials were used. **Veneer,** a layer of fine wood used as an outer finish, was common on furniture. Upholstery was used on the chairs, which were of deeply carved walnut, birch, and maple, instead of oak. **Turning,** which is carving done by machine, became popular.

The room looked more furnished, and the furniture was arranged in a more formal way. Some of the squareness of Jacobean furniture was gone.

Notice that the floor in Fig. 13-12 is bare. Rugs were not common. Small rugs were used as table covers and were seldom placed on the floor. Needlework was a favorite pastime. The picture over the mantle is an example of someone's sample stitches, naturally called a "sampler."

The **highboy** (high chest) was a new piece of furniture developed at this time. This highboy has brass hardware instead of wooden knobs. The Jacobean chest shown in Fig. 13-10, made

Richard Withington, Inc.

13-13. A gateleg table.

only a few years earier, was square in shape. The William and Mary highboy has curving lines on the base and the stretcher (the boards between the legs). The design shows new refinement and is more delicate.

Gateleg tables, Fig. 13-13, were typical of the period. The legs swing out to support the table's sides which could be raised or lowered as the occasion called for. Tables that could be folded to a smaller size were favored since the houses were crowded. Compare with the much simpler table shown in Fig. 13-11.

The small stool is an example of one of the most common seats used during the seventeenth century. Called a joint stool, it could alternate as a seat and a small table.

THE QUEEN ANNE PERIOD, 1720-1755

By 1720, when the **Queen Anne** style became popular, elegant townhouses were being built, Fig. 13-14. The houses of the restored town of Williamsburg, Virginia, show fine examples of this and later periods. Merchants persuaded more cabinetmakers to come to America. Soon furniture as fine as any made in Europe was produced here.

13-14. Georgian architecture was in vogue during the Queen Anne period.

13-15. To accommodate the full skirt this woman wears, a chair would have to have a wide seat.

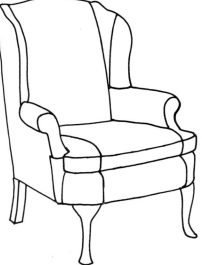

13-16. A wing chair.

The fashions of the day reflected a more elegant and leisurely life. The men wore broad-skirted frock coats and waistcoats with deep pockets. The women wore hoop skirts and jewels and beauty patches, Fig. 13-15.

Furniture design was influenced by clothing. Chairs were made without arms so women could show off their dresses to advantage when they were seated. Low-cut gowns were also popular. Although houses were more elegant, they were poorly heated, so the wing chair was invented to protect bare shoulders from cold drafts, Fig. 13-16. The wing chair has remained popular. The form is almost unchanged for use in our well-heated twentieth-century homes.

People spent much time at social eating and drinking. This is the period when the sideboard first appeared to aid in the serving of food. Another custom which led to the development of a special piece of furniture was the fact that ladies spent much time putting on beauty preparations. A hinged-top dressing table was developed for this purpose.

Inside, houses were decorated with paneling, carving, and moldings, and sometimes tile around the fireplaces. People were becoming involved with religion, politics, writing, and art. The furniture they selected for their homes is an indication of this.

William and Mary furniture departed slightly from the square and rectangular forms of Jacobean. Queen Anne was a real departure, being slender, graceful, and smaller in scale. This style was built on the reverse curve—a curve shaped like an "S." The shape of the chair back and legs in Fig. 13-17, and the legs and top of the highboy in Fig. 13-18 show this curve. On a chair leg it is called a **cabriole.** The chairs have a center piece shaped like a violin, often called

The Metropolitan Museum of Art, New York

13-17. A fiddleback chair with cabriole legs in front.

13-18. The top of this highboy shows the S curve. Note also the cabriole legs.

13-19. Dress styles, too, became more elaborate during later periods.

a **fiddleback.** Chair seats were upholstered in needlepoint or damask.

All of the intricate turnings of William and Mary have been replaced by curving lines. The shell was another characteristic of Queen Anne design. Notice the two fancy shells on the front of the highboy in Fig. 13-18.

THE CHIPPENDALE PERIOD, 1755-1790

During this period the French and Indian War, the Boston Massacre, and the American Revolution caused much upheaval. There was almost no middle class, and the differences in lifestyle between the rich and poor were very great. Fig. 13-19 illustrates the costumes worn by wealthy and fashionable people.

The elaborate interior styling of the Georgian home has had a great influence on interior design. It has been the inspiration for much of the architecture, furniture, and many decorative accessories which we have.

Thomas Chippendale, from whom this period got its name, published the first book on furniture design and his styles became very popular. **Chippendale** built ornate furniture with distinct Georgian and Orential characteristics. Fig. 13-20 shows an elegant interior furnished in the style of Chippendale. The square object by the fireplace is a pole screen, placed by women between themselves and the fire to protect their faces from heat. Oriental rugs and porcelain imported from China and England were often displayed. Wallpaper of Chinese inspiration and design, made in England or France, was favored at this time.

Some of the distinctive details of Chippendale designs were the S-shaped legs which ended in claw and ball feet and the pierced splat backs and ribbon backs on chairs, shown in Fig. 13-21. Chippendale furniture usually tended to be more generous in proportion than Queen Anne. Chippendale created the style known as **Chinese Chippendale,** characterized by straight legs and Chinese fretwork and carving, shown in Fig. 13-21. Chinese motifs were used on many items.

THE CLASSICAL PERIOD, 1758-1830

After the American Revolution, people lost their ties with England and designs more typically American came into being.

Many people in Europe and America—journalists, students, architects, designers, as well as the general public—were interested in and impressed with the discovery of artifacts in the ancient ruins of Egypt, Greece, and Rome. In addition, the current Greek struggle for independence caught the attention of Americans. Architects and designers were quick to adapt the ancient classical designs, producing the Greek Revival style.

The Metropolitan Museum of Art, New York

13-20. The wall covering in this Chippendale room has an Oriental design.

13-21. Notice the claw and ball feet on the table and the straight Chinese legs on the chair.

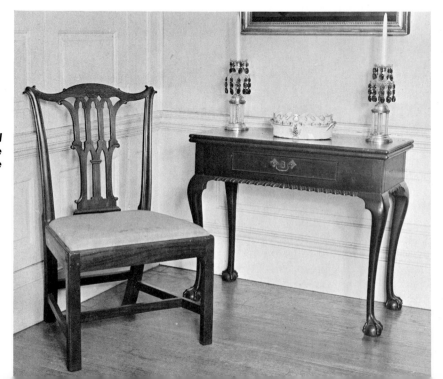

329

13-22. Clothing fashionable during the classical period.

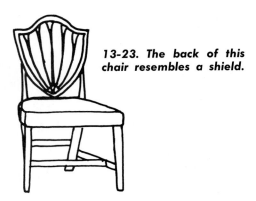

13-23. The back of this chair resembles a shield.

The **Hepplewhite** chair, shown in Fig. 13-23, is called **shieldback,** and the straight, tapered leg characterizes all furniture of Hepplewhite design. Classic shapes in silver and in lighting fixtures were typical of this period.

Sheraton furniture was very similar to Hepplewhite but was characterized by turned and reeded legs instead of straight legs, Fig. 13-24. **Reeding** is the beading or semi-cylindrical vertical molding on the legs. It is called reeding because it resembles reeds or stems of tall grass.

As we discussed earlier, designs move from the simple to the ornate. People tire of the elaborate, and the cycle begins all over again. A reaction to Chippendale's ornateness prompted people to accept the new classical styles, which were considered novel and fresh.

The new Greek Revival style, which began with light and graceful details, affected and influenced fashion design as well as houses and furniture. The woman's costume in Fig. 13-22 incorporated the classical Grecian high-gathered bodice and flowing lines. Details which originated in Greece, such as laurel branches and sprigs, were favorite motifs and were used to decorate the dress.

Furniture designs that developed during this period are referred to by the designers' names. Two English designers were George Hepplewhite and Thomas Sheraton, and the styles of this period bear their names.

Shreve Crump and Lowe

13-24. A Sheraton table with reeded legs.

Monticello/Ralph Thompson, Photographer
Chamber of Commerce, Cincinnati, Ohio

13-25. Exterior and interior design of the Federal period.

The backs of Hepplewhite chairs were round while Sheraton favored the straight line and designed chairs with rectangular backs. The forms were simple, light, and graceful.

Political changes initiated styles in furniture, houses, and the arts that were more American. American design types were Federal, Duncan Phyfe, and Empire—which was influenced by French and English Directoire designs. **Duncan Phyfe,** 1790–1825, a New York cabinetmaker, was most famous of the American designers who worked in the classical tradition. American furniture which had been given English names in the past was now called and known by the names of American designers.

The design of the interiors of **Federal** period houses were straight-lined and uncluttered. The room shown in Fig. 13-25 is an example of the Federal style. Furniture designed in this period reflected this simplicity of style. High ceilings,

13-26. Furniture designed by Duncan Phyfe.

plain walls, classical draperies, and marble busts were distinctive features.

Duncan Phyfe designed a style which was, in part, inspired by Napoleon's first empire. French motifs such as acanthus leaves, urn-shaped pedestals, dog's-paw and lion's-paw legs were favorites. The later examples of Duncan Phyfe furniture featured carved roses and leaf details which continued into the following Victorian period.

Duncan Phyfe's work was the last true hand-crafted furniture. Factories were springing up which began turning out machine-made products. Speed and volume were replacing hand crafting.

The room in Fig. 13-26 shows some of the finest Duncan Phyfe designs. The eagle over the

13-27. A dress popular during the early Victorian period. This type of costume inspired architectural details, such as wide staircases.

mirror is a general favorite of this period. The three-part table may be taken apart and used as three separate tables. Notice the curve of the chair backs. This curving line, only suggested here, becomes more pronounced in other designs of this period. It suggests a form that will evolve and become popular during the Victorian era that follows.

THE VICTORIAN PERIOD, 1830–1900

Mass-production made fashionable styles available to the working classes as well as the rich. Many styles flourished. Women wore costumes like the one in Fig. 13-27. Note the rich ornamentation. Elaborate detail was found not only in clothes and in architectural design but also in the furniture of the period.

Victorian period furniture started with styles that were simple and restrained. Then, as time passed, it became more and more elaborate. Finally, the public tired of the ornate and overdone designs, and a new style began.

The couch in Fig. 13-28 is an example of early Victorian design. The curving lines, inlaid conventional floral patterns, and the damask upholstery suggest the elaborate profusion soon to come. Rapid changes and developments in the textile industry made elaborately designed rugs and draperies available to the decorator. Textiles became popular in upholstered furniture, draperies, and even wall surfacing. To satisfy the demand for comfort, padded and tufted springs became common.

The interiors of the day were a mingling of many styles. Bric-a-brac was collected and displayed on "what-not" shelves. Pictures, statuettes, and fancy cut glass and art glass were cherished. Windows glowed with rainbow colors. Ornate carving crowded every surface, along with highly patterned rugs and wallpapers.

A favorite wood of the early Victorian period was rosewood—a dark red, tropical wood with a dark-brown grain that may be finished to a high luster. New methods made it practical to produce large pieces of veneer. A veneer of rosewood applied to a backing of pine was often used. Later, American black walnut was used as a solid wood rather than a veneer. Marble, iron,

The Metropolitan Museum of Art, New York
13-28. Victorian furniture was very elaborate.

and brass were also used extensively in furniture.

One of the most talented furniture craftspeople of the Victorian period was John Henry Belter of New York. He worked out a technique for bending and shaping wood after which he applied elaborate carvings. Natural motifs such as grapes, leaves, roses, and birds were his favorites. You can see that, with the invention of new tools, the manufacture of furniture was to have an important effect on the design as well as on the supply of furniture available. Machine-made versions of Belter's designs appeared in quantity, showing his influence and popularity.

Fig. 13-29 shows the interior of the Victoria Mansion. This lavishly decorated room typifies the kind of interior a person of wealth could command in the mid-nineteenth century. Outstanding features are ten great goldleaf mirrors from France, doors 3150 mm (10½ ft.) high, an intricately carved marble mantel, mural paintings, and gilded bronze chandelier. The ceiling is richly decorated with plaster ornament typical of the period, but even more outstanding are the panels of classical figures and cherubs painted by eleven artists who were brought from Italy for this one project.

Toward the end of the Victorian period, Henry Hobson Richardson designed the furniture shown in Fig. 13-30. Its primitive simplicity was a contrast to the elaborate Victorian crea-

13-29. It is difficult to find a spot in this room which has not been covered with some kind of ornament.
Victoria Society of Maine Women
Roger D. Calderwood

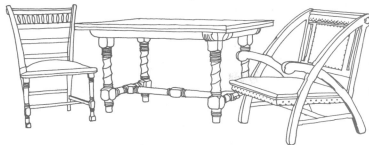

13-30. This furniture signals the Modern era.

tions. It is basically medieval, featuring rectangular forms and structural parts favored during the Middles Ages. This furniture complemented the interiors of the buildings Richardson designed. It is important because it suggests the Modern style, and it signaled the departure of Victorian extravagance.

TWENTIETH CENTURY STYLES, 1900–

Nothing did as much to change the course of design after 1900 as the Industrial Revolution. Rejecting the ornate styles of the Victorian period, designers became interested in the simple, almost perfect forms which machines can produce.

The Modern Period

As in housing, the Modern period in furniture is best known for simple, geometric forms, barren open spaces, and almost no use of ornamentation. Metal and plastic materials have become important. Function is instantly recognizable.

A famous school—the German **Bauhaus**—was founded prior to World War II by Walter Gropius. Gropius was one of those who initially recognized the difference between objects made by hand and those made by machine and founded his school of design for the machine age. A new look—**the machine-made look**—arrived.

Occupant, the chair in Fig. 13-31, which was designed by Eero Saarinen in 1953, has a pro-

file as graceful and pleasing as the best of any period. It is a classic Modern design and many similar chairs have been made in recent years.

Contemporary

Although the period in which we are now living can still be termed Modern, there is a general trend toward softening the harshness of the early designs. At each period in history there

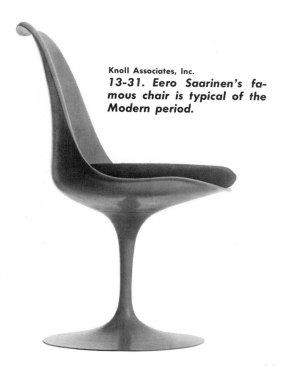

Knoll Associates, Inc.
13-31. Eero Saarinen's famous chair is typical of the Modern period.

were doubtless conflicting trends from which major styles emerged. Today, just as in the past, current trends are often in conflict with each other, and it is difficult to describe our contemporary style because we are too close to it to judge without prejudice. No doubt historians will someday find a name for today's style, but it won't be "contemporary." That word will be used by them to describe their own style.

There are, however, certain characteristics of contemporary designs which are identifiable.

● **It is not confined to one nation or continent; it is truly international.** The chairs in Fig. 13-32 were photographed on a field of snow to emphasize their space-age shape, which does not suggest any traditional design motifs or national characteristics. They are examples of the international style.

● **There is no reflection of preceding styles.** The designers want no tie with the past, even though they feel free to copy each other. For example, the chair illustrated in Fig. 13-31 has been copied by several manufacturers.

Although they are not considered contemporary, some designers continue to be inspired by styles of the past. While they do not copy the earlier styles, they are deeply influenced by them. These designers are located in all parts of the world, but they are not international. They are inspired by the earlier work of their own countries. These people are called **traditionalists.**

● **Contemporary furnishings usually emphasize the architectural materials—marble, wood, glass, stone, and plastics—which contribute interesting textural contrasts.** Furniture is arranged so the shape stands out in strong relief against the simple background. Bold design as well as color may be used. In Fig. 13-33, the texture of the rug contrasts with the smooth surface of the tables and the soft overstuffed chairs.

● **Furniture shapes follow more closely to the human form.** Before the time when plastic came into use in furniture manufacturing, people had fit themselves into the shape of a chair, whether it was a stone seat in primitive times, a crude wooden bench in colonial days, or a highly carved chair in the eighteenth century. In each case, the material used for the seat limited its form. Since a plastic can theoretically be shaped to fit a fat or thin individual, each chair could be formed to fit the person who was to use it. In practice, because of mass production methods, such individual shapes have not been made, but the new plastic material has provided a new type of comfort and new freedom of design.

● **Fluid forms have been coupled with the emphasis on convenience, resulting in modular units.** **Modules** are standardized pieces which fit together in various ways, like building blocks, so they can be arranged differently as the need arises. The storage unit in Fig. 13-34

Asko

13-32. These chairs show no national characteristics.

Fog & Morup
13-33. *Strong contrasts are used in this room.*

Campaniello Imports, Ltd.
13-34. *Note the simplicity of this room. It resembles the rooms of the Pilgrim period.*

Table 13-B.

FURNITURE STYLE CHARACTERISTICS

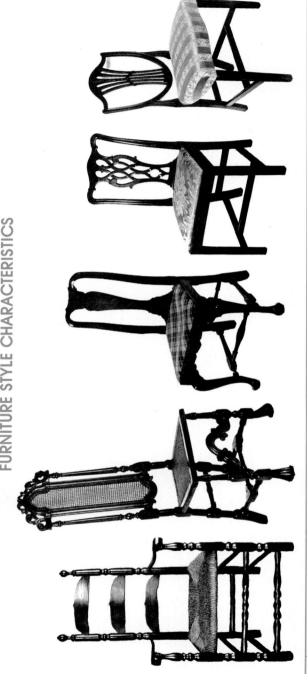

Period	Pilgrim: Jacobean 1640–1720	Pilgrim: William and Mary 1640–1720	Queen Anne 1720–1755	Chippendale 1755–1790	Classical: Hepplewhite 1780–1805
Common Materials	Oak and hardwoods	Fine-grained hardwoods such as birch, walnut and maple; walnut veneers	Walnut or maple stained to look like walnut; hardware made of brass; rich, imported fabrics used for upholstery	Mahogany	Mahogany, satinwood
Ornaments	Overall carving, half-turnings often painted black; bold and heavy	Caning used on chair seats and backs; veneers used; turning and carving delicate; chairs painted black or grained to look like walnut; feet carved	Carving limited to an occasional fan or shell on chests; hardware shows Chinese influence	Claw and ball feet on chair legs; open tracery on backs; fretwork	Bands of inlay, patterns of veneer; carving seldom used; shieldbacks on chairs
General Appearance	Rectangular lines and square forms; functional designs	A new lightness; chests and tables often veneered	Cabriole leg and fiddleback on chairs appear; simple forms and emphasis on quality; lines based on S-curve	A period of elegance; Chinese inspiration in carving, upholstery and hardware; cabriole or straight, untapered legs	Extreme classical refinement; light and delicate details; legs square and tapered

Period	Classical: Sheraton 1790–1805	Classical: Duncan Phyfe 1790–1825	Victorian 1830–1900	Modern 1900–
Common Materials	Mahogany	Mahogany	Dark brown or black walnut, rosewood	Plastic, metal, light-colored or bleached woods
Ornaments	Chair and table legs and bed-posts turned and reeded; carving preferred in swags, flowers, and "drapery"	Carving; gilding on metal	Floral designs, especially roses	Little surface decoration; bold colors, contrasting materials
General Appearance	Light and refined	Inspired by Egyptian, Greek, and Roman antiquities; chair and table legs often sabre-shaped; lyre-shaped table pedestals	Furniture mass-produced for the first time; machine carving, glued joints, flowing curves; romantic designs	Simple, functional, structurally sound designs; beauty of form and texture; fluid shapes; multiple-use furniture; many mechanical devices, such as TV, enclosed in furniture

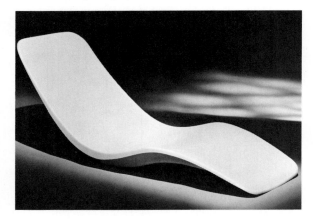

Sun & Leisure, Ltd.
13-35. Furniture which will stack.

Contemporary furniture is created of new materials such as plastic, glass, and metal; but the use of traditional materials such as beautiful wood and fabric is not ruled out. They give a feeling of warmth which would be lacking if only metals and plastics were used.

Table 13-B (Pp. 338-339) shows the characteristics of the important furniture styles.

REPRODUCTIONS AND OTHER TRADITIONAL PIECES

Today a combination of many styles of furniture is common. At present about 25% of consumers select contemporary designs, while the rest choose designs that are based on other pe-

is an example of the excellent design that has been developed for storage pieces. The segments of the couch in Fig. 13-33 also lend themselves to a variety of combinations.

Better use of space has led to the development of furniture that will stack, Fig. 13-35, and pieces have been designed to serve more than one purpose. Other examples are low, cube-shaped tables that may be used for seats or stacked for storage, sofas that convert into individual seats or beds, and storage units that form room dividers.

● **For the first time furniture has been developed by the engineer and the chemist.** Finishes that are durable and almost indestructible have been made possible. Experiments with other new materials have been a characteristic of recent design. For example, fiberboard is used to make unusual "paper" furniture in bright colors. Clear, see-through plastic is used to make "non-furniture" forms which seem to take up very little space since you can see through them.

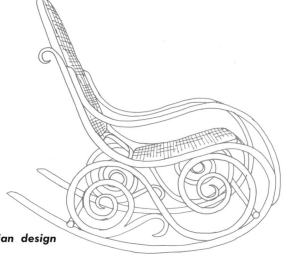

13-36A. This Thonet rocker is a Victorian design which is popular today.

Thomasville Furniture Industries
13-36B. Furniture in the style of Victorian designs.

riods or come from other countries. Fig. 13-36A. This means that todays interior may reflect greater individuality.

Designs from the past may be used in three ways. One is to furnish a home with antiques. This is difficult since scarcity and demand have made good antiques very expensive. Second is to select **reproductions** or accurate copies of originals. A third is to use furniture "in the style of" old designs. For example, "Victorian style" furniture may have many features that were popular during the Victorian era without being an exact copy of any one piece, Fig. 13-36B.

The antique furniture shown in this chapter is very expensive and rarely appears on the market. Fig. 13-37 shows a small booth in an antique show which featured less expensive

13-37. Real antiques at an antique show.

The Bartley Collection, Ltd.

13-38. An authentic reproduction of a Queen Anne lowboy.

country things such as a painted chair, an old hutch table, handmade quilts, a hooked rug, and various small accessories. While these are not rare forms they, too, are sought after today.

Reproductions, however, are widely available. Museums, historic houses, and furniture manufacturers offer selections. For example, the lowboy in Fig. 13-38 is an exact copy of a 1750 piece of furniture. The fine design and quality

crafting of this reproduction cost much less than would the original antique.

The Shaker reproductions shown in Fig. 13-39 are also true copies of museum originals. They come in kit form. All parts are sanded, ready for assembly, and the necessary hardware, paint or stain, and instructions are included. Because furniture parts are easy to package and ship, and the buyer does the handwork or finishing, antique design is available at a reasonable price. In 1980 the chairs cost less than $60. The kit includes the sturdy cotton tape to make the traditional Shaker style seat. The table is a copy of one used originally in the Shaker kitchen. It has a drawer for storage. The original of the dry sink was made about 1800.

Some people combine antiques and reproductions. All ethical manufacturers mark reproductions so they will never be confused with the antique original.

Furniture based on designs popular in the late 1800s is shown in Fig. 13-40. These pieces are Victorian in style. The tray table for example, has a base similar to those on the first sewing machines and suggests the fancy cast iron favored during this era. The forms of the bentwood arm chair, the roll-top section of the chest, the curved top mirror and shelves are all

Cohasset Colonials by Hagerty
George Cushing, Photographer
13-39. Reproductions which come in kit form.

13-40. None of these pieces are exact copies of antiques.

13-41. A setting with the country look.

Victorian features. While no piece is an exact copy of an antique, the charm of the period is captured.

Out of the new freedom characterized by the use of many designs from all periods, a new look has emerged. It is often called the country look and consists of homey color, texture, and material rather than a particular formal style. Natural wood, earthy colors, handmade items, plants, and pottery are typical of this look. The setting in Fig. 13-41 is an example. It includes a small chair based on a 1900 style oak chair and is shown with a modern pot, natural materials, and homespun fabric.

Another use of traditional design is to display old baskets, woodenware, or other handmade things as objects of art. This use of antiques is another instance of an original approach to design. The entryway in Fig. 13-42 features a hobby horse and carvings. Antique playing cards framed as pictures hang above a carefully refinished rolltop desk.

Case Problem A

A skilled cabinetmaker has been asked to make exact reproductions of chests that would have been used during the following times:

The Pilgrim Period, Jacobean
The Pilgrim Period, William and Mary
The Queen Anne Period
The Chippendale Period
The Classical Period, Duncan Phyfe
The Victorian Period
The Modern Period

Write a description of each chest as you think the cabinetmaker might design it, including the type of hardware and wood he might use.

Armstrong Cork Company

13-42. Antiques used as objects of art.

1. Who set the fashions when each of the furniture styles was popular? Was it a wealthy plantation owner—a political leader—a queen? Think about the groups of people who influence fashion today. Via television, we see inside homes that would not be open to us otherwise. Do you think it might influence furniture design to have wide publicity given to people who sit on cushions on the floor instead of using regular chairs?

2. Assume you are a furniture designer. What do you think the next style in furniture will look like? Explain your reasoning.

3. Find five pictures in magazines of Modern and contemporary furniture styles you think might become the valuable antiques of the future. Base your judgments on what you have learned about good design. Clip out the pictures, mount them, and attach a list of your reasons for selecting them.

14 How To Select Home Furnishings

Far left: Do you know how upholstered furniture is made? (Armstrong Cork Company)

Left: Appliances are a large investment and must be selected carefully. (Armstrong Cork Company)

Right: How would you inspect a chest of drawers before you made a purchase? (Armstrong Cork Company)

FURNITURE MATERIALS
Wood

Wood is still the most common furniture material. Most of today's furniture is made with veneers glued to a plywood base. Plywood consists of several layers of wood glued together at right angles to each other. With the excellent glues available today this results in a strong material which resists shrinkage or warping. Veneers can give beautiful wood grain effects. In this way fine woods are used economically and veneer construction is less expensive than solid wood.

Solid wood means that all exposed surfaces,

Fricks Reed Co.
14-1. A wicker chair, otto-man, and table.

tops, sides, door and drawer fronts are made of the solid wood named on the label. Wood on the inside, however, may be different.

Solid wood can be turned or carved. In case of damage it can be sanded and refinished since the interior is the same as the surface. There is no danger the surface will peel off, as with veneer.

Furniture is made of both hardwoods and softwoods. Hardwood comes from leaf-bearing trees. The hardwoods commonly used today include ash, birch, butternut, cherry, mahogany, maple, oak, pecan, and walnut. Softwoods come from trees with needles which remain green year round such as pine and fir.

The manufacturer selects woods to meet individual furniture requirements. For example, a chair might be formed from three or more different woods which could be stained or painted for a uniform color.

Finishes, the final coatings on the surface, often appear different from the real wood. For instance, birch may be stained to look like wal-

Terms To Know

bamboo	microwaves
carving	plain weave
case goods	satin weave
finishes	shaping
floats	solid wood
full warranty	twill weave
glides	warp
grounding	weft
joinery	welting
limited warranty	wicker

nut. All parts should blend in color and graining. The finish should feel smooth. A good finish does not scratch easily.

Wood products which have become popular in recent years are wicker, Fig. 14-1, and bamboo. **Wicker** is woven of pliant twigs and branches then usually painted. **Bamboo** is a fast-growing, tropical, woody plant which often appears in Oriental designs. The shelves on p. 17 are bamboo.

Metals

Metal furniture is strong and fairly easy to evaluate. The metals used in furniture manufacture include aluminum, iron, steel, brass, and copper. All have the advantage of being durable.

Aluminum is low in cost, lightweight, does not rust, is easy to care for, and is suited to outdoor use.

Wrought iron is durable and can be hammered and bent, making it suitable for accessories. Cast iron is more rust-resistant and may be used outdoors. For example, cast iron Victorian style garden furniture is popular.

Steel, when alloyed with chromium, does not rust and is often used for bathroom and kitchen accessories. Steel may be given a baked enamel finish suitable for indoor-outdoor use. Because of its strength steel is also used for furniture parts such as legs and frames.

Brass and copper are chosen for their beauty, color, and texture. Both take a high polish, but will tarnish if not protected by lacquer. Since they reflect nearby colors they blend with any interior. Both antique accessories and modern furniture in copper and brass are popular today.

The living room in a New York apartment is shown in Fig. 14-2. It illustrates the use of metal and metallic finishes to give the illusion of light and space. Although the room is furnished with

14-2. Metallic finishes can give a sophisticated effect.

Celanese House

14-3. The ball and claw foot on this leg was hand carved.

a large sofa and easy chair it does not appear crowded.

Since the construction details of metal furniture generally show, the consumer can see poor crafting. Joints should be smooth and sturdy, finishes should be durable. The major drawback of metal furniture is that it is difficult to repair.

Plastic

Plastic is a remarkably versatile material and its use has greatly influenced furniture design. Since it can be molded, unusual designs are possible. Mass production methods have made many pieces available at low cost. Since plastic may be used as a durable and easy to clean surface material, it has increased the variety of furniture available. Foamed plastic has revived the bulky look. Furniture made of this form of plastic has made comfort available at low cost.

Plastics come in a wide variety of colors and can be made to simulate other materials, such as wood or marble. They may be transparent or translucent. Transparent objects like the bookcase in Fig. 14-2 give the illusion of space and do not overcrowd a small room.

The disadvantage of some plastic furniture is

that it may grow dull and lose color. Repair and refinishing of most pieces is difficult or impossible.

BASIC CONSTRUCTION

Four important techniques are used in constructing furniture made of wood. **Shaping,** consisting of simple cuts, is used for parts such as legs and is done with saws and planes. **Carving,** the final cutting or design, by hand or machine is slow and expensive and must be done by skilled workers. The chair leg shown in Fig. 14-3 is an example of fine hand carving. Round members such as legs and posts are shaped by **turning** on a machine called a lathe. The basic method of holding the many parts of a piece of furniture together is called **joinery.**

Joinery

Wood breathes, it expands and contracts absorbing moisture from the air. The good cabinetmaker allows for expansion and contraction by choosing the right joint for the spot.

Joinery is especially important in **case goods,** which include desks, chests of drawers, and buffets. The drawers in a desk, for instance, must support the weight of the contents as well as constant pulling and tugging. The drawer joints must be tight and strong.

Good joinery is a clue to good cabinet making. The dovetail, mortise and tenon, and other joints are the age-old systems for bonding one piece of wood to another in ways that are harmonious with the wood's character. Some joints are concealed, others grace the piece with an interesting pattern. The most common joints are described and illustrated in Table 14-A.

In addition to joinery, modern glues are used for fastening wood pieces together rigidly. Nails, screws, and staples are also used.

Metal furniture can be all of one piece or joined by bolting, welding or riveting. Most metal joints are more than strong enough to hold up under normal family use. Plastic furniture is usually formed in a mold and has no joints.

Table 14-A.
COMMON FURNITURE JOINTS

Butt. Two pieces of wood glued or nailed together; very weak; dowels are sometimes added to strengthen the joint

Rabbet. A groove is cut in one piece of wood to receive the other; not a sturdy joint; should not be used on pieces which must withstand constant movement such as a drawer

Mitered. Two edges cut at 45° angles and joined to form a square corner; the joint is glued and sometimes reinforced with a staple or glue block; most commonly used on picture frames

Tongue and groove. The projection, or tongue, on one piece is inserted in a groove cut into the other; used in flooring materials and paneling as well as in furniture

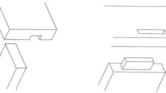

Dado. Similar to tongue and groove; generally used for holding shelves or drawer bottoms in fixed positions

Mortise and tenon. A projection on one edge fits into a hollowed-out space in the other edge; when glued forms a very strong joint which holds well under strain

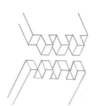

Finger or box. Edge cut into square notches which then fit together; since the notches are square they can sometimes be pulled apart; used on boxes and lower quality furniture

Dovetail. A series of flaring projections on one piece fit into series of grooves in the other; can take strong pulls or strains; a good drawer joint

Corner block or glue block. Used to reinforce joints; see also Fig. 14-4

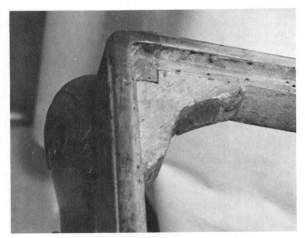

14-4. This corner block reinforces the leg.

UPHOLSTERY

The two sofa cushions shown in Fig. 14-5 illustrate the problem facing the buyer of upholstered furniture. These cushions are from two sofas purchased in a warehouse sale. They were comparable in price and purchased at the same time. Each has been in use for a few years. Note that the one on the left held its shape while the other did not. The fact that it may take weeks or months before the buyer is aware of defects makes returns difficult or impossible.

Frame and Springs

Upholstered furniture is generally made up of a wood frame, spring construction, padding, and an outer fabric covering.

The frame or skeleton structure of the piece is a vital, but unseen part. The fact that so much is concealed by the outer covering makes selecting upholstered furniture difficult. You must read labels and ask questions about the pieces being considered. See if hardwood, which was kiln dried to prevent warping, was used for the frame. Good joints and blocks add strength and are used in the best quality furniture. Screws, in addition to glue, generally hold better than nails at points of strain. Some furniture labels and manufacturer's advertising will include information on these details. Good manufacturers are proud of their products and provide adequate consumer information.

Another concealed detail is the spring. Coil springs are used on better large pieces, Fig. 14-6. In quality construction each spring is hand-tied and anchored to webbing or to steel bands at the back and base. Another type, the convoluted spring, is composed of zigzag strips of steel, and is satisfactory. It is generally found on pieces which have slender lines. Check to see if springs feel buoyant. They should not hit against the frame when bounced on.

A wide variety of fillings and paddings is used. These include curled hair which is expensive, rubber, urethane foam, dacron fiberfill, and cotton. Solid foam or urethane filling or stuffing wears better than bonded shredded foam. Foam is usually covered with a layer of polyester fiber. Kapok or sisal is often found in inexpensive furniture. Regardless of the filling used you should not be able to feel the framework through the upholstery.

14-5. Often poor crafting will not show up until furniture has been used a while.

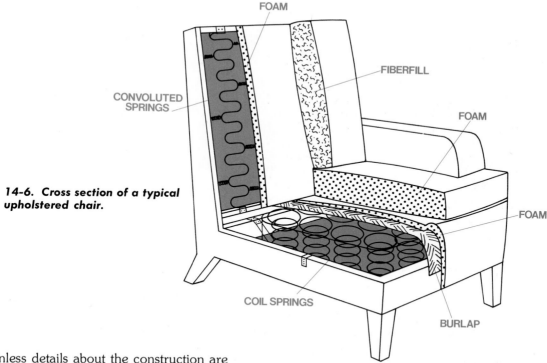

14-6. Cross section of a typical upholstered chair.

FOAM

FIBERFILL

CONVOLUTED SPRINGS

FOAM

FOAM

COIL SPRINGS

BURLAP

Unless details about the construction are given in the manufacturer's literature there is no way to evaluate the unseen parts. Fig. 14-7 shows the kind of label required by law, but the label offers little help in determining how the article of furniture will wear.

Some features of upholstered furniture may add extra wear. For example, loose back and seat cushions give twice the wearing surface because they can be turned. Extra arm covers protect arms that tend to wear and show soil first.

Upholstery Fabrics

The major features which determine suitability of a fabric are its appearance, feel, fiber, weave, color, pattern, cost, ability to resist sunlight and soil, flammability, and cleanability.

Fiber and weave affect the appearance and durability of a fabric. Each weave produces a fabric suitable for a particular purpose. Note the long threads, called **floats,** in the **satin weave** illustrated in Fig. 14-8. If this fabric is used

14-7. This tag gives construction details.

NO.
UNDER PENALTY OF LAW
THIS TAG NOT TO BE REMOVED
EXCEPT BY THE CONSUMER
ALL NEW MATERIAL
CONSISTING OF
BODY:
SHREDDED URETHANE FOAM   65%
URETHANE FOAM   30%
CELLULOSE FIBER PAD   5%
CUSHION: ( )
URETHANE FOAM   100%

LIC. NO. N. Y. 37943 (MISS.)

This article is made in compliance with an Act of the Dist. of Columbia approved July 3, 1926; Kansas approved March 1923; Minn. approved April 24, 1929; N. J. revised statutes 26; 10-6 to 18. La. Act 467-1948 Mass. 425. Licensed in Md. Licensed in Pa.

Certification is made by the manufacturer that the materials in this article are described in accordance with the law.

SOLD BY

Date of Delivery
Distributed By
Manufacturer's Name
Address

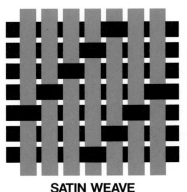
SATIN WEAVE

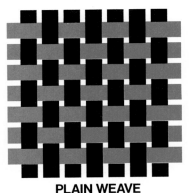
PLAIN WEAVE

TWILL WEAVE

14-8. Three common fabric weaves.

where it receives hard wear these threads will soon become frayed. The fabric should be positioned on the furniture so the wear is in the same direction as the floats. For example on a chair seat the long floats should go from front to back.

The simple one-over-one of the **plain weave** results in a flat fabric. When both the **warp** (lengthwise) yarns and the **weft** (crosswise) yarns are the same fiber and size, this weave results in a fabric which is balanced. That is, it is as strong in one direction as in the other, and should wear evenly.

The **twill weave** has a pattern which "steps down". This also results in a firm, strong fabric. Denim is a twill weave.

There are many variations of these weaves. You might like to make a collection of some of the fabrics commonly used for upholstery, such as brocade, corduroy, and velvet, so you can study their characteristics.

Non-woven and knitted fabrics are also used for upholstery. Leather is used on some expensive furniture. Vinyl, the most commonly used non-woven, is durable and easy to clean. Since it is non-absorbent it is less comfortable in hot weather than more absorbent woven fabrics. Knitted fabrics lack durability but are used in slip-on covers. Since the material may be

stretched these covers fit well and make it possible to recover some soiled or worn furniture.

Fabrics made of strong fibers, such as nylon or olefin in a tight weave such as a twill, should be selected for furniture which will receive hard use. Medium and darker tones and patterned fabric generally are less likely to show soil and wear. Protective finishes such as stain and water

14-9. This chair will not survive hard wear.

repellents extend the life of the fabric. Removable covers may simplify the problem of care.

Compare the chairs shown in Figs. 14-9 and 14-10. The Chippendale chair in Fig. 14-9 is upholstered in a silk damask pattern appropriate to the style of the chair. This is a delicate fabric which will not take hard wear. The fabric covers the edge of the chair, where many tacks have been used as part of the design. Changing the fabric would be difficult and time consuming. This chair is suitable for a formal room where it would receive little wear. In contrast, the furniture shown in Fig. 14-10 has a durable vinyl covering which will be easy to clean and the color is less likely to show soil. Each is an excellent but very different piece of furniture.

When judging upholstered furniture the outer fabric may be a general indication of quality.

Look at the crafting and finish. For example, the seams should be even and well-formed with no knots or thread ends showing. Hems and pleats should be even. Patterns should be perfectly matched. The cushions should be firm and well fitted. They should fit closely and evenly to each other. The **welting,** the cording used in the seams, should be straight and the fabric construction smooth. If there is a skirt it should be lined and hang straight. Deck fabric which covers the underside should be color-coordinated and tightly woven. The design and color must be appealing and the cost within your budget limits. When judging the fabric read the label for fiber content, color fastness, treatment (such as spot and stain resistive finish and flammability), and any guarantees. If there is a guarantee, be sure you know what it covers and for how long.

Peem Oy

14-10. Vinyl coverings are more durable.

14-11. This drawer is made with dovetail joints.

HOW TO SHOP

Don't hesitate to inspect a piece of furniture thoroughly before you buy. The exterior should be smooth and flawless. Note any hardware; it should be an appropriate design and of good quality. Next, you should inspect the construction and the quality of the unseen parts. The backs of buffets and chests should be recessed into grooves and screwed into the frame, not nailed or stapled on. A chest should feel heavy and well balanced. No spaces or gaps or glue should show where two pieces of wood are joined.

Pull out any drawers. Check to see if they slide easily. Look to see how the side of the drawer is joined to the front, Fig. 14-11. Look at the bottom of the drawer as shown in Fig. 14-12. This drawer has a well-made center guide and blocks added for extra strength. The bottom is unfinished, but it is smooth and carefully fitted into the sides.

With the drawers removed, look inside a chest, Fig. 14-13. The parts of case furniture that are not meant to be seen tell a lot about its construction. This chest is carefully made. Screws, which are stronger than nails or staples, have been used to hold the **glides,** wood strips which keep the drawers aligned. Another quality detail which shows only when the drawers are out is the dust shelf. This is a piece of wood beneath each drawer which prevents dust from falling on the contents of the drawer below. It keeps clothing from getting caught when a drawer is removed.

After you have examined the furniture itself, find out about store policies. Ask about delivery dates and charges. How are returns handled? Are exchanges possible? Reputable stores guarantee to repair or replace furniture delivered with scratches or other damage.

Study labels and guarantees. If they give little information—beware! Get fabric samples when possible to be sure that what you order is what you get. Find out about care techniques. Cleaning can be costly.

Table 14-B was compiled by the National Association of Furniture Manufacturers and suggests what to look for as you examine furniture in a store.

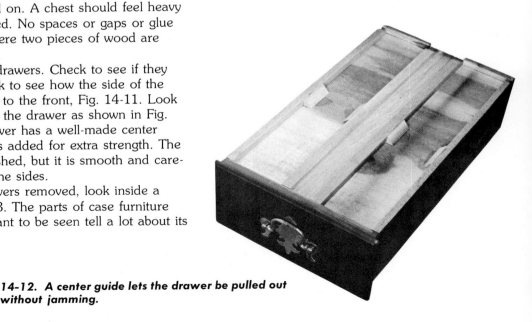

14-12. A center guide lets the drawer be pulled out without jamming.

14-13. *Glides and dust shelves indicate better quality case goods.*

BUYING AND RESTORING USED FURNITURE

Auctions, junk yards, thrift shops, flea markets, and garage sales are good sources of used furniture. Used furniture is often a good buy if it is well-constructed and well-designed. Look it over carefully, just as you would a new piece. Sometimes high quality used furniture can be refinished or reupholstered in up to date styles for the same amount or less than it would cost to buy a brand new piece of lower quality. Even more can be saved if you plan to restore the furniture yourself.

Reupholstery can be difficult and should not be attempted on more complicated pieces without the aid of someone with experience. Wood refinishing, however, is not as difficult as long as the wood is in good condition and not heavily carved. In either case, it is best to start with a small, simple, and inexpensive piece on which you can learn.

One of the simplest ways to restore furniture that you may not want to invest a lot of time and money on is to "antique" it. Antiquing has become popular because it consists of giving the furniture a base coat of paint, which may disguise a number of flaws. The paint is then gone over with a clear, dark coat which adds wood-grain and distressed effects, Fig. 14-14. There are many brands of antiquing kits on the market.

SELECTING MAJOR APPLIANCES

Major appliances include the refrigerator, freezer, range, dishwasher, washer, dryer, water softener, disposer, and trash compactor. Most apartments furnish a range and a refrigerator-freezer. In some cases certain appliances are considered as part of a house and are purchased along with it. Otherwise, you must buy your own.

Refrigerators

There are two main types of refrigerators: the conventional type with a single door and the combination refrigerator-freezer.

Conventional refrigerators have one door with a small frozen food compartment inside. This compartment is suitable for storing small quantities of frozen food for short periods of time.

Refrigerator-freezers are available in styles with the freezer on top or along the side. In these the freezer section can be used to freeze food, and store frozen food for longer periods of time.

Refrigerators may be purchased with manual defrost, automatic defrost, or frost-free operation. To defrost manually the appliance must be turned off. When the frost melts it is then wiped up by hand. In an automatic model the refriger-

Table 14-B.

CHECKLIST FOR SELECTING FURNITURE

Case Goods
- [ ] Do doors and drawers fit well?
- [ ] Do doors and drawers open and close smoothly?
- [ ] Do drawers have glides and stops?
- [ ] Are there dust panels between drawers?
- [ ] Are the insides of drawers snag-free?
- [ ] Are the drawer corners joined securely?
- [ ] Do long shelves have center supports?
- [ ] Are long doors of china cabinets attached with piano hinges?
- [ ] Does unit have leveling mechanism to square it to the wall and floor?
- [ ] Do large pieces have casters so that they will move easily?
- [ ] Is hardware secure and strong?
- [ ] Is the back finished, so you can use it away from a wall?

Upholstery
- [ ] Are the frame and corners well padded?
- [ ] Are there any visible lumps or bumps?
- [ ] Are seams and welts straight and are the sewing details nicely finished?
- [ ] Do patterns and stripes match at seams?
- [ ] Are patterns centered?
- [ ] Is heavy-duty furniture covered in a tight weave fabric?
- [ ] Do cushions fit snugly?
- [ ] Are cushions semi-attached or reversible?
- [ ] Are buttons sewn on securely?
- [ ] Are fabrics treated?
- [ ] Can you get protective covers for arms?
- [ ] Is the chair frame sturdy and does it sit squarely on the floor?
- [ ] Are the chair seats comfortable?
- [ ] Are corners braced and glued, and well supported?

Recliners and Convertible Sofas
- [ ] Does the mechanism work smoothly and quietly?
- [ ] Is it well balanced in each position?
- [ ] Do moving parts clear all fabric to avoid tearing?
- [ ] Are metal parts smooth with no sharp or rough edges?
- [ ] Is the frame strong and sturdy?
- [ ] Do the legs provide good support and stability?
- [ ] Is the outer cover a tightly woven fabric?
- [ ] Does the mattress have the amount of firmness you prefer?

Casual Furniture
- [ ] Are the joints on metal furniture neat and properly welded?
- [ ] Are metal edges smooth and free of burrs or sharp edges?
- [ ] Are decorative ornaments "double coined" the same on front and back?
- [ ] How many layers of paint and undercoating are there?
- [ ] Are straps replaceable?
- [ ] Are tops acrylic or tempered glass?
- [ ] Is rattan or wicker smooth?
- [ ] Are rattan or wicker joints secure?
- [ ] Does plastic furniture have smooth edges, surfaces, and sides?
- [ ] Is the plastic uniform in color, clean and free of bubbles, and impact resistant?
- [ ] Are the seams and joints well bonded?
- [ ] Is the gauge and weight of plastic appropriate for its use?

National Association of Furniture Manufacturers

14-14.

A. Read product directions carefully.

B. After sanding, apply the base coat.

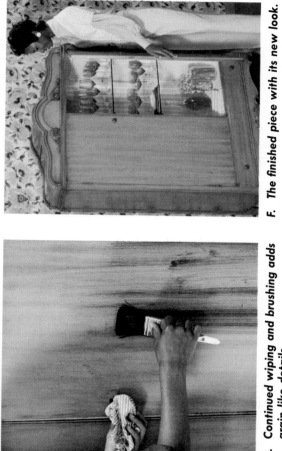

C. A clear glaze is brushed on over the base coat.

D. Most of the glaze is wiped off; the remainder sticks to carving and corners.

E. Continued wiping and brushing adds grain-like details

F. The finished piece with its new look.

PPG Industries, Inc.

ator portion defrosts automatically but the freezer part, which needs to be defrosted less frequently, must be done manually. In frostless models the refrigerator and freezer defrost automatically. The frost is eliminated by evaporation. The more automatic the appliance the more it generally costs both to purchase and to operate.

Some refrigerator-freezers have water and ice dispensers in the door. These may save energy because the door is opened less frequently. "Power-saver" switches and improved insulation are other features designed to reduce energy use. Details vary; many small conveniences may be included such as meat keepers, egg trays and produce crispers.

Recently designers have created a modular refrigerator. In appearance it resembles three dishwashers set side by side. Each module opens like a drawer and provides a different type of cooling. Each is opened separately, thus saving energy. The entire refrigerator fits into base cabinets rather than standing upright like conventional models.

Freezers

Families may purchase freezers to enable them to buy food in large quantities and save money, to preserve home-grown produce, to cut down on the time spent in shopping, or to have a variety of foods on hand for guests.

Freezers are available in upright and chest models. New models offer special features such as frostless operation, doors which can be locked, and signals which warn of power interruptions. Chest models cost less to operate than uprights of the same size. Since cold air is heavier than warm air, less is lost when the top of the chest type freezer is opened.

Ranges

There are several types of ranges available. The free-standing stove is counter height and may have one or two ovens and a broiler unit. The high-low range features two ovens—one above and the other below the counter. Both free-standing and high-low ranges have four surface cooking units at counter level. A third type is the slide-in range, which slips into the counter and appears to be built-in. Surface units and single or double ovens come separately and may be built-in if desired.

A special feature of some ranges is the self-clean oven. When set to clean, the temperature becomes hot enough to burn off food deposits. This feature adds to the purchase price and uses large amounts of energy. A second type of self-cleaning oven has a porous-ceramic coating on the oven walls. This coating absorbs and oxidizes most food deposits during normal cooking, but parts such as the racks and pans must be cleaned by hand. The ceramic scratches easily, which is a disadvantage.

Many ranges come with additional convenience features such as timers, clocks, electrical outlets, and rotisseries. New glass-ceramic cook tops are also available (see p. 285, Fig. 12-13).

Electric ranges require heavy duty (240 volt) electric service, and installing this wiring can be as expensive as the stove itself. The cost of wiring should be investigated carefully before purchasing an electric range.

Gas ranges must be connected to a gas line or fitted to use bottled propane gas. Pilot lights which burn continuously waste energy. Also, a drop in gas pressure may extinguish the light, and a return of pressure fill the house with gas, resulting in a hazard. An energy-efficient electric ignition pilot light is a desired feature of a gas range.

Microwave ovens heat only the food. The **microwaves,** which are similar to radio waves, pass through without heating most ceramics, glass, paper, and plastic. Once inside the food, they vibrate the food molecules at an incredible rate which, in turn, create the heat for cooking. Because food is cooked so quickly, it loses very little moisture. Cleaning the oven is easy because the interior walls don't heat up and food doesn't bake on. The oven walls come clean with a damp cloth. Because disposable paper or plastic plates can be used for cooking, dishwashing can be cut down. With microwave cooking only the food gets hot, not the kitchen, which is an advantage in hot weather. Another advantage is that the danger of fire is reduced. Because the oven remains cool it is easier for some elderly and handicapped people to use. Microwave ovens require 115 volts A.C. current for operation. This is regular household current so the need for special wiring is eliminated. Microwave cooking requires much less energy than conventional cooking. There is, however, concern over possible radiation leakage from microwave ovens and manufacturers must meet federal safety standards.

Clothes Washers

Washers offer a number of convenience features such as small load cycles, a choice of temperature and speed, and permanent press and soak cycles. Some offer water level controls. The washer shown in Fig. 14-15 features an automatic detergent, bleach, and fabric softener dispenser.

Washers require a drain, hot and cold water connections, and a 115-volt outlet.

Energy saving features include water level controls and separate wash and rinse-water temperature controls which allow for cold water rinses.

Clothes Dryers

Automatic moisture-sensing or temperature-sensing controls that shut the appliance off automatically are available on some new dryers.

Some include cycles designed for knit and permanent press fabrics. For safety all dryers stop when the door is opened. Most will stop when off balance.

Water Softeners

The minerals in hard water react with the alkali in soap and form a curd which may remain on clothes. Synthetic detergents are not affected by the minerals. However, the harder the water, the more detergent you have to use to clean effectively.

Hard water can be remedied with a water softener—either a water softening unit or packaged products. Water softener units may be purchased or rented, and the installers usually agree to service them periodically. An analysis of the water should be made before purchasing a water softener to be sure it will be effective. Local water companies can sometimes supply an analysis.

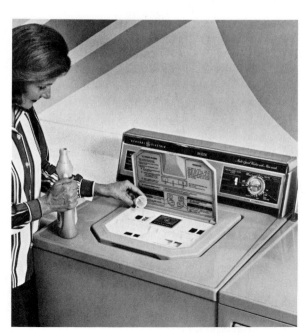

General Electric
14-15. A washer with built-in dispenser.

General Electric
14-16. A dishwasher with energy-saving features.

odorless, and sanitary. The disposers are attached to the drain under the sink. They grind up garbage, which is then flushed down the drain.

Two types of disposers are available. One can be fed continuously, and plates and other utensils may be flushed off directly into the disposer as it operates. The second type must be loaded and the stopper placed in position before the disposer will operate.

Disposers must be installed according to both electrical and plumbing codes.

Before installing a disposer, it is important to be sure the additional waste can be handled by the sewer system. Disposers are forbidden in some cities because of inadequate sewers. Cesspools and septic tanks must be large enough to hold the extra waste from the disposer.

Trash Compacters

Solid waste compressors are also available which compact such items as garbage, bottles, paper, and cans. This waste is sanitized and ejected in easy-to-handle cubes.

Safety and Security Appliances

Fire extinguishers used correctly may provide a margin of safety after the alarm has been called in to the fire department. Extinguishers must be maintained, however, so their contents remain active.

Smoke and fire detectors sound an alarm before smoke or flames are noticed and allow occupants to escape. They are one of the best fire safety measures available. Smoke reveals the presence of fire much sooner than heat

Dishwashers

Dishwashers are available in built-in, compact, and portable models, with a variety of wash and temperature cycles. Families should evaluate their needs since cycles range from power scrub for heavily soiled pots to gentle cycles for fine china. Dishwashers use less water than washing by hand, but the drying cycle uses a lot of energy. Some dishwashers can be turned off before this cycle and the dishes allowed to air-dry, Fig. 14-16.

Garbage Disposers

If the waste disposal system is adequate, mechanical garbage disposers are convenient,

does, a fact that makes smoke detectors better than heat detectors as early warning devices.

The Federal Housing Administration requires installation of smoke detectors in all FHA-financed houses and mobile homes. Many local building codes also require these devices in new homes. Two types are on the market. The first detects slow, smoldering fires and the latter is sensitive to fast, flaming fires. One of each kind provides backup against failure of the other. If the limit is one single detector, the battery-powered model might be the first choice. All battery models sound a warning when the batteries run low.

In addition to fire safety there is a growing need for protecting property from intruders. Many apartment buildings have security guards and electronic security devices to safeguard the tenants. In some areas owners of private homes install security devices. These systems detect when a door or window is opened or when a person enters their range.

Some salespeople have taken advantage of today's climate of fear to promote inadequate equipment and make unnecessary installations. Before purchasing any equipment assess your situation and study the alternatives.

HOW TO BUY APPLIANCES

Today's kitchen areas vary from rooms which are strictly utilitarian, where people cook-eat-and-run, to rooms where people spend a lot of time, enjoy gourmet cooking, and entertain guests. The first requirement of a satisfactory kitchen appliance is that it fits your family life style. Since the requirements of each buyer are different, only you can determine which appliances are important to you.

If your home is already built you should consider the problems involved in the installation of a major appliance before making the purchase. Some kitchens have built-in features which make changes difficult.

Some apartments will not allow certain appliances. For example, if a laundry room is already provided, the owner may not permit tenants to have their own washing machines. Free-standing and small portable appliances which can be adapted to different locations might be a wise choice for the person who moves frequently.

If you are building a new home, you may want to plan for space, plumbing, and wiring for appliances you may install in the future. For example, if you are saving for a dishwasher, and later for a washer and dryer, you can build removable counters equal to the size of these appliances. Later, portions of the counter may be taken out and replaced by the appliance. This means you must determine both the size of the equipment you plan to buy and arrange to have the necessary water, gas, and electric connections available where needed.

Study the market thoroughly to learn what choices are available to you. For example, study performance ratings published by consumer organizations and evaluate the information provided by the manufacturer and by salespeople. If possible observe demonstrations of the models you are considering.

One should look for energy saving features. The dishwasher illustrated in Fig. 14-16 with the power-saver option requires 40% less energy than the same model without this feature.

Safety is also important. The Underwriters' Laboratories, Inc. (*UL*) certification seal on an electrical appliance means that the product has been tested and meets their safety standards. Similarly the Association of Home Appliance Manufacturers' (*AHAM*) seal and the American Gas Associates (*AGA*) certified seal mean that the appliance meets their safety and performance standards. All automatic gas appliances should have safety devices that shut off the gas if the pilot flame goes out. The appliances should be properly vented where necessary.

Look for a product warranty which should clearly state what is covered. A **full warranty** covers all parts, labor, and other cost involved in the repair of any defect within a specified time limit. A **limited warranty** generally covers only a few specified parts and may or may not cover labor or shipping costs. Be sure you understand what the warranty does and does not cover before making a purchase.

USE AND CARE OF APPLIANCES

Be sure to follow installation instructions which come with the appliance. You must also follow your local building code which may specify such things as the use of non-combustible materials in certain locations, plumbing and wiring standards, and installation by licensed workers.

All appliances should be properly installed to prevent shock and fire. Appliances installed by a competent electrician will be grounded to protect the user from shock. **Grounding** means that one wire is connected to a water pipe, or to a copper rod or pipe driven into the soil. If a system is not grounded, it is possible for a person to receive a shock when touching metal parts.

Mail the warranty registration card to the manufacturer. Failure to do this may void the warranty. Keep instruction booklets and follow all care and service suggestions.

If an appliance is not satisfactory, do not attempt to fix it yourself. First check to be sure it has been installed correctly and that you are following operating instructions. Warranties are nearly always void if the appliance has been tampered with by anyone not approved by the manufacturer.

If you have a complaint you should start with the store where the item was purchased. They may send you to a service center approved by the manufacturer. If the store or service center does not correct the problem, write or call the manufacturer. Many have toll-free numbers and take immediate steps to correct problems. If the problem is still not resolved you might call your local Better Business Bureau or consumer protection agency.

Electrical cords should never be roughly handled so that they are damaged. For example, they should never be nailed to the wall or run under a carpet where they will be stepped on. They should always be removed by the plug—never pulled out by the wire. Never overload a circuit by plugging too many appliances into one outlet.

As a safety precaution, keep appliances clean and in good repair. For example, a refrigerator should be defrosted regularly so it is not loaded with a heavy coat of frost. The cooling unit should be cleaned to remove dust and lint which could cause the motor to become overheated.

ACTIVITIES

1. Plan a "treasure hunt". Look around the school to see if you can find examples of the types of joints listed in Table 14-A.

2. If there is a woodworking class in your school ask your teacher if the instructor can talk to your class about furniture construction.

3. Discuss the changes that would occur in your family life style if you had no major appliances except a stove in your home.

4. Visit an appliance store and look for labels which give the estimated yearly energy cost of the appliance. Many models will feature energy efficiency details. Make a list of the energy details on one or more labels.

5. As a class project select a piece of furniture and refinish it. Perhaps you could refinish an item used by your school. Your teacher or some parent might supply a piece that needs to be refinished.

ACTIVITIES

6. Select a major item of furniture or equipment. On a comparison shopping trip study two or more examples of the product. How did they differ? Which would you choose? Justify your selection.

7. Select advertisements for a major piece of equipment such as a refrigerator or stove. Make a list of the words or phrases in the advertisements which are helpful. Do the advertisements give the information you need to make a major purchase? Draw a line through all of the words which are not informative. Arrange the advertisements to show the most and least helpful.

8. At a fabric store, ask for small clippings of ten upholstery fabrics. Take notes on the fiber content and special qualities of each, such as stain-resistance. Put the samples and information into a notebook.

15 Designing and
Furnishing
a Room

Far left: This room is designed around one idea. By studying it you can tell a lot about the people who live here. (GAF Corporation)

Left: Window treatments and the use of light are important design elements.

Right: Accessories help personalize a room.

PLANNING TO BUY

Home furnishings can be costly and the wise consumer plans carefully before shopping. For example, you may be tempted to use an unusual and exciting color combination, or you may become enthusiastic about a new fabric or accessory. If you buy without a plan, you may realize, all too late, that these items do not fit in with what you already have. Or on the spur of the moment you may buy a new piece of furniture on sale, then find that it does not fit the space you have. Because it was on sale you

Terms To Know

bracket light
broadloom
carpeting
cornice light
cottage curtains
cove lights
draperies
draw curtains
fixtures
fluorescent tubes
focal light
glass curtains
incandescent bulbs

looped weave
patterned weaves
plaid weaves
rug
selvedge
shag weaves
soffit lighting
stained glass
structural lights
textured weaves
valance
valance lighting

cannot return it. As a result, you may have to live in a room you do not enjoy because you cannot afford to change it.

It requires discipline to think of realities such as dollars and cents or accurate measurements, along with the fun of decorating. However, keep in mind that money and space limitations generally come first when you are furnishing or decorating.

When you move into your first home, you may have a few pieces of your own furniture and may need to add only a few more. On the other hand, you may need to buy enough furniture to get started. This means that you will have to decide what you can buy immediately and what you can do without until you can afford it. Of course, regardless of how little furniture you start out with or how little money you have to spend, you want a home that is attractive and pleasant to live in. This requires careful planning. And although it takes time and thought, the planned approach to decorating usually gives the most satisfactory results.

- **Provide for special interests.** To feel comfortable in your home, you must be able to participate in those activities which you enjoy. A good furnishing and design plan provides for those activities. For instance, someone who enjoys reading will probably want a large, comfort-

able chair and an adequate reading lamp. These items will be among the first this person will buy, and an apartment or house will have to accommodate them. Sometimes personal interests can assist in the decorating process. The woman who uses the bedroom in Fig. 15-1 collected the antique furnishings and made the patchwork coverlet herself.

- **Look for versatility.** Thoughtful planning based on present as well as future requirements will help stretch your housing dollars. This means selecting furniture which is versatile or can be adapted to more than one use or location. For example, the table shown in Fig. 15-2A and B can be used in several ways. In A it is shown extended for use as a dining table. In B it is shown closed. In this view it is being used in an efficiency apartment as a place for one person to eat and to provide a convenient spot for a reading lamp and other objects. It might also be used as a hall table or as a side table in a dining room.

Another wise choice may be modular furniture which can be grouped in many combinations to fit a wide variety of rooms.

- **Have in mind a basic style.** When selecting style, remember that what you like is most important. Do you prefer a contemporary design or traditional? Perhaps you would like a design based on the style of another country such as Japan or England. Do you want the room to be simple or ornate; formal or informal? This may determine the style you choose.

Some styles may be mixed. For example, Early American Windsor chairs and simple contemporary tables might be attractive together. If you plan to mix periods and styles, try to select pieces that are similar in scale and degree of ornateness. Colors should blend and textures should be related. For example, several large, dark, highly carved pieces might be harmonious.

Matched sets such as a living room set can give your home a store-window look. This usually is not as distinctive as a room furnished with pieces individually selected to reflect your taste.

15-1. *A room should reflect the interests of the person who lives there.*

A

Ethan Allen, Inc.

15-2. This versatile table is especially suitable for limited spaces.

B

Remember too that your tastes may change again later. Furniture which can adapt to different "looks" or color schemes might be the best investment.

The modern chair in Fig. 15-3 has a durable hardwood frame which can be completely unbolted and taken apart in sections. It is simple to pack and move and very easy to recover with new fabric. The only tool needed to reupholster it is a staple gun. Since the upholstery can be easily changed it can be adapted to fit many decorative schemes.

● **Simplify the chore of moving.** Because their lives are not settled yet, young people may move frequently. Moving is tiresome and may also be costly. The more it's simplified, the easier it is to do.

Oversized furniture often presents problems to the mover, especially if doorways, corridors, and window openings are narrow. One example is a king-size bed with matching box springs. Since the spring is rigid and wide, it may be impossible to get it up a narrow stairway or around a sharp corner; or it may not even go through a window opening.

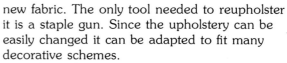
Metropolitan Furniture Corporation
15-3. This chair is easy to move and to recover.

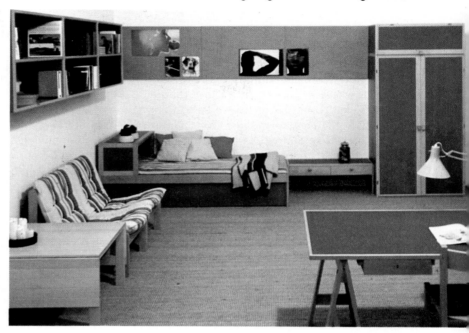

Danish Furniture Manufacturers
15-4. An entire roomful of furniture which would be easy to move.

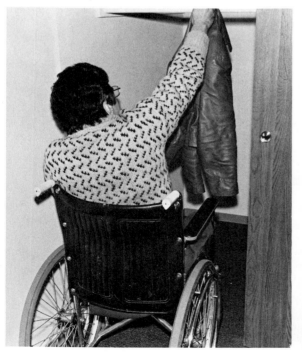

The furniture in Fig. 15-4 is lightweight and simple and would be easy to take from place to place.

● **Account for special needs.** Some people have special needs and limitations. For example, an elderly person may not be able to do much housework. Then furniture which requires little maintenance is preferred.

Well-chosen furnishings can make a home more convenient for a person in a wheelchair. For example, easily reached bookshelves and tables that are wheelchair height are helpful. Heavy chairs may serve as a steady handgrip. Lamps with switches at a convenient height and storage cupboards with low shelves help a person to be independent, Fig. 15-5. All furniture

Boston Housing Authority
15-5. The elderly, ill, or handicapped may have special needs. The pole in this closet is fixed at a handy wheelchair height.

371

should be placed to provide wide clear passageways. Floors should be covered with wall-to-wall carpeting or a hard surface flooring which has no loose edges.

A family with small children might consider safety paramount. They would avoid furniture with knobs that could be unscrewed and perhaps swallowed. They would not select furniture with sharp corners and would be sure no lead-based paint had been used as finish. The furniture shown in Fig. 15-6 is carefully designed with the special needs of children in mind. The chair seats as well as the foot platforms are adjustable.

● **Don't exceed your budget.** No selection will be truly satisfactory if it does not fit your budget and no one but you can say what that amount should be. Only you can decide how much you have to spend and how you should spend it. However, once you've decided on a budget, stick to it. To get the most for your dollar is to buy the most suitable items which fit within your budget. You may not always be able to afford some of the things you like.

Table 15-A can help you determine your preferences and which items you need.

ORGANIZING THE SPACE

You have already learned how to draw a floor plan and make furniture templates. It is best to do this for each room you plan to furnish. Analyze your activities carefully so that you will allow enough space. You may want to review the information on judging space requirements and making templates in Chapter 11. Remember, take the outside measurements of the furniture. Once you have the furniture measured, make a template for each piece to the same scale as your floor plan. On each template, identify the piece of furniture and list its dimensions.

If you were a professional decorator, you would also want to determine how an arrangement would look in an elevation. For example, Fig. 15-7A shows a floor plan with a sofa and two tables. The tables are centered in front of the sofa.

Figure 15-7B is a drawing showing how the scene would look in real life. Notice the different heights of the tables. The two tables appeared to be similar when seen only on the floor plan. It is obvious, however, that its height makes one table unsuitable for the location

Westnofa Furniture
15-6. The table may be used alone. The chair heights may be adjusted as the children grow.

Table 15-A.
PLANNING TO BUY

How long do you plan to live there? Will you move frequently? _____
Will you be living alone? _____
Will you work at home? _____
Do you have hobbies which require extra space or storage? _____

Do you plan to entertain guests frequently? _____
Do you have any skills, such as sewing or painting, which will be helpful in decorating? _____

Your Possessions	What You Have	What You Need	Money You Can Spend	Your Possessions	What You Have	What You Need	Money You Can Spend
Beds				Curtains			
Chests				Lamps			
Chairs				Coffee table			
Sofas				Storage cabinets			
Dining table				Range			
Dining chairs				Refrigerator			
Bookcases				Clothes washer			
Area rugs				Clothes dryer			
Draperies				TV set			

Your Home	Size	Number Windows and Size	Number Doors	Architectural Details	Light Exposure	Colors You Can't Change	Colors You'd Like To Use
Living room							
Bedroom							
Bedroom							
Bedroom							
Kitchen							
Bath							
Bath							
Family room							
Utility room							
Dining room							
Other							

shown. You must always keep in mind that a floor plan does not show height.

Next, plan the furniture arrangement. Keep in mind the activities that will take place in the room as well as the space needed for these activities and for the furniture.

● **A well-furnished room gives a feeling of balance.** There are several ways to achieve this. When you place the cut-out templates on your room floor plan, think also of the height of the furniture. Avoid grouping tall pieces together—it is better to alternate tall and low, Fig. 15-8. If all of the furniture is low, select one piece such as a table and make it appear tall by placing a picture or mirror above it. But keep pieces which go together in proportion. For instance, a tall table lamp does not look in proportion be-

side a low sofa. Avoid a concentration of large items in one area—distribute them around the room. There should also be a balance between the amount of space occupied by furniture and that required for movement. Lamps should not be clustered in one area, but should be distributed so that the room is evenly lighted. Materials and textures, too, should be considered in a balanced arrangement. Regardless of the sizes and shapes of the furnishings, the room would not look balanced if all of the upholstered furniture were on one side of the room and all of the wood pieces on the other.

● **Furnishings should be considered in relation to the architecture of the room.** A fireplace, a group of windows, a work of art, or a doorway may provide a focal point about which

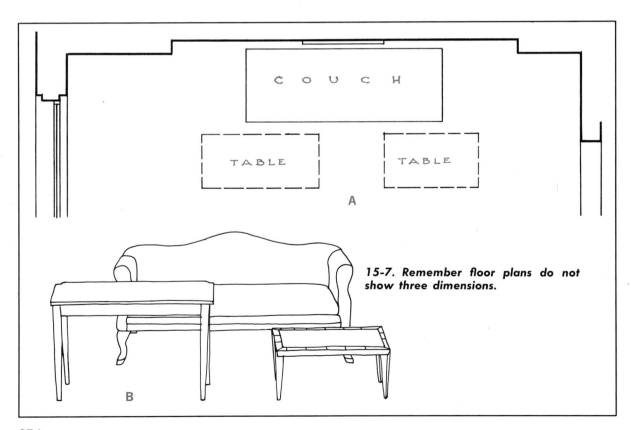

15-7. Remember floor plans do not show three dimensions.

Joao Isabel
15-8. The head of this bed is high, the table is low, the chest falls between the two heights.

furniture may be arranged. If the room has no real center of interest, furniture may often be grouped to create one.

● **Furniture may help to minimize an undesirable feature of the room.** For example, two conversation groups may be arranged so that they help to reduce the apparent length of a long, narrow room, Fig. 15-9. Large pieces of furniture tend to make a large room appear smaller, and small pieces make the room appear larger.

● **Large pieces should be placed against the walls.** This is why large cabinets, secretaries, and chests of drawers are unfinished on the back. In a bedroom the head of the bed should be placed against a wall, although in some modern rooms the bed is in the center and a chest of drawers placed at the head. Unless a room is very large or long, a sofa should not be placed crosswise away from a wall. No furniture other than an occasional chair or TV set should be set on a diagonal.

● **Furniture should be grouped for different activities.** For example, you may have a grouping of a sofa and chairs for conversation; sofa, chairs, a TV set, and several snack tables for watching TV; desk, chair, lamp, and bookcase for reading; small table, telephone, lamp, and chair for phone calls. If you entertain, you may prefer several conversational groupings.

● **Keep in mind the space needed for movement or traffic lanes.** The room in Fig. 15-10 is carefully planned for movement. People sitting in the conversational grouping also have easy access to the door and the rest of the room.

By moving templates around, you will find a furniture arrangement you like. You may also discover that there is not enough space for all the furniture you would like to have. In that

375

15-9. The bookshelf and window valance also add height to this low-ceilinged mobile home living room.

case, re-evaluate your activities and determine what furniture you can do without.

Fig. 15-11 shows two different approaches to the problem of furnishing the same studio apartment. In each case, one room serves as a combination living room, dining room, and bedroom, with space for books and television. The activities of the tenants have been considered, and the space has been well planned for the furniture and for ease of movement. Let's analyze each room arrangement.

The studio apartment in A is occupied by two women. Does this room meet their needs? They

have a comfortable area in which to sleep. The dining table also serves as a study table, and the bookcase is adequate for the books they will have. The screen separates the bedroom area from the living-dining area and provides privacy in case one woman wants to retire earlier. The separate living-dining area serves for viewing TV or entertaining friends informally. Can you think of any way to improve this arrangement without buying furniture?

Now let's look at the same studio apartment occupied by a single man as in B. Does the room arrangement meet his needs? The sofa-

House Beautiful Magazine, Otto Zenke, Decorator,
Ernest Silva, Photographer

15-10. *Although this room has more than one furniture grouping, it is easy to walk through.*

bed is ideal. During the day the combination of the sofa and the love seat makes a good conversation area for guests. Note that there is enough space so that the sofa-bed can be opened each night without having to move any furniture. The large bookcase is ample for a book collection and could even hold a stereo. The dining table seats four comfortably. For larger parties, the table can be moved to the center of the dining area and extended. What would you do to improve the arrangement without buying additional furniture? Has the tenant made a good choice of furniture? Give reasons for your answer.

If this were your apartment, how would you furnish it now? Why?

DEVELOPING A DECORATING SCHEME

A successful room usually is the result of a decorating theme which reflects the personality of the owner. You can achieve individuality if you select furniture, draperies, wall and floor coverings, and accessories that reflect your personal interests. Your preferences in color, texture, and style are also important in developing an individualized decorating scheme.

The Theme

Begin with objects or ideas you like. Your clothes are good clues to the colors and textures you prefer. Look at the clothes in your closet and at the articles you have collected. Do you like traditional or contemporary; simple or elaborate; quiet or dramatic? Often a favorite picture, lamp, or collector's item may provide a ready-made theme.

The room in Fig. 15-12 was designed around the owner's love of birds and the outdoors. The natural wood of the sideboard blends with the rattan chairs and wood floor. The many plants give a fresh, open-air effect. Do you think the person who lives here would be comfortable with mahogany Chippendale furniture with damask upholstery?

In combining rugs and carpeting, draperies,

upholstery, and wall finishes, it is usually advisable to follow the rule that one pronounced pattern is enough. If the draperies, for example, show an exciting floral design, the walls and floor covering should be plain. If the walls are papered in floral, geometric, or scenic patterns, the draperies and carpeting generally should be in a solid color, and the solid color should match one of the colors in the pattern. Keep in mind that, while too little pattern may make a room dull and lifeless, competing patterns can be confusing and exhausting.

The interior shown in Fig. 15-13 is a good illustration of the use of pattern. Note that although the rug and carpet are quite different the same arrow-like device or pattern is repeated in each, which makes them harmonious. Neutral colors with no pronounced pattern are used elsewhere in the room.

The Color Scheme

Always plan your color scheme before you buy anything. There is often more than one way to decorate a room. It may be much easier to get the fabrics and accessories for one color scheme than for another. You may want to review the section on color schemes in Chapter 2.

Before you decide on a final decorating scheme, you will find yourself making many adjustments in your mind as you analyze the kind of furniture you want or have, its placement, and the color you like. But always keep in mind that this is your home. Decorate it to suit your personality.

BACKGROUND FURNISHINGS
Wall Treatments

A symmetrical spacing of windows or doors often suggests a formal, traditional room, while a lack of symmetry may call for a more informal and contemporary approach.

The use to which a wall will be put may establish the design of the entire room. For example, a wall devoted to storage or covered with paintings serves a function beyond that of a divider.

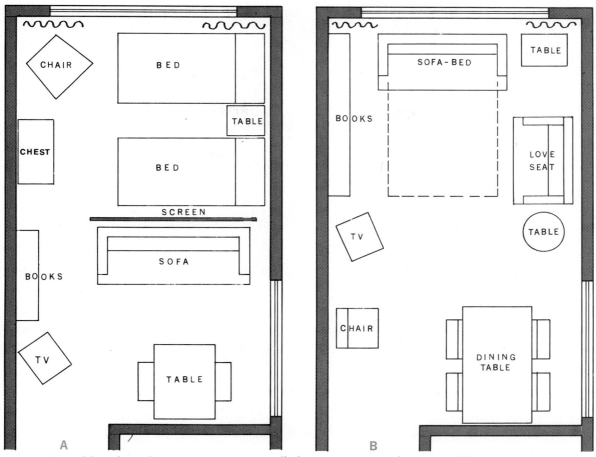

15-11. Although studio apartments are small, furniture arrangement can add to their comfort.

Whether wall areas are large or small, light or dark, and open or closed may also suggest the appropriate style of decoration and furnishing.

Today, there is an increasing tendency to do the unusual or unexpected in decoration. Walls may be covered with scenic murals, Fig. 15-14, or wall-to-wall carpeting may be used as floor-to-ceiling wall covering or walls may be painted white and the ceiling black to create a sky-high illusion. "Non-walls" or dividers in the form of curtains, strings of beads, or other non-rigid materials are common.

Changing the color or pattern of room surfaces offers a quick and inexpensive way to create a new look in a room. The easy to apply wall covering used in Fig. 15-15 (page 382) has created a crisp and cheerful room. Table 15-B (page 383) shows the most popular wall finishes.

Arranging Decorative Items on a Wall

USING THE PRINCIPLES OF DESIGN

When decorating a home, walls provide important areas for display. Pictures and other

15-12. A room should have a unifying idea or theme.

Couristan, Inc.

15-13. *Patterns may be mixed if they have similar features.*

General Electric
15-14. *This mural has been made from a photograph of a deep pine forest.*

15-15. Sunny gold checks make this kitchen cheerful.

Table 15-B.
DECORATIVE WALL FINISHES

Material	General Appearance	Use	Advantages	Disadvantages
Paint, flat finish	Soft and dull; textured effects available; many colors	Any wall	Fast-drying, fade resistant; easy to apply; solvent-based are more durable; inexpensive	Harder to clean than semi-gloss
Paint, semi-gloss and enamel	From soft sheen to high gloss	Any wall, wood trim on doors and windows	Fast-drying, fade resistant; easy to apply; solvent-based are more durable; inexpensive; easy to clean	
Wallpaper	Large variety; some made of fabrics; scenic murals also available	Any wall	Wide price range; many different decorating effects possible	Can be difficult to apply and maintain
Fabric	Wide variety of colors and patterns	Any wall	Wide price range; interesting effects; easy to install	Not all widths are practical; must be chosen carefully
Panels, wood or plastic	Natural or imitation wood grain, stone, brick; shiny or textured surfaces	Any wall with few doors, windows, etc.	Easy to install; usually permanent; rich effects possible	Can be expensive

items give a room a warm, personal look. They make it more homey. These displays might include posters, small snapshots attractively mounted, photographs enlarged to poster size, prints, paintings, or a collection of maps marked to show places or events. Fabrics are popular wall decorations today. Interesting fabric hangings might include handweaving, needlework, macrame, or well-designed printed fabrics.

Items on a wall look best when arranged according to the elements and principles of design. Not all the guidelines will apply in every situation, but it's wise to begin with them.

The contrasting wall arrangements in Fig. 15-16A and B show how the principles of proportion and unity and variety can be applied. In A, the pictures are scattered about with the large ones crowded to the right side and the small ones spaced farther apart on the left. This

results in poor proportion. The parts do not relate to each other; there is too much variety and no unity. In B, the large rectangular pictures are distributed throughout the grouping, giving proportion. The round and triangular forms still add variety but seem to fit in as part of the whole. The outer edges of the grouping form a rectangle, which gives unity by making the grouping a recognizable form.

Unity is also a consistency of style. A common character is kept throughout a design.

In Fig. 15-16C, the formal mirror, the ornately framed picture, the primitive fish, and the small unframed rectangle lack unity. Because of the diversity of forms and subjects, the result is confusion. In D, unity is achieved by using three paintings with frames of similar style and proportion. D also represents formal balance.

In Fig. 15-16 the composition in E is not bal-

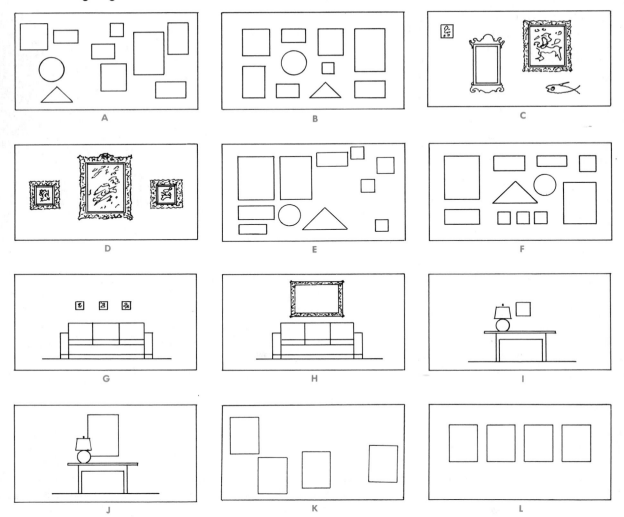

15-16. Picture arrangements should be based on the principles of design.

anced. The large frames are all on the left side of the wall, which results in a lopsided effect. If you imagine each of these forms as solids, the left side would be much heavier than the right. In F, the two large pictures are placed at opposite sides and the remaining decorations are evenly distributed between them. Because of the

even distribution of weight, this arrangement has balance and stability.

Furniture, accessories, and nearby wall decorations should relate to each other in size. They should be in proportion. In G, the three small pictures look silly in proportion to the sofa and the surrounding wall area. In H, the large picture complements the sofa. The same effect might have been achieved with a grouping as long as the outer size of the grouping was not larger than the area covered by the large picture.

Well-planned wall decorations often reduce the need for major pieces of furniture by providing a point of emphasis in a room. Handsome prints or posters, which may cost very little, can be very effective. Poor and good arrangements are shown in I and J. In I, the picture over the table is small in relation to both the lamp and the table. In fact, the picture and the lamp are so similar in size that they compete with each other. As a result, neither dominates. In J, the large picture is obviously the most important element in the composition. It provides the necessary emphasis, and the result is satisfying.

In K, the arrangement of pictures forms no obvious pattern. There is no regular spacing, nor is there any continuity of lines, either vertical or horizontal. Shapes are not repeated in a regular pattern. Consequently, there is no rhythm. In L the four pictures are spaced evenly giving a series of repeated accents which result in rhythm.

MAKING YOUR OWN ARRANGEMENT

For most people it can be difficult to visualize how items will look once they are on the wall. Items which seem to balance in your imagination may not balance when hung. This can result in a wall full of nail holes or adhesive hangers which have to be removed or repaired. There are two methods of planning groupings which avoid these problems.

Method A

1. Collect the items you wish to group together. Trace their outlines on paper and cut them out.
2. Using masking tape, place the paper silhouettes on the wall in the arrangement you wish to use. Move the silhouettes until you have a pleasing arrangement. Stand back from your work to be sure it's as satisfactory from across the room as from close up.
3. Place the hangers and hang the grouping.

Method B

1. Place a large piece of paper on the floor in front of the wall space you're going to use. Butcher's paper or grocery bags cut apart and taped together to form a large piece work well.
2. Place your items on the paper in the arrangement you think you want. Move them around until you think they look best. Stand back and check your work from a distance.
3. Trace the outlines of the items in their proper positions on the paper with a felt tip pen or crayon.
4. Hang the entire piece of paper on the wall with masking tape. Pound in the nails through the paper. If you're using adhesive hangers, cut a hole in the paper and attach them directly to the wall.
5. Hang the items over their silhouettes on the paper. Remove the paper carefully.

Whenever possible, visit museums and art galleries to see how pictures are framed and displayed by professionals. Study arrangements pictured in professional books and magazines.

Hang single pictures at eye level.

Hang pictures so the wire does not show. A triangle of wire is distracting since it takes the eye upward. If the wire must be exposed, two vertical wires are less distracting.

Pictures placed on highly patterned wall paper can result in confusion. The problems of design-on-design are a challenge, even for the experienced decorator. If you feel that a patterned wall paper needs a decorative object, a mirror is a good choice since it reflects the color and pattern of the surrounding room.

Frames should complement the subject. For example, a small print calls for a simple frame, while a large oil painting might require a wide gold frame.

Uneven numbers of pictures are generally more pleasing than even numbers because they seem less stiff and formal. One or three are bet-

385

15-17. These shades are custom-made.

ter than two, because two may look like "eyes." Sets of pictures which function as a unit may be an exception, such as a pair of portraits or pictures of the four seasons.

All wall hangings are enhanced by proper lighting. There should be enough light to show the color and texture, but it should not distort the colors. The light must be placed so that it is not reflected by glass or painted surface.

Paintings and other decorations should not be hung where damage might result from dirt. They should not be placed over a heating vent, or close to a chair or sofa where someone might lean against them.

Window Treatments

The principal types of windows are illustrated on p. 202. Different methods may be used to control the amount of light and air entering through the window, to restrict the view from either the room or from outside, and to afford protection against weather and vandalism.

ON THE EXTERIOR

Awnings may be used on the exterior to reduce sun glare and to protect an open window from rain.

Shutters—hinged, roll-down, or sliding—may be used for physical protection. In parts of the country where violent wind storms occur frequently, shutters are essential to protect the window glass. The hinged shutter is commonly used as decoration, even though in the past its use was more functional.

Metal grilles are generally used for decoration. However, they can also be used for security purposes on basement and first floor windows.

SHADES AND BLINDS

Window shades give good light control and privacy and have the advantage of reasonably low cost. They are easily cleaned and offer a wide variety of decorative possibilities. The room in Fig. 15-17 calls for specially coordinated shades because of the unusual shape of the windows. The lower shades roll down from the crossbeam to the floor. However, the matching shades on the upper windows are attached to the crossbeam and roll up to the sloping ceiling. The ends of the shades are finished off at an angle which matches the sloping ceiling. The decorative effect is complete—no other window treatment is required.

Window shades may also aid in heat control. For example, insulated shades made of heat reflective fabric which was developed for the space program are available. These may be applied to the interior surface of the window frame and they function as a storm window in reducing heat loss. Since they eliminate light they are used at night and during very cold weather on windows where light or the view are not important. Semi-transparent shades made of reflective film in colors such as gold, silver, or bronze may be used to reduce heat penetration and to protect fabrics from sun-fading.

Besides fabric, shades can also be made of slender strips of bamboo. Since they are water-resistant, they are often used to protect porches and balconies. However, their decorative possibilities make them useful in other areas, too.

Venetian blinds made of wood, metal, or plastic, are popular because they permit complete light control. The most commonly used blind consists of a series of horizontal slats which may be tilted or raised by cords. Vertical slats are available. Vertical blinds are also made of shade cloth and come in a wide range of colors, Fig. 15-18.

An inexpensive window shutter of white plastic is illustrated in Fig. 15-19. Although the shutters are decorative, they help to keep out bright sunlight. Other window treatments that give an open effect include strings of beads, plastic spheres on cords, macrame, and potted plants.

Window Shade Manufacturers Assn.

15-19. Folding shutters which control light as well as disguise a heating unit.

Window Shade Manufacturers Assn.

15-18. Vertical blinds.

CURTAINS

Glass curtains hang closest to the window glass and are usually lightweight, translucent, and unlined, Fig. 15-20A They may remain over the window in a fixed position or may be drawn open. Those attached to doors or casement sash are referred to as casement curtains.

Draw curtains are probably the most popular form of window covering today. They are attached to a rod or track above the window so that they may be easily drawn open or closed. Figure 15-20B shows draw curtains.

Cottage curtains consist of separate glass curtains for the upper and lower halves of a window. The upper curtains are usually tied back to the window jamb. Cottage curtains provide privacy, but do not cover the window completely.

A

B

C

15-20. Common types of window coverings.

DRAPERIES

Draperies are generally made of an opaque fabric and are usually lined, Fig. 15-20B. They hang at each jamb of the window for its full height. In the case of a formal interior, they extend to the floor. A **valance** consisting of the same material with a wood or cardboard backing can be used across the top of the window. Draperies and curtains are often used together in an infinite variety of materials and forms. Draperies may be hung from a track known as a traverse rod. They may be tied back, criss-crossed, tiered in several rows, hung in swags, or formed over cardboard or wood, as in Fig. 15-21B.

In a modern house with many large windows,

draperies help to reduce sun glare, provide privacy, and eliminate the area of blackness that a large window presents at night. Draperies also provide insulation against heat loss. They absorb sound and help to exclude many outside noises from the room.

In decorating a room, draperies can focus attention on an important window, disguise unattractive features of a room, or change the apparent proportions of a wall area. They can be used to conceal uneven plaster or unsightly pipes. Draperies can add color and richness to the interior. They form an important part of the color scheme, not only in the interior but also on the outside. If the color of unlined draperies differs from room to room, the exterior view of the house probably will not be harmonious. If they they are lined, one color may be chosen for the lining that will be uniform throughout the house and will complement the exterior. Apartment leases often specify white draperies or white linings to unify the exterior appearance.

STAINED GLASS

Very popular during Victorian times, stained glass is once again fashionable in home decoration, Fig. 15-20C. **Stained glass** panels are created by forming sections of colored glass into a design and holding them together with strips of lead. Making stained glass is an art and stained glass windows can be expensive.

Floor Coverings

Rugs and carpets contribute much to the character of a room. They provide color, warmth, and texture. Besides adding comfort, they are sound absorbent. In many cases they reduce the time spent on housekeeping.

A **rug** is finished on all four sides and is available in standard room sizes and shapes. **Carpeting** comes by the roll in broadloom widths of 3600 mm (12 ft.) or 4500 mm (15 ft.) and can be purchased in any length. **Broadloom** means the carpet was woven on a wide loom and does not refer to any other special qualities.

A red Oriental rug and a wall-to-wall carpet have been used in the room shown in Fig. 15-13. Note that the Oriental rug in the background is finished on all four sides. Rugs generally have a fringe on two sides and a **selvedge,** or finished edge, on the other two sides. In contrast, the carpeting which is in the foreground goes to the wall and is fastened to the floor. A rug may be moved to equalize wear. It can be sent to a cleaner and is part of the owners' home furnishings. The carpet which is fastened to the floor cannot be moved easily and is considered a part of the house. In most cases when a family moves, the wall-to-wall carpeting is left behind.

Carpeting comes in five basic weaves: patterned, plaid, shag, textured, and looped. **Patterned weaves** are like that in Fig. 15-13. The type of pattern used can be anything from floral to geometric. **Plaid weaves** follow the plaids used in clothing, such as tartan. **Shag weaves** have become very popular in recent years. They consist of long, "shaggy" pile, from which they get their name. Shag carpeting is shown on p. 355. **Textured weaves** are those in which the pile is cut different lengths to form a textured design. This is also called "sculptured" carpeting. In a **looped weave,** the pile fibers remain uncut, forming loops.

The most important fibers used in carpeting today are listed in Table 15-C.

The initial cost is important in selecting floor coverings. It is often better to select a rug of good quality, made of an inexpensive fiber, rather than a cheap version of a more expensive rug. For example, a quality porch rug might be a better choice than a cheap, imitation Oriental.

Carpets or rugs should be selected with the character of the house in mind. Since carpeting is a long-term purchase, try to choose a color and pattern that will not become dated during its life. Also, be sure to choose a color that will not fade in sunlight.

Versatility should be considered. For example, when selecting a floor covering for a small

Table 15-C.
RUG AND CARPET MATERIALS

Material	Advantages	Disadvantages
Wool	A natural fiber; resilient and long-lasting; many attractive colors	Must be moth-proofed; wide price range
Nylon	Durable, easy to maintain; resilient	Can create static electricity
Acrylic	Wool-like; easy to clean	Must be treated for flame resistance
Olefin	Low cost; includes the indoor-outdoor variety	
Polyester	Low cost; easy to clean; multiple use	
Grasses	Especially suitable for warm climates; natural fibers	Not especially durable

apartment, keep in mind that you might move to a house or larger apartment. Two small rugs might be used in separate rooms in a small apartment, and later combined in one large room.

Small rugs or carpets may also be used to define activities. For example, in a studio apartment, a small rug under a dining table and another one in the living area would tend to separate the activities. This would make the apartment appear as two rooms.

Special needs dictated by location should also be considered. If one or two areas in a room will get extremely hard wear, it might be well to select small rugs rather than wall-to-wall carpeting. Worn areas in wall-to-wall carpeting might mean the entire room must be recarpeted but the small rugs could be replaced as required.

If you live in an apartment or buy a home already carpeted, you may have to make do with the carpeting since to replace it can be expensive. Oftentimes a decorative scheme can be carried out using the carpet color as a base.

In order to save the carpeting in the mobile home in Fig. 15-21A and B, rust was chosen as the basic color. What was done to change the color of the walls?

LIGHT

Light is also an important tool in decorating. Different types of lights vary in color. The color of light affects the apparent color of fabrics, wood, and other surface materials. For example, a green sofa under a light which has yellow tones will appear to be yellow-green. Light may be focused to highlight decorative objects, to "wash" walls, and to accent window treatments or planting.

Lighting may assist in creating moods. For example, a room with low illumination, such as candlelight, creates a party mood. Good general illumination provides a business-like atmosphere. A small area of light is intimate and friendly; large areas of light are more impersonal.

Lamps and light fixtures should complement the style of the furnishings in the room. How do the lamps differ in Fig. 15-21A and B? However, this should not influence you to select a lamp which might not give the correct amount of light. Chandeliers, lamps, and other fixtures come in a wide variety of sizes, colors, and shapes. They can be selected to complement any decorative theme and also to provide good light.

A

15-21. A room redesigned around carpeting color.

B

Planning Good Lighting

Good lighting results from both the quantity and quality of the light. Sewing, reading, and some hobbies require focal light. **Focal light** is concentrated on a spot which requires a higher level of illumination. Fig. 15-22 shows the use of focal lights to illuminate entryway mirrors and to highlight a display shelf.

A home should have an adequate supply of lamps so they can be permanently placed. There should be no need to shift a lamp from one area to another to achieve good lighting.

Most utility companies have lighting consultants who can recommend minimum light levels for various tasks. Lists of recommended levels have been published by the U.S. Department of Agriculture, by the Illuminating Engineering Society, and by manufacturers of lighting equipment. These lists may be used as guides. However, keep in mind that each situation may differ. The reflecting quality and color of the surface to be lighted as well as the color of the surrounding area will affect the lighting. For example, a lamp with bulbs totaling 150 to 200 watts should supply ample study light. However,

if a student is working in a room which has dark walls, dark furniture, and little or no general light, the one lamp may be inadequate.

The light in any room may be improved by rewiring and by adding new fixtures. However, lighting may also be improved without this additional cost. When the surfaces of a room have high reflective qualities, light is increased. Paint the walls and ceiling white or a light color to increase the usable light. Keep the fixtures clean so that all of the light available shines through. Never put fixtures or bulbs into water; never screw a wet bulb into a socket; never touch a hot bulb with a damp cloth.

Types of Lamps and Light Fixtures

Incandescent bulbs are available in many sizes made of clear or opaque glass and in assorted colors. Sometimes part of the globe is covered with metallic reflective coatings. Incandescent bulbs also come in decorative shapes designed to be used without shades, and in clear shapes which resemble a candle flame. The flame-like bulbs are designed to be used in sconces and chandeliers.

Since the temperature of the bulbs rises when lighted, this must be considered when selecting shades or covers. Space must be allowed for air to circulate around the bulb. Fabric shades that come too close to the bulb may burn.

Fluorescent tubes produce three or four times as much light as an incandescent bulb of the same wattage. Fluorescent light is "colder," both in color and temperature than an incandescent light of the same size. The "coldness" or bluish appearance may be avoided by selecting one labeled "warm white."

Fluorescent tubes come in several colors. All may provide adequate light for visual needs, but the decorative effect may vary drastically. It is

American Plywood Association
15-22. These ceiling fixtures provide focal light.

15-23. Tiffany shades give this room character. Note the bases are different.

wise to check the effect of all lights on the colors in the room where they will be used.

In a lamp, the quality and quantity of light is determined by bulb size, the placement of the bulb, and the size and type of shade, if there is one.

Exposed bulbs are one of the most common causes of glare. All lamps and fixtures should be shaded or placed so that the bulbs are hidden from view. Occasionally, special bulbs designed for use without shades may be selected. Light reflecting from a shiny surface produces indirect glare, so care should be used in placing lamps.

It is desirable to have a shade which is slightly translucent to avoid uncomfortable brightness. The shade will reflect the most light if the inside is white and has a smooth but not shiny surface. Shades are usually considered part of the decorative scheme, as in Fig. 15-23.

Table and floor lamps are generally used to provide focal light. They are also used along with lighting fixtures and structural lights to provide general lighting. Many combinations may be made to provide the light needed for good sight and the desired decorative effect.

Correct lamp height is determined by the eye

level of the user. The lower edge of the shade should be at the eye level of the person using the lamp. When a floor lamp is correctly placed, the light will come from behind the shoulder of the reader. The lamp may be either to the right or to the left of, but not directly behind the chair.

When shopping for a lamp to be used for reading and study, look for the tag which states, "This is a Better Light, Better Sight Bureau Study Lamp." These improved lamps give the maximum of glare-free light. When correctly placed, they provide excellent light.

Fixtures are generally attached to the wall or hung from the ceiling, as in Fig. 15-22. Many kinds are available. Fixtures should harmonize with the surroundings, provide an inconspicuous but adequate source of light, and be safe.

Structural lights are built into the room and include valance, cornice, cove, soffit, bracket, ceiling, and wall lights.

Valance lighting is located near the ceiling. A valance is open at the top and bottom and is generally placed above the draperies. The light, placed behind the valance, shines down over the drapery or wall and is also directed toward the ceiling.

A **cornice light** is mounted on the wall at ceiling height. It is closed at the top so it directs light downward. Cornice lights are used to highlight pictures, drapery, and wall hangings.

Cove lights are attached to the wall near the ceiling. They are directed toward the ceiling and reflected by the ceiling to the room below.

Soffit lighting is used in areas over sinks and cabinets or to light a bathroom mirror.

A **bracket light** is similar to a valance light except that it is located on the wall at a lower level than ceiling height. Many types of brackets which are complete, self-contained units are available. They may be used for general lighting, over a sofa or bed, or to highlight wall decorations.

ACCESSORIES

Accessories contribute to successful interior design. Accessories commonly used on the wall include pictures, wall hangings, mirrors, sconces, or such decorative items as wood carvings or framed collections or trophies.

Tables and mantels offer places to display favorite decorative objects such as candlesticks, bowls, vases, or sculpture.

Plants and flowers complement most color schemes.

Accessories are an important part of the total appearance of most rooms, and the principles of design and color should apply to their use. Small objects show off more effectively if they are not crowded. A room may appear confused and cluttered if many things are scattered about. It is usually more effective to arrange them in some sort of order or grouping, so the small items count as a unit.

Case Problem A

Joe and Lynn Sanchez are both lawyers. They've purchased the condominium in Fig. 15-24. They entertain clients in their home so they need the large dining room. They intend to use the second bedroom as a home office and must arrange it to accommodate two desks which measure 750 × 1500 mm (2½ × 5 ft.). The only other piece of furniture they will bring with them is a king-size bed.

The condominium is located in an area where much of the natural environment is preserved. Owners may enjoy bike trails, canoeing, and nature walks. Balconies and windows are placed to take advantage of the view. Both Joe and Lynn enjoy the outdoors and intend to use furniture which will reflect this interest. They will also have many plants. Plan a furnishing and decorating scheme for them.

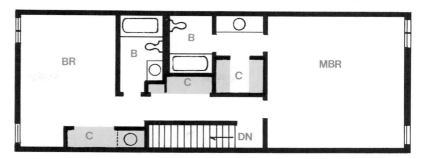

SECOND FLOOR

15-24. Illustration for Case Problem A.

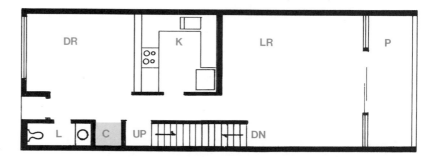

FIRST FLOOR

395

Pretend that you are decorating your first apartment, shown in Fig. 15-25, which you will furnish to suit your own taste.

This is a studio apartment with a living area that is used as a combination living-dining room and bedroom.

All of the walls and ceilings are painted off-white except for the tiled wall in the bathroom. The wall-to-wall carpet in the living room is avocado green.

The small kitchen has walnut cabinets, avocado green appliances, and beige vinyl floor tile. It is equipped with a range, refrigerator, sink, and garbage disposer.

The bathroom has beige and white ceramic tile floors, with walls tiled five feet up from the floor. The bathroom fixtures are a deep beige. The dressing area has the same beige vinyl floor tile as the kitchen.

The lease states that you may change the color of the walls, but when you move you must pay for the cost of repainting the walls their original color. If you install paneling or any other material on the walls, you must pay for the cost of having it removed. You must also provide your own draperies which must be lined in white.

Draw the apartment to scale, including the elevations.

Study the features of the floor plan. Note that there is a large floor-to-ceiling window on the terrace side of the room. Below the window is a low radiator. Next to the window is a sliding glass door which permits you to go out on the terrace. Note the irregularities in the living room walls. There is a pass window between the kitchen and the living room. How will these features affect your furniture arrangement?

How will the color limitations influence your color scheme now and in the future? Would it be worth the cost of having the walls painted twice (now and when you move) to get a more harmonious color scheme? Why do you suppose that many apartments have walls painted off-white? Can you think of color schemes that would not harmonize with the avocado green carpet? What, if anything, could you do about a wall-to-wall carpet if the color were not part of your preferred color scheme?

Furnish this apartment on a low or medium-low budget.

A tiny apartment such as this one calls for multiple-use furniture. However, you will want to select furniture that will be usable in future homes, too.

Study the plan and analyze your activities. Where will you eat? What kind of a bed will you have? Will you have enough seating space when you entertain? Think in terms of your present and future needs.

Decide on the furniture you will need. Make templates for the furniture and develop a suitable arrangement. Make up a color scheme. Make a shopping list, and secure at least two prices for each piece of furniture and any other items you will need. Don't forget items such as bed linens, towels, and cleaning equipment.

Summarize your ideas for the room as follows:

• Describe the orientation of the room. What direction does it face? What kind of a view does it have?

• Describe your activities, and style and color preferences.

• On the scale floor plan and elevations, draw the final furniture arrangement you have selected. Give your reasons for selecting each piece of furniture.

(Continued)

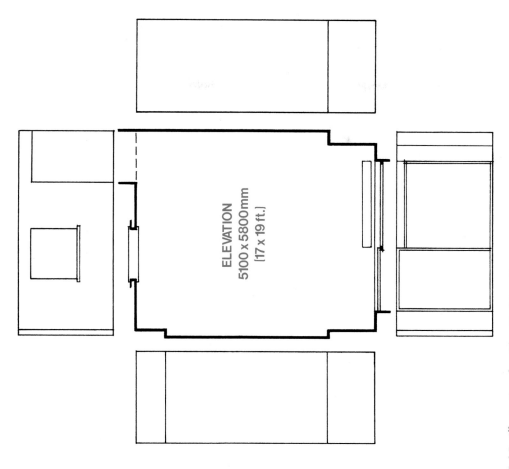

ELEVATION
5100 x 5800mm
[17 x 19 ft.]

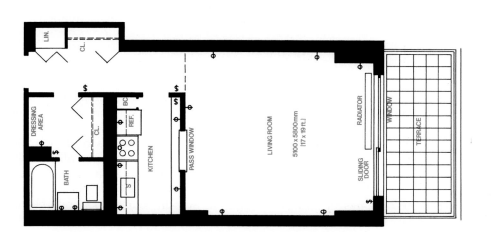

15-25. Illustration for Case Problem B.

**Case
Problem
C**

• From the shopping list, make a list of the final items you would want to buy. Classify them as *Essential, Nice But Not Necessary, Luxury.* Give your reasons. Did you stay within your budget?

• Describe your decorating theme. Why did you select it and how does it relate to your future plans?

• Make up a color plan, showing samples of colors and fabrics you will use for all areas (see Chapter 2). Why did you select this color scheme? Were you handicapped or helped by the colors already in the apartment?

• What have you learned from the case problem that will help you when you are ready to furnish your own home?

A C T I V I T I E S

1. Make a collection of pictures showing nontraditional furniture. For example, baskets used for storage or seats, sewer tiles for end tables, or cushions used as chairs.

2. Selecting and furnishing an apartment involves compromises. Choose a partner. Assume that you will be roommates for one year or longer, and that you will share the apartment in Fig. 15-11A. Study the plan together and decide how you would buy and arrange furnishings to provide for your separate interests. List or make a sketch of the major pieces and tell where they will be placed. How will you decorate? The landlord will allow you to paint or paper the walls. You must buy your own curtains or draperies. Could you arrange this apartment so that it would be satisfactory for both of you? If not, explain.

3. Visit the model rooms in a large furniture store. Describe several decorative details which might be used in a small apartment. Did you see any features which might be used in a room at home? Describe them.

4. Visit the lobby of an airport, hotel, motel, or other public building. Write a brief description of the atmosphere that the decorator created. Did you see any features which you consider to be less than successful? For example, a floor covering which was an interesting color but which showed dirt badly. What features did you especially like?

5. Study the home sewing sections in the collection of pattern books of a fabric store. List and describe the home sewing projects that you find most appealing. How could one of them be used in a decorating plan for a room in your present home?

6. From your library or local utility company, secure a copy of the recommended lighting levels for visual tasks. If you were to improve the lighting in your home, what changes would you make?

7. Visit a lamp display in a department store. Observe the designs in lamps and fixtures. Do any vary greatly from the standard design associated with lighting? Has lighting quality been sacrificed because of design? Discuss in class.

8. Make up a bulletin board display showing the latest window treatments featured in home decorating magazines. Would it be possible for you to duplicate these window treatments? Discuss in class.

9. You might wish to collect samples of carpeting made from each of the major fibers. Experiment with removing different stains from each one and test a small sample of each for flammability. A comparison of different-priced samples of the same type of carpeting will also help you to judge quality. If small doormat-size samples can be obtained, it might be interesting to tape them down in a high traffic area in your school and observe their wearing qualities.

16

When You Buy a Home

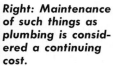

Far left: Homes with custom-designed features, such as the built-in tub, are usually more expensive. (Armstrong Cork Company)

Left: In this bath, other expense was kept to a minimum by the clever use of wall coverings and accessories.

Right: Maintenance of such things as plumbing is considered a continuing cost.

The type of home—whether it be a custom-built house, a used house, a mobile home, or a condominium—is one factor determining price. But the costs of home ownership involve more than the initial cost. They include, in addition to the down payment, the closing costs of the purchase. They also include continuing costs such as mortgage payments, interest on the mortgage, taxes, maintenance, and repairs.

Look through the "Homes for Sale" classified ads in your local newspaper and notice the wide range of prices, perhaps from several thousand dollars to several hundred thousand dollars. What causes this great variation in

Terms To Know

abstract of title	graduated payment
appraisers	mortgage
assessed valuation	interest
assessment	market value
bid	mortgages
closing costs	passing title
collateral	principal
continuing costs	right-of-way
conventional loan	setback
deed	site plan
easement	VA loans
FHA loans	

prices? Unlike most other consumer products, homes have no specific standards that can be used to determine prices. They differ in style, location, design, and features, and they differ just as much in price. Even two similar homes in the same neighborhood may vary greatly in price.

As we discuss prices, keep in mind that, while the price is an important gauge of value, it is not the only gauge. The value of a home to you depends on how it is suited to your needs and how much you are willing to pay for it.

Since the majority of people prefer living in single-family houses; this chapter will discuss those in greater detail.

CONDITIONS THAT AFFECT PRICES

Essentially, a house is a shelter, an enclosure. In the United States, because of the temperate climate, a house usually consists of a floor, walls, and a roof. It needs doors for entry and exit and windows for light and ventilation. Generally, a house is divided into specialized living areas such as food preparation and eating, social, rest, and hygiene. In this society, a house

Compix

16-1. This home made of foam sprayed over plastic balloons may not be suitable for everyone.

16-2. This home is easy to enlarge.

must also have plumbing, wiring, and in most areas of the country, heating.

The features of a basic house are affected or modified by any number of conditions, which influence the price of the house.

● **Climate.** Some types of construction are more expensive than others. For example, in areas with regular seasons of cold weather, the frame of the house and the roof must be strong enough to support the weight of heavy snow. Roofs are usually sloped so that snow and ice slide off. Foundations must extend below the deepest penetration of frost to avoid damage from freezing. This adds to the cost. Insulation and expensive heating systems are also needed. If the heating system uses oil or gas as a fuel, a chimney is required to get rid of the products of combustion.

In warmer climates such as in the south, the heating system may be simple and inexpensive. Footings may be placed only 450 mm (18 in.) deep and still be safe because the ground does not freeze. But in warm climates air conditioning may be desirable.

In hurricane or high-wind areas, mobile homes and house roofs may require cables to anchor them to the ground. Bad weather may delay building activities, which in turn adds to the construction cost. For example, in the north frozen soil could delay excavating a foundation or installing underground facilities.

● **Design.** Generally, it takes no more material to build an attractive house than an ugly one of the same size. However, good design in a house requires the talents of an architect, which adds to the initial cost of building. Good

design also may make a ready-built or older home more desirable and may increase its value because of the willingness of people to pay more for an attractive home. Some styles, too, are more acceptable than others. For example, in some areas a contemporary house may be more difficult to sell and may result in a lower price, Fig. 16-1.

A house which cannot be altered economically may be more difficult to sell. The house shown in Fig. 16-2 is an example of a style that lends itself to change. Note the new unpainted portion. The attic was not useful because of the steep slope of the roof. The roof was raised as shown by the new construction to create a more usable second floor.

Lending agencies tend to be conservative in their judgment of architectural style. Since the value of a house is determined partly by the price a buyer will pay, the lender is apt to look with greatest favor on a design which has wide appeal. If a proposed design is too advanced or experimental, financing may be more costly to the owner.

● **Location. Appraisers** are people professionally trained to estimate the value of a house.

Royal Berry Wills and Assoc.
16-3. A beautiful site adds to the value of a home.

Appraisers say that the three most important features which determine value are: 1. Location. 2. Location. 3. Location!

Many factors determine the value of a location. Its desirability as a residential area, its closeness to public transportation and shopping, the appearance and maintenance of homes in the area, the quality of the school system, and the distance from industrial or commercial areas. Two houses of equal value will be priced differently if one is in a desirable residential location and the other in a deteriorating area.

The location of the house in Fig. 16-3 affects its value. Although the house itself would still be attractive on a barren site, the large trees and stone wall enhance its appearance and make it more valuable.

● **A new buyer's changes.** When purchasing an older home, the buyer may want to make major changes in some of the features. For example, the kitchen and bathroom may have to be updated. Perhaps a dismal basement may be turned into an attractive recreation room. The costs of these changes add to the price of the house.

Expensive changes may occur in new houses, too. Often, when building a house, an owner is unable to imagine the completed home by just looking at the floor plans. Only after construction has started does the owner realize that changes will have to be made. Orders for materials and equipment may have to be cancelled, sometimes for a fee. Completed work may have to be removed and replaced; plumbing and wiring may have to be relocated. Such changes greatly increase the initial cost of the house.

● **Individual preference.** Most people want to express their own individuality. This desire to

be different may add to the cost of the home, Fig. 16-4.

For example, let's compare two older homes in the same neighborhood. Both have five rooms, a bath, a basement, and a two-car garage. One is an average house with no extra features. The other house has parquet floors, a tiled fireplace, built-in walnut china cabinets and book cases, marble sink tops, and built-in cedar closets. A buyer with a personal preference for these features would be willing to pay the higher price asked for this house.

The same may apply to new construction. For example, two six-room houses built in the same area look somewhat alike from the outside, but one cost $37,000 to build and the other $57,000. What caused the price difference? The owner of the $57,000 home specified

Armstrong Cork Company
16-4. The owner of this home wanted counter dividers installed, which added to the cost of construction. Is it a feature you would want? Why?

custom-built kitchen cabinets with built-in deluxe appliances and a fireplace in the family room as well as in the living room. In addition, the living and dining room walls were paneled in expensive imported wood. An entertainment center was built into the family room with television, stereo, book shelves, and storage. None of these features interested the neighbor who built the $37,000 house.

Generally, it is more economical to build a house of materials that are readily available. However, if the buyer wants to use unusual materials, such as rare woods that have to be special-ordered, the cost of the house will increase.

● **Labor costs.** Labor costs represent a large portion of the total cost of constructing a new house. Often there are ten or more trades involved in house construction—plumbers, electricians, carpenters, tile setters, plasterers, heating and air conditioning specialists, painters, flooring contractors, brick masons, and roofers.

How a builder plans a project to make efficient use of labor has an important bearing on the cost of construction.

● **Zoning regulations and building codes.** A builder may be required by zoning to pay for street paving, sidewalks, and underground electric power service before being permitted to construct a house; the cost must be added to the price of the house. Or zoning may require an excessive **setback,** the distance from the building to the property lines, resulting in a large and often costly lot size. Often, a building code is so worded that it will unintentionally prevent the use of new materials or new construction methods that might result in lower costs.

Zoning regulations and building codes vary from town to town as well as in different parts of the country.

● **Taxes and assessments.** It is almost impossible to determine the effect of taxes on the cost of construction. Taxes make up a part of the cost of every piece of material and equipment and every hour of labor required to build a

house. The builder also pays for building permits and other fees required during construction. All of these taxes are passed on to the buyer and represent a sizeable percentage of the total building cost.

Once the house is completed, the buyer will be obliged to pay a yearly property tax to the city or town based on the assessed property valuation. The **assessed valuation** is the value of the property as determined by the locality for tax purposes. It differs from **market value,** which is the amount the property will bring when sold. While the property tax does not add to the initial price of the house it may affect the price an owner can get when the house is for sale. If the property tax is high the owner may have difficulty in finding a buyer willing to pay this tax. A lower price may have to be accepted by the owner in order to make a sale.

Before investing in a particular area, learn what your tax obligations will be. High taxes also contribute to high rents, and in some cities landlords' tax costs are listed by them as separate items on rental bills to make tenants aware of increases. High taxes may also result in higher prices of items in stores. Taxes generally reduce your ability to meet other living expenses. Therefore you have two choices—either cut expenditures so that enough can be budgeted for taxes, or avoid locating in areas where taxes are high.

Assessments, too, add to the cost of owning a house and may affect the price. An **assessment** is a charge made to the owner by a locality for the owner's share of the cost of an improvement such as widening a street or installing new sewers.

● **Economic conditions.** When inflation occurs, real estate traditionally increases in value, and construction costs rise. During the inflation of the 1970's house prices rose by about 10% each year. During a period of deflation, real estate prices and construction costs decrease as a rule.

A period of high employment and good wages can bring a demand for housing that ex-

PPG Industries
16-5. The solar heating system installed in this home was more expensive initially, but will save a great deal in fuel costs.

ceeds the supply. When this happens, house prices tend to go up. When unemployment occurs such as during a long strike that may affect many industries, local house prices may go down.

Too, economic conditions generally vary from area to area. Industrial areas with high employment usually have greater housing costs because of the relatively higher wages, labor shortages, and increased construction costs. Areas that are not industrialized or that have little commerical activity may have more unemployment and a greater labor supply. Consequently, house prices may be lower.

● **Utilities.** The cost of utilities may make one house more expensive than another of similar design. For example, it generally costs less to connect to a sanitary sewer than to install a septic tank and leaching field. It may be more economical to connect to a locality's water main than to drill a deep well for water. Underground electric power lines are generally more expensive than those running overhead. One type of heating system may be more expensive to install than another.

The fuel selected for heating and cooking may also indirectly affect the price of the house. In different parts of the country one fuel may be cheaper to use than another, Fig. 16-5. If a house uses the more expensive fuel, a prospective buyer may take this into consideration and offer less than the seller is asking.

● **How much the buyer is willing to pay.** The final and most important influence in determining the price of a house is what a buyer is willing to pay for it. If a house has features that

appeal to a number of buyers, the owner will naturally sell to the one who will meet the price or come closest to it. On the other hand, if a house is not attractive, is out of date, or does not have any outstanding features, it will appeal to fewer people. The owner may have to lower the price to compensate for the disadvantages.

Let's take as an example an older home offered for sale in a well-established, well-maintained neighborhood. A supermarket and shopping center had recently been built about a block from this house. The owner asked what was considered to be a fair price for the home.

Several young couples with small children were interested in the house itself, but they felt that because of the nearness of the shopping area the traffic would be unusually heavy and dangerous to the children. A few couples who had no children thought that the nearby shopping area might be too noisy.

A retired couple also looked at the house; they had been forced to sell their home because an expressway was to be built in their locality. They not only liked the well-established neighborhood, but they also had several close friends living in the area. Since the couple did not own a car, they were happy to find a location within walking distance of a shopping center. Unfortunately, they lived on a fixed income and could not meet the owner's price. However, they made a reasonable offer. After a period of time, because no other offer had been made, the owner finally decided to sell to the retired couple at the price they were willing to pay.

THE TYPE OF HOME
The Used House

Should you buy a house that needs remodeling? Since there are many unknowns in remodeling, obtain accurate estimates for all that needs to be done. Plumbing, wiring, and heating equipment may be out of date in an older house. Add the cost of all the changes to the purchase price. Then compare the value of the finished building with the cost of new construction or a used home in better condition. Will the finished house be worth the total cost? Also, the neighborhood must be evaluated. Are other homes being maintained or improved? Is the neighborhood attractive or is it degenerating?

It is often easier to finance a new house than an old one. Smaller down payments and longer payment periods are generally available for new houses.

The Development House

Prices frequently go up after the area has been developed. The first owners may gain from the increased values if they choose an area which develops in a desirable fashion.

If buyers select a development house wisely, many uncertainties can be avoided. Usually, they can obtain a firm price before the work starts if one of the models is to be built for them. However, they should investigate the quality of the builder's work and reputation for living up to agreements. This type of building is highly competitive, so the cost per unit of area is usually low. The developer may offer financing or assistance in obtaining the financing.

However, construction costs may vary according to the type of construction. It is up to the buyers to decide whether they consider the price reasonable for the design and neighborhood.

Some developers offer the option of purchasing a partially finished house. The parts which

Mobile Homes Manufacturers Assn.
16-6. Although mobile homes are less expensive to buy, their resale value is low.

require the labor of experts are completed; but painting, interior finishes, completion of the second floor interior, planting, drives, and walks may be some of the areas left unfinished for an owner to do. The owners have the advantage of lower costs, but the disadvantage of living in an unfinished house if they do the work after they move in. If they prefer not to move in until completed, they have the cost of two homes, which may cancel out the savings usually made by buying an unfinished house.

The Custom-built House

The plans and specifications for a custom-built house are submitted to several reliable contractors for an independent written **bid,** or cost estimate, from each. To the selected bid are added the architect's fee, the cost of the land, and other extras such as the cost of building permits. This provides a total cost estimate before construction begins. Since the custom-built house is one of a kind and may call for many special features, the cost per square meter may be high.

Mobile Homes

Economy is one of the major advantages of mobile homes. They require little upkeep, and the purchase price is low. They are inexpensive to heat and maintain. For example, the mobile home shown in Fig. 16-6 was priced in 1979 between $22,000 and $25,000, depending on location. This includes shipping, assembly of the house, and hookup to water and power. Curtains, draperies, and carpets are included in the price of the mobile home. It is very important for the buyer to calculate the items which are and are not included in order to compare types of homes.

In some communities, the mobile home may be financed and sold as an automobile. This makes it possible for the buyer to avoid many of the complications of real estate taxes and costs. However, the value of a mobile home may depreciate rapidly since it is often considered to be an automobile. This means that the resale value

might be less than that of a comparable conventional house.

Insurance premiums for a policy on a mobile home may be higher than the same coverage for a conventional house because of differences in construction and greater suspectibility of mobile homes to wind and fire damage.

In the cost must be included moving by professional movers who will block and unblock the unit, mask the mirrors, tie down the furniture, stow loose items, and even pack the china. In order to move the unit themselves the owners would have to have it registered, equipped with brakes, lights and a hitch. They would also have to know highway requirements in every state through which they plan to move. For all practical purposes, mobile homes are really not very mobile.

Utilities and site rentals must also be taken into consideration. A mobile home may not be installed just anywhere. Land must be zoned to permit their use.

Co-op Apartments

The buyers own co-op apartments so of course do not pay rent. This does not mean that they live without costs, however. Like other home owners, they are responsible for taxes, maintenance, repairs, and all of the other costs that go with ownership. They pay a monthly amount, usually called a maintenance fee, to cover these costs. Someone is hired to manage the building and grounds and to arrange for necessary repairs and improvements.

Condominiums

Buying a condominium involves as many details as buying a house. The condominium owners pay a fee to cover the cost of maintenance. They also pay real estate taxes.

HOW TO JUDGE THE PRICE OF A HOUSE

How do you judge the price of a house? One way is to hire a professional appraiser to give an opinion of its value. Most buyers, however, want to make their own evaluations since personal taste affects their judgment of price.

Average Price Per Room

One way to compare several houses for sale in similar neighborhoods is to determine the average price of a room in each house. This gives a rough comparison of the houses on the basis of the price per room.

To use this method, total the number of rooms in each house. Features such as a garage, porch, hall, basement, patio, or swimming pool are counted as a "room."

Suppose you look at three houses, each of which has five rooms and a two-car garage, Table 16-A. House A costs $37,800 and has a basement. House B costs $46,800 and has a basement, a finished family room, and an outdoor patio. House C costs $50,000 and has a basement, a finished family room, a utility room with a completely furnished laundry and sewing area, and an outdoor patio. The average price per room for these three houses is estimated.

Of the three, the $50,000 house has the lowest cost per room while the $37,800 house has the highest. Perhaps House A is located on a beautifully landscaped lot, or the rooms are unusually large or designer decorated. In addition to the price per room, you will want to compare construction, room sizes, and storage space.

Construction Costs

A more accurate way to judge whether the price for a particular house is fair is on the basis of construction costs. When judging a house for sale, compare its cost to the cost of building it new. Construction costs tend to set the prices on all houses. When construction costs go up, the prices of all houses, new and old, tend to rise.

PURCHASING A HOUSE

Once you decide to purchase a particular house and are willing to pay the price that is asked, several important financial and legal steps must be taken.

Preliminary Steps

- **The agreement is signed.** A house may be purchased directly from the owner of the property or through a licensed real estate broker who represents the owner. When a buyer has made a firm offer to buy, and it has been accepted by the owner, they enter into an agreement which is sometimes known as contract of purchase, offer to buy, offer to sell or contract for sale. This is an important agreement because it is in writing and is therefore legally binding.

The agreement includes a description of the real estate and its legal location. It covers only real estate or real property, and not personal property. Real estate or real property includes land and anything attached to the land such as buildings, fences, and even the shrubbery. It also includes anything permanently attached to the buildings such as built-in storage cabinets. Anything that is not attached to the land or permanently attached to the buildings is considered personal property and is not affected by the sale. Furniture, a car, a boat, animals, and clothing are examples of personal property.

Fig. 16-7 shows both real and personal property. The buildings, fences, trees, and shrubbery are real property and will be included in the agreement if the land is sold. The horse is not fixed to the ground and is therefore considered personal property. If the owner wants to sell the horse, a completely separate sales agreement for the animal's purchase will have to be made.

The real estate sales agreement should clearly state the conditions of the sale and any exceptions.

The agreement should include the total price and the deposit that is to be paid. It should also state that the sale will be complete only if the seller has clear title to the property. The agreement should also set the time limits for payment of real estate taxes. Usually the seller pays taxes

Table 16-A.
AVERAGE PRICE PER ROOM

	No. Rooms	Garage	Extras	Total Rooms	Total Price	Price Per Room
House A	5	1	1	7	$37,800	$5,400
House B	5	1	3	9	$46,800	$5,200
House C	5	1	4	10	$50,000	$5,000

until the date of the sale and the buyer pays them for the balance of the year.

In addition, the agreement should describe any condition that affects the use of the land such as a right-of-way or an easement.

A **right-of-way** gives a person legal passage over another person's land. Fig. 16-8 shows an example of a right-of-way.

A new possibility for legal battles appears to be access to sunlight. For example, what would happen if a solar collector on the roof of one house were blocked from sunlight by the construction of a building next door? Laws in this country give landowners the right to obtain light from directly over their property but not across abutting land. The Ohio house shown in Fig. 16-9 obtains all of its heat from the sun. If a tall building were to shade the three collectors, a serious loss to the owners would result.

An **easement** is a limited, nonrevocable right given to a person or company to use property which belongs to someone else. For example, a

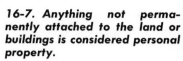

16-7. Anything not permanently attached to the land or buildings is considered personal property.

411

16-8. The road leading to the rear house actually belongs to the owner of the house in front.

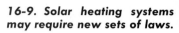

16-9. Solar heating systems may require new sets of laws.

16-10. Local governments often have easements for utilities.

utility company may have an easement to run a utility line through a person's property, as shown in Fig. 16-10.

- **A deposit is paid.** When the agreement is drawn up, a deposit or small down payment is made to indicate the intention of the prospective buyer to purchase the property. As a rule, the agreement states that the deposit will become a part of the purchase price.

- **The title search is made.** Before a real estate purchase can be legally completed, the seller's ownership of the property must be established. This is called a title search and is usually carried out by a lawyer who specializes in this work. The buyer pays for the title search.

The records of all previous sales, from the time the land was first obtained by grant from the government to the present, must be investigated. The search also reveals any outstanding debts against the owner which involve the property, and taxes and assessments that have not been paid. If there are such debts, the buyer should be sure the seller pays them before the sales transaction is completed. Otherwise, the buyer becomes responsible for these debts when assuming ownership of the property.

A clear title gives the owner full legal right to

use and control the property. The house shown in Fig. 16-11 is an example of what can happen when the title to a house is divided. One half is kept clean, painted, and in good repair by that owner. The other half is neglected. The value of the repaired part of the house is diminished because that owner does not have control of the entire house.

When the title search and the necessary investigation of ownership have been completed, a document known as an **abstract of title** is prepared. Technically, an abstract of title is no guarantee of ownership or that the title is clear or not clear. It is a true and faithful copy of all records covering the land in question, and it is up to the buyer and the buyer's attorney to evaluate those records. Quite often, a title is covered by title insurance which protects the buyer against financial loss caused by errors in the search.

The buyer should also have a licensed land surveyor establish the limits of the property and prepare a plot or **site plan.** This indicates the location of all boundaries and records the shape

16-11. The value of this house is affected by the owner who does not keep the property in repair.

of the property by giving dimensions of the sides and the angles formed at the corners. If this is done, future disagreements with neighbors may be avoided. An attorney should be retained to protect the buyer's interests in the transaction and to see that the papers are legally correct and complete and that costs are accurate. The attorney draws up the agreement and makes certain that the seller's deed complies with it. The attorney also checks the mortgage arrangements with the bank or other lender.

The Mortgage

Most people cannot accumulate enough money to pay cash for a house, so the majority of homes are purchased with **mortgages.** The buyer makes a down payment and borrows the balance. The buyer must determine the amount that can be safely put into the down payment, and the lender must determine the amount that will be loaned. The house is then held as **collateral,** or security on the loan.

New forms of mortgages which make buying easier may increase ownership. Owners now occupy over 63% of United States housing. That is the highest percentage in the world. The highest percentage of owner-occupied homes is in the middle-west. For example, in Indiana and Iowa over 70% of homes are owner-occupied. **Graduated payment mortgages** are designed to appeal to young buyers. Lower monthly payments during the first five years are required than with fixed payment mortgages. At present a 10% down payment is necessary and a number of states require monthly payments which cover the interest portion of the loan.

The amount a person may borrow depends on what the lender thinks the house is worth and what the lender believes the borrower will be able to repay. A lender generally has an appraiser determine the property's worth. In deciding what a borrower can repay, the lender evaluates such facts as credit record, age, income, and earning potential.

The borrower, or mortgagor, is generally required to make monthly payments. These payments reduce the principal and pay the interest and other charges. The **principal** is the total amount borrowed and the **interest** is the amount charged for the use of that money. A schedule is set up by the lender for repayment, depending on the length of time allowed to pay off the loan.

Investment laws may limit the amount of the loan that any bank can make. This is usually stated as a percentage of the total price of the house. These regulations change often so a borrower should learn what the loan limits are at the time of purchase.

The borrower should shop for the most favorable mortgage terms possible since there may be some variation in interest rates. Financial institutions such as savings and loan associations, life insurance companies, and commercial and mutual savings banks generally make mortgage loans. In some communities private individuals may also make loans.

Making arrangements for a mortgage may take several days or it may require several months. When the loan is assured, the borrower may safely sign the agreement and make the down payment.

There are three types of mortgage loans: conventional, FHA (Federal Housing Authority), and VA (Veterans Administration). VA loans are also called GI loans.

A **conventional loan** is a transaction between a borrower and a lending institution. The lending institution uses its own money at its own risk and must absorb any loss that may occur.

Conventional loans may contain a provision which enables the borrower to finance appliances along with the house. Since only two parties are involved, it may be possible to arrange a conventional loan in a relatively short time. The lender takes a greater risk when making a conventional loan since it is not insured. For this reason, the amount loaned may be smaller.

For those who can afford little or no down payment because of low income, special assistance is available. These include FHA and HUD loans. Information on these assistance payment programs is available from the agency involved or from most banks.

FHA loans are issued through the Federal Housing Authority, which insures the bank or other lending agency against any loss. The borrower pays for this insurance, which is collected by the lender and passed on to the government. Since the lender is protected against loss, a higher percentage may be borrowed. FHA loans may run up to 35 years. Down payments are relatively low. The long payment period and small down payment make home ownership possible for many who could not qualify for conventional loans. If a borrower wishes an FHA loan, the lender will make arrangements for an FHA appraisal of the property, and FHA determines whether or not the loan is to be granted.

VA loans may be made to any person who has served 90 days or more in active military service and has been discharged or released under honorable conditions. Interest rates may be favorable compared to other loans. Veterans who are planning to purchase property should check the regulations governing VA loans to evaluate the advantages of this type of loan.

INTEREST RATES

Interest rates depend on economic conditions and on the number of people who wish to borrow. They are also regulated by state and federal rulings.

When you borrow money for a mortgage, you are really buying time. You are buying the privilege of paying for the house sometime in the future instead of now. For this privilege, you are charged a percentage or interest on the amount borrowed.

The more time you buy, the more it costs. For example, if you borrow $27,000 for 15 years you pay less than you will if you borrow the same amount for 25 years. A small down payment and long payment period is very ex-

Table 16-B.
COSTS OF A MORTGAGE LOAN

Original price of house	$45,000.00					
	Loan A			Loan B		
Down payment	$6,750.00			$18,000.00		
Total borrowed	$38,250.00			$27,000.00		
Interest rate	$9\frac{1}{4}\%$			$9\frac{1}{4}\%$		
Loan fees	$765.00			$540.00		
Length of mortgage	15	20	25	15	20	25
Monthly payment (Principal and interest)	$412.18	$369.15	$358.94	$277.89	$247.29	$231.23
Total interest paid on mortgage	$29,192.40	$43,596.00	$62,682.00	$5,020.20	$14,349.60	$24,369.00
Total cost of house	$74,192.40	$88,596.00	$107,682.00	$50,020.20	$59,349.60	$69,369.00

pensive. Note in Table 16-B that the largest amount borrowed ($38,250) for the longest time (25 years) cost $107,682, or more than twice the value of the house! The larger the down payment and the shorter the loan period, the lower the dollar cost. The table shows the importance of a large down payment as well as the importance of repaying a loan in as short a time as possible.

Based on a survey done by the National Association of Home Builders the national median price for a new home in 1978 was $45,000. While that sounds like a lot of money, median price means that half of all of the houses cost less than $45,000—some a lot less. Two-thirds of the new home buyers were buying with the money realized from the sale of a previous home. People buying their first home usually choose a cheaper house—a manufactured house, a mobile home, one of the so-called basic houses (no frills, perhaps some work still to be done by the owner), or a house on which the owner does work to hold the price within the budget.

Individuals and government agencies are developing other low-cost alternatives. For example, the Virginia Housing Development Authority has designed a two-story "stick-built" house to sell for around $20,000. The house is constructed at the site but it has been designed primarily for economy.

Buying a home is not easy but a study of incomes and prices reveals that it was even more difficult in the past. In 1900 the median price of a home was $4,881, but the median family income was only $490 per year. Then almost ten years of income was required to pay for a home. While the price of houses has increased there has also been a notable increase in income, making home ownership more possible today than at any time in history.

AFTER THE SALE
Transfer of Ownership

The transfer of ownership from seller to buyer is known as **passing title** or passing papers. The written document transferring ownership is known as a **deed.** The deed must be signed, delivered to the new owner, and recorded immediately in the proper government office as prescribed by state law.

Closing Costs

Closing costs involve the fees and charges made as part of the sales transaction. They may range from a few dollars to several hundred dollars. The buyer should get an estimate before the purchase. All of these costs must be paid at the time of the sale, so the buyer should be certain that money is available.

Closing costs may include all or most of the items on this list:
- Title search
- A survey to establish the boundary lines
- Mortgage application fee
- Legal fee for lender's attorney, which buyer pays
- Legal fee for buyer's attorney, Fig. 16-12
- Title insurance
- Fire insurance adjustment
- Property tax adjustment
- Mortgage tax
- Recording fees
- VA or FHA service charges, if these loans are used

Additional Costs

If an older home needs improvements or a new home needs completion before it can be lived in, the buyer must have money available.

The actual cost of moving is another expense involved in buying a house. Sometimes families rent a truck and do their own moving with the help of friends. However, if large amounts of furniture, heavy furniture and appliances, or valuable possessions such as antique or art collec-

tions are involved, the buyer would be wise to use a professional mover. A professional mover will give a cost estimate for the move and will also carry insurance on all the items. Since professional movers generally must be paid in cash when the furniture is delivered to its destination, the buyer should have enough money on hand to pay the bill.

When people move into another house, they generally wish they could buy new furniture, too. In some cases, however, new furnishings are a necessity, and these, too, should be considered as additional costs of buying a house. For example, a family living in an apartment that has a completely equipped kitchen may have to purchase a range and a refrigerator when they move into a house. Another family that has used a conveniently located laundromat may find that they have to purchase a washer and dryer when they move to an area with no laundromat facilities.

If the newly purchased house is far from public transportation, the family may have to purchase a second car.

The buyer of a house should take care to allow enough money for these additional expenses. Unfortunately, many buyers attempt to make as large a down payment as possible. As a result they find they are short of cash and unable to take care of some of these expenses.

Stock Boston/D. Kra & Hwohl
16-12. Because of the many legal matters involved, a home buyer must have an attorney.

CONTINUING COSTS

Continuing costs are those the homeowner must continue to pay until the debt or loan has been repaid and the house is sold. These costs include principal payments and interest, property taxes and assessments, property insurance, utilities (telephone, water, fuel, electricity), maintenance, repairs, and improvements.

Before purchasing a house, the buyer should itemize all of the continuing costs to make sure that monthly payments can be met. Unfortunately, failure to allow for these expenses has sometimes led to costly mistakes in the selection of housing.

Property Taxes and Assessments

A $60 tax rate applied to real estate valued at $25,000 would be $60 × 25 or $1,500 a year. And tax rates increase in times of general inflation. As you can see, the tax rate and the value of your property will have an important effect on your living cost.

Property Insurance

Many lending agencies require the home buyer to file a fire insurance policy with them. They also have the insurance company notify them if the borrower fails to make payments on the policy.

Fire insurance is available in a wide variety of policies. Generally, there are degrees of coverage from the most basic to a comprehensive all-risk policy. The cost of the policy depends on the coverage.

The standard home insurance policy covers only fire, smoke, and lightning damage and certain types of water damage.

Instead of this basic coverage most people prefer to protect themselves against loss by purchasing a broader policy. This contract is known by various names, such as "Homeowners Protection Plan," and includes coverage for such things as wind, hail, and smoke damage; explosions; civil disturbances; and theft.

Insurance coverage is so broad and so many different types of policies are available that a homeowner can get coverage for almost any combination of hazards.

The Homeowners Warranty Program (HOW) sponsored by the National Association of Home Builders (NAHB) is a program designed to provide the homeowner with ten years of insurance protection against major structural defects. Their definition of a major structural defect is damage to the load-bearing portion of the house, such as settling. This plan helps the buyer find reliable builders, provides for fair and speedy handling of disagreements over defects, and, since it can be transferred to another owner, it helps increase resale value. The HOW program is also available on condominiums and townhouses but not on mobile homes.

When selecting insurance, keep in mind the types of losses that might occur and the potential amount of the loss. If you try to insure against all possible risks, the cost may be so high that no funds are left for other purposes. Most people select basic coverage and add whatever additional coverage their budget permits and circumstances seem to require. The basic guide to purchasing any type of insurance is to guard against catastrophe. Most people can recover from small losses, but very few can afford large ones.

Utilities

Utilities include telephone, water, electricity, and fuel for cooking and heating. There may also be a service charge for the use of sanitary sewers or trash pick-up.

The major expense is usually fuel, such as gas, oil, or electricity for heating, and electricity for air conditioning. The cost to heat a house will depend on the size of the house, its construction, the type of insulation, and the efficiency of the heating system. Heating costs will be lower, of course, in a mild climate or where winters are short.

If the house is a new one and there is no record of the cost of heating, the fuel company can give an estimate. If the builders have constructed similar houses, they may have records available. If you are buying an older house, the owner or realtor may provide you with copies of fuel bills. Or you may secure the information from the utility company.

Maintenance, Repairs, and Remodeling

The cost of maintenance and repairs depends greatly on the condition of the house, the owners' pride and their ability to do the work without costly assistance. If many repairs are needed, it is wise to get estimated costs from painters, plumbers, and other tradespeople before purchasing the house. In ordinary houses that are in good condition, a maintenance and repair allowance of one to two percent of the price of the house is common. For example, on a $40,000 house this would be $400 to $800 a year. This amount would usually pay for paint and only minor repairs. It would not be suffi-

cient to also cover a major repair such as a new furnace or a new water heater.

Remember, however, that a dollar comparison is only one consideration. Your pleasure and satisfaction have value, also. To save interesting old structures is one of the most pressing and rewarding challenges facing communities today. Repair of the derelict house in a good neighborhood is often economically sound. However, money spent on a good house in a blighted area is very seldom good economy. Neighborhood improvement is very important.

Fig. 16-13 shows an example of successful remodeling. The large, one-family house was neglected and deteriorating. However, it was structurally sound and in a good neighborhood. The original floor plan was easily converted into an attractive two-family apartment. Now it is not only appealing in appearance, but it has also proven a wise investment for its owner.

Case Problem A

George and Lettie Harris have been married for four years and are expecting their first child. They live in an apartment but have decided to purchase a house. George is a plumber and Lettie is a bank teller, but she will leave her job shortly because of her pregnancy. Both George and Lettie come from large families. They have many close relatives living out of town, so they frequently have overnight and week-end guests.

George and Lettie have discussed their finances with their banker and with the real estate agent. They have finally located two houses that they can afford. Now they must select one to buy.

House A is a new, six-room ranch of frame construction. It has three bedrooms, one large and two small, all with large closets; an L-shaped living-dining area; a bath; and a kitchen equipped with range and refrigerator. There is no basement, but there is a utility room with a furnace and water heater and enough space for a washer and dryer. The house has an attached two-car garage and a small cement patio. The lot measures 15 × 43m (50 × 140 ft.). The house sells for $35,000.

House B is a 20-year-old Cape Cod of frame construction. It has two medium-sized bedrooms with small closets; a living room; a dining room; a bath; and a kitchen. The kitchen comes equipped with a fairly new range, but the owner is taking the refrigerator. There is an attic which can be remodeled into one large or two small rooms. The house has a divided basement with a finished family room in one half and a utility room in the other. The utility room has a furnace, a water heater,

(Continued)

16-13. Remodeling a structurally sound home can be a good investment.

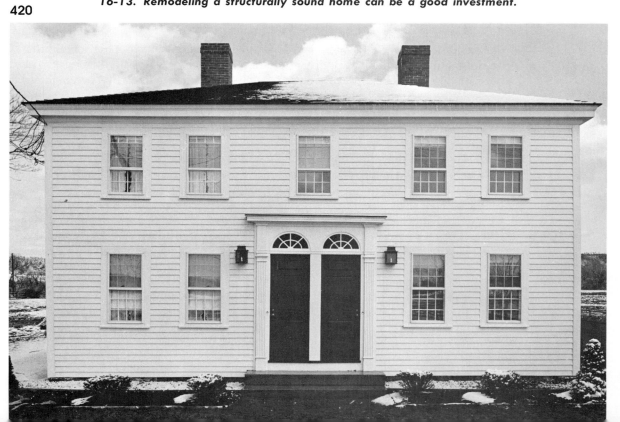

**Case
Problem
A**

and a completely furnished laundry center with an automatic washer and dryer. There is a one-car garage attached to the house with a breezeway. The lot is 24 × 43m (80 × 140 ft.). The house costs $32,500.

Use the cost-per-room method described in this chapter to evaluate both houses. What else will have to be considered in making the decision? Why? If you were George and Lettie, which house would you select? Why?

ACTIVITIES

1. Look at two or three houses for sale in one neighborhood. Select either all two-bedroom or three-bedroom houses. Using the cost-per-room method described in the preceding section, determine which of the houses is the best value for the money. If you were purchasing a house, which of these would you select and why?

2. Write a real estate advertisement offering the house or apartment building in which you live for sale. Limit the advertisement to 50 words. Think of all of the points you should mention. For example, you might include the style of architecture, location, size, amount of land, special features, and facts about the area. Look at some advertisements of property similar to yours. Do they include the price? Discuss the pros and cons of including each item. If the house needs some repairs, should you mention what is needed? Why?

3. Obtain information from a moving company regarding costs, local and long distance, and the type of insurance available. Find out about their rules, what obligations they assume, how they determine charges, and when the charges must be paid.

4. Make a collection of advertisements of houses for sale. Select all two-bedroom or all three-bedroom examples. Make a chart showing the price range. Discuss the reasons for the differences in price.

5. Find out the current interest rates charged by various lenders in your community.

6. Secure copies of forms such as a mortgage, deed, abstract of title, and loan application. Study and discuss these in class.

7. If you know people who have recently remodeled houses, ask them what prompted them to make the changes. Do they believe their investments were worthwhile?

8. Collect pictures of home improvement ideas and arrange them on a bulletin board.

17 Should You Buy or Rent?

Far left: When you own a home your color choices are unlimited. (Sterns and Foster)

Upper left: A used home usually costs less and can be remodeled.

Lower left: In these apartments the colorful awnings are provided. (Stock Boston/Elizabeth Hamlin)

Right: Mobile homes are less expensive to purchase but depreciate quickly. (Family Circle Magazine/Elyse Lewin and Vincent Lisanti)

Generally, a decision to either rent or buy a home is based on the amount of money you have to spend and on the economic and social advantages that are most important to you. The decision is a personal one that you will have to make for yourself. The ideal solution for one person may be a poor answer for another.

When making the decision, it is well to remember that what may be right in housing today may be wrong tomorrow. The housing market is changing. In some locations, it may be more advantageous to rent; in others, to buy. New methods of construction may make certain forms of housing more economical than others;

┌─ Terms To Know ──────────────────────

  equity

traditional styles may become old-fashioned. Huge apartment complexes may offer more advantages than a house.

Not too long ago, apartments were a small part of housing; most buildings were usually modest units for about eight or ten families. Today, apartments make up from 25 to 30% of all new housing units being built, according to the National Apartment Association. Huge apartment complexes house thousands of families. Small-scale furniture and appliances are specially designed for apartments.

An apartment in a converted building may lack some modern features, but it may offer advantages such as more space for the money. It might also be in a more convenient neighborhood.

A duplex house may provide many of the advantages of a single home for the tenant. The owner of a duplex may find the income from renting half of the house reduces the cost of housing and makes ownership possible.

Evaluate the advantages and disadvantages of buying and renting in light of your own needs and wants. Your final decision may not always be the most economical one. However, whether you choose to rent an apartment such as the one in Fig. 17-1 or buy a house such as the one in Fig. 17-2, your decision should be the most satisfactory solution for your needs.

THINGS TO CONSIDER

Perhaps the greatest single advantage to buying a home is that when you have finished paying for it, you own it. A renter owns nothing. A renter's monthly payments may be as much as those of a homeowner, but there is no return on the investment. There are, however, many economic and social factors to consider.

● **Inflation and deflation.** Many years ago, there was a belief that any kind of debt was undesirable; credit purchases were frowned upon. However, this attitude changed during the period of inflation that followed World War II.

Many people who borrowed money to buy

17-1. Are your lifestyle and budget best suited to an apartment?

Royal Berry Wills and Assoc.
17-2. Do you plan to own your own home someday?

homes after World War II profited by taking on this debt. The value of the dollar declined and long-term debts were paid off in dollars worth less than the dollars borrowed. In other words, if you borrow a dollar which is worth 100 cents and pay it back with one that is worth 50 or 60 cents, it is the same as borrowing 100 dollars and returning only half. In general, those who bought property during the past 35 years and kept it for at least five years before selling probably realized a profit due to inflation.

However, it is well to remember that the reverse may also be true. If there is deflation or a depression, the dollar does not lose value, but it may become increasingly hard to earn money. This situation could work a hardship on those who buy a house when prices and interest rates are high and who must pay off loans with money which has become hard to earn.

● **Return on the investment.** An increasing population and a limited amount of land tend to raise real estate values. Unlike other investments which suffer sudden and drastic fluctuations in value, changes in housing occur slowly. The alert owner may anticipate a trend before any serious loss occurs.

Too, homeowners are likely to take good care of their property. The person who is skillful in using a home workshop or in gardening may make many repairs and improvements. These may add value to the home.

Investment for profit is seldom a primary reason for purchasing a home. However, a home represents the largest single investment most people make. The equity built up through mortgage payments may be one of the family's major forms of savings **Equity** is the money the owner has paid on the mortgage after interest

425

17-3. Equity can be used to remodel or repair a home.

(and sometimes taxes) has been deducted from the payments, plus the down payment. The homeowner adds to the equity or savings with each monthly mortgage payment. If the house is sold the equity will be returned to the seller as cash.

However, it is well to remember that a house cannot always be turned into cash quickly. But if money is needed, it is generally possible to use the house as security for a loan. The homeowner in Fig. 17-3 used the equity as security on a loan to remodel the house.

- **Monthly costs.** The homeowner's monthly payments are based on the actual cost of the property. Most homes are purchased with borrowed funds. The payment period of these loans extends over long periods of time—15, 20, even 30 years. Once the terms of the mortgage are arranged, a person may estimate with some accuracy the monthly and yearly costs of housing for many years. Taxes may rise and there may be some increase in the cost of repairs, but these amounts can usually be anticipated. Therefore homeowners can be assured that their housing costs will not change much for many years.

Generally, a renter's monthly costs are lower than an owner's, comparing units that are similar in size, location, and features. The renter pays a monthly rent which the building's owner uses for maintenance, property insurance, and other costs. Rent increases can occur every year or so, and during periods of inflation, even oftener. Rents can also go down.

However, renters have control over the cost of housing subject to the terms of the lease. If expenses must be reduced or if they want a more luxurious apartment, renters can move.

- **Financial risk.** If a renter is offered a better job in another area and decides to move, it may be done with a minimum of expense. The homeowner, however, may have to buy a second house while the first remains unsold.

When a renter's income is suddenly reduced the solution may be to move to less expensive quarters. If a owner cannot meet mortgage and tax payments, the owner may have to sell at a loss or the property may be lost by foreclosure.

If a neighborhood deteriorates, a renter may move. An owner, however, may have to sell at a loss in order to move. If a home becomes outdated, the renter may move to more modern quarters while a homeowner is faced with the expensive task of remodeling. However, the seller of an older house may have purchased it when prices were lower and may sell it for less and still make a profit. The owner or builder of a new house may have paid so much for it that to reduce the price means losing money.

Many people feel a sense of security in owning a house, in having a place that they can call their own. They look forward to the years when the mortgage will be paid and their only housing expense will be taxes and maintenance costs.

- **Family size.** Budget demands in a family's first years mean that most cannot afford a good-sized 2 or 3 bedroom house. However, if a house is purchased which is comparable in size and cost to a small apartment, young buyers soon find it is not suitable for a growing family. They must sell and find a new home, a procedure which is not as simple as changing apartments.

Very few houses are designed to make enlargement reasonable or practical. The three-stage house shown in Fig. 17-4 is an exception. The basic house compares favorably in size and cost with an apartment and has been called "the home with a built-in future." A family room is one addition. Two bedrooms, one bath, and a storage loft make up another possible addition. In this house no load-bearing walls need be removed. No material need be wasted. For example, the kitchen window, which must come out when the family room is added, will be used elsewhere. The expanded house is planned so it will fit most standard-size lots. At each stage the house looks complete.

- **Taxes.** The homeowner has income tax advantages which result in cash savings because interest payments and local property taxes may be deducted from gross income in determining taxable income. If the house is sold at a profit, and another, more valuable, house is purchased

within a year, income tax need not be paid on the profit from the first house. If a homeowner over the age of 65 sells a house at a profit, this person may deduct some or all of the profit from income when calculating income taxes owed.

Taxes are more likely to be stable in established areas where the schools and utilities already exist. In some areas, property taxes are so high that they exceed the rent paid for similar housing. This is one of the reasons some retired people who live on fixed incomes are selling their houses and renting apartments.

- **Business and financial experience.** Owning their own home may give young people valuable experience in managing money and making business decisions.

Many credit agencies consider home ownership important when making credit recommendations. Since the homeowner must make monthly payments, a reputation for promptness and responsibility can be achieved.

Some homeowners spend a great deal of time and thought on the selection of materials and equipment for their houses. They discuss these problems with knowledgeable people and gain skill in buying. Often the homeowner becomes interested in the business decisions made by community officials, since these may affect local taxes and assessments. The value of real estate is affected favorably by good government. How tax money is spent on public services and educational facilities becomes of great importance to the owner.

- **Altering the property.** The homeowner may redecorate or remodel without asking permission from anyone. In Fig. 17-5, two homeowners cut plywood for a recreation room addition. Improvements to make a house more livable can add to its value, provided they are well done. Work you do yourself is less expensive since you save the cost of labor.

A renter may have to live with certain inconveniences which the building's owner does not want to change.

- **Maintenance and repairs.** Homeowners generally have more opportunity for developing

American Plywood Association

17-4. This home is specially designed for adding-on.

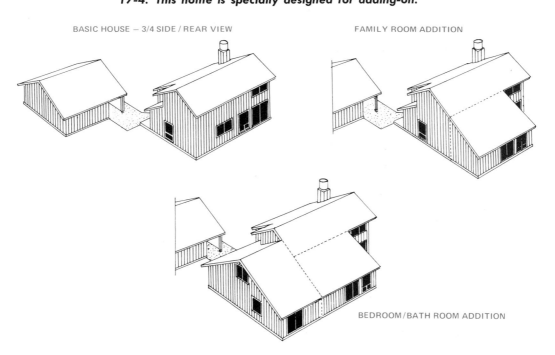

BASIC HOUSE – 3/4 SIDE / REAR VIEW

FAMILY ROOM ADDITION

BEDROOM/BATH ROOM ADDITION

creative activities and hobbies than renters. For example, a person with a creative flair may spend enjoyable hours refinishing furniture, painting walls, and achieving artistic effects in the house without concern for landlords or lease restrictions.

The garden work, painting, and other home repairs that one person looks upon as a hobby may be sheer drudgery to another. An apartment offers freedom from all of these tasks, allowing more time for leisure activities. Maintenance problems such as snow removal and lawn mowing are taken care of by the management. If the plumbing, the wiring, or a built-in appliance needs repairs, it is up to the management and not the tenant to have it serviced.

- **Recreation.** A house may provide extra space such as a basement, a family room, or

17-6. Few apartment renters can have a garden.

even part of a garage for creative activities, a workshop, or hobbies. A yard such as the one in Fig. 17-6 can be a great source of pleasure for an enthusiastic gardener. Children, too, can share in these activities and develop hobbies and interests of their own.

Many people enjoy chores that accompany home ownership such as mowing the lawn and shoveling snow because it gives them a chance to be outside and get exercise.

Many of the newer apartments have recreational facilities for the tenants. Some may have a tennis court and a club house or recreation room that tenants may use for social activities. Some of the larger apartment complexes may have a golf course, gymnasiums, indoor swimming pools, and even shopping facilities.

Many apartments, especially the larger ones, provide organized social activities. These include bridge parties, classes, exercise sessions, and social gatherings. Family-type apartment complexes may have day nurseries or baby sitter services.

- **Privacy.** Generally, except for emergencies, no one may enter a person's house without per-

World Wide Photos, Inc. (UPI)
17-5. Making changes is something homeowners can do when they choose.

mission. However, the manager may enter a rented apartment or house at reasonable times or in case of an emergency.

Some homeowners enjoy the freedom of being able to go outdoors into their own private yard whenever they want to relax or talk to neighbors. Others enjoy the freedom to entertain as many guests as they want whenever they like.

In an apartment, the closeness of neighbors sometimes limits the kind of entertainment. For instance, close neighbors would not want to hear loud parties late at night. This does not mean, of course, that home ownership gives a person the right to show disrespect for neighbors.

● **Safety.** Apartment buildings generally must conform to the safety standards established by local building codes. Some apartments also have additional safety features. These may include guards or janitors on duty day and night, and security locks on apartment and entry doors. Some may have closed circuit television cameras in the lobby that relay pictures of anyone in the lobby onto a television set located in the tenant's apartment. All of these extra precautions help a tenant to feel safer and to be less concerned about theft of personal property.

Home owners must take steps to insure the safety of their homes themselves.

● **Pride of ownership.** Some people appreciate the privilege of owning property. Perhaps they or their ancestors came from countries where home ownership was either forbidden or so difficult to attain that few were able to enjoy it. Owning a home gives them a sense of freedom and accomplishment which apartment living could never provide.

● **Community interest.** Since an owner is less likely than a renter to change residence, an owner may be more inclined than a renter to develop community interests. Neighbors are important since the homeowner knows they are likely to live nearby for a number of years.

Home ownership and social responsibility should go hand in hand, and a realization of this may be considered another benefit of home ownership.

● **Your work location.** A young person may change jobs several times before deciding on a career. Home ownership may restrict movement and limit the person's job opportunities.

Transportation problems in large urban areas are serious. During rush hours, even expressway traffic slows down. The homeowner who commutes long distances in heavy traffic and pays for parking must add this to the cost of a house in the suburbs. Those who cannot drive may find themselves isolated in a suburban location which has either limited public transportation or none at all. The tenant in a downtown apartment may save both the time and money usually spent in commuting.

Case Problem A

Lisa and Tony Gerardi have been married for five years and live in an apartment. They have no children. Tony has a fine job with an excellent future on the administrative staff of a large national firm. Promotions occasionally involve moving to another city. Lisa studied interior decorating. She does not work but is active in community affairs.

Lisa wants to buy a house; Tony does not. Lisa is bored with apartment living. She feels that a house would give her a creative outlet. She could decorate the house as she wished and add to her antique furniture collection. The apartment is too small for any more furniture. She could garden, which she enjoys. She also likes to give dinners for large groups and feels crowded in the small kitchen and dining area in the apartment.

Case Problem A

Tony is concerned that a house will tie them down. He enjoys the freedom of apartment living. He does not have to take care of chores such as mowing the lawn, shoveling snow, raking leaves, and doing minor house repairs. Instead, he has leisure time for his hobby of stamp collecting and for golf and fishing. He reasons, too, that if they buy a house he might not be able to take advantage of a future job offer that might involve a transfer. If they owned a house, it might be difficult for them to sell it, and they might lose money.

What solution would you offer for Tony and Lisa? Give reasons for your decision.

ACTIVITIES

1. Discuss this statement, "The advantages of home ownership are largely social and those of renting are economic." If you had to make a choice now, would you rent or buy? Why?

2. Visit an apartment for rent and a house of comparable size for sale. Compare all of the facts you are able to learn regarding the economic and social advantages of each.

3. List the social and economic advantages of home ownership *in your area* for a single person; a young, newly married couple; a couple with two school-age children; and a retired couple. In each case, which advantages do you think are most important?

4. Do you think that a young, newly married couple should buy a house if they can afford one? Give reasons for your answers.

18 How Much Can You Afford?

Far left: With careful shopping and attention to good design, even a handsome room such as this can be furnished at moderate cost. In 1981, the items in this room were priced as follows: sectional, $1000; side chairs, $100 each; coffee table, $200; cube table, $100; stack tables, $150; lamp, $150; rattan chest, $150; curtains, $150.

Left: The pillows are hand made. The dacron fill cost $6, the cover fabric $9. The plant was purchased at an auction for $25.

Right: The owner also made the wall hanging; cost of materials, $15.

THINGS TO CONSIDER

Although there may be a variety of housing available, its cost may restrict your choice and eliminate many of the possibilities. Your income is probably the most important guide to the amount you can safely spend on housing. However, your savings, debts, anticipated income, and family situation should also be considered.

● **Your income.** As a rule, the higher the income, the smaller the percentage of the total that is usually spent on housing. Payments for housing may range from as much as 35% in the lower to less than 13% in the upper income levels.

• **Savings.** The amount of savings or assets that you can turn into cash may affect your decision to rent or buy. Generally, a specific percentage is required as a down payment on a house. A 20% down payment on a $50,000 house requires $10,000 in cash.

It is advisable not to spend your last cent on a down payment. Some savings should be reserved for buying costs and for emergencies. If you do not have enough savings for a down payment and an emergency reserve, you would be wise to rent until you build up your savings.

• **Your debts.** When considering an application for a mortgage loan, lending agencies such as banks take into account the amount of debt you have compared with your savings. Therefore anyone with many bills and no savings generally cannot borrow the money needed to purchase a house. Most lending agencies have charts showing debt limits that families at different income levels can handle. However, the matter may best be discussed with a bank official who can advise you regarding financial matters.

• **Your financial potential.** In buying a home, you must be prepared to make a specific payment each month. This includes the mortgage, interest and property taxes, and insurance. In addition, there will be the cost of maintenance and repairs.

Before deciding to make a financial commitment that you must keep for many years, you will need to consider your financial potential. Do you have job security? Are there other job opportunities in the area? Do you have a job that calls for frequent moves? For example,

employees in some administrative training programs in large industries are expected to move to different cities as the jobs demand, Fig. 18-1. Such constant changes may cancel out some of the economic advantages of home ownership.

Your choice of career will also have great influence on the type of housing you select since a career often determines the income you can anticipate.

For many years lending agencies ignored the total income of the family. This rule has been relaxed and the income of two or more workers may be considered. Age is also less of a factor. Now one-third of all buyers are under 30 years of age, and one in eight is under 25. Singles represent 25% of all buyers in some parts of the country.

• **Your family situation.** People with families face many situations that will influence their choice in housing. They must consider the size of the family or the size they plan to have. There are greater financial obligations if the family is large—education, transportation, clothing, and possible illness. How old are the family members? It may be acceptable for a young, healthy family to assume a long-term debt. Would it be equally wise for older people who may not have many years of good health ahead of them? If a family has a member who is chronically ill and in need of costly medical care, they may not be able to spend as much on housing as their income level might suggest. Can you think of other situations when it might be unwise for a family to take on the burden of home ownership?

HOW TO ESTIMATE HOW MUCH TO SPEND

Once you have determined the limits you can safely spend on housing, you may want to compare them with the following traditional guides. Although your own personal finances, and not rigid rules, should dictate your final decision, these guides may help you to evaluate your own situation. Keep in mind, however, that in some locations housing costs have increased more rapidly than wages, and people have found that they must spend more for housing than the guides suggest.

These guides are based on the assumption that you will not increase spending in other areas such as purchasing a car or furniture or remodeling the house extensively.

- **A family may spend from 1.5 to 2.5 times their annual income on a house.** To follow this guideline, multiply your annual income by 1.5 and 2.5. For example, if you have an annual income of $12,000, you may spend from $18,000 ($12,000 × 1.5) to $30,000 ($12,000 × 2.5) for a house.

Under favorable conditions, if the family is young, healthy, and ambitious, the maximum may be safe. If, however, they are older, ill, or have uncertain job prospects, perhaps the low figure should be the guide.

- **A week's take-home pay equals a month's rent.** When deciding how much you can afford to spend on rent, this rule may be used as a guide. If your take home pay is $145 a week, then you should not pay more than $145 a month for an apartment. In many cities, however, it is almost impossible to find suitable low-cost apartments.

Frequently two people share an apartment and expenses. Then each of the two roommates may pay up to one week's wages for the rent. Thus, if the two people make $145 a week apiece, together they may spend $290 for housing.

- **A family can afford a house that costs 100 times a month's rent.** If you pay $200 a month in rent, your monthly budget will not change substantially if you purchase a house for $20,000 (100 × $200). If your rent is $350, then a house costing $35,000 will not increase your housing costs.

NEW FURNISHINGS

As prices vary greatly from home to home, they also vary in furnishings. For instance, a single square of vinyl floor tile can cost as little as $2, while the same size square of wood parquet

Stock Boston/Bohdon Hrynewych

18-1. This district manager has been transferred three times to different areas of the country.

can cost $50. A table lamp can cost from $25 to $600. Of course prices change all the time, and in recent years they have steadily gone up. Perhaps the best way to learn how much things cost is to visit all kinds of stores, from the least expensive to most expensive. But remember that price does not always indicate quality, Fig. 18-2. The price of an expensive brand-name item includes the cost of all the advertising which made the brand famous. Oftentimes a less well-known brand may contain the same quality of materials and workmanship but the price is less because less advertising was done.

Note the price of the furniture you like and measure the pieces so you can work them into the floor plan later. Also, begin to make a price list of the pieces you may need. Look at several brands so you will have the price information available when you begin to determine your budget limitation. Try to get two or more prices for each item you may want to buy. This is one way to stay within your budget limitations.

Prepare a shopping list. It helps you to know, before you make any purchases, whether or not all of the essential items are available in the desired colors and sizes. If you find that some are not available, you can revise your plan, and you will not have wasted money on unsuitable objects.

Making a Budget

After you have established what your housing costs will be, you must make your furnishings budget from what money is left. This is why it is wise to consider both together. You would not want to rent an expensive apartment and have nothing left with which to furnish it.

Generally, the money spent for furnishings amounts to one-half of one year's income. For instance, if you earn $12,000 a year, you would plan to spend $6,000 on furnishings. Of course you would not spend this money all at once, but over two or three years. Experts recommend that a person have about one-fourth of this amount available in cash to keep from having too many credit obligations.

THE AMOUNT SPENT ON EACH ROOM

One guideline for a home furnishings budget suggests the following approximate allowances: living room 40%, dining room 20%, master bedroom 25%, second bedroom 15%. However, your personal needs and life style should determine how much you spend and on what room.

The money spent on each room is usually divided in this way: furniture 65%, floor coverings 20%, window coverings 10%, pictures and other decorative items 5%. These percentages are approximate.

The size of the rooms and their number will influence how you adjust your budget. Also, if you can repair, refinish, or remodel furniture, make curtains and draperies, hang wallpaper, and paint, the amounts you spend will be affected.

A THREE-YEAR PLAN

Because furnishings are costly, they must be purchased over a period of time. Most people will want to buy the essential pieces first, and then the less essential. For instance, for your bedroom you might need a box spring and mattress, storage space such as a chest or dresser, a window covering, and a lamp if there's no ceiling light. Table 18-A shows a three-year buying plan which would be suitable for many people.

You are probably asking yourself, "Why not decide on a budget at the very beginning, before making plans?" If you have not prepared an overall plan, you may select items at random.

Fricks Reed Company

18-2. This wicker furniture is of good quality but still relatively inexpensive.

Table 18-A.
A THREE-YEAR BUYING PLAN

Room	First year	Second year	Third year
Living room	Sofa Side chair or easy chair Table for lamp Lamp or two Window covering Carpeting, if needed	Coffee table Occasional tables Draperies, if desired Additional lamps	Area rugs Desk Accessories
Dining room	Table Four chairs	Carpeting or rug Window covering Storage unit, such as sideboard	Draperies, if needed Extra chairs Accessories
Bedroom	Box spring and mattress Chest of drawers for each person Lamp, if needed Window covering	Mirror Lamps Floor covering Bedside table	Draperies, if needed Chair Accessories

Later as you can afford more, you may find that you have selected the wrong color or the wrong piece of furniture. For example, because a plan was not thought out, you may have two pieces of furniture that provide more drawer space than you need, while shelf space may be lacking.

Keep in mind, too, that it is costly to buy special items just for a home you may not occupy very long. Unless they are inexpensive and intended only for temporary use, the items you purchase should be adaptable to future homes—and this involves sound thinking and thorough planning.

Decide what your budget will allow. You know how much money you have and how much you will be able to spend. The logical approach is to put your plan on paper. Then determine if your plan is financially possible.

Using Credit

If, after careful planning, you do not have cash for a necessary item, the use of credit may be justified. There are many kinds of credit accounts. Careful comparisons should be made before making a choice. Remember that credit is a form of borrowing and you always pay for it. The payment may be in interest, usually a percentage of the amount loaned, or the goods will have been marked up to include the cost of the credit. True annual interest rates are limited by law; however, they may be very high.

When should credit be used? When the purchase of the item results in savings greater than the credit cost. For example, a new freezer or refrigerator may reduce food bills an amount greater than the cost of the credit. The purchase of a new sewing machine might result in savings in clothing cost. Credit might be used to take advantage of items on sale. However you must be sure savings are large enough to justify the use of credit. In some cases it might be advisable to use credit in order to keep cash for emergencies.

There are many types of charge accounts. It is important to investigate each and see which is best for you. Major retail stores generally offer some version of the following:

- **Thirty-day accounts.** Charges must be paid within thirty days and no interest is charged.
- **Budget charge accounts.** These have three to six month payment periods. One and one-half percent per month (which is 18% per year) is generally charged.
- **Revolving accounts.** Under these accounts charges up to a given amount are permitted each month. Interest rates of 12% to 18% are charged on the unpaid balance.
- **Installment-sales credit accounts.** These may cost from 12% to 42% annually, and fixed monthly payments are required. Their use is limited to major items such as appliances. Be sure to check the terms of this type of agreement. The rates may be as much as three to five times as high as the terms for loans of other types. There are other pitfalls to watch out for, such as a wage assignment clause which means the creditor can take part of your salary if you fail to pay. Another clause may make all payments due at one time if one payment is missed. The merchandise might be repossessed or taken back even though a number of payments have been made. Before using this type of credit you may wish to investigate some other loan options.

In addition to these credit plans, local banks and credit unions usually offer various kinds of small loans which could apply.

Consumer law requires the lender to disclose the following facts in writing—cash price, down payment, total amount financed, finance charges, annual percentage rate of finance charge, late charges, total payments and amounts of payments. Even so, contracts can be confusing and not to the advantage of some customers. Don't sign anything you haven't read or do not understand. Don't agree to any contract without comparing the cost of the credit as well as the cost of the merchandise.

Case Problem A

John and Anna Greenberg are planning to purchase an automatic dryer. Anna wants to buy it now on the installment plan. John wants to wait until they can pay cash. Their old machine has broken down and they are using a public laundromat. Which approach is most convenient? Which approach is cheapest? What factors would have to be considered in determining the advantages of each plan? Give reasons for your answers.

ACTIVITIES

1. Investigate the different charge plans available in four local department stores or other retail businesses. Make a list of them and then write what you think are their advantages and disadvantages.

2. Interview people in your community or members of your family to find out what problems they have with charge accounts. If possible bring sample billing statements and study them in class.

3. Go to your local credit bureau to find out how it operates and the type of information recorded. Find out how someone's inaccurate record can be changed.

4. If there is a commerical bank with a small-loan department in the town where you live arrange an interview with the manager and find out:
   - How a person's credit status is investigated.
   - What fees the bank charges in addition to the stated interest.
   - What the bank does if the borrower is late in making the required payments.

PART 6 CAREERS

19

Job Opportunities in Housing

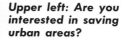

Far left: Are you creative? Would you enjoy redecorating this entry? (Armstrong Cork Company)

Upper left: Are you interested in saving urban areas?

Lower left: Do you like working outdoors? Perhaps construction work would appeal to you.

Right: Are you independent and do you like working on your own? You might want to own your own business.

Housing touches the lives of everyone. For this reason, it is a field which offers a great variety of career opportunities on the professional, semi-professional, and skilled trades levels. Some jobs require a college degree while others offer apprenticeship training. There are also many specialized training programs in vocational and trade schools as well as adult education courses.

HOW TO DECIDE ON A CAREER

The first step in establishing career objectives is not to think of any particular career but to

┌─Terms To Know────────────────

architect
architectural
    rendering
civil engineer
drafter
electrical engineer
housing manager
land developer
mechanical
    engineer

mortgage risk
    financer
property manager
real estate broker
research
structural
    engineer

begin by taking a serious look at yourself. You must clarify in your own mind the direction in which you want to go.

Certain personal characteristics are needed for success in some careers. What are yours? Are you enthusiastic? This is a requirement for most selling jobs. Have you a good health record? Some jobs are more physically demanding than others. For example, a realtor spends many hours driving and walking to show houses to prospective buyers or tenants. What special talents or skills do you have? For example, do you like to work with your hands? This would be an asset in many jobs in the construction field. Perhaps you have a good speaking voice. You might consider a career in real estate or as a consumer representative. Both jobs require the ability to speak well.

It is important to recognize your limitations as well as your skills. For example, engineering calls for an aptitude in mathematics. If you do not have this aptitude, look to other fields for a career choice. The important point is to build on your own strengths and aim for a job that calls for the talents you have.

If you are not sure what you would like to do as a career, consider what you like to do now.

The hobbies you pursue and the people and school classes you like may be clues to the type of job you would enjoy. If you especially enjoy courses in art, public speaking, and writing, you might consider writing a home furnishings column, promoting household equipment, working as an interior designer, or selling real estate. If you prefer painting or handicrafts, you might work as a carpenter, painter, or designer. Do you like chemistry? You might be interested in research work, looking for new materials for houses and furnishings. Do you enjoy meeting new people? Retailing or industrial sales might be the career for you. Would you prefer a job that helps others to improve their living conditions? You might consider a career in urban development or city planning. Do you like to have your work planned by others or do you prefer to set up your own guidelines? Would

Lawrence Eagle Tribune
19-1. Work-study programs can help you define your interests.

you be willing to take risks to make a profit? Have you the drive and independent spirit to succeed on your own? You must answer these and many more questions.

Taking advantage of a work study program while you are in school may help you test your interest and skills in a career area. In Fig. 19-1 students from a vocational-technical high school carpentry department are shown building a house. Proceeds from the sale of this house will be used to finance the next house. Each student has an opportunity for work experience.

Setting Goals

What do you want to accomplish? When you establish long-term goals, it is easier to decide on the intermediate steps you need to take to reach your ultimate goal.

Your financial goals are important in selecting a career. Some salaried positions will never bring great financial rewards because there is little opportunity for advancement. If financial gain is important, learn first what salaries can be expected in the careers that you are considering. In careers where you may own the business, such as interior design or real estate, the income is limited only by your ability and desire to work.

Do you want to continue to live in the same town? Willingness to move to another city may influence your career decision. If you want to work as a furniture designer, for example, you may have to move to the areas where large furniture factories are located. Would you be willing to move to a less desirable climate to pursue a career?

What skills will you need and how will you learn them? In considering any type of work, try to determine what the demand will be for certain skills in the future. Study "Help Wanted" columns in newspapers that are published in cities where you would like to work. These advertisements are an indication of the employment situation. Remember, however, that many good jobs are never advertised.

Two specialized publications are useful in studying careers. They are the *Dictionary of Occupational Titles, Vols. I and II* (Washington, D.C., U.S. Department of Labor) and *The Occupational Outlook Handbook* (U.S. Department of Labor, Bureau of Labor Statistics). Look at the job categories in these publications that are related to the field of housing.

You can obtain much information about careers in the public library. There you will find success stories of people who have worked in the field of housing, stories about companies manufacturing products for the home, and information about equipment and research. You may write for college catalogues to learn what courses are required in some of the fields that interest you.

After you have established general career objectives, get as much information as you can about the careers that seem appealing to you. For example, if you are interested in construction work, talk to a builder and learn about the requirements for employment. You may even be able to get a part-time job during the summer. This will give you an opportunity to see if you enjoy the work. If your interest is interior design, you might arrange an interview with an interior designer.

Obtaining experience in a specific job may be difficult while you are in school. Experience, however, is a broad term. Many different jobs have common qualities. For example, you gain experience in working with people when you do volunteer work in a hospital. This experience may be helpful if you are seeking a job in retailing or in any field where you have to work with many people.

Take advantage of the experience of your school counselors and teachers. If you are interested in a career in housing, they may recommend courses that will be beneficial and suggest sources of information.

CAREERS IN HOUSING
Architecture

An **architect** specializes in designing buildings which meet the needs and wishes of the client.

Andersen Corporation
19-2. Architects need creative talent.

The glass cube home in Fig. 19-2 shows the creative skill of an architect who took advantage of new developments in insulating glass to design a home for people who wanted an unspoiled view.

The architect also assists in the selection of a builder and supervises construction to be sure that the builder follows the drawings.

Although architecture is a rewarding career, it has some disadvantages. A long training period and a difficult state examination are required before you can become a registered architect. Generally, years of experience are needed to become established in the field. Also, there may be periods when business is slow since the construction industry is affected by the state of the economy.

A five-year college course in design, engineering, and liberal arts leads to a Bachelor of Arts degree in architecture. If you choose to major in structural and mechanical design, the degree is known as a Bachelor of Science in architecture.

In design courses, the student learns to design buildings and prepare drawings. Courses in color theory, interior design, and city planning are also included. The engineering courses include structural concrete and steel design and plumbing and electrical work.

In general, eight years of experience in the office of a registered architect are considered essential, unless the person has completed five years of schooling in an accredited school of architecture. In this case only three years of office work may be required.

The required office experience is generally limited to drafting. However, the exposure to other architects in the office, to contractors, and to clients is a valuable part of the beginner's training. The questions and answers you hear in an office give you a fund of information which could never be obtained in college classes.

Drafting

Detailed drawings by a **drafter** are needed to enable a contractor to construct a building. These are usually referred to as working drawings. They are developed from preliminary sketches made by the architect and indicate materials to be used, important dimensions to follow, and the extent of work to be done by the contractor. They are drawn on thin tracing paper from which blueprints, or blue or black line prints, may be made. These are needed for the owner's record, for the building permit, and for the contractor's use.

The drafters who prepare these drawings must have patience, good eyesight, and steady hands, Fig. 19-3. They should also be able to anticipate the questions which the builder might ask and must produce drawings which answer those questions. Drafters must also have some knowledge of construction.

An architectural drafting certificate is granted in some vocational and trade schools upon completion of a two-year program. This program usually includes courses in design, architecture, English, mathematics and physics.

Opportunities for advancement depend largely on the person's willingness to learn and on the opportunities in a given location as well as on the economic times.

Model-making

Model-making is related to architecture. A model is a miniature of a proposed building. The model enables the client to see the appearance of the planned structure in three dimensions and to make revisions in design before construction. Some models include adjacent buildings so the client is able to judge the appearance of the finished building in relation to its setting.

The model-maker must know how to interpret architectural drawings, be able to do the precise work required, and have the patience and ability to create a three-dimensional scale miniature of the proposed structure.

Most model-makers have art school training and work as apprentices.

Architectural Rendering

An **architectural rendering** is a drawing showing in perspective the appearance of a completed building.

The architectural renderer must be skilled in drafting and able to interpret architectural drawings in order to draw a correct perspective. The person who prepares architectural renderings works with such artist's tools as pencil, pen and ink, watercolor, and tempera paint.

Courses in rendering are available at most schools of architecture.

Landscape Architecture

The landscape architect is concerned with site work such as grading and paving roads and parking areas and with the selection of planting, rather than with the building itself. The landscape architect's professional services include design, preparation of site plans, and supervision of construction and planting.

The landscape architect must be trained in horticulture, and must understand which plants will thrive in a certain location, the time required for growth, and how vegetation will appear at maturity.

To be a landscape architect, you would follow a training program similar to that of an architect. In addition, you would need graduate work in your special field.

Fields related to landscape architecture offer many opportunities for self employment such as landscape service, Fig. 19-4. These jobs may be handled by one individual, responsible for a few

Stock Boston/Tyrone Hall
19-3. This drafter prepares a working drawing.

19-4. This landscape architect is landscaping the grounds in a new subdivision.

World Wide Photos
19-5. Mechanical engineers review a blueprint.

grounds, or by the large contractor who manages teams of workers and provides equipment.

Engineering

An ever-increasing complexity of construction methods, materials, and mechanical equipment has called for new kinds of engineering. The engineer works with the architect as a consultant and gives professional assistance in the design of a building. The principal engineering classifications are structural, mechanical, civil, and electrical engineering.

The **structural engineer** is concerned with the physical stability of a building.

The structural engineer estimates the weight the structure must support, calculates the pressure of wind against the walls and roof, determines the force likely to be exerted by earthquakes, and also figures the amount of horizontal pressure against foundation walls from the weight of earth fill. Having done this, the engineer designs a structure capable of resisting these forces.

The **mechanical engineer** is concerned with the selection of heating, ventilating, air conditioning, and plumbing equipment required for a building and with the design of ducts, piping, valves, and temperature controls. In Fig. 19-5, mechanical engineers review building plans on the construction site.

The **civil engineer** is responsible for site planning. This includes grading or cutting away high land and filling low areas, planning for the disposal of storm water to minimize soil erosion and eliminate puddles, designing systems to remove sanitary waste, and laying out roads, driveways, parking areas, and sidewalks. Preparing a site for construction is shown in Fig. 19-6. This may involve blasting to remove rock.

A four-year college course for a degree in civil engineering includes a basic core of mathematics and natural and engineering science.

The **electrical engineer** determines the owner's requirements for lighting and for such equipment as ranges, fans, motors, ovens, heating elements, and air conditioners and calculates the amount of electric power needed.

Interior Design

The interior designer is usually a graduate of a school of art, interior decoration, or design. Although a degree is not required, the well-trained person is more likely to succeed. Before working independently, the beginner should have work experience with an established designer.

Generally, an interior designer is retained by a person wishing to decorate a home. The designer recommends colors, fabrics, furniture, and accessories and makes sketches of proposed room arrangements. The interior designer gathers samples of materials and photographs of

furniture. These are generally presented to the client for final selection. Since the designer has access to many material samples which are unavailable to the client, this phase of the service is important.

Frequently, designers have their own shops. They may also be employed by retail stores which sell home furnishings. They may decorate model apartments for rental agents, furnish rooms to be photographed, write articles for magazines, or design home products and decorative fabrics.

This career calls for creative flair and a knowledge of design and furnishings. Many of the rooms shown in this text were decorated by interior designers. A home economics background, including knowledge of fabrics and sewing, may be an asset.

19-6. Civil engineers are responsible for site planning.

A major disadvantage is that this service may be considered a luxury. People are not required by law to employ an interior designer, whereas you must have a set of blueprints in order to obtain a permit to build. If the budget is tight, the services of the interior designer may be omitted.

Kitchen and bath design is a relatively new speciality. These designers generally work for a manufacturer or for a firm which plans residential and commerical kitchens. They would design new products and improve those in production. They might work as free lance artists doing work on their own.

Another design speciality is lighting. These designers are generally employed by a utility company, lighting equipment manufacturer, or an engineering firm designing new products or planning new installations. Interior designers may choose to teach or combine work in the field with part-time teaching. Employment opportunities in all design fields are best in medium-size or large cities.

Real Estate

Careers in real estate include six major fields of specialization: brokerage, property management, mortgage risk financing, appraisal, research and education, and land development.

The **real estate broker** aids those who wish to buy, sell, rent, or lease real property.

If you plan to be a real estate broker, you should enjoy selling. You should be outgoing and enthusiastic and enjoy organizing your own day. You should be able to adjust to changing conditions and schedules. This is a good career if you like to work with others and enjoy giving service.

A good education is a definite asset, and practical and technical knowledge are important. Fields of study offering degrees in business administration or land economics provide a good background. Community college courses, seminars, institutes, and correspondence courses along with experience in selling and office procedure contribute to the necessary practical training.

The **property manager** handles every aspect of income-producing property for the owner. This consists of advertising, leasing, tenant relations, collections, accounting, and maintenance.

The property manager may handle apartments or commercial developments such as office buildings, shopping centers, and industrial complexes.

Wise management of real estate means a great deal to the owner since it should result in safeguarding investments and in a maximum profit. A good manager must be able to keep a complete and accurate record of expenses and receipts and must be trained in the management of income.

The manager must know enough about building construction and equipment, and the cost of alterations and repairs, to appreciate the value of good work done by specialized trades. The manager should have the ability to oversee repair work, hire and supervise maintenance personnel, and must be tactful in dealing with others. The manager must know how to manage real estate at a profit.

The **mortgage risk financer** finds mortgages for investors, aids investors in gaining a return on their money, and aids purchasers in acquiring and financing real property. This may be all or a part of the business of many real estate firms.

To enter this field, you should have managerial ability, and be able to understand the mortgage market. You should also be able to appraise property. You should have an administrative mind and be interested in finance and banking. A formal education is preferred with a degree in business administration and/or banking and finance.

The **appraiser** must be able to give an estimate of property value and must be able to prepare a written report based on the following: the cost approach, the income approach, or the market data approach. All of this requires an orderly, analytical mind. As an engineer would attack a problem through careful investigation and analysis, so must the appraiser work without bias or prejudice.

The educational requirements consist of a college education with degrees in business administration, mathematics, or accounting. Technical education in the principles of appraisal is essential. This may be acquired by constant self-education through special courses, by studying publications covering up-to-date appraisal methods, and through courses sponsored by the American Institute of Real Estate Appraisers. Designation must be received for appraiser qualification.

Compensation for appraisal service is usually a fixed fee, never a commission. If you are an employee of an appraisal firm, your compensation will be a salary.

There is a constant demand for real estate appraisers by real estate firms, financial institutions, insurance companies, and branches of government. The opportunity for advancement is almost unlimited, depending on individual performance and excellence.

Research is becoming a new, vital field in real estate. It consists of gathering information in all categories of real estate such as planning, production, marketing, and financing and in investigating the efficiency and production of construction materials. It also includes the analysis of cost trends, especially construction costs, in all parts of the country.

In general, to consider this field, you should be research-oriented, of a scientific mind, and prefer to work individually.

Education should include formal schooling in business administration, law, engineering, sociology, and land economics. Advanced degrees and teaching experience may be of great value.

The **housing manager** is primarily concerned with people, may provide a number of social services, and is responsible for the operation of the physical property in a way that benefits the tenants.

People in the field of housing management work in low-income housing, limited-profit housing, housing for the aged or other government-assisted housing, and in cooperatives.

This field offers a variety of career opportunities. Large developments may have one or more resident managers responsible for maintenance, tenant selection, social programs, community relations, and social service. There may be several levels of employment in each category. For example, the job titles in management might include management aide, assistant manager, resident manager, and supervisory manager. Also, people with special skills may be employed to take charge of programs designed to improve the nutrition of the tenants or to supervise some service such as meals-on-wheels. An expert in child care might operate a nursery school.

Land Development

Of vital importance to our nation is the planning and development of home neighborhoods, shopping areas, commercial and industrial centers, and multi-family projects. To function as a **land developer** requires a knowledge of real estate including site procurement, cost analysis and financing, installation of improvements, construction, merchandising, and management, Fig. 19-7.

To consider land development as a career you should be willing and able to take risks for large gains. You should have executive ability, be able to accept responsibilities under pressure, have keen judgment, and a good knowledge of construction. This would come with experience.

Degrees in business administration, engineering, or architecture are desirable. An important requirement is experience in some phases of land development.

Construction

Construction work may vary from repairing houses to building skyscrapers. The skilled trades in construction include painters, carpenters, tile setters, bricklayers, electricians, plumb-

19-7. Land development requires a knowledge of real estate.

terity, and the ability to measure accurately. Most building trade unions require a grade of 85, but an acceptable score is usually determined by the program director.

When applicants are accepted for training, they are assigned to work under the supervision of a skilled person. The trainee, such as the carpenter's apprentice in Fig. 19-8, learns new skills through on-the-job training.

During the training period, the apprentice is paid a beginning wage which is usually 50% of the union rate, with periodic advances. Upon completion of an apprenticeship the wage is equal to the starting union rate.

In addition to field work, the apprentice is required to attend classes for one day a week, generally on Saturday. Good attendance is essential.

The apprentice program may last four years.

19-8. A carpenter's apprentice.

ers, plasterers, roofers, and flooring specialists. Training may range from the self-taught to those who attended vocational schools. Many in this field prepare for their work through apprenticeship programs.

In many areas, apprentice training programs are run by trade unions and are open to those who pass an aptitude test. Since the size of a class is usually limited to the training facilities, a would-be apprentice might have to wait for a class opening. A high school diploma or a trade school certificate may be of value to the applicant, but it is not essential for acceptance in some programs. For example, if you were interested in carpentry, an aptitude test would reveal whether you have good space perception, dex-

During this time students may supplement their incomes with part-time jobs since continuous employment cannot be guaranteed.

Construction work usually depends on weather, general business conditions, and the amount and character of building activity. Often conditions in one trade will affect the work of another. For example, if the shipment of an essential building material such as steel or concrete is delayed, an entire construction project might be held up. Generally, trade unions have an employment service for members, which normally assure continuous work.

Large-scale construction projects such as apartment house complexes or large housing developments may offer more continuous employment than working for an individual. Assignments for apprentices are more likely to be available in large firms.

Fletcher Drake

19-10. Large buildings require many workers.

19-9. Construction jobs often call for ingenuity as well as physical strength.

Fletcher Drake

Construction jobs call for the ability to work well with others. Many require physical stamina. The person shown in Fig. 19-9 is skilled in the use of heavy mechanical equipment. Since the work varies widely and many problems arise, ingenuity and resourcefulness are also requisites for success.

Work in the construction industry ranges from the small job to large-scale projects such as the one in Fig. 19-10 which require many employees with specialized skills. For instance a painter must be dexterous in handling tools and must also have a good color sense. Often a client will specify an exact color desired. Some clients depend on the advice of the painter in selecting colors. The successful painter is able to antici-

451

pate problems and make accurate estimates of the time and amount of materials that will be required for a job. No special school experience is required. However, courses in vocational training might open job opportunities.

Another skilled craft is tile setting. The tile setter must be adept in the use of materials and tools. Accuracy is essential in order to make dependable estimates of the time and materials that will be required for a job.

The underground portion of a building must be waterproofed, another important trade.

Bricklaying is another important trade in the construction industry. The job involves cementing bricks together with mortar to make a straight wall. The work not only calls for skill and manual dexterity but also for physical stamina and good health. The bricklayer must lift heavy bricks, climb and work on scaffolds, and work outdoors in a variety of weather conditions, Fig. 19-11.

If you are interested in any of the trades, your most valuable training is to work with an experi-

enced and capable person. Contact local trade unions for information on apprenticeship programs. In addition, a good general education with some courses in business will be helpful, especially if your goal is to go into business for yourself.

Building Materials

There are many careers related to the development, promotion, and sale of construction materials. Included are such materials as aluminum, brick, concrete, flooring, glass, lumber, wall coverings, plaster, paint, tile, and waterproofing compounds. In almost every community, opportunities may be found in these specialties.

To qualify for this work, people must be trained in the particular area such as sales or research. They must also understand the properties of the materials used. The training required varies with the materials, the complexity of the job, and the involvement with other trades.

For the self-motivated individuals who like to work on their own, the field of building materials offers wide diversity and many opportunities for self-employment. Businesses can range in size from a one-person operation to one with many employees. There are small businesses related to all of the fields mentioned in this chapter as well as many others. The shop in Fig. 19-12 specializes in stoves, fireplace accessories, and other items related to heating.

Another career area in building materials is in research. More than ever before, the building industry is looking for new materials and techniques to solve housing problems. Beginning positions in research are open to those with bachelor's degrees and training in basic research. Advanced positions may call for a mas-

UPI
19-11. Bricklayers must have physical stamina.

19-12. Some people enjoy having their own business.

ter's and often a doctoral degree. In addition to knowledge in the field of research, competence in mathematics and statistics is necessary. This field calls for self-discipline since there may be many hours of routine, detailed work. Projects may take weeks or even years to complete. Meticulous care is required. In Fig. 19-13, a research worker checks the timing on an experiment.

Home Furnishings

Numerous career opportunities exist in the field of home furnishings. These jobs range from advertising and sales to upholstering furniture.

Selling home furnishings offers vast opportunities for careers. Frequently a salesperson will specialize in one area of home furnishings such

as appliances, carpeting, or furniture. A knowledge of the product, experience in selling, and enthusiasm are essential for advancement in this field.

Career possibilities in the home furnishings field exist for those who enjoy working with their hands. Cabinet-making, refinishing furniture, and restoring antiques require a knowledge of woods and finishes and the ability to use tools. An understanding of historic design is helpful. These jobs call for patience since careful, accurate work is required. Sometimes research must be done to determine the correct materials or colors to use.

Many firms are small and employ people with special skills to design and make custom furniture. Those shown in Fig. 19-14 are making brass beds.

Upholstery and drapery-making also require skillful hand work, a knowledge of color, an

19-13. Researchers must enjoy detailed work.
E.I. Du Pont De Nemours & Co., Inc.

19-14. Artisans such as these have special skills.

understanding of textiles, and a background in design. Skill in specific techniques may be acquired in schools offering courses in these subjects. On-the-job training may also be available for beginners in decorator workshops and large upholstery studios.

In most careers in this area, a knowledge of furnishings, including materials, styles, and construction, is essential. An understanding of interior design will be of value.

Some of the courses that will provide a background in this field include art history, furniture design, interior design, textiles, marketing, and advertising. Some high schools and many colleges offering courses in this field arrange for field work experience for students. On-the-job training is invaluable in this area.

Service

Generally, this field includes the repair and maintenance of equipment and appliances, the care of buildings and grounds, and any other services performed for householders. This is

one of the most rapidly growing career categories for several reasons. Today's appliances and equipment generally require a trained specialist to maintain or repair them. Also, many people would rather pay for service than forfeit their working or leisure time to do maintenance or minor repair work.

The list of service careers is almost endless. One of the major areas is servicing household equipment such as appliances, furnaces and air conditioners, and stereo and television sets. Outdoor maintenance is another service area that is booming. This includes the care of lawns, plants, and shrubbery and the removal of snow. Equipment rental agencies have become popular. Here the householder may rent anything from a punch bowl set and tableware for a large party to furniture, a lawn mower, garden equipment, or a snow plow.

Cleaning is another service in great demand. This includes housecleaning, rug and carpet cleaning, and window washing. Exterminators specialize in getting rid of insects and rodents.

Some service companies eliminate undesirable odors in a house.

Commercial moving is another service career area. Movers sometimes employ a consultant to help customers plan their moves. The consultant may give advice on the preparation of an inventory, the insurance to be carried, and hints on packing, shipping, and unpacking furniture and dishes. Some nationwide movers even provide information on schools, churches, and civic activities in the area to which a customer is moving. The consultant may lecture to civic groups on the problems of moving and prepare informative booklets for prospective customers.

The field of service offers an enterprising individual an opportunity to start a business without a large investment, either in time for training or in working capital. Often, service may be rendered at hours other than regular working hours. For example, people who work prefer to have appliance repairs made in the evening. This makes it possible to start a service career as a second job without an interruption of income until you become established and have a full-time business.

Opportunities for self-employment are generally better in more populated areas. However, vacation areas with seasonal homes may also afford opportunities. A second business might be developed during the off-season.

What to do to prepare yourself as a service specialist depends to a large extent on the field that interests you. Frequently, equipment manufacturers offer repair courses. You may also work with someone already established in the speciality. A trade or technical school may have a course in the work of your choice.

Work in the service field calls for sales skills since the problems of selling a service are similar to those of selling a product. To succeed in the service field, you must have imagination and promotional ability. Business skills such as record-keeping, inventory control, and advertising are an asset.

Manufacturing and Utility Companies

Most utilities employ people who help consumers make decisions regarding appliance purchases. They also try to solve consumer problems in the use of either the appliance or the fuel. Many of these jobs require sales ability. Others are in public relations where the ability to express ideas is of great importance. Usually, these careers involve meeting the public and demonstrating household equipment.

Utilities and manufacturers generally require home economists for their home service departments. Additional on-the-job training is provided in demonstrating the equipment and helping consumers, Fig. 19-15. As a rule, the sales departments are staffed by people who are interested in a sales career and in working with the public.

UPI

19-15. This home economist demonstrates computer kitchen equipment.

Government

The increasing role of government in housing has created a number of opportunities for employment in this field.

Government employees must pass a civil service examination or be appointed to their positions by elected officials or others empowered to do so. Occasionally, professional consultants are retained temporarily to offer advice on specific problems.

The types of employment in government housing are varied, but essentially they are either creative or administrative. The creative jobs may include the service of architects, city planners, and engineers; while other employment includes work in urban planning, neighborhood improvement, public housing, and housing for the elderly. Training in social work may be required in some of these jobs.

In the second group, administrative, the field broadens to include many special services in government offices. Administrative personnel have a variety of duties. For example, the director and assistants shown in Fig. 19-16 manage completed housing projects, guide professional assistants who are working under contract, represent the government in questions involving tenants, inspect work under construction, and approve requisitions for payments to contractors.

Employment requirements may include citizenship, residence in a specific area, special training, education, and physical fitness. The requirements vary widely depending on the job and on whether the government is federal, state, or local.

Urban renewal is the federal government's effort to cope with the problems of urban housing needs. These projects include many agencies, both public and private, and are directed toward upgrading economically and socially depressed neighborhoods.

Boston Housing Authority

19-16. Housing managers must enjoy working with people.

More Career Information

If you require additional information, you may write to professional and trade associations which represent the field of your choice. Two publications which list the associations and their addresses can be helpful.

The National Trade and Professional Associations of the United States and Canada, and Labor Unions, published by Columbia Books, Inc., Washington, D.C., has a Key Word and Geographic Index. All organizations concerned with one field, or within one geographical area, are listed together.

The Encyclopedia of Associations (3 vols.), published by Gale Research Co., Book Tower, Detroit, Michigan, is a guide to both national and international organizations. It gives detailed information on nonprofit American organizations listed by interest. For example, under "furniture," you will find: Furniture Rental Association, National Association of Bedding Manufacturers, National Home Furnishings Association, and many others.

When you request information from any organization, state definitely what you want. Do not ask for "anything available." Instead, ask specific questions or request literature on certain types of jobs.

ACTIVITIES

1. Select three jobs which you think might interest you. What are your qualifications?
• List any skills or desires that you may have such as an artistic talent or a preference for outdoor work.
• List your work experience, including volunteer and special school assignments.
• List any hobbies and interests that might indicate skills that would be useful. For example, if you are interested in making model planes, you may have the manual dexterity needed for carpenter work.

Analyze these qualifications. Do any of them show an aptitude for or an interest in any of the housing careers discussed in this chapter?

2. Analyze your needs and preferences. What are your ambitions?
• What are your financial and social ambitions?
• Do you wish to be self-employed?
• Do you plan to go to night school? Trade school? Junior college? College?
• Would you be willing to work full-time and go to school in the evening to earn a degree?
• In what part of the country would you want to work? Are there any limitations on the types of jobs available in that area?
• In some careers such as architecture or engineering, a person spends many years getting the education and experience needed to become a success. Would you be willing to spend the time and money needed to gain the necessary education and experience?

Analyze your answers to these questions. Would any of the career areas in housing help you to fulfill these ambitions?

3. Analyze the answers you gave in questions 1 and 2. Review the housing careers discussed in this chapter and select one that might appeal to you. Get the following information on that career from the library: specific educational requirements, apprentice training programs, availability of jobs, experience needed, salary levels. Report the results of your research to the class.

BIBLIOGRAPHY

ARCHITECTURE AND HOUSING

Andrews, Wayne. *Architecture, Ambition and Americans: A Social History of American Architecture.* New York: Free Press, 1966.

Beyer, Glenn H. *Housing and Society.* New York: Macmillan Co., Inc., 1965.

Keats, John. *The Crack in the Picture Window.* Boston: Houghton Mifflin Co., 1956.

Mumford, Lewis. *Interpretations & Forecasts.* New York: Harcourt Brace Jovanovich, Inc., 1973.

Mumford, Lewis. *Sticks & Stones—A Study of American Architecture and Civilization.* New York: Dover Publications, 1955.

Neutra, Richard. *Survival Through Design.* New York: Oxford University Press, Inc., 1969.

Newmark, Norma L., and Thompson, Patricia J. *Self, Space and Shelter.* San Francisco: Canfield Press, 1977.

Rapoport, Amos. *House Form and Culture.* Englewood Cliffs, NJ: Prentice-Hall, Inc., 1969.

Smith, Don, and Smith, Jo-an. *The Housebuying Checklist.* New York: Avon Books, 1975.

Sommer, Robert. *Personal Space: The Behavioral Basis of Design.* Englewood Cliffs, NJ: Prentice-Hall, Inc., 1969.

Watkins, A. M. *How To Avoid the 10 Biggest Home-buying Traps.* New York: Hawthorn Books, Inc., 1972.

BASIC DESIGN

Evans, Helen Marie. *Man the Designer.* New York: Macmillan Co., Inc., 1973.

Feldman, Edmund Burke. *Varieties of Visual Experience: Art and Image and idea.* New York: Prentice-Hall, Inc., 1973.

Lockard, William Kirby. *Design Drawing Experiences.* Tucson: Pepper Publishing, 1976.

ECOLOGY AND NATURAL RESOURCES

Anderson, Bruce. *Solar Energy and Shelter Design.* Harrisville, NH: Total Environmental Action, 1973.

Coonley, Douglas R. *Design with Wind.* Harrisville, NH: Total Environmental Action, 1974.

Daniels, M. E. *Fireplaces and Wood Stoves.* Indianapolis: Bobbs-Merrill, 1977.

DeChiara, Joseph, and Koppelman, Lee. *Manual of Housing and Design Criteria.* Englewood Cliffs, NJ: Prentice-Hall, Inc., 1974.

Farallons Institute. *The Integral Urban House. Self-reliant Living in the City.* San Francisco: Sierra Club Books, 1978.

Gropp, Louis. *Solar Houses.* New York: Pantheon, 1978.

Murphy, John A. *The Homeowner's Energy Guide.* New York: Thomas Y. Crowell Co., 1976.

Nattrass, Karen, and Morrison, Bonnie M. *Human Needs in Housing: An Ecological Approach.* Millburn, NJ: University Press of America, 1977.

Skurka, Norma, and Naar, John. *Design for a Limited Planet. Living with Natural Energy.* New York: Ballantine Books, 1976.

Wedin, Carol S., and Nygren, Gertrude L. *Housing Perspectives.* Minneapolis: Burgess Publishing Co., 1976.

FURNITURE

Bishop, Robert. *Centuries and Styles of the American Chair, 1640–1970.* New York: E. P. Dutton & Co., Inc., 1972.

Boericke, Arthur. *Handmade Houses. A Guide to the Woodbutcher's Art.* San Francisco: Scrimshaw Press, 1973.

Boger, Louise Ade. *Complete Guide to Furniture Design.* Rev. ed. New York: Charles Scribner's Sons, 1969.

Colonial Williamsburg Foundation. *The Williamsburg Collection of Antique Furnishings.* New York: Holt, Rinehart and Winston, Inc., 1974.

Ehrenkranz, Florence, and Inman, Lydia. *Equipment in the Home.* New York: Harper and Row, Inc., 1973.

Hennessey, James, and Papanek, Victor. *Nomadic Furniture.* New York: Pantheon, 1974.

Howell-Koehler. *Step-by-Step Furniture Finishing.* New York: Golden Press, 1975.

McDonald, Robert J. *Upholstery Repair and Restoration.* New York: Charles Scribner's Sons, 1977.

Moody, Ella. *Modern Furniture.* New York: E. P. Dutton & Co., Inc., 1973.

Nutting, Wallace. *Furniture Treasury.* 3 vols. New York: Macmillan Co., Inc., 1974.

O'Neil, Isabel. *The Art of the Painted Finish for Furniture and Decoration.* New York: William Morrow & Co., Inc., 1971.

Stillinger, Elizabeth. *The Antiques Guide to Decorative Arts in America, 1600–1875.* New York: E. P. Dutton & Co., Inc., 1973.

Sunset Editors. *Furniture Upholstery and Repair.* Menlo Park, CA: Lane Publishing Co., 1970.

Wicks, Harry. *Furniture Refinishing.* New York: Grosset & Dunlap, 1977.

Williams, Patricia M. *Buying Home Furnishings.* New York: St. Martin's Press, 1975.

Winchester, Alice, eds. Antiques Magazine and *The Antiques Treasury of Furniture and Other Decorative Arts.* New York: E. P. Dutton & Co., Inc., 1959.

Wright, Louis B.; Tatum, George B.; McCoubrey, John W.; and Smith, Robert C. *The Arts in America: The Colonial Period.* New York: Charles Scribner's Sons, 1966.

HISTORIC HOUSES

Camesasca, E. *History of the House.* New York: G. P. Putnam's Sons, 1971.

Conran, Terence. *The House Book.* New York: Crown Publishers, Inc., 1976.

Drury, John. *The Heritage of Early American Houses.* New York: Coward, McCann and Geoghegan, Inc., 1969.

Grieff, Constance M. *Great Houses from the Pages of Antiques.* Princeton, NJ: The Pyne Press, 1971.

Tunis, Edwin. *Colonial Living.* New York: World Publishing Co., 1976.

Tunis, Edwin. *Young United States.* New York: World Publishing Co., 1976.

Whiffen, Marcus. *American Architecture Since 1780: A Guide to Styles.* Cambridge, Mass.: M.I.T. Press, 1969.

INTERIOR DESIGN

Alexander, Mary Jean. *Designing Interior Environment.* New York: Harcourt Brace Jovanovich, Inc., 1972.

Allen, Phyllis S. *The Young Decorator.* Provo, UT: Brigham Young University Press, 1975.

Apartment Life Editors. *The Apartment Book.* New York: Harmony Books, 1979.

Brett, James. *The Kitchen: 100 Solutions to Design Problems.* New York: Watson-Guptill Publications, 1977.

Conran, Terence. *The Kitchen Book.* New York: Crown Publishers, 1977.

Faulkner, Ray, and Faulkner, Sarah. *Inside Today's Home.* New York: Holt, Rinehart and Winston, Inc., 1975.

Faulkner, Sarah. *Planning a Home. A Practical Guide to Interior Design.* New York: Holt, Rinehart and Winston, 1979.

Halse, Albert C. *The Use of Color in Interiors.* New York: McGraw-Hill Book Co., 1968.

Helsel, Marjorie Borradaile. *The Home Decorator's Color Book.* New York: Simon and Schuster, Inc., 1972.

Naar, Jon, and Siple, Molly. *Living in One Room.* New York: Random House, 1976.

Schram, Joseph F. *Modern Bathrooms.* Menlo Park, CA: Lane Publishing Co., 1966.

Skurka, Norma, and Geli, Oberto. *Underground Interiors.* New York: Quadrangle Books, Inc., 1973.

Stepat-Devan, Dorothy. *Introduction to Home Furnishings.* Riverside, NJ: Macmillan Co., Inc., 1971.

Bibliography

Wallach, Carla. *Interior Decorating with Plants.* New York: Macmillan Co., Inc., 1976.

Whiton, Sherrill. *Interior Design and Decoration.* Philadelphia: J. B. Lippincott and Co., 1974.

PERIODICALS

Antiques Magazine; Architectural Digest; Architectural Forum; Architectural Record; Better Homes and Gardens; Changing Times; The Kiplinger Magazine; Consumer Reports; Country Journal; Das Haus (German); Design From Scandinavia (Denmark); Domus Overseas (Italian); Forecast for Home Economics; Futurist; Good Housekeeping; Home Furnishings Daily; House Beautiful; House and Garden; House and Home; Interior Design; Interiors; Journal of Home Economics; La Maison Francaise (French); Mother Earth News; Progressive Architecture.

INDEX